ETHICAL STANDARDS

& Clinical Forms

for
Licensed Mental Health Counselors

Samara C. Kezele Fritchman
Licensed Counselor [LMHC]   National CE Presenter
Employee Assistance Specialist [CEAP]   Critical Incident Responder [CIR]

Fritchman

Tacoma, WA 98406
www.samdia.com

Samara C. Kezele Fritchman
Licensed Counselor [LMHC]   National CE Presenter
Employee Assistance Specialist [CEAP]   Critical Incident Responder [CIR]

ETHICAL STANDARDS & CLINICAL FORMS
- For Social Service and Mental Health Professionals
- For Academic Programs in Counseling Psychology

All rights reserved. No portion of this book may be reproduced or transmitted electronically without authorized consent of the author.

© **2013** Samara C. Kezele Fritchman, CreateSpace Publishing Platform*
© **2014** Samara C. Kezele Fritchman, CreateSpace Publishing Platform *Text Revisions/Content Updates*
© **2019** Samara C. Kezele Fritchman, Kindle Publishing Platform *Text Revisions/Content Updates*
© **2021** Samara C. Kezele Fritchman, Kindle Publishing Platform *Text Revisions/Content Updates*

Visit www.samdia.com for contact information

Fritchman, SCK (2013,2014,2019) Tacoma, WA, Fritchman (Publisher)

ISBN-13: 978-1492-1330-7-0
ISBN-10: 1492133078

Printed in the USA
Kindle Publishing Platform
https://kdp.amazon.com/
Updates 2019 by Samara C. Kezele Fritchman
Cover Design by Samara Fritchman and Sean Bonsel
Editing: Val Dumond (author of *Grammar for Grown-ups*) [2013]*
Proofreaders/Re-edits: Beth Williams, Sarah Brewer, Laci-Jo Estes [2014, 2019]

Library of Congress Cataloging Number: 2013912758
1. PSYCHOLOGY
2. BUSINESS
3. ETHICS
4. NON-FICTION

This book is perfect for Academic Institutions

There are Research Suggestions
throughout the book,
and there is a comprehensive
Research Section with tips for searching
the Internet for helpful charts, your state's relevant
information, and codes/laws.

Contact the Publisher/Author: www.samdia.com
for bulk order discounts

Kindle Publishing Platform, ISBN-13: 978-1492133070

A practical and useful reference book.

We need timeless principles to steer by in
running our organizations and building our
personal careers. We need high standards...
The ethics of excellence.

— Prince Pritchett

ETHICAL STANDARDS & CLINICAL FORMS

IMPORTANT NOTICE: Over the years I have shared my information with many sources and posted documents on the Internet for counselors to open, save and share. I have received information from a variety of sources—bits and pieces of statements, ideas, thoughts, and insights from others without notations of who's the original source. If you recognize material in this book that you claim authorship to, please let me know. This book is a print on-demand book and its content is easily changeable to denote credit or remove the information.

CASE EXAMPLES: Any case examples used within this course do not reflect actual individuals. They are adapted from actual cases, but identifying information has been changed and new elements added to protect the privacy of clients, except for those cases that are public knowledge.

CAVEAT: Ethical standards are written broadly, in order to apply to professionals in varied roles, and the application of an ethical standard may vary depending on context. Ethical standards are not exhaustive. For many ethical issues, the fact that an ethical standard does not specifically address a specific issue does not means the specific issue in question is necessarily ethical or unethical. Ethical codes are not intended to be a basis of civil liability. Whether a counselor has violated their ethical standards does not, by itself, determine whether the counselor is legally liable in court action, whether a contract is enforceable, or whether other legal consequences occur. This information is not intended to provide all of the details of the HIPAA Privacy Rule or any other laws or guidelines. This material also does not constitute legal advice. If there is any discrepancy between the provisions of the HIPAA Privacy Rule, other laws, or regulations and the material in this book, the terms of the laws, rules, professional guidelines, and regulations will govern in all cases. This information is not intended to describe all of the national mental health associations' guidelines, but to ensure that readers are guided by their professional code(s) of ethics, state licensing regulations, and others laws relevant to their state. Ethical dilemmas are varied and complex. Ethical decision-making can be difficult as well as time-consuming. Sometimes, mental health counselors are still left with a little ambivalence and uncertainty following their decision. It is always important to keep in mind the importance of supervision, consultation, and legal advice regarding any mental health practice ethical dilemma. This cannot be overstated.

Also, when I use the term counselor, I am referring to all mental health professionals regardless of their licensing.

DISCLAIMER: All samples are intended as guidelines only. For use in your own setting, forms must be personalized to reflect your state's relevant laws and regulations, your licensing requirements, and your own actual policies. You also need to modify sample forms or sample text so it is applicable to your clients, settings, and the type of work you do. Sample clinical forms and sample text ideas are provided "as is," without warranty of any kind. Sample clinical forms are not intended to be a substitute for legal, ethical, or clinical advice or consultation. States vary in laws, statutes, and licensing boards' requirements. Readers should take extra care to know their state's health/safety codes and laws/statutes that are relevant to (but not limited to): minors' rights, protective services, mandatory reporting, and licensing board's ethical guidelines. You must modify the forms so they comply with your state laws, professional organizations' codes of ethics and your state licensing board's guidelines.

ALWAYS CONSULT WITH YOUR PROFESSIONAL COLLEAGUES, FOLLOW COMPANY POLICIES, DISCUSS WITH SUPERVISOR(S), AN ATTORNEY, OR YOUR INSURANCE COMPANY'S RISK MANAGEMENT DEPARTMENT BEFORE IMPLEMENTING A NEW FORM.

ABOUT THIS BOOK: It was my intent to create a text book that's a useful and helpful resource guide. The information is not presented in an exhaustive manner. Rather, I've presented key bits of information. You, the reader, can further explore various topics and areas of need or interest. Throughout the book, there are assignments that will help guide research and challenge your knowledge on ethical and legal issues.

This book will help you sort out fact from fiction; ethical issues from legal issues; and, their applications in practice. Through this book, you will gain an understanding and an appreciation for the purpose and necessity of ethical standards. The core realities of these value-based and value-laden approaches to mental health care pivot on ethics and ethical competencies. Competence, within the field of psychology, is as important as any other standard and possibly more important, because all the knowledge that is available to practicing counselors is constantly growing and changing. This makes competency a lifelong goal that is never quite satisfied. There are many ethical guidelines and necessary competencies that guide professional counselors. Furthermore, attention to culture and diversity issues have been articulated into ethical standards and understanding culture is critical for counselors. Why? Because, every professional counselor's individual cultural orientation and every client's individual cultural orientation are both present in each and every counseling session. Values and principles, along with adherence to ethical standards, do define a counselor's practice; and, these values and philosophies must remain consistent with ethical guidelines for the profession.

ETHICAL STANDARDS & CLINICAL FORMS

FROM LIVE SEMINARS TO BOOK FORMAT

I have covered a variety of topics associated with ethics and mental health counseling in live seminars for thousands of attendees over 30 years. Each of these ethics seminars are six-hours long. On the following pages, I have shared the materials covered in these seminars, along with additional information that time does not allow for in the seminar format.

SOME OF THE SEMINAR TITLES ARE:
- ETHICS—Necessary and Essential Information for Mental Health Counselors
- REQUIRED ETHICAL COMPETENCIES—Codes, Standards, and Ethica lExpectations
- CULTURAL COMPETENCIES—A Multicultural Approach in Healthcare
- COMPLEX CLIENTS—Ethical Standards, Communications and Interventions
- SUICIDE--Prevention, Assessment and Treatment

www.samdia.com
Samara Claudia Kezele Fritchman
Washington State Licensed Mental Health Counselor (LMHC #MH00005086)
National Certified Counselor; NBCC (NCC #53560)
International Certified Employee Assistance Professional;
International EAPA.org, (CEAP #032468)
Employee Assistance Professional-Clinical; International EAPA.org, (EAS-C)
Critical Incident Responder Certified Clinical Trauma Professional, Evergreen Certification, (CCTP #307805)

EAP SeSamara has 40+ years of experience working with all levels of staff spanning a variety of job classifications, ethnic backgrounds, and educational levels within a wide variety of industries providing consulting, counseling and professional development training services as an external employee assistance professional. Samara holds degrees/professional education in: business/human science, counseling psychology, legal studies and adult learning. She has taken several time/task specific work assignment throughout her career with Pierce College [Professor], Tacoma Housing Authority [Drug Education Liaison], Shelton Chamber of Commerce [Director of Operations], Subway Development Company [Director of Operations], Tacoma Community College [Instructor/Counselor], Tacoma Rescue Mission [Education and Career Advisor].
For career details, visit: www.samdia.com

1991 BA: Bachelor of Arts, Business and Human/Behavioral Science; Evergreen State*
1994 MA: Master of Arts in Counseling Psychology; St. Martin's College^
1999 JD: Juris Doctorate (US Legal Studies); [Did not take the bar; not an attorney] Columbus University~
2007 PhD: Educational Psychology (Adult Learning/Curriculum/Process); Columbus University~

*The Evergreen State College, public liberal arts college (Accredited by Council on Higher Education) ^St. Martin's College, MAC Program (Accredited by Council on Higher Education) ~Columbus University: Academic /Professional Dev. Programs; Distance Education (Accredited by World Association of Universities)

Samara offers continuing education (CE) approved seminars for licensed health care professionals and clock-hour approved seminars to educators and administrators in private/public schools, serving Washington State. In addition, she provides training seminars for small businesses, corporations, and non-profits 501(c).

SHE HAS PROVIDED REGIONAL AND NATIONAL SEMINARS ON A VAST ARRAY OF TOPICS FOR 30+ YEARS.

Please visit her website for details:
WWW.SAMDIA.COM

TABLE OF CONTENTS

Refer to INDEX for detailed listing of topics

Preface 1

Part 1: Ethical Standards—Guidelines 3

Part 2: Ethical Standards—Competencies 165

Part 3: Ethical Standards—Multiculturalism 211

Part 4: Sample Clinical Forms 259

RESEARCH..529

State-by-State Research 530

Codes of Ethics: Need to Know 540

Ethical Decision Making..541

References 547

INDEX of all topics 555

Bulk Order for Academic Programs 568

Digital Forms: Ordering Information......................................569

*Ethics are
the defining
quality that
distinguishes
individuals
as professionals
—regardless of
treatment modality
—ethics remain
a crucial part of the
counseling process.*
Samara Claudia Kezele Fritchman

PREFACE

I have taught ethics seminars to mental health counselors for over 20 years. The challenge of writing this book was to make it timeless. Laws change, ethics are revised, and states change licensing requirements. But the fundamental elements of ethics in the mental health profession are timeless. I chose to make this a resource book so you, the reader, can participate in building your knowledge base relevant to the counseling profession and more specifically, relevant to the environment in which you will, or are, providing counseling services.

Ethics is the defining quality that distinguishes individuals as professionals. Regardless of the choice of treatment modality whether best practices, complementary or alternative approaches—ethics remains a crucial part of the counseling process. Ethics is the defining quality that says, "I am a professional." Professionals don't cross the line to inappropriate boundaries or fail to provide informed consent. Professionals don't mishandle clients' records or allow their personal problems to affect their counseling. Professionals don't practice outside their area of competence or provide counseling outside their basis of competency.

A counselor's primary responsibility is to promote the well-being of their clients. In general, their clients' interests are primary. And confidentiality is vital. However, responsibility to the larger society or specific legal obligations may, on limited occasions, supersede this confidentiality owed clients (e.g., mandatory reporting).

Ethical issues that violate ethical standards are not an ethical dilemma; violations are right vs. wrong situations. A true ethical dilemma is a right vs. right situation, where there are two (or more) choices, each having merit. Ethical dilemmas are often context driven—the type of work being done; the type of clientele; and, issues of social justice, fairness, and equity. These are the ethical issues that counselors struggle with in this helping profession.

TO START WITH, HERE ARE A FEW ETHICAL GUIDELINES:

- Counselors must remain alert to and avoid conflicts of interest that interfere with the exercise of professional discretion and impartial judgment.
- Counselors should not take unfair advantage of any professional relationship or exploit others to further their personal, religious, political, or business interests.
- Counselors only provide services to clients in the context of a professional relationship based on valid informed consent.
- Counselors take reasonable steps to ensure that documentation in clients' records is accurate and reflects the services provided.
- Counselors should base practice interventions on recognized knowledge; empirically-based knowledge relevant to effective counseling.
- Counselors refrain from initiating an activity when they know, or should have known, that there is a substantial likelihood that their personal problems will prevent them from performing their work-related activities in a competent manner.

Licensed mental health counselors must maintain and promote high ethical standards. These high ethical standards also protect, enhance, and help improve the integrity of the mental health care profession. Value-based and value-laden approaches to mental health care pivot on ethics, and the personal values, principles, and standards of a counselor define their work.

Continuing education, active discussions through consultations, and responsible implementation of and adherence to ethical standards are vital.

PART 1

ETHICAL STANDARDS: GUIDELINES

A counselor's ability to be compassionate with healthy boundaries is key

A UNIQUE PROFESSION

In counseling, the counselor is his or her own instrument. Their ability to be compassionate, with healthy boundaries, is key. With compassion, a counselor dethrones him/herself and puts the client foremost. Compassion is strongly linked to emotions, and empathy is expressed by behavior and action. Most individuals enter the counseling profession because of a sensitization to people's sufferings. This sensitization could be from their own struggles or from watching those close to them struggle with personal issues, addictions, and traumas.

Good therapeutic work comes from personal energies, both positive and negative.

Everyone leaves childhood with blessings and talents, developed or natural, and with incidences of good luck (being in the right place at the right time, and taking advantage of that good fortune). In our lives, there have been and are people who helped us, encouraged us, or told us we had value.

HERE ARE SOME QUESTIONS TO ASK YOURSELF:
- Who took a special interest in you and encouraged you?
- Who believes or believed in you?
- Who has been or is your mentor?
- Who has been your inspirational model?
- How are you blessed? (Remember, blessings come from adversities, too)

But, everyone also leaves childhood with wounds. The problems that stain psyches can become a great source behind the compassionate ability to help others. The injuries suffered in childhood can invite healing. An example: Using anger in a constructive and creative way to write some injustice or change the world to make it a better place.

HERE ARE SOME QUESTIONS FOR SELF-REFLECTION:
- How have you been wounded?
- What would you like to change?
- If given one hour on prime time TV to influence the world—what would you talk about?
- How can you turn your wound(s) in to a blessing and a contribution?

Ethical issues are common in every profession. However, in mental health work, which relies heavily on relationship building and can directly impact the health and welfare of clients, ethics poses even greater responsibilities and challenges. The word ethics is derived from both the Greek word ethos, which means character, and the Latin word mores, meaning customs. Ethics defines what is good for both society and the individuals. Though closely related, laws and ethics do not necessarily have a reciprocal relationship. While the origins of law can often be based upon ethical principles, laws do not prohibit many unethical behaviors. Likewise, adherence to certain ethical principles may challenge a mental health counselor's ability to uphold the law.

ETHICAL STANDARDS

Ethical standards are created to help professionals identify ethical issues in their practice and provide guidelines to determine what is ethically acceptable and what is ethically unacceptable behavior. What makes mental health work unique is its focus on a person's well-being, as well as its commitment to the well-being of society as a whole.

ETHICAL DILEMMAS

Ethical dilemmas are varied and complex. The ethical decision-making process can be difficult and time-consuming. Sometimes mental health counselors are still left with a little ambivalence and uncertainty even following an ethical decision. Typically, there will be more than one person involved with the ethical decision-making process. It is always important to keep in mind the power of supervision and consultation regarding mental health work. When a counselor avoids consulting with colleagues about a clinical relationship, boundaries, conflicts of interest, or any clinical situation, then that avoidance can be a sign that there's room for concern. Counselors who are reluctant to consult colleagues for advice need to ask themselves: Why?

INTEGRITY AND OBJECTIVITY

If a counselor loses their integrity or their objectivity, or both, then indeed, the quality of client care will be diminished.

ETHICAL CODES

From time-to-time we may encounter writings or workshop presentations with a tone of absolute authority and unquestioning certainty, suggesting that some among us are ethically infallible. These authorities come across as above the mental mistakes, personal biases, limited perspectives, convincing rationalizations, and accidental blunders that can trip up the rest of us. We are fallible and capable of making simple errors, finding ourselves in sticky situations, or finding ourselves heading down slippery slopes.

"Ethical codes" in the mental health profession exist to help guide the services provided and the counselor providing the services. Codes strive to enhance social justice and promote the dignity and worth of a client. They stress the importance of human relationships and treating people with dignity. Ethical codes help monitor counselor competence. Codes summarize broad ethical principles that reflect core values related to and linked with the mental health profession. Ethical codes help counselors identify relevant considerations when professional obligations conflict, or ethical uncertainties arise. And, ethical codes help socialize counselors new to the field of mental health care.

"Ethical decision-making" is the ability to reason with ethical principles and arrive at a decision that elicits ethical professionalism. Our ethical responsibility is an on-going process that aims to resolve ethical dilemmas, while promoting the best interest of clients. We are faced with complex clients in complex situations, such as drug dealers, sexual predators, domestic abuse, criminal conduct of a client, duty to warn and protect, child protective services, and a multitude of issues surrounding minors. An understanding of ethical codes, relevant laws, and state requirements are vital for making appropriate decisions!

LAWS AND CODES

"Laws" are pre-determined rights and wrongs. Laws can be, and are, periodically challenged, overturned, or a new precedence is established. Professionals should be highly aware of the rules in their specific field of mental health care. They must remain aware of how their behavior may appear to a sometimes accusing or suspicious public.

"Ethical codes" are morality-based requirements and interpretations. Ethical dilemmas in the mental health profession are often complex, so a useful guideline would be to examine the problem from several perspectives and avoid searching for simplistic solutions. When there is a problem, ask yourself if it is an ethical, legal, professional, or clinical problem. Is it a combination of more than one of these? If it's ethical, seek ethical guidance from codes. If it's professional or clinical, seek consultation from supervisors or colleagues. If it's a legal question, seek legal advice.

USEFUL QUESTIONS WHEN FACED WITH ETHICAL ISSUES:
- Is it related to a client and what they are or are not doing?
- Is it related to a client's significant other and what they are or are not doing?
- Is it related to you, the counselor, and what you are or are not doing?
- Is it related to the institution or agency and their policies and procedures?

THREE SIMPLE TESTS:
These tests help ensure that a selected ethical course of action is appropriate.
1) Testing Justice: Assess your own sense of fairness by determining whether you would treat others the same in the same situation.
2) Testing Universality: Ask yourself whether you would recommend the same course of action to another counselor in the same situation.
3) Testing Publicity: Ask yourself whether you would want your behavior reported in the press.

ETHICS

"Ethics" is closely related to professional competence. Ethically, counselors maintain clinical competence through education, continuing education, advanced training, clinical supervision, clinical experience (the learning curve), and a commitment to ethical codes. Competence generates confidence! Clients put their trust in counselors, and a fundamental expectation is competence. In a complex field where individual and social values vary and are ever-changing, the need to interact fairly must be given some direction and consistency by rules. Ethical codes exist with the goal of being effective in modifying human behavior—specifically, the behavior of mental health professionals.

In providing services, counselors represent themselves as competent within the boundaries of their education, training, license, certification, consultation received, supervised experience, and any other relevant professional experience. When seeking employment, counselors accept employment only on the basis of existing competence or with the intention to acquire, as quickly as possible, the necessary training. A colleague accepted a job in a sexual predator program although he had never worked in this field. He accepted employment based on his existing competence, along with the "intention" to acquire other necessary competence. Of course, he followed through by attending training seminars relevant to this field and by working closely with an experienced supervisor/mentor.

Ethical codes are moral-based requirements and interpretations. Laws can be defined as standards, principles, processes, and rules that are adopted, administered, and enforced. Both codes and laws regulate behavior. In addition, state licensing boards having specific licensing requirements. Individuals applying for a license must possess good moral character and comply with the rules and regulations pursuant to that state board. They must demonstrate competence through education, certification, and experience. And individuals must never use their professional relationships to further personal self-interest. All counselors are at risk of making ethical mistakes or finding themselves thrown into an unexpected ethical dilemma. Many things can trip them up—mental mistakes, personal bias, limited perspectives, convincing rationalizations, and/or accidental blenders. There are ethically troubling categories, such as blurred dual or multiple relationships, conflicted relationships, and a myriad of complex counseling settings.

STATE-TO-STATE

Traveling from state-to-state, I have a clear understanding of how laws and codes can vary. This book imparts the importance for each reader to be guided by their state's licensing regulations, their state's statutes and laws relevant to ethical practices, state requirements, mandatory reporting, as well as minor laws and statutes in order to make the most appropriate ethical (and legal) decisions. The following (page 10) is a list of items that vary from state-to-state. For state laws and codes relevant to the counseling profession and more specifically to your licensing, check with your state board or your state's counseling association relevant to your specific licensing.

YOU NEED TO RESEARCH AND CLEARLY UNDERSTAND YOUR STATE'S LAWS AND YOUR LICENSING BOARD'S REGULATIONS REGARDING:
- Mandatory reporting laws and regulations
- Bartering policies
- Requirements for reporting impaired colleagues
- Information regarding counselors and sexual relations with clients
- Laws regarding minors and mental health care
- Laws regarding minors and emancipation
- Record keeping and record retention requirements
- Definition of "standard of care" and "scope of practice" for your licensing

LICENSING BOARDS

Remember, licensing boards have requirements for individuals to be licensed as mental health professionals. Individuals must possess good moral character and comply with the rules and regulations pursuant to their state board. They must demonstrate competence in their education, certification, experience, and supervision. And, they do not use professional relationships to further personal self-interest.

"Mandatory Ethics" describe minimal duties and professional expectations to remind counselors of basic ethical responsibilities and what to avoid. Mandatory ethics describes compliance with the "must" and "must nots" of ethical responsibilities. In the ethics of mandatory or minimal duties, counselors are not praised for fulfilling them, but they can be blamed for not fulfilling them. Mandatory ethics are enforceable through administrative and legal systems.

"Aspirational Ethics" involve the highest standard of conduct to which a professional can aspire by understanding the moral fiber behind the codes. Ethics of aspiration go above and beyond the minimum requirements. Aspirational ethics help cultivate certain habits of mind and heart that are called virtues, or attitudes for collaborative and respectful living. In the ethics of aspiration, it is not just about fulfilling the minimum, enforceable, ethical guidelines; it is about conducting oneself in a praise-worthy manner that demonstrates an understanding of the moral fiber behind the ethical codes.

HISTORY OF ETHICS CODES

Codes of ethics have been developed by all the national mental health associations and all state boards. Being a member of a professional association not only exposes you to a wealth of knowledge, but it also provides assistance with ethical issues. When individuals identify with the mental health profession, they are pledging to practice in an ethical and responsible manner. In addition to this allegiance, and the professional ethics and standards of practice it promotes, the counselor also has a duty to support the values, rules, laws, and customs of the society they are a part of and work with. Regardless of the specific association(s) that counselors choose to join, it is a priority that every counselor follows their codes of professional conduct outlined by the state's licensing board. State licensing laws and licensing board regulations identify basic competencies for mental health practice. Failure to follow the ethical codes of one's profession may result in sanctions, fines or expulsion from the profession, and if sued, in a legal judgment against the counselor.

Every professional association is interested in and concerned about ethics. Whenever associations are considering additions or revisions, they strive to do so based on the critical incidents gathered and compiled from the general membership. This is useful information. Associations strive to identify ethical principles that address realistically the emerging dilemmas that the diverse membership confronts in the day-to-day work of mental health care.

Unfortunately, there is a long-standing history of misconduct in the healthcare industry. The Hippocratic Oath refers to abstaining from intentional wrongdoing and harm. This oath sought to rectify injustice hundreds of years ago.

In more recent history there's the story about Sabina. In 1906, Sabina, a 19-year-old Russian-Jewish refugee in a deep state of dementia, given to spells of silence when she was not blurting out tales of Wagner's heroes and heroines, was sent to the Zürich Psychiatric Hospital. Carl Jung took her on as his first patient and was anxious to test out his practices of word association and dream therapy on this unusual case. In the course of treating her, he battled his growing sexual and emotional attraction. The two become sexually involved. Although there were no codes of ethics as we think of them now, Jung felt the pressures of his actions. But, he defended them in a note to Sigmund Freud, stating, "The preservation of my clinical relationship with Sabina could only be rounded out by sexual acts."

ETHICAL STANDARDS & CLINICAL FORMS

Sabina, who eventually was cured (according to Jung), became a psychoanalyst. Freud is brought into the story, first by Jung's correspondence and then at a social meeting where Sabina so charmed him with her contradictions of his theories that he invited her to join him on a tour of America. As evidenced by diaries and letters of Sabina, discovered in 1977, she was a frequent topic of discussion between Freud and Jung.

DO SOME RESEARCH:
What was the climate of psychotherapy and sexual relationships like during these earlier years in psychotherapy? See what you can discover about this time in Zürich. Aside from Freud and Jung, who were the key counselors?

RESEARCH
- Watch the movie "A Dangerous Method" (It's about Sabina)

QUESTIONABLE, UNETHICAL, AND UNPROFESSIONAL BEHAVIOR

Unfortunately, there's a lot of questionable, unethical, and unprofessional behavior. Common characteristics of counselors who demonstrate questionable behavior include:
- They are unaware or misinformed of ethical standards
- They offer treatment outside their specific scope of practice
- They might display insensitivity to the needs of others
- They might exploit clients by putting their own needs first through self-serving act
- They reveal interpersonal boundary issues through their inappropriate behaviors
    - Those counselors who are generally ethical, can occasionally blunder due to oversight or distraction

COGNITIVE JUSTIFICATIONS

There is a history of cognitive justifications and rationalizations by counselors who have engaged in unethical behavior. Codes of ethics are needed.

OVER THE YEARS, I HAVE HEARD JUSTIFICATIONS, SUCH AS...

"What I did was not unethical, because no one ever complained about it before." This doesn't change anything.

"What I did was not unethical, because I can name others who did the same thing." This just means that others are also engaging in unethical behavior.

"What I did was not unethical, because I was under a lot of stress." If the stress was so great that it lead to unethical behavior or boundary violations, then the question is whether the counselor was still counseling when impaired by too much stress.

"What I did was not unethical, because the client asked me to do it." Client consent is irrelevant. Clients cannot consent to ethical violations. Why? Because the counselor has the influential position of power, and exploitation of transference feelings, and/or the exploitation of the counselor's knowledge of a client are relevant concerns.

WHAT ABOUT THIS COGNITIVE JUSTIFICATION?

"What I did wasn't unethical as long as I know that legal, ethical, and professional standards were made up by people like you who don't understand the hard realities of counseling, and the people involved in enforcing these standards are dishonest, stupid, and they are conspiring against me."

A code of ethics cannot and will not guarantee ethical behavior. Codes summarize principles and socialize practitioners to the profession, but codes are the minimal behavioral statements and expectations. Ethical codes are not the maximum of what counselors are to live up to—they are the minimum. Minimum competency is the fulfillment of our licensing requirements; maximum competency refers to our intellectual and emotional competencies and our aspirational ethics. Competence is difficult to define and assess. A counselor needs to get input and feedback from trusted colleagues, family, and friends as a measure of their competency.

ETHICAL STANDARDS & CLINICAL FORMS

THE ETHICAL COUNSELOR
SPECIFIC ETHICS-RELATED VALUES
- Relational Connection: The ability to form healthy relationships with clients and colleagues
- Autonomy: Acknowledging the right of others' self-determination
- Going Good: (Beneficence) A desire to reduce human suffering and improve the welfare of others
- Do No Harm: (Nonmaleficence) Mindfulness to do no harm
- Competence: Committed to the value of being exceptionally skilled
- Humility: An awareness of personal limitations and weaknesses
- Professional Growth: The continual seeking of formal and informal learning opportunities
- Openness to Complexity and Ambiguity: Recognizing the uniqueness of people and their presenting problems
- Self-Awareness: Attending to one's emotional needs as well as unfinished personal business

HOW ARE CODES USED

Codes are used as a measure of a professional's competence, a complainant's validity, and the appropriateness of a regulatory board's actions. Each licensing board in each state has developed criteria to measure the conduct of the professionals they license. Their concern is whether conduct falls below the standard of care.

Actions and behaviors, relevant to state licensing board complaints, are typically sorted according to "severity"—least to the greatest.

"Least severity" is when a counselor's conduct caused no harm to a client (but counselor's behavior was outside the standard of care) or minimal client harm. A minimum disciplinary action could include reprimand, training, monitoring, supervision, probation, and psychological evaluation. Oversight for [x] years (number of years is determined by the licensing board's administrative process), which may include reprimand, training, monitoring, supervision, psychological evaluation, probation, and suspension are options for the sanction(s).

"Moderate severity" is when conduct caused moderate harm or risk to the client. A minimum disciplinary action could include suspension, probation, practice restrictions, training, monitoring, supervision, and psychological evaluation. Oversight for [x] years, which may include suspension, probation, practice restrictions, training, monitoring, supervision, psychological evaluation, and possibly revocation of license are options for the sanction(s). The duration for the disciplinary action typically spans [x] to [x] years, (span of years is determined by the licensing board's administrative process) unless there is revocation of the license.

"Greatest severity" is when conduct causes severe harm or even death to a human client. A minimum disciplinary action could include suspension, probation, practice restrictions, training, monitoring, supervision, and psychological evaluation. In addition, the licensing board may require the counselor to acquire additional education and demonstrate knowledge or competency. A maximum disciplinary action could include permanent conditions such as a revocation of a professional's license.

RESEARCH
- Research your state licensing board: What are the criteria for measuring the conduct of professionals licensed in your state?
- What are their sanctioning policies and processes?

RESPONDING TO A LICENSING BOARD INVESTIGATION

The probability of being investigated by a state licensing board is generally small, but it is greater than being sued. Many board complaints are never investigated. If the board decides that the complaint has no merit or decides not to investigate for any reason, you may not even know that a complaint was ever filed against you. Remember, the duty of the boards is to protect the public and regulate licensed mental health counselors. Licensing boards are a consumer protection agency. They are there for the protection of the consumers—our clients.

LICENSING BOARD INVESTIGATORS

Do not meet with a licensing board investigator without your legal representative. Meeting with an investigator without your attorney can be a most dangerous error. The reason for an attorney is to protect your rights in response to certain questions, so you do not unknowingly incriminate yourself. If a licensing board investigator is friendly and casual, keep a professional distance. Do not talk about the case nor release any records without legal representation. If an investigator shows up at your office, asked for their business card and tell them that your attorney will contact them. Do not allow them to pressure you to do anything; you have the right to legal representation.

Do not assume that a lack of harm to a client will end an investigation. Boards often focus on whether you provided services below the standard of care, rather than focusing on harm. They are concerned about whether you violated any state laws or administrative or professional guidelines, more so, than whether or not your client was harmed by your treatment. A claim of harm by a client is more an issue for civil courts. Talking about the investigation to anyone who will listen can do more harm than good. Remember, sometimes what you say can be held against you.

If a complaint is filed against you, contact your malpractice insurance carrier and get in touch with a knowledgeable attorney who has experience in administrative law and specifically with your state's administrative codes. Help your attorney identify experts on the issue at hand and how a certain expert's stance could benefit you. Be active in your defense and understand that it may take a long time to resolve. Focus on self-care and have strategies in place to manage your stress.

BOARD INVESTIGATIONS

Never take a board investigation lightly, and do not assume that your innocence will automatically be acknowledged. Never assume the complaint lacks merit; don't assume that your initial explanation will cause the complaint to be dismissed. Licensing boards have a very complex and detailed process to follow in order to fulfill their mandate to protect the public.

Seek legal advice and try to get an insurance policy that covers phone contact with an attorney. It is worth the extra cost. Having an insurance policy that includes coverage for investigations by licensing boards often includes attorney telephone consultation. Do not respond to a letter from the board unless you have consulted with an attorney. Let an attorney respond respectfully and professionally to any complaint.

Do not turn any material or clinical records over to the board without getting legal advice. The board is likely to have a right to review the clinical records related to an ongoing investigation, but the rules of evidence are quite complex and, at times, confusing. Let your attorney advise you about what to turn over to your licensing board.

INSURANCE COVERAGE

BEST PRACTICE IN TODAY'S WORLD IS TO HAVE AN INSURANCE POLICY THAT OFFERS THE FOLLOWING COVERAGE:
1) Liability (1 million/5 million)
2) A minimum of $25,000 coverage to defend your license if a complaint is filed against you with your licensing board. This amount can be increased by paying an additional premium fee.
3) Don't forget to ask about landlord coverage or "slip and fall" coverage, if needed and relevant to your situation.

Also, consider having a policy that provides [x] number of hours, per calendar year, for phone consultations with an attorney. Another option is to check your state counseling association to see if they provide this service as a benefit of membership.

ETHICAL STANDARDS & CLINICAL FORMS

RESEARCH
- Internet search for insurance policies; compare at least three (Annual cost and benefits)
- Try CPH & Associates or HPSO, as well as policies available through your professional association(s)—*compare their rates and benefits. (Author is not making a recommendation or an endorsement for any particular company or association)*
- Check you current policy—*does it include:*
  - Telephone contact hours with an attorney who specializes in mental health laws?
  - Coverage for investigations by licensing boards?
  - Risk Management advice?
  - A web site that addresses risk management concerns for mental health practice in your state?

ETHICS DIFFERS FROM THE LAW

Ethics often holds us to a higher standard, because the law does not prohibit many unethical behaviors. However, laws and ethics do overlap and many laws come from ethical violations.

Laws impose legal obligations; codes impose professional standards.

When a licensed counselor commits an ethical violation, an option for the injured party is to take them to court. That court then makes a decision and that decision is referred to as "case" or "court" law. When case law is significant, state legislation can enter a bill to create a new "legislative" or "statutory" law.

WHAT WOULD MAKE LEGISLATION LOOK CLOSELY AT A COURT DECISION?
- When there is a negative discovery
- There were severe adverse consequences
- The event is high profile

THE CORNERSTONES OF ETHICS

THE CORNERSTONES OF ETHICS ARE:
   1) Do no harm
   2) Do not exploit clients
   3) Do not continue counseling if your professional judgment is impaired

These three statements are the cornerstones of our professional ethics. When ethical committees sit down to write or revise ethical codes, they weigh what they are doing against these cornerstones. Keep these three items in mind, as they bear much relevance to the information that will be covered throughout this entire book.

Licensed counselors, ethically, are to include a statement in their consent or professional disclosure document stating clearly that they adhere to their ethical guidelines. If a counselor's ethical responsibilities conflict with the law, regulations, or other governing legal authorities (licensing boards), counselors make known their commitment to their ethics code and take steps to resolve the conflict.

If the demands of an organization conflict with their ethical codes, then counselors clarify the nature of the conflict, make known their commitment to their ethics code and, to the extent feasible, resolve the conflict in a way that permits adherence to the ethics code.

If the conflict cannot be resolved, and the counselor's ethical responsibilities conflict with the laws, regulations, and other governing legal authorities, then the counselor "may" adhere to the requirements of the law, regulations, or other governing legal authorities. This is an interesting statement because the word "may," in essence, is saying you have a choice, which you do. Sometimes, counselors take a stand against a law, regulation, or governing authority because they believe that not taking a stand would cause greater harm to a client. Sometimes we see civil disobedience.

For example, in the earlier years of managed care, counselors found themselves in conflict when they were asked to diagnose or document in a manner that promoted reimbursement rather than an accurate representation of what existed. It took individuals who were willing to take a stand for justice to promote change.

MORAL PRINCIPLES

The "moral principles" underpinning ethical codes are viewed as foundational elements of ethical guidelines. Ethical guidelines cannot address all situations that a counselor is forced to confront. Therefore, understanding both the cornerstones of ethics (do no harm; do not exploit clients; do not counsel if your professional judgment is impaired) and these moral principles (that support the cornerstones of ethics) are vital for attaining an "aspirational ethics" standard that influences your actions.

THE MORAL PRINCIPLES ARE:
- Autonomy
- Fidelity
- Doing Good (Beneficence)
- Do No Harm (Nonmaleficence)
- Justice

Understanding these moral principles helps counselors clarify issues involved in any given ethical situation. By exploring an ethical dilemma using these moral principles as a guide, the counselor can gain a better understanding of the conflicting issues.

"Autonomy" is the principle that addresses the concept of independence. The essence of this principle is allowing an individual the freedom of choice and action. It addresses the responsibility of the counselor to encourage clients, when appropriate, to make their own decisions and act on their own values. There are two important considerations in encouraging clients to be autonomous. First, help the client understand how their decisions and their values may or may not be received within the context of the society in which they live, and how they might impinge on the rights of others. Second, consideration for the client's ability to make sound and rational decisions must be given. Clients incapable of making competent choices, such as children, and some individuals with mental handicaps or emotional instabilities, should not be allowed to act on decisions that could harm themselves or others.

"Fidelity" involves the notion of loyalty, faithfulness, and honoring commitments. Clients must be able to trust the counselor and have faith in the therapeutic relationship if growth is to occur. Therefore, the counselor must take care not to threaten the counseling relationship, nor leave obligations unfulfilled.

ETHICAL STANDARDS & CLINICAL FORMS

"Doing Good, also called beneficence," reflects the counselor's responsibility to contribute to the welfare of the client. Simply stated, it means to do good, to be proactive, and to prevent harm when possible.

"Do No Harm, also called nonmaleficence," is the concept of not causing harm to others. This principle is considered, by many, to be the most critical of all the principles. This principle reflects both the idea of not inflicting intentional harm and not engaging in actions that risk harming others.

"Justice" does not mean treating all individuals the same. The formal meaning of justice is "treating equals equally and unequals unequally, but in proportion to their relevant differences." If an individual is to be treated differently, the counselor needs to be able to offer a rationale that explains the necessity and appropriateness of treating the individual differently.

RESEARCH
- Research the formal meaning of justice listed above.
- Create some examples of how it applies to clinical work.

SCOPE OF PRACTICE

Counselors are to practice within their "scope of practice" which means to practice within their licensed profession, professional education, and competency.

An example of a scope of practice for a "licensed professional counselor" might read: The application of principles of human development, learning theory, counseling, group dynamics, an etiology of mental illness and dysfunctional behavior to individuals, couples, families, groups, and organizations for the purpose of treatment of mental disorders and promoting optimal mental health and functionality, etc...

An example of a scope of practice for a "licensed marriage and family counselor" might read: The diagnosis and treatment of emotional and mental disorders, whether cognitive, affective, or behavioral with you in the context of relationships, including marriage and family systems, etc...

An example of a scope of practice for a "licensed social worker" might read: The diagnosis and treatment of emotional and mental disorders based on knowledge of human development, the causation and treatment of psychopathology, psychotherapeutic treatment practices and social work practice. Treatment modalities include but are not limited to diagnosis and treatment of individuals, couples, families, groups, or organizations, etc…

An example of a scope of practice for a "licensed clinical psychologist" might read: The diagnosis and treatment of psychological disorders and the performing of psychological testing, etc…

RESEARCH
- Contact your licensing board, state association, or national association and ask for a copy of your "scope of practice."

STANDARD OF CARE

"Standard of Care" usually relates to the process of the work with the client, the decisions made, although not always the decision itself, and rarely the clinical outcome alone. We cannot guarantee specific clinical outcomes, and the law does not impose a "duty to cure." Counselors are not expected to be perfect, and counselors do not guaranteed positive or desired results. Another way of looking at standard of care is by comparison—comparatively the level of practice one counselor provides in relation to other reasonable and relatively prudent professionals.

Counselors are held to the same standard as others in the same profession or discipline who have comparable qualifications and provide comparable services. The standard of care is a most important concept in mental health. Careless mistakes or errors in judgment do not necessarily put a counselor below the standard of care.

Standard of care is not a standard of perfection, nor is it defined by any particular theoretical philosophy or specific psychotherapy or treatment orientation.

Standard of care is typically based on legal-professional-community principles, where risk management guidelines are geared towards reducing the risk of malpractice for counselors. Standard of care is not determined by the therapy outcome. If the counselor uses a treatment process that falls within the standard of care, and they are not negligent, but the outcome is negative, they are not necessarily below standard of care. Standard of care is not a fixed standard. It continues to evolve and develop as more counselors practice in new or modified therapy interventions.

Periodically, studies are done on code violation allegations that are related to standard of care. Poor practice is the failure of a counselor to provide services within accepted standards and it is the focus of such studies. These studies typically reveal findings of incompetence in conjunction with other forms of unethical behavior.

Examples, of being outside scope and standard, include a lack of minimum competence, training, education, supervision, or certification and licensing. A counselor using old testing materials instead of current ones, or not staying current on trends, interventions, and ethical code requirements are examples of being outside scope of practice and standard of care.

Counselors can demonstrate ignorance or lack of skill when they fail to understand or demonstrate "best practice" knowledge. It is important that licensed mental health counselors, through various ways, stay current in their counseling practice. Professional development includes, but is not limited to, on-going consultation and supervision, peer review, coursework, certification training, seeking additional schooling through graduate degree work or academic participation, professional membership, and periodical reading.

Counselors need to demonstrate knowledge of current laws and regulations regarding the practice of psychotherapy. State counseling associations typically strive to stay current on changes in laws or regulations that impact counselors. Thus, membership with a state association can be very helpful.

RESEARCH
- Internet search for these key words: mental health + competence + standard of care + study
- What recent studies did you find?
  - What were their conclusions regarding competence and standard of care?

Standard of care is derived from statutes. Every state has many statutes, affecting such areas as child abuse, elder abuse, domestic violence reporting, duty to warn and protect, and so forth. Certainly, if a state statute mandates that a counselor act in a certain way, not doing so lies clearly below the standard of care. In most states, licensing board regulations govern many aspects of the counseling practice, such as: Rules about who can and cannot take the licensing exam; and, rules about mandated continuing education, licensing fees, and regulations regarding supervision are common.

Case law also affects standard of care. Tarasoff vs. Regents is the famous California case that created a duty for counselors to warn an intended victim. Since this case in 1976, many other states have obligated their licensed counseling professionals to do the same. Also HIPAA regulations address standard of care; ethical codes of professional associations outline standard of care; consensus of professionals and communities impact standard of care; insurance companies and litigating attorneys influence standard of care. There is no one textbook, court case, or set of rules that completely defines the standard of care.

A negative outcome, such as a client's suicide, is not sufficient proof of sub-standard care. A client who sues a counselor must establish that the counselor acted below the standard of care. Sometimes sub-standard care is the outcome of intentional or negligent acts. More often it is errors in judgment. The standard of care is primarily determined by testimonies from expert witnesses. Attorneys on both sides present conflicting expert testimonies about standard of care. Adding to this complexity is the fact that there are hundreds of different theoretical philosophies and therapeutic orientations. Many different types of communities and cultures make the concept of standard of care extremely complex and controversial.

Many codes of ethics state: "These ethical codes are not intended to be a basis of civil liability." Codes of ethics are not supposed to be simply equated with the standard of care, which is the basis for civil liability. Ethical codes further state: "The issue as to whether a counselor has violated ethical code standards does not by itself determine whether the counselor is legally liable in a court action, whether or not a contract is enforceable, and whether or not any other legal consequences occur."

RESEARCH

- Look at your association's code of ethics. Are there statements like the ones listed above?
- Are you in a specialized area of counseling? (sex therapy, forensic, body therapy)
- Identify associations for several specialized fields of therapy.
  - What elements in their code of ethics speak directly to the professional specializing in a specific area of practice?

Remember, standard of care is not a fixed standard. It continues to evolve and develop as more counselors practice in new or modified therapy interventions. Changes can also come through the publication of new research findings, new therapy guidelines, or the advancement of new theoretical processes.

Complying with standard of care means that counselors act in a prudent and reasonable manner. The proof of this compliance is almost exclusively found in a counselor's clinical records.

Good records go hand-in-hand with quality care: Documentation of diagnosis, assessment, mental status and details of presenting problems, treatment planning, progress notes, test results, consultations, crisis interventions, documentation of special phone calls or contact with others involved with the care of the client, clear informed consent, appropriate office policies, and termination details—all are necessary and essential for quality care.

RESEARCH
- One way to evaluate if conduct by a licensed counselor is within standard of care is to ask these questions:
  - Does the behavior violate any state or federal laws, licensing board regulations or an ethical principle?
  - Would a respected colleague, who uses a similar theoretical orientation, working with similar clients, in a comparable community, do the same?

FIDUCIARY DUTY

A "fiduciary relationship" is a professional relationship based on trust. It is a relationship in which the professional counselor acts in the best interests of the client. Clients come to counseling seeking help from people they believe they can trust. A fiduciary duty provides the highest standard of care. A "fiduciary" (in this situation, a "licensed counselor") is expected to be extremely loyal to the person to whom the duty is owed (the client). In a fiduciary relationship, a licensed counselor must not put their personal interest before this duty, and they must not personally profit from or receive personal gain at a client's expense. When a fiduciary duty is imposed, equity requires a stricter standard of behavior. The licensed counselor has a duty not to be in a situation where personal interests and fiduciary duty conflict; they are not to be in a situation where the fiduciary duty conflicts with another fiduciary duty (e.g., counselor is counseling both the rapist and the victim); and, they are not to be in a situation to profit from the fiduciary position without expressed knowledge and consent, meaning there should be a written consent that includes financial agreements.

In the mental health profession, a fiduciary duty is a legal obligation of the licensed counselor to act in the best interests of the client. The counselor is the fiduciary—someone trusted with the care of another. A counselor's fiduciary responsibility and relationship with the client typically begins when the client signs a consent form for care. Virtuous counselors upholding their fiduciary relationship would be motivated to "do good" and possess a high degree of self-understanding and awareness. They would also comprehend the "mores" (the collective moralities) of their communities in relationship to the cultures they interact with and their clients' diversities.

ETHICAL STANDARDS & CLINICAL FORMS

EXTRATHERAPEUTIC

The term "extratherapeutic" refers to a counselor's behavior that involves "actions of self-interest" and "exploitation." This can include a "perception of self-interest." An example of this could be when a counselor uses a counseling sessions with a client for their own cathartic dialogue. When a counselor self-discloses too much, it can be perceived as self-interest. Remember, the session is about the client, not the counselor.

Extratherapeutic does not represent two words accidentally put together—"extra" and "therapeutic." It has nothing to do with going the extra mile as in "extra."

EXPLOITATION CAN OCCUR IN MANY WAYS BUT THE TWO COMMON FACTORS ARE:
    1) Intimacy issues, concerns, violations
    2) Power differentiation

There are special characteristics of the counselor/client relationship, which places the counselor in a position of greater power and authority. The relationship, in essence, renders it "unfair" for the counselor to gain any benefit at the client's expense.

What if a counselor was seeing clients in a hot tub? What if they were nude? What if their counseling practice was in a nudist colony? Would that change anything?

RESEARCH
- **Internet search this phrase: "The glory days of nude psychotherapy".**
  - **What did you discover?**

COMPLAINTS

Complaints come from many sources: Clients, agencies, insurance companies, and colleagues. What about friends? A counselor went to a western tavern with a friend. After too many drinks, an argument started between the friends and ended in a fist fight. The counselor knocked his friend to the floor; as the friend lay there, the counselor said, "You are a crazy, paranoid, bipolar, obsessive-compulsive idiot." The friend filed a complaint with the licensing board stating he was diagnosed inaccurately, and inappropriately, in public.

When a complaint is received, questions are asked: "What is motivating the complaint? Does it make sense?" Then facts and data are collected as the complaint is further investigated. The conclusion a complaint results in dismissal, summaries, actions, or what is commonly referred to as sanctions. Sanctions can include a letter to a counselor's file, a supervisor appointed, suspension, or revocation of the counselor's license. Referring back to the above complaint: There was no fiduciary relationship between the counselor and the friend. The friend was not a client. However, the counselor did receive a letter from the licensing board (which was placed in his file) that emphasized the importance of the ethical responsibility to uphold the integrity of the counseling profession, which his public behavior failed to do.

ISSUES OF FRAUD

Remember, licensing boards have licensing requirements. Individuals are to be of good moral character and comply with the rules and regulations of the licensing board. They are to demonstrate competence and they are not to use professional relationships to further personal self-interest.

"Fraud" carries severe sanctions because fraud demonstrates a lack of good moral character. For example, fraudulent billing or fraudulent misrepresentation of qualifications can be met with severe sanctions.

ETHICAL STANDARDS & CLINICAL FORMS

LICENSING BOARDS, CIVIL, AND CRIMINAL COURTS

Licensing boards deal with violation of behavior standards and impose sanctions. These are administrative actions. Civil courts seek monetary damages for negligence, or breaches of duty owed to clients. Determinations of guilt are made by a preponderance of the evidence. Criminal courts seek sentencing, deal with felony crimes, and determinations of guilt are determined by evidence beyond a reasonable doubt.

RESEARCH
Contact your licensing board for the following information:
 1) Disciplinary process
 2) Chart of sanctions
 3) Examples of cases and sanctions

YOUR RECORDS ARE VERY IMPORTANT

In the case of administrative litigation (when a complaint has been filed against you with your licensing board) it is often not the counselor's word against the client's, but the client's word against the clinical records. Many boards make the decision whether to pursue a case based on experts who develop their opinion from reading the client's complaint and the counselor's records, but not necessarily interviewing the counselor themselves.

Records should reflect a counselor's competence and their decision-making ability. Records should show that the counselor has the capacity to weigh available options; records should show a rationale for treatment selection; and, records should reflect the counselor's knowledge of clinical, ethical, and legal relevance.

It is important to document all special occurrences, such as important phone calls, emergencies, issues of dangerousness, mandated and other reporting, consultations, testing, referrals, and contact with family members or other individuals known by the client. (More on records later)

ETHICAL STANDARDS & CLINICAL FORMS

*Counseling is a unique profession
providing great opportunities
to help others*

IT IS A UNIQUE PROFESSION

Counseling is a unique profession providing great opportunities to help others. It can be rewarding to directly work with people and their problems and often being able to see the results of the work. The collaboration and networking with other professionals and large professional organizations can support many needs. It is a diverse field offering many different opportunities. But it has its downside. It can be emotionally draining and can be professionally isolating. Working with non-compliant, manipulating, or self-sabotaging clients can be extremely frustrating.

When I was in graduate school learning how to "do counseling," and I looked forward to the opportunity to eventually work with real clients. When conducting mock therapy sessions, I did exactly what I was taught to do in graduate school. I used my training in appropriate body posture and reflected on what I thought I heard my mock client say. However, after actually providing real services to real clients, I recognized something important—the learning curve is on-going.

There is a learning curve. I entered the field like many others, wanting to help people. Therefore, early on in my career I was quite frustrated about being less effective then I had envisioned. Then, older and wiser and more experienced, I learned that such frustrations are common. Counseling is a profession that works with vulnerable people who are struggling with issues of resistance, denial, sabotage, rage, and chronic failure. Counseling is challenging.

THE MENTAL HEALTH PROFESSION AND THE MEDIA

Unfortunately, beliefs are formed about the mental health profession through media, and media does not always represents the mental health profession appropriately. If a TV show and movies that involve counseling, it typically includes unethical behavior. These portrayals diminish the professional reputation through off-color (unethical) interactions. Movies, such as *What About Bob, Mumford, Analyze This (and That), As Good as it Gets, Prime,* and *Goodwill Hunting* are fraught with unethical behavior. Take some time and watch these TV shows: *Frasier, The New Adventures of Old Christine, Two and a Half Men, Seinfeld, Golden Girls, The Office, Bob Newhart,* and *Growing Pains.* Look for the movies and TV shows or episodes that involve counseling and you'll find unethical behavior.

Read the comic strips, or check out greeting cards (those that have something to do with counseling) and you'll see references to unethical behavior. This is why our ethical codes state that counselors are to conduct themselves in such a manner that helps uphold, protect, enhance, and improve the integrity of the profession. Counselors are to help advance the values, ethics, knowledge, and mission(s) of the counseling profession. We protect, enhance, and improve the integrity of the profession through appropriate study and research, active discussion, and responsible behavior. For a list of TV shows and movies, keyword search: "TV shows and movies that are relevant to counseling" using www.wikipedia.org

CLIENTS' VULNERABLE NATURE

Who are our clients? Often they are needy, victimized, frightened, overwhelmed, vulnerable, depressed, angry, lonely, grieving, desperate, young, elderly, disabled, discriminated, sick, weak, frustrated, and ashamed. Clients come to counseling feeling guilty when change has not been maintained. They often blame themselves for their conditions and are embarrassed. They are easily frustrated that understanding does not mean feeling better. The stigma of receiving mental health counseling or being diagnosed with a mental health condition still exists.

THE ISSUE OF FAMILIARITY

A measure of "familiarity" naturally exists in the counseling relationship. There is a long continuum of what can and is considered relational intimacy, or familiarity. Familiarity is a relational intimacy. Don't be thrown by the word intimacy, because this is not about inappropriate intimacies between a counselor and a client. What does this mean? It means there exists in the counseling relationship a relational intimacy because of the familiarity we have with clients. Imagine a long line and label this line relational intimacy. At one end of it is the beginning of familiarity—knowledge of a client's fears, concerns, and struggles—a knowing of the client's mental processes. At the other end of the continuum would be inappropriate intimacies, or familiarities. Because of the work in counseling, the relationship with clients exists on this relational intimacy continuum. The challenge is to keep appropriate boundaries in place so that the relationship does not move too far down the continuum to the inappropriate end. Ethical codes that address boundary issues are vital, necessary and needed.

EMPATHY AND WARMTH

A counselor's empathy and warmth can be a potent medicine or an ethical concern. Empathy and warmth must be tempered with appropriate boundaries. Take the issue of hugging a client. There is nothing in ethical codes that tells you whether or not to hug a client. There is nothing in the ethical codes that tells counselors how to hug a client. A counselor has to take many things in to consideration: The diagnostic criteria of the clients they work with, the culture of the clients they serve, the counselor's personal style and temperament, the age of their clients, the type of counseling provided, and the setting in which the counseling is delivered. I know counselors who do not hug their clients; I know counselors who hug their clients all the time.

I went to see my very first counselor when I was 19 years old. She was a lovely old woman. I enjoyed my session. At the end, she asked if I would like to return, and I said I would. As she was standing by the door she picked up her appointment book and we decided on the next appointment time; she wrote out an appointment card for me. After she handed me the appointment card, we stood looking at each other face-to-face, and I wanted to give her a hug. I moved in, arms outstretched; she stepped backwards, smiled and put her hand in front of her, stopping me in my tracks. She looked at me and said, "I know what you'd like to do; you want to give me a hug." I thought, not anymore, that moment has passed. She said, "Let me show you how to hug." I was thinking I'd stepped into the Twilight Zone. She said, "Do what I do," and she put her right hand on her left shoulder, her left hand on her right shoulder, then bent her knees with a bit of a bounce, smiled, and said, "Hug, hug."

My gestures were not as enthusiastic, and I could hardly wait to get out of there. Once outside, I deposited the appointment card in the first trash receptacle I saw and never called or went back. I understand now what she was doing—she had a boundary. Unfortunately, she did not inform me about this boundary, and I was taken by surprise. If, in her consent form, she had included a diagram of stick people demonstrating the appropriate technique for a hug, I would have been with the program. Boundaries are very important in the mental health profession, but shock and surprise do not promote good client relations.

Ethical codes are necessary, but not sufficient
and must be tempered by experience and context.

BOUNDARY CROSSING

Boundary crossings are defined as non-exploitive deviations from standard practice. What is "standard practice" and how is it defined? It is one counselor and one client in a confidential setting. Boundary crossings may encompass benign and beneficial departures from established counseling norms. There is a virtual explosion of healthy controversy and thoughtful writings on the issue. Is it possible to tell which boundary crossings are therapeutically helpful; which are therapeutically contra-indicated as harmful; which might be common or even unavoidable in certain communities, settings, or cultures? The meaning of boundary crossings and their appropriate application can only be understood and assessed within the context of therapy. The context of therapy consists of four main factors: Client, setting, therapy, and counselor.

CLIENT FACTORS:
- Culture and history, including history of trauma, sexual and/or physical abuse, age, gender, presenting problem, mental state, and type and severity of mental disturbances, socioeconomic class, personality type and/or personality disorder, sexual orientation, social support, religious and/or spiritual beliefs and practices, physical health, prior experience with therapy and counselors, etc.

SETTING FACTORS:
- Outpatient versus inpatient; solo-practice versus group-practice; office in medical building versus private setting versus home office; freestanding clinic versus hospital-based clinic; privately owned clinic versus publicly run agency, as well as the presence or proximity of a receptionist, staff, or other professionals. It also includes locality, whether its large, metropolitan area versus small, rural town; affluent, suburban setting versus poor neighborhood; or university, school or other academic settings; culturally-bound settings, major urban settings, remote military bases, prisons, or police department settings.

THERAPY FACTORS:
- Modality: Individual versus couple versus family versus group therapy; short-term versus long-term versus intermittent therapy.
- Intensity: Therapy sessions several times a week versus once a month; child versus adolescent versus adults and the level of intervention. Intense and involved versus neutral or casual relationships; length of counseling, long term relationship versus the beginning of therapy versus middle of therapy versus towards termination of therapy.

- Therapeutic orientation: Psychoanalysis versus humanistic versus group therapy versus body counseling versus eclectic therapy. In addition, there are therapeutic relationship factors such as the quality and nature of the therapeutic alliance (secure, trusting, tentative, fearful, or safe connection). Other factors include idealized or transference relationship issues, familiarity or distanced, presence or absence of dual relationships and type of dual relationships, if applicable.

COUNSELOR FACTORS:
- Culture, age, gender, theoretical philosophy, therapeutic orientation, faith and belief issues, scope of practice (training and experience).

Although it may seem obvious, knowledge of ethical codes and state laws are essential in framing the background for boundary crossing considerations. Clear expectations and boundaries, whenever possible, strengthen the counseling relationship. Obtaining informed consent, sticking to time limits, protecting confidentiality and explaining its limits, and documenting case progress (including being explicit about any overlapping relationships and out-of-office therapies) diminishes the risk of misunderstandings between client and counselor. Ongoing consultation and discussion of cases, especially those involving boundary crossings and dual roles, provides an opportunity for counselors to gain additional perspectives.

THE PROHIBITION AGAINST DUAL RELATIONSHIPS ORIGINATES FROM TWO SOURCES:
1) Appropriate concerns due to the power differential between counselors and clients, along with the ethical requirements to protect clients from harm or exploitation, and 2) Traditional counseling that emphasizes neutrality and careful transference work, and the concern that impairment of a counselor's judgment can occur. Many sources warn counselors of the dangers of dual relationships in general. Professional organizations, consumer protection agency (state licensing boards), and, in some states, legislative laws, agree completely with counselor-client prohibitions against sexual relationships. A concern for exploitation and client harm is the basis for all these protective policies and guidelines.

"Boundary crossings" occur when we deviate from standard norms, but when done, they are done for the client's benefit—the boundary is changed to assist the client. My colleague who works with individuals with eating disorders deviates from standard norms, regarding boundary crossings, when she goes shopping with a client, has a meal with a client and spends time with them after that meal.

ETHICAL STANDARDS & CLINICAL FORMS

Boundary crossings have the potential for creating a dual relationship, but they are not a dual relationship when the purpose of the boundary crossing is therapeutic. The purpose for boundary crossings should be relevant to theory orientations, the boundary crossing is always discussed with the client, and informed consent is obtain.

You can create a boundary-crossing plan (not unlike a suicide safety plan) or an addendum to your consent regarding planned boundary crossings. And of course: Document–document–document. Remember, boundary crossings are not necessarily boundary violations.

RESEARCH
- Is it possible to tell which boundary crossings are therapeutically helpful?
- Which are therapeutically contra-indicated as harmful?
  - Which might be common or even unavoidable in certain communities or cultures?

BOUNDARIES

Boundaries in therapy define the therapeutic-fiduciary relationship or what is also called the "therapeutic frame." They distinguish psychotherapy work, or clinical relationships, from other relationships, such as social, sexual, and business. Therapy is never "clients with benefits."

- THERAPEUTIC BOUNDARIES are necessary for ethical therapy and includes time and place of sessions, type of work being done, the client's condition(s), fees, and confidentiality/privacy.
- RELATIONAL BOUNDARIES are needed between the counselor and the client, and these include self-disclosure, physical contact, gifts, contact outside of therapy.

CULTURAL COMPETENCE

Boundary crossings are non-exploitive deviations from standard practice. Non-explotive boundary crossings often reflect the setting, type of therapy, or "client culture." Ethics requires counselors to have an understanding of the various cultures they work with and receive education regarding social diversity. A counselor's cultural competence is an ethical requirement. Gender, culture, and spirituality are elements of therapeutic processes. Such factors shape identities and defines one's behavior. Gender, culture, and spirituality influences the levels of understanding and the effective responsiveness that competent counseling professionals need to consider in a culturally and spiritually diverse society. Mental health issues are viewed through an individual's unique gender, cultural, and spiritual world view. Everyone has been affected by and identifies with culture(s).

Although significant developments in gender, multicultural, and spiritual/religious research have further defined professional competencies, the impact of globalization and subsequent cultural/ethnic diversity has had a growing influence on professional practices which, more than ever, necessitates a broader base of understanding for human development. Gender, culture, and spirituality intersect and impact interventions and treatments used by counseling professionals. In today's global society, consequences of not attending to these significant contextual dimensions may limit the counselor's ability to assist their clients and may even thwart their growth and development.

"Cultural diversity" embodies the many factors that individuals bring to therapy. In 1991, I had the opportunity to work as a drug education liaison with gangs. Quickly, I had to gain an understanding of this culture—the initiation rituals, rivalries, language, and the hierarchy of power. Culture is not limited to race, creed, and color. Culture can be a group of people with a common agenda that closely and significantly binds them together. As a tall, blonde, Caucasian woman, I stood out in this area of town. Actually, I was both a novelty and a curiosity as I wandered around asking individuals if they belonged to a gang, and if they would talk with me. I think being a novelty and a curiosity are what kept me safe. Also, the organization that hired me printed my business cards; they printed the name of the agency, my name, and, instead of the title "drug education liaison," they printed "drug liaison." During the term of the six-month grant, I never had the card reprinted correctly. The misprint was a point of humor that opened dialog.

ETHICAL STANDARDS & CLINICAL FORMS

Ethics requires counselors to always consider and respect a client's spiritual/religious beliefs. However, exploring religious and spiritual beliefs and using religious and spiritual interventions are two different things. Exploring spiritual and religious beliefs is a more passive process, while using religious and spiritual interventions is an active process that needs clear informed consent, preferably in writing. A spiritual intervention, such as prayer, should not be used without the consent of the client.

Woven through the social context of gender role assignments and life experiences is the spiritual/religious realm. Spirituality/religion is a part of culture and forms meaning, value, and direction for individuals. Therapeutic problems may surface when an individual is faced with events that lead to existential dilemmas and examination of their human condition in relationship to their faith and beliefs. The search for a place in the larger collective has often been found in religion and spirituality. It is found in diverse communities. Treating various psychological conditions requires the assessment of an individual's spirituality and religious beliefs.

"Cultural diversity competence" is reflected in a counselor's ability to respond effectively to people of all cultures, classes, races, ethnic backgrounds, sexual orientations, and faiths/religions in a manner that recognizes, affirms, and values the worth of individuals, families, tribes, and communities, and protects and preserves the dignity of each. Counselors demonstrate cultural competence by being knowledgeable about culture, especially cultures they work with on a regular basis. Counselors who work with specific cultures inevitably join in honoring client accomplishments, rituals, and life transitions: Native American clients in some of their sacred rituals, Latino clients in weddings, Catholic clients at confirmations, or Jewish clients for bar or bat mitzvahs, to name a few.

"Culturally competent counselors" recognize and appreciate the strengths found in cultures and they take into consideration the nature of social diversities and oppression concerns. "Bar-coding" is a term used to refer to unearned privilege and unearned oppressions. People are born into positions of privilege or oppression; and sadly, people are labeled—by themselves, others, their communities, or as a reflection of their privilege or oppression. And labels can promote opportunities, but more often they create obstacles. Mental health counselors should understand and value diversity cross-culturally, conduct cultural self-assessment, acquire and integrate cultural knowledge into their practice, and adapt to the diversity of cultural contexts. Positive talk climates are descriptive, spontaneous and empathetic, oriented toward problems, and express equality.

Many well-meaning counselors make common errors when working with diverse cultures: Insensitivity to nonverbal cues, gender bias, over emphasis of cultural explanations for psychological difficulties, or vice versa. Counselors can promote an ethical practice in cultural competence by displaying materials that reflect cultures and ethnic backgrounds of clients and provide printed materials that are of interest to and reflect cultures of the people served. Treatment aids, such as play therapy and games, should reflect the cultures of those served and should be incorporated into the counseling practices. A counselor's cultural competence can also be seen by their understanding that beliefs and concepts of emotional well-being vary from culture to culture.

BOUNDARY VIOLATIONS

"Boundary violations" include wrong, unethical, and possibly illegal behavior between a counselor and the client. Self-interest or personal gain by the counselor is a result of boundary violations. This self-interest has nothing to do with being paid for services rendered, nor the personal satisfaction a counselor can feel from doing their job well. Boundary violations are reflected in self-interest gained by a counselor at the expense of the client. In other words—exploitation.

Boundary violations can be a by-product of boundary crossings. Boundary crossings are defined as non-exploiting deviations from standard practice; these boundary crossings can reflect the counseling setting, the type of therapy provided, or the client culture. But whenever we cross boundaries, we are gaining more familiarity with our clients. And sometimes that familiarity leads to boundary violations.

Counselors who go to people's homes (e.g., hospice, family services) gains familiarity. As we gain familiarity, boundaries can get blurry, and this increases the potential to continue a slippery slide down the continuum towards the slippery slope of boundary violations.

A client's consent is never a defense with boundary violations, because of the respective roles. The counselor has the fiduciary responsibility to act in the best interest of the client, and boundary violations reflect self-interest. When a counselor exploits a client, it is universally regarded as unethical; it is considered in every jurisdiction to constitute malpractice; and, in some states certain types of boundary violations are a criminal offense.

Clients are injured by boundary violations. Injuries include sexual dysfunction, anxiety disorders, psychiatric hospitalizations, increased risk of suicide, depression, dissociative behavior, internalized feelings of guilt, shame, anger, confusion, hatred, inability to trust, and feelings of worthlessness and humiliation.

SEXUAL BOUNDARY VIOLATIONS

Our ethical codes of conduct are very specific about sexual boundary violations. Counselors do not engage in sexual intimacies with clients; counselors do not terminate therapy to circumvent these standards; and, counselors do not accept individuals with whom they have engaged in sexual intimacies, as clients.

Association codes of ethics vary regarding relationships with clients who are previous clients. Please keep in mind that association codes of ethics are revised periodically, so the information shared here may very well have changed since the publication of this book. But, nonetheless, it helps to make this point clear. The American Psychological Association states that psychologists do not engage in sexual intimacies with "current" clients. The American Counseling Association prohibits intimate relations for five years after the termination of the counseling relationship.

The National Association of Social Workers prohibits engaging in sexual activities or sexual contact with current clients, but goes on to say that if social workers engage in conduct contrary to this prohibition or claim that an exception to this prohibition is warranted because of "extraordinary circumstances" it is the counselor who assumes the full burden of demonstrating that the former client has not been exploited. These above statements do leave open the possibility of an intimate relationship with a previous client. Most licensing boards adhere to "once a client, always a client." Since it is your state that issues your license, it is vital that you adhere to your state licensing board's codes of professional conduct.

With that said, let's look at a typical precedence set in case laws regarding counselors who have had sexual relations with clients. Although paraphrased, consider the guilty verdict to read something like this: "Do not engage in sexual intimacies with the clients except in the most "unusual circumstances" and if sexual intimacies are engaged in, the counselor bears the burden of proof to demonstrate that there has been no harm, exploitation, or impairment of the counselor's judgment."
Take another look at these words: Do not engage… except… most unusual circumstances… if you engage…. Can it be any clearer? Case law is written with

broad strokes; it becomes precedence that subsequent cases can be weighed against. Case laws (court decisions) are not as clear and specific as legislative or statutory laws. Look at this statement again: Except in the "most unusual circumstances." The social workers' code of ethics states something similar. If social workers engage in conduct contrary to the prohibition against sexual relations with previous clients, a claim with an exception is warranted because of "extraordinary circumstances."

So what would be an example of a most unusual and extraordinary circumstance? Here's one: You are a hard-working, ethical counselor who is going to take a ten-day vacation to a tropical paradise. The day of departure arrives and you are at your office finishing up your final chart notes. You rush to the airport and board the plane just before the doors are closed. You take your seat in first class (remember this is a fantasy). You're on your way. However, you have no idea that a previous client of yours is sitting in the economy section of the plane. After several hours the pilot announces the initial decent. Tragedy strikes; the plane goes down! Even a greater tragedy. Everyone perishes except for two people—you and your client. You make your way to a deserted island and go about the business of survival. Reflecting on your association's code of ethics, you think you recall a two-year, or was it revised to five years, waiting period before entering into an intimate relationship with the previous client. You are a very ethical counselor, so you start notching off the coconut tree. After a few years you throw your hands up in the air and say, "This is a most unusual and extraordinary circumstance!" Then, five years later, when you are rescued from the island, you find yourself in a lawsuit. I believe, under these circumstances, you'd be found not guilty.

As mentioned earlier, "once a client, always a client" is the general rule of thumb. Although the prohibition against sex with clients reaches back beyond Freud, beyond the Hippocratic oath, as far back as the code of the Nigerian healing arts. It was only with systematic research that began in the 1950s that the profession began to understand the depth, pervasiveness, and persistence of the harm that can result when counselors abuse their role, power, and trust. When people are hurting, unhappy, frightened, or confused, they seek help from a counselor. They may be depressed, perhaps thinking of suicide. They may be suffering trauma from rape, incest, or domestic violence. They may binge and purge, abuse drugs and alcohol, or engage in other behavior that can destroy health, and sometimes be fatal.

The therapeutic relationship is special, characterized by exceptional vulnerability and trust. Unfortunately, small percent of counselors do take advantage of client trust and vulnerability and of using the power inherent in the counselor's role. By its nature, the counseling relationship is unequal. Clients make themselves vulnerable by sharing intimate details of their lives with their counselors. Clients invest trust in counselors, relying on the counselor's judgment for help. Often, clients view their counselors as powerful, parent figures, and clients may interact with the counselor in a childlike way. Many clients idealize, admire, and experience sexual attraction or romantic feelings toward their counselors.

Competent, ethical counselors recognize that these client responses are normal, but they also realize that the power imbalance between counselor and client negates the possibility of an equal, consenting relationship. Counselors who encourage clients to act on these feelings abuse their position of trust. They misuse the relationship to gratify their own needs, failing to fulfill the responsibility to help the client. Such manipulation is a violation of the client's trust in a form of abuse, even if the client appears to consent or even initiate the sexual contact.

Many believe that the power dynamics in the therapeutic relationship so closely resemble those in a parent-child dyad that sex between counselor and client is psychologically equivalent to incest. Unfortunately, sex between counselors and clients occurs more frequently than it should. Counselors are fiduciaries for their clients, and this role should prevent them from engaging in any activity that is not in the client's best interest. The law recognizes this. Clients harmed by sexual or other self-serving exploitation may seek remedies in civil suits for monetary damages, criminal sanctions, and licensing board actions.

RESEARCH

- Check with your association on their latest research regarding this issue
  - Check the Internet
- Boundary crossing or boundary violation?
  - Ponder the best and worst outcomes for any boundary crossing or boundary violation
  - Consider the research on the topic and discuss the issue with a trusted colleague

TOUCH IN THERAPY

Touch in therapy can have a degree of therapeutic intervention appropriateness and cultural relativity. Counselors must avoid risky physical contact, sexual harassment, and the use of derogatory language. But, touch can be deliberately employed to intentionally and strategically enhance a sense of connection with the client. Touch can also soothe, greet, relax, quiet down, or reassure the client.

THERE ARE MANY TYPES OF TOUCH IN PSYCHOTHERAPY:
Ritualistic or socially accepted gestures for greeting and departure, conversational markers, consolation or reassuring touch, grounding or reorienting touch, and celebratory or congratulatory touch. Some counselors utilize touch as part of their theoretical clinical intervention. This could include bioenergetics, Gestalt, or hypnotherapy.

Sexual, hostile, and punishing forms of touch are all unethical and depending on the laws in various states, they could be illegal in counseling. These forms of touch are counter-clinical and should always be avoided.

While preventing a client from hurting him or herself, or others, it may require some physical intervention, but physical punishment by a counselor is never appropriate in the context of counseling. Counselors who are in a clinical practice that requires client restraint should be trained in restraint procedures so they can remain in the highest standard of care.

HARM

Ethical violations become an issue of negligence, and negligence, whether intentional or unintentional, that causes harm, can place a counselor at risk of legal action.

THREE ELEMENTS MUST EXIST TO FILE A MALPRACTICE SUIT:
1) A professional, fiduciary relationship existed
2) There was negligence on the part of the counselor
3) There are damages defined and claimed by the client

"Unintentional Harm" could be potentially harmful professional behaviors or work shortcuts, a lack of knowledge, or incompetence. But, unintentional harm is still negligence. "Intentional Harm" refers to professional predatory offenders—counselors who enjoy using their power and authority to control and dominate or to fulfill their needs. These are individuals who are personally (for selfish reasons) motivated to establish a close or intimate relationship with the client. Categorically, intentional harm is a severe form of negligence.

"Negligence" can be, but is not limited to, a counselor's improper use of interventions, failure to appropriately refer, or wrongful termination. Negligence can be a failure to properly analyze and predict the effects of your acts on a client's behavior or the counselor may have recklessly acted without regard to the effect of their behavior on the client. Negligence can be a counselor detrimentally influencing a client's behavior, such as recommending that a client go have an affair. Negligence can result from a counselor's interventions that worsen the precise emotional disorder(s) for which the client retained the counselor to treat. Negligence can be the creation of new traumas stemming directly from a counselor's interventions or behaviors towards a client.

Common negligent violations are typically centered on boundary issues, competency concerns, counselor misrepresentation, fraudulent or improper billing or documentation, confidentiality breaches, poor record-keeping, and atypical types of practice or settings. Violations can also occur from unclear informed consent or not getting a client's informed consent. To obtain true "informed" consent, as the law interprets that duty, a counselor should advise a client of known or foreseeable risks associated with therapy, and verbally explain any limits of confidentiality.

INFORMED CONSENT

The history of informed consent dates back to a court in England in 1776. It concluded that consent needed to be obtained before a physician touches a patient. In 1914, a court in New York City determined that the patient, not the doctor, had the right to decide treatment. In 1957, a United State's court upheld that a patient must be informed of both their diagnosis and treatment options. The term "sufficient disclosure" came from a United State's case in 1972 meaning that a physician must provide sufficient details regarding a patient's diagnosis and treatment options whether or not the patient asks. The physician has a duty to volunteer the information. Informed consent assumes that patients are generally unlearned and unknowledgeable, and that there is not an equality between the patient and the physician. Because of this inequality, the physician must take reasonable steps to ensure that any consent is informed.

INFORMED CONSENT LEGAL STANDARDS:
1) Professional element refers to the information a reasonable provider would offer to a patient or client in a similar situation.
2) Materiality refers to the amount of information the average patient or client would deem adequate enough to decide whether to accept or reject treatment.

Before providing mental health services, counselors truthfully inform clients of their training and credentials and inform clients of their right to withdraw consent for treatment at any time. Counselors truthfully inform clients of the risks, hazards, and relative benefits of all proposed mental health treatments and of alternative treatments. Counselors obtain written informed consent from clients and secure client consent for all counseling and related services. This includes any video/audio-taping of client sessions, the use of supervisory and consultative help, the application of special procedures and evaluations, and the communication of client data with other professionals and institutions. If the counselor is supervised, that fact is disclosed and the supervisor's name and role indicated to the client in the informed consent. Counselors take care that: 1) The client has the capacity to give consent, 2) The client reasonably understands the nature and process of counseling (the costs, time, and work required; the limits of counseling and, any appropriate alternatives), and 3) The client freely gives consent to counseling, without coercion or undue influence.

Counselors respect the necessity for appropriate informed consent regarding the structures and the processes of counseling. Early in counseling, counselor and client should discuss and agree upon several issues: 1) The nature of and course of therapy, 2) Client's issues and goals, 3) Potential problems and reasonable options and/or alternatives to counseling, 4) Counselor's area of expertise, 5) Confidentiality and its limitations, 6) Fees and financial procedures, 7) Limitations about the times, availability, and access to the counselor, including directions in emergency situations, and 8) Reason for terminating the clinical relationship. *See "Checking the Validity of Informed Consent" for more details.*

THE PATIENT'S RIGHTS ACT

A few key points from the Patient's Rights Act are: 1) The client has the right to privacy, and privacy is the right to decide the time, place, manner, and extent of self-disclosure; 2) They have a right to autonomy and self-determination; 3) They have the right to be a participant in treatment decisions; and, 4) They have the right to refuse treatment. There are many other issues addressed in this act, such as living wills, power of attorney, euthanasia, dignity and worth.

RESEARCH
- Web search "Patient's Right Act" and read

HIPAA PRIVACY DISCLOSURE

Health Insurance Portability and Accountability Act (HIPAA). *Disclosure document is required by law and explains the use of a client's Private Health Information (PHI).* THERE ARE THREE KEY FORMS RELEVANT TO THE HIPAA PRIVACY RULE: 1) Notice of privacy practices, 2) Authorization form, and 3) Client consent form. HIPAA is the industry standard that establishes "best practices" regarding client confidentiality. HIPAA takes precedence over other state laws on the subject, except when state laws offer even more stringent client protections. HIPAA is about consent and confidentiality. Confidentiality is about protecting clients and preserving therapeutic relationships. Professional counselors are not to discuss with others (except when allowed or required by law) what was disclosed in counseling sessions. This creates a safe environment for clients by protecting them from harm and protecting their privacy. Counseling needs to be a safe place for people to confess problems without fearing what they have shared will be disclosed without permission.

HIPAA NOTICE OF PRIVACY PRACTICES

To comply with HIPAA disclosure, a Notice of Privacy Practices, in written form, is given to clients at their first office visit. HIPAA also requires that you obtain the client's written acknowledgment that this notice was received and then that acknowledgment is filed in the client's record. A client's refusal to sign the acknowledgment should be documented and filed in the client record.

> **RESEARCH**
> - Web search for a downloadable copy of HIPAA's "Notice of Privacy Practices" and read the document
> - Web search for your state's privacy laws relevant to mental health care
>   - Compare the two documents
>   Note: a notice of privacy practice can be tailored to reflect your practice policies and your state's privacy laws. State privacy laws should continue to be followed if they are more stringent than the HIPAA regulations.

HIPAA AUTHORIZATIONS

The HIPAA privacy regulations do not require client's consent to use their private health information (PHI) for routine disclosures, such as those related to "treatment, payment, or healthcare operations" (TPO). However, the regulations do mandate that you obtain written client consent before releasing their information for any reason other then TPO. You also need to identify situations in your practice were special authorization is needed and develop and utilize an authorization form . A signed copy (of any/all client authorizations) is retained in the client's record.

> **RESEARCH**
> - Web search for a sample copy of HIPAA's "Authorization Form" and read the document. How would you tailor it for your practice?

ETHICAL STANDARDS & CLINICAL FORMS

CLIENT CONSENT FORM

Counselors need to have an informed consent document for clients to read and sign. INFORMED CONSENT SPECIFIES: 1) The type of work you do, 2) Who you are, 3) The financial arrangements, and 4) Limits of confidentiality. *See "Informed Consent" section for more details.*

By signing a consent form, a client agrees to enter into a therapeutic relationship with the counselor. The signing of a consent form also obligates the counselor to act in the best interests of the client. A fiduciary relationship is established. Clients have a right to make decisions about their own health and medical conditions. But counselors have a responsibility to obtain informed consent. Informed consent is also a legal and ethical obligation to provide relevant information to clients regarding expectations of therapy and limitations of confidentiality, preferably, "before" the onset of assessment and treatment.

The essence of informed consent is designed to anticipate questions of reasonable clients thus preventing future misunderstandings and frustrations, yielding a "therapeutic culture of safety."

Famous failures to get informed consent include the US government in 1932, Tuskegee Syphilis Study where individuals being treated were unaware that they were being treated with placebo. In the 1990s, hospitals were testing for AIDS without patients' knowledge. A testing center administered the Stanford IQ Test for placing kids in classes. The agency was sending one letter to the school and a different letter to the parents. When this was discovered the agency defended what they were doing by saying, "The report we send to the school is accurate; the report we send to the parents is soothing and positive."

ENSURE CONSENT COMPREHENSION

In instances when clients are not literate or have difficulty understanding the primary language used in the practice setting, take steps to ensure the client's comprehension. This may include providing clients with a detailed verbal explanation, or arranging for a qualified interpreter or translator if needed. In instances where the client lacks the capacity to provide informed consent, counselors should protect the client's interests by seeking permission from an appropriate third party. In such instances, counselors seek to ensure that the third party acts in a manner consistent with client's wishes and interests.

Take reasonable steps to ensure a client's ability to give informed consent. In instances where clients are receiving services involuntarily, counselors should provide information about the nature and extent of services and about the extent of a client's right to refuse service. Clients mandated into a treatment program lose some self-determination, autonomy, and possibly, some confidentiality. The legal system can take away rights; you as a mental health counselor cannot. A client who is mandated into a treatment program for sexual offenders, after being released from prison, has lost some of their rights outlined in the Patient's Rights Act. But, these rights were taken from them through appropriate legal proceedings. Such a client, who does not comply with their treatment program, risks further legal action.

> **RESEARCH**
> - Search the Internet for three sample mental healthcare consent forms
>   - Begin to write your consent form
>   - Rework your current consent form

Ethically, counselors only provide services to clients in the context of a professional relationship based on valid informed consent. The language in an informed consent is to be clear and understandable and written for the purpose of informing clients about the services, risks related to the services, limits to services, alternatives, and many other elements of the counseling process.

INFORMED CONSENT: THE PROFESSIONAL DISCLOSURE STATEMENT

A counselor's consent form can include their "Professional Disclosure Statement" (PDS), or this information can be provided in a separate document, flyer, or brochure. This is a written document that a counselor gives to clients. This document has information about the counselor's identifying information, counselor's state license number, education, relevant continuing education or certifications, and a list of the associations or organizations the counselor is a member of in good standing. A counselor should include a statement that they abide by their codes of ethics outlined by the associations they belong to and by their state's code of professional conduct. A PDS also identifies a counselor's therapeutic philosophies, treatment orientations and interventions.

ETHICAL STANDARDS & CLINICAL FORMS

It can include information regarding a counselor's target market (e.g., adults, children, couples, families; specialty; outpatient versus inpatient; etc.). There should be sufficient detail in a PDS to enable a potential client to make an informed decision about whether or not to accept treatment from a specific counselor. If a counselor is an intern (has not yet met all the requirements for licensing), they must explain this in the document and identify that they are under supervision, provide the name of their supervisor.

RESEARCH
- Search the Internet for three sample professional disclosure statement
  - Create your PDS
  - Rework your current PDS

FINANCIAL ARRANGEMENTS

Information regarding fees can be included in the informed consent document or in a separate document. Typically, a financial arrangement is a separate document from the informed consent.

Financial arrangements must include what the client will be charged, and whether you accept benefits or not (bill insurance companies for the client or not). If a sliding scale is used, then a sliding fee policy needs to be explained. Money is a complex issue facing counselors and clients, especially at the beginning of treatment, and many counselors tend to avoid this important topic. Provide details explaining the fees and consequences of missed sessions, late cancellations, debt collection policies, insurance reimbursement, etc.

Come to an agreement as soon as possible with clients on the fee structure: Full fee, sliding scale, no fee, bartering, and insurance assignments (or not). Different settings often require different approaches to fee setting. And ethically, counselors do not have an obligation to treat people who cannot afford their fee or those who, for whatever reason, do not pay.

> **RESEARCH**
> - Find three samples of mental healthcare financial arrangement documents by searching for counselors who have the document posted on their web sites
>   - Create your own

INFORMED CONSENT DOCUMENT

Keep a copy of your informed consent along with a copy of the HIPAA Notice of Privacy Practices in a clear and prominent location at the service delivery site. Placing these documents in a binder located in a waiting area makes them accessible for clients to read. If the informed consent is electronically signed by the client, a paper copy must be provided, if requested. Whenever it's revised, make the revised document available to current clients. If a counselor maintains a practice website, these documents should be available on the website.

CONTENT CHANGES COULD BE DUE TO:
1) Permitted uses or disclosures, 2) Clients' rights, and/or 3) Counselor's legal duties or other privacy practices described in these documents.

INFORMED CONSENT AND WHAT TO EXPECT IN COUNSELING

Informed consent is vital! The Patient Rights Act, HIPAA, and "best practice" dictates its necessity. Informed consent is a cornerstone of health care, not just a legality. It is a moral responsibility to honor and secure. Informed consent helps clients understand what to expect in counseling—the course of treatment, interventions, alternatives, and what is expected from the client. Surprise (and shock) regarding a counselor's intervention often leads to failed therapy and even complaints. Counseling in today's world is an exchange of information; it is seeking collaboration regarding treatment options; and, it is seeking an agreement on treatment plans.

INFORMED CONSENT AND THE RISKS ASSOCIATED WITH COUNSELING

There are risks (and benefits) for all mental health counseling, but there are "three significant risks" that should be made clear to potential clients. The first significant risk is that the client's presenting symptoms/concerns/issues do not improve with counseling. The second significant risk is that the client's issues could worsen. And the third significant risk is that, possibly, during the course of counseling, new issues/concerns/symptoms could arise. Consent forms need to address risks.

RESEARCH
- **How would you word these risks in your consent?**
- **Think of various forms of counseling—*what additional risks are relevant to these various therapeutic interventions?***

TERMINATION OF SERVICES

Abandonment (see next page) is not the same as treatment termination. Counselors should have a clear understanding of when a therapeutic relationship should end.

THE THERAPEUTIC RELATIONSHIP CAN BE DISCONTINUED WHEN:
- The client is not benefiting from therapy
- The client may be harmed by the treatment
- The client needs a higher level of care
- Client's issues are outside of counselor's expertise
- Client no longer needs therapy
- There are conflicts of interest that are unresolvable
- Counselor's objectivity has been compromised
- The client has threatened the counselor

It's important for counselors to maintain their influential position. Remember that too much self-disclosure can diminish it. Sometimes, as the counselor, you need to make the decision that a client must seek treatment elsewhere for any of the above reasons. The counselor's influential position, in the clinical relationship, helps when such decisions need to be made.

ABANDONMENT

"Client abandonment" is defined as the premature termination of the professional treatment relationship by the counselor without adequate notice, without therapeutic reason, or without the client's involvement. This unilateral termination of the clinical relationship is a form of negligence. Abandonment occurs when a counselor inappropriately ends treatment, such as halting needed therapy with no notice. In comparison, many times counselors and clients continue with therapy beyond the point of necessity. While dependent clients can make it difficult to end treatment appropriately, the counselor must sometimes make the therapeutic decision to appropriately end the clinical relationship, even when the client does not want it to end.

TERMINATION AND INFORMED CONSENT

One of the reasons information on termination/referrals is in the consent form is to help educate the client. Counselors should take some time, as early on as possible in the clinical relationship, to verbally discuss with the client termination and referral information. This can help head off termination or referral dilemmas.

PRE-TERMINATION COUNSELING

Counselors provide pre-termination counseling and suggest alternative service providers whenever possible. This may not be possible in all cases, such as if, or when, a client abruptly stops attending therapy.

TERMINATION AND REFERRAL

Termination/referral is a time to evaluate the work that has (or has not) been accomplished. Celebrate the progress and talk about the goals that have not been reached. Treatment plans are vitally important; they are the road map, as well as the gauge, to monitor progress and weigh the appropriateness or necessity for terminating the clinical relationship or for making a referral.

ETHICAL STANDARDS & CLINICAL FORMS

INTERRUPTION OF SERVICES

Paramount consideration must be given to the welfare of the client and to the continuity of care. Counselors (in solo or private practice) ethically are required to have a transfer plan in place to ensure continuity of care in the event that services are interrupted by factors such as counselor unavailability due to relocation, illness, disability, or death. *See "transfer plans" section for more information.*

> **CAVEAT:** Always follow company policies regarding termination of services, referrals and interruptions of services, as well as ethical guidelines. The client's welfare and best interests are paramount. And, client abandonment is a serious issue, ethically and legally. Make you have a transfer plan in place.

CONFIDENTIALITY EXPECTATIONS

Clients come to therapy expecting confidentiality. Therapy would be ineffective without the trust that confidentiality breeds. Effective therapy depends upon an atmosphere of frank and complete disclosure of facts, emotions, memories, and fears.

HISTORY OF CONFIDENTIALITY

Until the dawn of the 19th century, mental illness was perceived as being supernatural, demonic possession, or "lunatics" bound in chains at asylums. It was not until post World War II that "de-institutionalization" of the mentally ill begin. Historical concepts of mental illness, combined with the essence of personal disclosures that are sensitive, embarrassing, and could denote that they are less than normal, contributed to the social stigma associated with mental health counseling, a stigma that still, unfortunately, exists.

Since clients come to counseling expecting confidentiality, it is vital to discuss with clients the nature of confidentiality and its limitations. Ethically, we are required to discuss with clients, as early as possible in the relationship, the limits of confidentiality that exist (mandatory reporting, duty to warn and protect, child protective services, adult protective services). Counselors protect clients' confidential information at all times, including during legal proceedings, to the extent the laws provide.

While confidentiality is an ethical concept, breaches of confidentiality are a legal issue.

Privileged information is information that is protected by law; confidential information is information between people; personal information is information that is private, secret, and sensitive to an individual; and, public information is information known by others. Counselors have a primary obligation to take reasonable precautions to protect confidential information, obtained from a client, that is stored in any medium, recognizing that the extent and the limits of confidentiality may be regulated by law, established by institutional rules, or by company policies. Counselors should protect the confidentiality of clients' written and electronic records and other sensitive information, taking reasonable steps to ensure that client records are stored in a secure location and format; that client records are not available to others who are not authorized to have access.

"Confidentiality" is an ethical concept, and simply put, means that what is shared within the therapeutic relationship will not be voluntarily disclosed by the counselor. Confidentiality is essential because it fosters trust, which is the bedrock of the therapeutic alliance. "Privilege" is a legal concept that protects clients from their counselor being forced to disclose confidential information. Privilege is distinguished from confidentiality in that disclosure is typically involuntary. In other words, confidentiality "binds" the counselor not to reveal client material even if the counselor feels "inclined" to do so, and privilege protects client information from inappropriate disclosure when "pressed" by legal authorities.

Counselors should not disclose identifying information when discussing clients with consultants or colleagues, unless the client has consented, or there is a compelling need for such disclosure (to prevent harm to the client or others).

Counselors may disclose confidential information when appropriate with valid authorization from a client or a person legally authorized to act on the behalf of a client, or when required by law to do so. In all instances, counselors should disclose the least amount of confidential information necessary to achieve the desired purpose—only information that is directly relevant to the purpose for which the disclosure is made.

CONFIDENTIALITY IS BASED ON FOUR PRINCIPLES

CONFIDENTIALITY IS BASED ON FOUR IMPORTANT PRINCIPLES:
1) The principle of "autonomy" is related to client self-determination.
2) The principle of "privacy" demands respect for clients' intimate secrets.
3) The principle of "pledge of silence" states that counselors strive to protect their clients' secrets from disclosure.
4) The principle of "utility" explains that confidentiality in therapy is useful to society and society relinquishes its right to certain information and accepts the risk of not knowing some problems in exchange for its members to improve their mental health.

With self-reported previous crimes, the principles of confidentiality are very relevant, especially the principle of utility. Can we breach confidentiality when a client confesses a previous crime? Duty of care issues can be violated when we breach confidentiality. If a state has a "duty to report law" regarding past crimes, it typically permits, but does not require disclosure of these crimes by counseling professionals. It is essential that counselors are cognizant of their own state's statutes before breaking confidentiality.

Ethical codes state: "When uncertain as to whether a particular situation or course of action may be a violation of a code of ethics, counselors consult with other colleagues or seek legal advice." Counselors are subject to liability both for failing to report when reporting is mandated and for reporting when a report is not required. Counselors also need to be careful not to use their influential position to press clients to turn themselves in when they've shared previous criminal activities.

"Utility" (the fourth principle of confidentiality) explains how confidentiality in therapy is useful to society and that society relinquishes its rights to certain information and accepts the risks of not knowing some problems in exchange for the members of society to improve their mental health. Even after the client is not a client, this rule still needs to be honored. However, when the revelation of information helps to avert a criminal act, then the confidentiality rule does not apply. Reporting would fall under duty to warn and protect—which is mandatory—compelling counselors to disclose the confidential information.

ETHICAL STANDARDS & CLINICAL FORMS

RESEARCH

How would you react to a client's confession of their direct involvement in a murder (from their past)? Consider the four principles of confidentiality (page 59), especially "utility."

- What if children witnessed the crime. Would this change your ability to report?
- What questions would you ask a client? How would you go about exploring their current involvement in criminal activities?
- What if you had the following statement in your Informed Consent and had verbally discussed with the client when you explained the limits of confidentiality: *I reserve the right to report to appropriate authorities information you share about previous criminal acts*
- What could be a comment a client might say that would cause you to fear for your own safety?
- Discuss this issue with colleagues and share your thoughts.
- Web search this issue for any state legal cases that pertain.

NOTE: *Always remain aware of your state's requirements and laws that affect this issue; laws change—stay current.*

CAVEAT: Questionable past activities of clients, such as in criminal behaviors, need to be carefully handled. The advice of an attorney cannot be overly emphasized. Although ethical issues of confidentiality are involved, the legalities need to be discussed with an attorney. Remember, a breach of confidentiality is a legal issue. Also, legal counsel should be sought when or if a minor was involved, in any way, even if they were only present in a home or in another room etc., during the crime—*seek legal advice*!

COMPLEX ISSUES INVOLVING CONFIDENTIALITY

COUNSELOR SAFETY: If a client makes a threat towards the counselor, the counselor can report the threat and client information to law enforcement.

DUTY TO WARN/PROTECT: If there is threat of harmful intentions to themselves or others then the counselor is required to inform the proper authorities.

FUTURE CRIMES: The police need to be called if the client plans to commit a serious crime. The confidentiality of the client is sacrificed, if the future security of the public is at risk.

PAST CRIMES: When a client admits to a past crime that they committed, what should the counselor do? In such a scenario, confidentiality of the client takes a higher priority, since the crime has already been committed and avoiding it is not a possibility. However, if a client admits to a past crime that involved a minor, then consultation with an attorney cannot be over emphasized.

These are difficult and complex issues and counselors should consult legal advice if they have any doubt about their obligations.

CONTINUING THE CLINICAL RELATIONSHIP: REGARDING CLIENT REPORTED PAST CRIMES

Do you need to continue seeing a client that you are uncomfortable with because of what they have disclosed to you? Actually, if what they have told you impairs your professional judgment and diminishes your objectivity, then, ethically you should not continue counseling them. However, you cannot abandon them. These are the situations where you need to consult with colleagues, speak to your insurance company's risk management department, or seek legal advice.

Discuss the referral situation with the client and the ethical necessity to refer. You can explain that what they have shared is confidential and you will take every precaution to protect their confidential information (if this is true and you are not required to report what they have shared). Without disclosing details, you can ask colleagues if they would accept a client who has reported (whatever the past crime is), which does not fall under mandatory reporting. You assist clients with continuity of care, never abandon them or your fiduciary duty to act in their best interests.

PRINCIPLES OF CONFIDENTIALITY AND CLIENT RECORDS

Let's turn to the protection of the client's confidential and sensitive secrets, which can be difficult, especially if the counselor has made note of everything the client has said in the chart notes. Insurance companies can ask for copies; records can be subpoenaed. With self-reported past crimes, each counselor must make their own decision about the amount of detail to put in a clients chart. Certainly, records are to accurately reflect services, but counselors make clinical judgments often in regards to the amount of detail. By documenting in detail specific information clients share, a counselor could be compromising the client's confidentiality in regards to non-mandatory, non-reportable previous crimes. I can share what is typically done—counselors use psychotherapy notes for such matters.

PSYCHOTHERAPY NOTES

"Psychotherapy notes" are also known as "Shadow Notes" or "Clinician's Confidential Notes" and, sometimes, "Process Notes." Mental health counselors are permitted to maintain psychotherapy notes separately from the rest of the chart. These psychotherapy notes may represent personal notes used to record or analyze group, individual or family therapy, and unlike the rest of the chart do not have to be disclosed to the client. Anything that is kept in a client's chart is NOT a psychotherapy note. HIPAA provides special protection for psychotherapy notes, but, in order for clinical-related notes to qualify as "psychotherapy notes" they must meet certain conditions that include: 1) Being maintained separately from the client's other healthcare records, 2) Not being the only source of information for treatment or payment, and 3) Being solely for the use of provider that created them. The third point is key: these notes are solely for the use of the counselor who created them. Whether or not a counselor uses psychotherapy notes is a personal, professional decision.

Regarding process notes: Many counselors take more detailed notes during a session and then use those notes to formulate what they choose to place in the client's record. If the counselor destroys those process notes, then they are not psychotherapy notes; if the counselor keeps the process notes in the client's file, then they are not psychotherapy notes. However, if the counselor keeps the process notes in a separate file, separate from the client's chart—then they become psychotherapy notes.

RESEARCH
- Check the Internet for information about psychotherapy notes.
- HIPAA allows special protection for psychotherapy notes, what does this mean?
  - Are they discoverable in legal proceedings?
- When would you consider using psychotherapy notes?
  - With a difficult client? To document in detail things being said or done?
  - What other scenarios can you think of?
- Why would you not want to use psychotherapy notes?
- How are electronic health records handling the creation and storage of psychotherapy notes (or sometimes called "Clinician Confidential Notes)?

Technology and Science have complicated ethics

TECHNOLOGY AND ON-LINE ISSUES: ETHICAL ISSUES AND CONFIDENTIALITY

Technology and science have complicated ethics. Modern digital technologies have raised many complex clinical, ethical, and legal issues for counselors. E-counseling has gained momentum, and there are many professional, well-designed sites used by many consumers seeking counseling. With e-counseling, clients no longer have to worry about looking a counselor in the eyes; anonymity is a major appeal for this counseling format. "Counseling" is a professional relationship and activity in which one person endeavors to help another to understand and to solve his or her problems; the giving of advice, opinion, and instruction to direct the judgment or conduct of another. "Psychotherapy" is the treatment of a disorder. E-counseling is not psychotherapy, and a diagnosis is never given. Since insurance companies do not compensate for e-counseling, there is no need for a diagnosis.

The online counselor should carry professional liability coverage for online-based counseling. Most counselors and licensing boards assert that counseling takes place in a counselor's own state. This is where they are licensed, and where they are subject to the rules of their state licensing board. Mental health counselors who want to be an on-line counselor should confirm that on-line services are not prohibited by their applicable state or local statutes, rules, regulations or ordinances, codes of professional membership organizations and certifying boards, and/or codes of their state's licensing boards.

Counselors provide on-line counseling services only in practice areas within their expertise. Mental health counselors do not provide services to clients in states where doing so would violate local licensing laws or regulations.

RESEARCH
- **Call your state licensing board or state association and ask them for their official stance about online mental health counseling**
  - **Ask for a written copy of their statement to be mailed to you**

… ETHICAL STANDARDS & CLINICAL FORMS

E-COUNSELING CONSENT CONSIDERATIONS

Professional counselors take reasonable steps to secure and verify the true identities of clients, and obtain alternative methods of contacting clients in case of emergency situations, if at all possible. Counselors providing e-counseling should require clients to execute client informed consents stating that the client acknowledges the limitations inherent in ensuring client confidentiality of information transmitted through on-line counseling, and acknowledge the limitations that are inherent in a counseling process that is not provided face-to-face.

If counselors electronically transfer client confidential information to authorized third-party recipients, they do so only when both the professional counselor and the authorized recipient have "secure" transfer; the recipient is able to effectively protect the confidentiality of the client's information being transferred; and, the informed written consent acknowledges the limits of confidentiality relevant to on-line counseling.

Develop an appropriate in-take procedure for potential clients to determine whether on-line counseling is appropriate for the needs of the client. Counselors need to warn potential clients that on-line counseling services may not be appropriate in certain situations and, to the extent possible, inform the client of specific limitations, potential risks, and/or potential benefits relevant to the client's anticipated use of on-line counseling services. Mental health counselors diligently try to ensure that clients are intellectually, emotionally, and physically capable of using on-line counseling services, and that they understand the potential risks and/or limitations of such services. They develop individual on-line counseling plans that are consistent with both the client's individual circumstances and the limitations of on-line counseling. Counselors who determine that on-line counseling is inappropriate for the client should avoid entering into or immediately terminating the on-line counseling relationship, and encourage the client to continue the counseling process through a more traditional method of counseling.

CONFIDENTIALITY AND E-COUNSELING

Counselors ensure that clients are provided sufficient information that adequately addresses and explains the limitations of computer technology in the counseling process in general and the difficulties of ensuring complete client confidentiality of information transmitted through electronic communications over the Internet through on-line counseling. Professional counselors inform clients of the limitations of confidentiality and identify foreseeable situations in which confidentiality must be breached in light of the law, in both the state in which the client is located and the state in which the professional counselor is licensed. On-line counselors must be aware of the means for reporting and protecting suicidal clients in their locale, and also be aware of the means for reporting homicidal clients in the client's jurisdiction.

THE FUTURE OF ONLINE COUNSELING

As for the future of online counseling, it is believed that as technology evolves, the field is likely to continue developing. Consumers are using the Internet to find many products and services, so some form(s) of mental health service is likely to continue to be available in the years ahead.

E-MAIL AND TEXT MESSAGES

In counseling today, best practice is to limit the amount of information that a potential, current, or past client shares via e-mail or texting. If you have a web site that allows potential clients to e-mail you, limit the space they have to share information. You want to avoid a long e-mail that details their past and current life details. An e-mail outlining suicidal intentions from a person seeking a counselor places counselors in a difficult position with ethically gray boundaries. So limit the number of words in a box on your e-mail response form. Also, texting needs to be controlled. Clients should understand that e-mail and texting should never be used in an emergency situation. Encourage clients to call your office phone, which has this message: hang up and call 911 if this is an emergency.

SOCIAL MEDIA AND CONFIDENTIALITY

Some counselors may choose to add a statement to their office policy or consent form stating that they do, or preferably, do not engage in social networking with previous or current clients. If you do interact with clients on social media sites, define the parameters of such involvement. Questions to consider: What is the context of the therapy with a particular client? Who is the client? Why did the client post a friend request? What is the meaning of the request? What is the nature of the therapeutic relationship? What does connecting with the client via social media mean for the counselor?

> **RESEARCH**
> - **Would you interact with clients via social media?**
> - **When do you think such interaction would be beneficial to a therapeutic relationship?**
> - **What are the dangers?**

INTERNET SEARCHES

Is it okay for counselors to search for information about their clients on the Internet? Not without informed consent. If a counselor is going to do an Internet searches on clients, there needs to be a statement in their informed consent document that states: At times I may conduct a web search on clients. If you have concerns or questions regarding this practice, please discuss it with me.

Clients have the right to privacy. Privacy is the right to decide what, when, where, and to what extent they want to self-disclose. If a counselor Internet searches a client they are taking away the client's right to privacy. Why would a counselor want to do Internet searches? What happens when a counselor finds clinically significant information about their client online? A counselor may discover that his or her new client has filed several board complaints against former counselors—is this information going to impair your judgment in working with this client? Would you still be able to work in the client's best interest? What if a counselor finds out that a client has an active and violent porn website which the client has not mentioned during therapy, even though therapy focuses on issues of intimacy or sexual addiction?

Counseling, traditionally, is a process in which clients present information, issues, or concerns. If the counselor uncovers clinically relevant information then they are placed in a position of being the ones to present the information or withhold the information—either choice could interfere with the therapeutic relationship and potentially harm or exploit the client, or impair the counselor's judgment.

RESEARCH
- **Would you consider an Internet search on a new client without informing them? With informing them?**
- **What about an established client? What reason could you think of that would compel you to do a search?**

Searching purposely is different than stumbling upon client information while on the Internet. Before the Internet, counselor would stumble upon information about a client in a local paper or at a community event. When, or if, they come across client information accidentally, they could choose to mention, or not.

OTHERS CALLING ABOUT A CLIENT

THERE ARE TWO SCHOOLS OF THOUGHT: 1) Counselors who believe you should listen to what you're being told, and 2) Counselors who believe you should end the call and not listen. First, there are some states that require counselors to take action to protect a client from harming themselves or others, if a client's family member or significant other has given information to the counselor. With this aside, whether or not to listen to the information from a third-party would be the counselor's decision. Remember, unless you have a signed authorization in place from the client to speak with a specific individual, a counselor does not even confirm whether or not the person is a client. The response is: "I cannot confirm whether or not this person is or isn't a client." If you do listen to information from a third-party then what do you do with the information? Do you tell the client about the call and what was shared; or, don't tell the client? Ethically, the information should be discussed with the client to maintain a trusting therapeutic environment.

RESEARCH
- **Which school of thought do you agree with? Why?**
- **Look up this case: Ewing vs. Goldstein, 2004.**
  - **How does this case apply to the above information?**

*Counselors always discuss
with clients
the limits of confidentiality*

CONFIDENTIALITY EXCEPTIONS

Counselors always discuss with clients the nature of confidentiality and its limitations. They strive to protect client's confidential information at all times, including, during legal proceedings, to the extent that the law provides.

WHEN COUNSELORS DISCLOSE MEDICAL INFORMATION THERE ARE TWO QUESTIONS THAT ARISE: 1) Can I disclose this confidential client information without the threat of liability for unauthorized disclosure? 2) Do I have a duty to disclose this confidential client information?

CONFIDENTIALITY EXCEPTIONS: MANDATORY REPORTING LAWS

Confidentiality exceptions include situations where counselors are required by law to disclose. Mandatory reporting requirements exist to fulfill the duty to warn and protect; this is an exception to confidentiality. Reporting to child and vulnerable adult protective services is another. When there is a serious threat to the health or safety of a client or someone else, a counselor has an obligation to disclose private health information to reduce or prevent a serious threat. Under these circumstances, counselors only make disclosure to persons, organizations, or agencies that are able to help prevent the threat.

CONFIDENTIALITY EXCEPTIONS: HIPAA'S NOTICE OF PRIVACY PRACTICE

There are many other special circumstances outlined in HIPAA's Notice of Privacy Practice: treatment–payment–operation (TPO), treatment alternatives, health-related products and services, release of information to family and friends involved in care, military and veterans, workers' compensation, public health risks, health oversight activities, lawsuits and similar proceedings, law enforcement, deceased patients/clients, organ and tissue donation, national security, inmates, and research.

Take the time to read, thoroughly, a HIPAA Notice of Privacy Practices.

ETHICAL STANDARDS & CLINICAL FORMS

Another exception of confidentiality, outlined in HIPAA's Notice of Privacy Practice, addresses the issue of healthcare providers speaking with each other regarding the care of a client within an agency, or with a supervisor. However, it is best practice for a private practice counselor to get consent from their clients if they wish to consult with other private practice counselors. Never discuss client cases in informal settings. When clients find out that their counselor has shared information about them in informal settings with colleagues who had no relevant connection to their care, they could file a complaint that has merit.

AUTHORIZATION FOR RELEASE OF INFORMATION

When a client has authorized a release of information the counselor may communicate their confidential information according to the authorization.

If a client revokes a previous authorization, then the counselor will no longer act on or disclose the private health information for the reasons previously described in the authorization.

RESEARCH
- Get a copy of a HIPAA Notice of Privacy Practice and see if all of the above items are listed in it
- If not, which ones are missing? Why?
- Get a copy of an "authorization for release of PHI" form from www.hhs.gov/ocr/privacy, and then three additional copies...
  - One from a large medical facility
  - One from a smaller mental health care clinic
  - One from a counselor in private practice
- Do they vary? If they do, why? What would your form look like?

ADDITIONAL EXCEPTIONS OF CONFIDENTIALITY: COURT ORDERED TREATMENT

If an individual is court ordered into treatment there might be additional exceptions to confidentiality. There could be a requirement that the counselor reports back to the courts or reports to a specific individual identified in the court documents. If a sexual offender is released from prison and required to enter a treatment program there is a required treatment compliance. This client's progress, most likely, will be reported back to the court or to a parole officer, or whoever mandated them into therapy. There are consequences for not complying with the treatment requirements.

EMERGENCIES

Emergencies trump confidentiality. If individuals require emergent care, those providing the care will talk to whoever is available, and try to seek consent. However, the primary necessity is providing care.

GROUP THERAPY

Group therapy has confidentiality issues. Only the licensed counselor is required to maintain confidentiality. Any one else attending a group therapy session can share what was said with other people. This, of course, is why there are group therapy agreement documents that participants sign stating that they will maintain confidentiality and respect the privacy of the other individuals.

RESEARCH
- Find three consent forms for group therapy and compare them.
    - Get them from agencies or counselors who offer group sessions
- Would you add or delete any of the items in the samples?
    - Web search Alcoholics Anonymous and look at their policies for group AA meetings. Compare this to your other samples.

OTHER EXCEPTIONS

When there are active investigations by the Department of Social Services; when records or a counselor's presence is court ordered; when information is readily available to others; when there is communication between healthcare providers involved with the care of an individual; or, when there is administrative/legal proceedings—exceptions to confidentiality exist.

RESEARCH
- Go to your state's Dept. of Social and Health Services
  - What are their policies for "active investigations"?

CONFIDENTIALITY EXCEPTIONS AND INVOLUNTARY COMMITMENT

Involuntary commitment has elements of confidentiality exceptions. The priority is to help the individual get the care that is needed in a timely manner or to keep an individual in the treatment facility for a specific period of time. Involuntary commitment can occur (or a person can be detained) when there is a likelihood of serious harm to others, or to the individual themselves, or due to grave disability. Grave disability is defined as a condition in which a person, as a result of a mental disorder, is in danger of serious physical harm resulting from a failure to provide for their essential human needs of health or safety, or they manifest severe deterioration in routine functioning evidenced by repeated and escalating loss of cognitive or volitional control over their actions and is not receiving such care as is essential for their health or safety. A person can be detained by a Designated Mental Health Professional (in most states) for up to 72 hours without a court order. If the client is not ready for release within the 72 hours, a petition for involuntary treatment is filed seeking detention for up to 14 calendar days. If the client elects to have a contested hearing, then a judicial officer decides the outcome. There is no right to a jury trial. The legal standard is preponderance of the evidence. If the client requires treatment beyond 14 days, then a petition seeking detention for up to 90 calendar days is filed. The client has a right to a jury trial. The legal standard is clear, convincing evidence. If the client requires treatment beyond 90 days, then a petition for 180 calendar days is filed. The petitioner cannot ask for another 90 days. The legal standard is clear, convincing evidence.

RESEARCH
- **Look up information regarding involuntary commitment for your state**
- **Does your state use this term: Designated Mental Health Professional, or another?**
  - **If you had a client who you believed met the criteria for involuntary commitment, what would your first step be?**
  - **Second? Third? And so on...**

EXCEPTIONS TO CONFIDENTIALITY: COUNSELOR IMPOSED

Finally, if a counselor has added additional limits of confidentiality to their consent form and verbalize these limits of confidentiality to their clients then they have created additional exceptions. Examples of this could be: risky behaviors that are not covered under mandatory, such as fire starting, injury to animals, excessive drinking or drug abuse, HIV client engaging in unprotected sex, eating disorders, cutting. All of these are situations where there is a "substantial likelihood" of "serious and foreseeable harm" to self or others.

A counselor could add a statement in their consent form regarding previous criminal activities stating: "I reserved the right to report to law enforcement previous criminal activities reported by clients, such as murders or bank robberies." However, if a consent form reads like the Miranda Rights: you have a right to remain silent; anything you say can and will be used against you, this would dilute what counseling is about—helping clients share.

RESEARCH
- **Would you put any of the additional limits of confidentiality listed above in your informed consent? Which ones? Why or why not?**

CONFIDENTIALITY AND COUNSELING

For a client to be fully candid with a counselor it is of the utmost importance that clients understand the limits of confidentiality. Counseling is a specific place where individuals with secrets can share and seek help.

EXCEPTIONS TO CONFIDENTIALITY: MANDATORY REPORTING

When the law compels breaches of confidentiality, it is related to mandatory reporting. Mandatory reporting encompasses the Warn and Protect Laws and Protective Services. Mental health counselors are mandatory reporters in all states. Counselors are required to report because they have frequent contact with at-risk populations—infants and children, people who are elderly or dependent, individuals with mental illness or developmental disabilities, and residents of nursing homes and other healthcare facilities. All states recognize the different types of abuse, but each state might define them differently. Make sure you know your state's definitions for: physical abuse, neglect, sexual abuse, emotional abuse and any other relevant definitions. Some states also provide definitions in statutes regarding: parental substance abuse or defines abandonment as child abuse.

Three exceptions to confidentiality concern harm to self or others: 1) Where there is a reasonable suspicion of child abuse or vulnerable adult abuse, 2) Where there is a reasonable suspicion that a client may present a danger of violence to others, and 3) Where there is a reasonable suspicion that a client is likely to harm themselves. In all of these situations, the counselor is either allowed or required by law to break confidentiality in order to protect the client, or someone else against whom the client has made a threat. And if a client ever threaten the counselor, then the counselor can always report for their own safety and protection.

MANDATORY REPORTING: CHILD AND VULNERABLE ADULT PROTECTIVE SERVICES

Children and vulnerable adults are populations that cannot protect themselves. Protective laws provide a number of protections for these populations, including overall safety and protection from all forms of abuse. These laws can vary from state- to-state, but many child and vulnerable adult protective laws share similar elements. Federal and state laws and departments of social and health services in each state are involved with enforcement and they define child and vulnerable adult abuse and neglect.

HERE ARE SOME TYPICAL DEFINITIONS:
A "Child" is defined as an unborn or recently born person, a young person especially between infancy and a person not yet of majority age. The age of majority is the threshold of adulthood as it is conceptualized and recognized in law. It is the chronological moment when minors cease to legally be considered children and assume control over their persons, actions, and decisions, thereby terminating the legal control and legal responsibilities of their parents or guardians over and for them. Depending upon state law, this usually happens at some point between 18 and 21.

A "Vulnerable Adult" is defined as a person age 18 or over who resides in a nursing home, assisted care facility, or in a care home. It also includes adults who receive personal care or support to continue living independently in their own home. Adults who receive social care services or any services provided in an establishment for a person with learning difficulties would be a vulnerable adult. Vulnerable adult definitions include adults who have a learning or physical disability; a physical or mental illness; chronic or otherwise, including an addiction to alcohol or drugs; or a reduction in physical or mental capacity. Disabilities are a dependency upon others in the performance of, or a requirement for assistance in the performance of, basic physical functions. In addition, severe impairment in the ability to communicate with others, or impairment in a person's ability to protect him or herself from assault, abuse, or neglect are defined as disabilities.

"Physical Abuse" is generally defined as "any non-accidental physical injury to a child or vulnerable adult" and can include striking, kicking, burning, or biting, or any action that results in a physical impairment.

"Neglect" is frequently defined as the failure of a parent or other person with responsibility for the child or vulnerable adult to provide needed food, clothing, shelter, medical care, or supervision such that the child or vulnerable adult's health, safety, and well-being are threatened with harm. In a few states, failure to educate the child as required by law is defined as neglect. Some states specifically define medical neglect as failing to provide any special medical treatment or mental healthcare needed by the child or vulnerable adult.

All states include "Sexual Abuse" in their definitions of child and vulnerable adult abuse. Some states refer in general terms to sexual abuse, while others specify various acts as sexual abuse. Sexual exploitation is an element of the definition of sexual abuse in most jurisdictions. "Pornography laws" pertaining to child protection typically prohibit the sharing, purchasing, filming, or e-mailing any print, photo or video that depicts children being exposed to or participating in sexually explicit situations. This includes minors engaged in sexual behaviors, obscene conduct or the display of a child's genitals when done in a sexual manner. The selling or buying of children for use in child pornography also falls under child protection laws. The advent of the Internet created a need for child protection laws regarding children's online usage and access. Some child protection laws require schools, libraries, and other public places to install special software on all computers that are accessible to children.

Almost all states include "Emotional Maltreatment" as part of their definitions of abuse or neglect. Typically, language used in these definitions is "injury to the psychological capacity or emotional stability of a child or vulnerable adult as evidenced by an observable or substantial change in behavior, emotional response, or cognition" as evidenced by "anxiety, depression, withdrawal, or aggressive behavior."

"Parental Substance Abuse" is an element of the definition of child abuse or neglect in some states. Circumstances that are considered abuse or neglect in some states include parental exposure of a child to harm due to the parent's use of illegal drug or other substance; manufacturing of a controlled substance in the presence of a child or on the premises occupied by a child; allowing a child to be present where the chemicals or equipment for the manufacturing of controlled substances are used or stored; and, the use of a controlled substance by the caregiver that impairs the caregiver's ability to adequately care for the child.

Several states include "Abandonment" in their definition of abuse or neglect, generally as a type of neglect. It is considered abandonment of a child or vulnerable adult when the parents or caregivers whereabouts are unknown, the child or vulnerable adult have been left by the parent or caregiver in circumstances in which the child or vulnerable adult suffers serious harm, or the parent or caregiver has failed to maintain contact with the child or vulnerable adult or to provide reasonable support for a specified period of time.

RELATED CHILD PROTECTIVE LAWS

Various laws covering vulnerable populations offer differing definitions of abuse and different penalties for failing to report. But there is a lot of common ground, such as any evidence of physical injury, neglect, sexual or emotional abuse, or financial exploitation. By law, mandatory reporters must report suspected abuse or neglect of a child or a vulnerable adult, regardless of whether are not the knowledge of the abuse was gained in the reporter's official capacity. And, the mandatory reporting for issues of abuse and neglect involving children, or vulnerable adults, is typically a 24-48 hour obligation. (Know and follow your state's laws and regulations)

A mental health counselor's duty is owed to these vulnerable populations. Counselors do not have the responsibility to investigate; their responsibility is to report to appropriate agencies if they have reasonable suspicion. If you are uncertain as to whether or not to report, you can always call child protective or adult protective services and ask for a consultation. Always document in your clinical record the date, time, and who you spoke to; ask for a copy of the intake report for your file, if possible. Reporting to protective services is a limit of confidentiality that must be explained in your consent form, according to HIPAA's Notice of Privacy Practices, and ethically you should take the time to discuss this limit of confidentiality with new clients.

Then, if, In the course of therapy, a client speaks to you about their involvement or knowledge of abuse or neglect or abandonment of a child or vulnerable adult, they knew they were placing you in a position of reporting. Many times, clients need your assistance, support, and initiation regarding these issues.

ETHICAL STANDARDS & CLINICAL FORMS

RESEARCH
- What is the "Age of Majority" for your state?
- Look up laws regarding "protective services" for your state
- Since states vary regarding mandatory reporters, make a list of all mandatory reporters for your state
    - When would you need to make a report?
    - How does your state define: abuse, neglect, abandonment, etc.
    - What are the pornography laws for your state?
    - Do you have the phone numbers for Protective Services?
- Call them and ask for information regarding your responsibilities as a licensed mental health professional
    - Some states exempt psychologists from having to report abuse if they are told of the abuse by the abuser. Does your state have such an exemption? Why do you think such an exemption might exist?

MANDATORY REPORTING: DUTY TO WARN AND PROTECT

In the counseling profession, duty to warn and protect applies to cases where the client is dangerous to themselves, others, or has made a threat against a specific target (e.g., building, transportation, etc.) In these situations, the counselor must breach confidentiality to keep the client or their target safe. If their state requires them to make an attempt to personally contact and warn an identified victim (a specific person) who is in imminent danger, the counselor must do so. States do vary in their interpretation of this duty to warn an intended victim. Some states require the counselor to make a reasonable attempt to contact an identifiable person, the intended victim. Other states do not require the counselor to do this. However, all states require that the counselor take action by contacting local law enforcement or other medical personnel involved in the care of the client, to help advert a threat of harm to themselves or others. The word "threat" typically refers to "physical harm."

As mentioned above, the necessary actions required to discharge the duty to warn in regards to contacting an intended victim varies from state-to-state. States with a "Required Standard" have statutory laws that require counselors to make an attempt to contact a third-party identified person when a client has made a threat towards that specific person.

If the counselor is unaware of how to contact the individual, or is uncertain as to who the individual is, then their duty to warn would be fulfilled by contacting local law enforcement, or other medical personnel involved in the care of the client.

States with a "Permissive Standard" give permission through statutes for counselors to warn of serious threats, but the permission to warn is limited to notifying medical or law enforcement personnel, not the threatened person or persons.

States with a "No Statutory Standard" do not provide any statutory language for counselors to address the duty to warn an intended victim, although some of these states have implemented the duty through court decisions.

States that have established a duty to warn also vary as to what type of threat triggers the duty. Some states require or permit any disclosure of confidential information to prevent a general threat to the public at large. Other states require or permit disclosure based only on the basis of a threat to harm a specific individual or group of individuals. Know which standard applies to your state.

As counselors, we need to assess the threat. Is it one of self-harm or harm to another person, several persons, a building, or means of transportation? Is the threat to a specific individual or the general public? What are the details disclosed regarding the threat and under what circumstances? Does the client possess the means and capacity to carry out the threat? Does the criteria for involuntary commitment apply? Who needs to be warned to discharge your duty? Regarding time frame, a counselor has 24-48 hours (in most states) to report to the appropriate authorities once they have made the decision that the report needs to be made. Counselors report in "good faith" and, by doing so, they have immunity from prosecution. The law compels the counselor to report under these situations, so a counselor doing so in good faith should not fear prosecution from the client. Counselors have a responsibility for making difficult determinations regarding the assessment and treatment of clients, and this includes taking steps to assure client safety and the safety of others. Counselors need to review the following when considering reporting: 1) How much time has passed since a threat was made? 2) Does the client possess the means, motive, opportunity, and capacity to carry out their threat? 3) Is the threat of harm to a specific individual or does it represent a general threat to the public at large? 4) Who needs to be warned to effectively discharge the duty—the intended target? Law enforcement? Another treating healthcare provider?

RESEARCH
- Look up "Duty to Warn/Protect" laws for your state
- Web search these legal cases: Tarasoff vs. Regents, Jablonski by Pahls vs. United States, and Ewing vs. Goldstein. How have the other cases expanded on the Tarasoff Case?
  - Is your state a required, permissive, or no statutory standard state?
  - What types of threats would establish a duty to warn for you in your state?

CLEAR AND IMMINENT DANGER VS. SERIOUS AND FORESEEABLE HARM

Relevant cases, after Tarasoff, have impacted the reporting obligations and the terms of duty to warn and duty to protect, as well as who is the identifiable victim and if foreseeable harm can be anticipated. Ethical codes are making the shift from "clear and imminent danger" to "substantial likelihood of serious and foreseeable harm" when considering the need to break confidentiality. "Serious and foreseeable harm" allows a broader scope of circumstances where counselors need to considering reporting. Codes of ethics specify that counselors should consult with other professionals when in doubt as to the validity or necessity for breaching confidentiality, but if the threat is believed to be real, time for consultation may not be prudent.

HOMICIDE RISKS

It is impossible to predict with 100% accuracy "dangerousness" ahead of time. The art of counseling involves learning to discern what the client is really saying. When someone says, "I wish someone else was dead" are they talking homicide or just expressing frustration with their current stress level or relationship difficulties? How do we distinguish between a client who vents in scary ways and those who may carry out their threatening words? Assessing seriousness and imminence of danger is fraught with trouble. The best predictor of future violence is a history or pattern of past violence. The violent–angry–impulsive person will show a history of violence, such as assaults, hitting and injuring others, destroying or damaging property, and injury to self.

These individuals reveal impulsive anger or rage that is explosively triggered by various people or events and the person quickly gets out of control. They show a tendency to hurt others and vengefully react when angry. They project blame onto others and are critical and condemning of others.

Typically they are unable to receive criticism from others and justify their anger and harmful expressions. Unable to forgive, they tend to hold grudges and resentment over a long period of time. Suppressed anger (the denial of anger in the face of obvious evidence) and repressed anger (the denial of an anger problem contrary to history) are both characteristic of a violent–angry–impulsive person.

Good documentation is essential in every case, but with dangerous and threatening clients, is critical. Make sure you have a treatment plan and you update it regularly. In your case notes record specifically what the client says, your assessment of the threat, what you did, and why you decided to do it.

RESEARCH
- Find a sample assessment for homicide evaluation
- You can find one on line...
  - What would you add or change?

SUICIDE RISKS

There is no pure legal duty to prevent suicide—the duty is to intervene appropriately. The law recognizes the limits of being able to stop a determined person from suicide. The duty to intervene is judged according to the degree of suicidal risk exhibited by the client and the counselor's ability to accurately assess and control that risk. The counselor's liability increases as the risk of suicide increases and the counselor is able to foresee the client's actions and pro-actively intervene. A counselor in an inpatient facility can control the client's behavior more than in an outpatient setting; liability is greater when suicide occurs in a hospital, day treatment, or residential care facility. Indeed, the counselor working in an inpatient or restrictive treatment setting has a strong duty to intervene in the life of someone judged to be a substantial risk for suicide.

Suicide is not only one of the riskiest cases for a counselor clinically and personally, but legally as well.

Assessment of suicidal risk involves gathering information from multiple sources across a number of key variables. The essential two-part question of suicide assessment is: 1) Is this person at risk for committing suicide, and if so, 2) How serious is the risk? A competent counselor will assess this risk according to history, trait, mood, personality, diagnosis, and situational factors. Begin counseling with the assessment of suicide risk. The easiest way to get information about suicide risk is to ask questions at the beginning of counseling. Incorporate questions about suicidal (and homicidal) behavior in clinical assessment forms. This gives direct access to these issues at the start of the professional relationship. Structuring assessments so as to ask these questions in an initial interview puts clients more at ease because they see it as a part of the routine followed with all new clients.

Professional counselor liability for suicide cuts across two issues: 1) The setting in which the crisis arises and the nature of the alleged harm, and 2) Whether it involves failure to take preventative action to avoid suicide or whether the clinical behavior caused the suicide.

SUICIDE SAFETY PLANS

In years past, counselors used what was called a "no suicide contract." They would have clients sign a document stating that they would not commit suicide, but these documents have been found unenforceable in court law. They also lack a treatment plan. Counselors need to use a "suicide safety plan." A suicide safety plan is a written document. It is a set of instructions that you create with your client as a contingency plan should the client begin to experience thoughts about harming themselves. It will contain a series of gradually escalating steps that they can follow, proceeding from one step to the next, until they are safe.

A SUICIDE SAFETY PLAN SHOULD INCLUDE THE FOLLOWING ELEMENTS, IN THE SAME ORDER AS PRESENTED:
- When the plan should be used: making the client familiar with what types of situations, images, thoughts, feelings, and behaviors might precede or accompany suicidal urges. The client writes an example such as: "When I feel suicidal, I tend to isolate myself and not take good care of my health."
- What the client can do to calm or comfort themselves when they are feeling suicidal: create a list of activities that are soothing. The client writes examples such as: "I will take a hot bath or listen to music."

- What are the client's reasons for living: create a list of the reasons; it is easy to get caught up in the pain and forget the positives and such a list helps the client refocus their attention on the reasons to keep going until suicidal thoughts and feelings pass. The client writes examples such as: "My children, my spouse, my faith in God are reasons to live."
- Who the client can talk to: keep a list of contacts that the client can talk to if they are unable to distract themselves with self-help measures. List names, phone numbers, and other contact information.
- Who the client can talk to if they need professional assistance: create a list of all professional resources available to them, along with the phone numbers, e-mail addresses, and other pertinent contact information (psychiatrist, counselor, crisis hot line).
- How can the client make their environment safe: plan what steps clients can take to keep themselves safe. This may involve removing or securing any items that they are likely to use to hurt themselves, or going to another location until their suicidal urges or thoughts pass. This may also involve getting another person involved to help them. The client writes examples such as: "When I am feeling suicidal, I will ask my brother to keep me company." Or "When I feel like hurting myself, I will go to a public place, like a mall, restaurant, or library to distract myself."
- If they are still not feeling safe: if all other steps have failed to keep the client safe, then have a plan, such as going to the nearest hospital emergency room and asking for assistance. If they do not feel safe to get to the hospital on their own then they should call 911 or a trusted family member or friend to help them.

RESEARCH
- **Check the Internet for sample suicide safety plans**
  - **Create a template for use with your clients**

THESE SITUATIONS THAT CAN BE CONFUSING...

Activities that do not meet the legal requirements for mandatory reporting under mandatory reporting laws can be confusing and difficult for counselors.

WHERE CAN YOU TURN TO FOR ADDITIONAL INFORMATION?
- MINORS ENGAGED IN SEXUAL ACTIVITY—refer to your state's statutory rape laws; this information is easily found on the Internet by searching the words: "statutory rape laws" by states.
- CLIENTS WHO HAVE AIDS/HIV OR OTHER COMMUNICABLE DISEASES who are engaging in unprotected sex—talk with your local health department.
- ADULT CLIENTS OF DOMESTIC VIOLENCE—call the National domestic violence hotline for consultation or information, or talk with your state's Department of Health to determine if there are mandatory reporting requirements for domestic violence.
- CLIENTS WHO ARE SEVERELY DISABLED due to drug and alcohol abuse who continue to drive or engage in other activities or work in safety sensitive positions—consult with colleagues or contact your insurance company for an appointment to speak with an attorney or someone in their risk management department. Sometimes, situations like these, can fall under the duty to warn and protect laws.
- CLIENTS WHO ARE SELF-IDENTIFIED SEXUAL PREDATORS (they have never been arrested, charged or convicted) who engage in risky situations (work at a place where children are or volunteer in an organization for children)—consult with colleagues, talk with an attorney, or contact your insurance company's risk management department. Sometimes, situations like these can fall under the duty to warn and protect laws and/or child protection or pornography laws.
- CHILDREN (UNDER THE AGE OF MAJORITY) AND MARRIAGE—search on the Internet using these key words: "marriage, age requirements" by states.

RESEARCH
- Where else could you get more information or guidance?
- Research each of the previously listed situations for your state
- Would you ever consider adding statements in your consent creating additional limits of confidentiality? *(e.g., If you speak to me regarding past crimes I reserve the right to contact local law enforcement.)*
  - Why? Or, why not?

Reporting to law enforcement, contacting an intended victim, or speaking to another healthcare provider in relation to duty to warn and protect is a limit of confidentiality that has to be explained in your consent form and verbalized to new clients at the onset of a clinical relationship, preferably before assessment and treatment. Ethically counselors are to take the time to discuss the limits of confidentiality with new clients to ensure their understanding and to provide the opportunity for them to ask questions. Once counselors have done this, and then the client speaks about reportable situations, they can be reminded that what they have communicated requires reporting.

CAVEAT: When in doubt regarding mandatory reporting: 1) Consult with colleagues, 2) Call your professional association's ethical department, 3) Call your insurance company's risk management department, 4) Call for a consultation with your state's protective services, or 5) Seek legal advice. However, if danger is imminent, then time may not allow for consultation(s) before the need to contact law enforcement, or initiating involuntary commitment, to keep the client or others safe.

*Your records need to be
clinically relevant
and
protective of your work*

CLINICAL RECORDS

Ethically, you are required to keep records on clients and these records need to include the client's name and relevant information, written acknowledgment that they have received the HIPAA Notice of Privacy Practices, a signed and dated consent form, clinical session notes that reflect the dates of contact (in-person, by phone, or via technology), presenting symptoms/issues/concerns and/or diagnosis, all notes regarding consultations, reporting, or other special situations.

Counselors are also required to have fee arrangement documents, which the client has signed. This document should be kept in their clinical file. Counselors ethically are to establish and maintain billing practices that accurately reflect the nature and extent of services provided and that identify who provided the service in the practice setting. When setting fees, counselors should ensure that the fees are fair and reasonable for the type of work done, and for the community the services are being provided.

Your records need to be clinically useful and protective of your work.

ETHICAL STANDARDS & CLINICAL FORMS

RECORD GUIDELINES

SOME GUIDELINES ARE:

1) Clinical notes are to reflect services, 2) Assessments support diagnosis, and 3) Diagnosis supports the treatment plan. Not keeping clinical records is beneath the "standard of care" doctrine and would be unwise to ignore.

S.O.A.P. NOTES

RECORDS NEED TO REFLECT:

1) What client is thinking (Subjective), 2) How the counselor is thinking (Objective), 3) The counselor's clinical judgment(s) (Assessment), and 4) The proposed direction(s) (Plan).

The "S.O.A.P. note format" has been around for a long time and is a useful way to structure clinical records. Many electronic records follow a "D.A.P. Format" which stands for: Data (Data includes both Subjective/Objective), Assessment, and Plan. When counselors work for an organization or agency, they need to follow that agency's record-keeping format. If a counselor is in private practice, they have the freedom to choose a recordkeeping format. Counselors are required to accurately document what occurs during a counseling session, and the S.O.A.P. format is designed well.

COUNSELORS NEED TO ASK THESE TWO QUESTIONS:

1) What are the mental health needs of this client? and, 2) How can these needs best be addressed?

Some suggestions for the "subjective" portion of the notes would be to keep client quotations to a minimum. When client quotations are overused it makes the record more difficult to review for client themes and to track the effectiveness of interventions. If you use quotations, record only keywords or a very brief phrase—these can be very useful especially when a client has spoken something significant that would be helpful to refer back to at a later date. The subjective has to do with what the client is presenting to you that is directly related to how they are feeling, thinking, or perceiving. The subjective is what the client brings.

Suggestions for the "objective" portion of the clinical notes would be to keep the information factual—what you see. The counselor's observations include any physical, interpersonal, or psychological findings that the counselor witnesses. Information should be stated in precise and descriptive terms and avoid labeling observations with value-laden language.

The "assessment" portion of the clinical notes is a summarization of the counselor's clinical thinking regarding the client's problem(s)—what the counselor is thinking and why. This portions serves to synthesize and analyze the data from the subjective and objective portions of the notes. These are the clinical impressions.

Some counselors keep personal or shadow notes separate from the client's file (e.g., psychotherapy notes, see below; topic was also covered earlier).

The "plan" section describes the counseling interventions used. It has two parts: 1) The action plan: Interventions, educational instruction, treatment progress, and treatment direction, and 2) The prognosis: The probable gains to be made by the client given a diagnosis, the client's personal resources, and the motivation for change.

> **RESEARCH**
> - Do you use S.O.A.P formatted notes? If not, Why?
> - Search the Internet for examples of S.O.A.P. notes

PSYCHOTHERAPY NOTES (Previously discussed on page 62)

"Psychotherapy notes" are also known as "shadow notes" or "confidential notes" and sometimes "process notes." Mental health counselors are permitted to maintain psychotherapy notes separately from the rest of the client's chart. These psychotherapy notes may represent personal notes used to record or analyze group, individual, or family therapy, and unlike the rest of the chart do not have to be disclosed to the client. Anything that is kept in a client's chart is NOT a psychotherapy note. HIPAA provides special protection for psychotherapy notes, although, in order for clinical-related notes to qualify as psychotherapy notes they must meet certain conditions that include: 1) They are maintained separately from the client's main healthcare record, 2) They are not the only source of information for treatment or payments, and 3) They are solely for the use of the provider that created them.

Many counselors use what they call "process notes" during sessions. During the clinical session, the counselor takes down much of what is being said on process notes. At the end of the session they dictate or otherwise enter portions of their notes into the client's paper or electronic record of the session.

If they shred the process notes then technically those notes are not considered psychotherapy notes. They were simply notes that helped the counselor process the counseling session. However, if the counselor retains the process notes and keeps them in a separate place from the client's record, then they meet the criteria for psychotherapy notes.

RESEARCH
- Do an Internet search on the words "psychotherapy notes and HIPAA" and read more about them
- Think of reasons why a counselor might want to use shadow notes
- Do you see a downside to keeping these confidential notes?
- If you used "process notes" during a session do you dictate chart notes from them and toss them or do you save them?

GOOD RECORDS REFLECT A COUNSELOR'S COMPETENCE

Clinical notes are very important because clinical records reflect a counselor's competence in: 1) Decision-making abilities, 2) Their capacity to weigh available options, 3) Their rationale for treatment selection, and 4) Their knowledge of clinical, ethical, and legal relevant issues.

Counselors should always document special occurrences like telephone calls with clients or client's family or friends (counselors only engage in conversations with such individuals, if a client has authorized them do so), emergency situations and issues of dangerousness, mandated and other reporting that is done, including any consultations with agencies. Counselors document in a client's records any additional consultations they have with colleagues or other care providers, testing and testing results, and referrals. Equally, it is important to have information on the termination of the therapeutic relationship.

CLINICAL NOTES

Good records help counselors provide quality care by providing continuity, and they do not need to rely on their memory to recall details of their clients' lives and the treatments provided. Not keeping any clinical session notes is below the standard of care, is unethical, and in many states, illegal. In the case of administrative litigation (licensing board investigations), civil or criminal action, it is often not the counselor's word against the client, but the client's word against the clinical records. Also, in case the treating counselor becomes disabled, dies, or cannot continue to provide care, records help the next treating counselor with information so the client's continuity of care continues.

WHAT ABOUT THE AMOUNT OF DETAIL IN A SESSION NOTE?

The amount of detail is determined by your employer, electronic record format, the services or evaluations you are providing, who retained you for a specific service and the amount of detail they are expecting, and also, by your personal choice if your are self-employed.

A girlfriend of mine went to see a counselor with her 13-year-old daughter at the request of the court. She got a copy of the clinical notes and showed them to me, specifically wanting to know about the fifth paragraph. The first four paragraphs were typical of a counseling session for such an evaluation—mother presented with child…regarding divorce…child feels…mother identifies concerns…etc. Then came the fifth paragraph, which read, "Mother is tall and thin. She is wearing a royal blue dress with rhinestone accents around the neck and sleeves. She is wearing matching royal blue suede high-heeled shoes. She has rings on four fingers, each hand, and three gold necklaces and large hoop gold earrings. She arrived at the office wearing a knee-length faux fur coat." The next paragraph returned to typical clinical session notes.

My friend wanted to know what that paragraph was about. My reply, "I think she was the fashion police." Really, that part of the note was disjointed. If the counselor was trying to make a point she did not make the point clear. When we write something in a clinical note there needs to be relevance to why we have written it down—connect the dots.

ETHICAL STANDARDS & CLINICAL FORMS

RECORD RETENTION

Adhere to your state's requirement for record retention, especially when you are in private practice.

Typically, most states, it has been seven years from the last time you saw a client or seven years after a minor client turns eighteen. Although several states now require ten years.

If you are a preferred provider on insurance panels, check your contract. Most insurance providers now require counselors to keep clinical records a minimum of ten years. If you work for an organization or agency, adhere to their record-keeping retention policies. Always maintain records for the most stringent length of time relevant to the work being done. Different areas of health care require different lengths of time.

Private health information records can only be destroyed by incineration (burning) or by shredding. Electronic records are typically stored forever because simply erasing data does not mean it has been he erased from the hard drive. Replacing hard drives can be expensive.

RESEARCH
- What is your state's record retention requirement if you were in private practice?
- Check your Preferred Provider Contracts: What is the length of time they require for record retention?
- If you are using electronic records do you have encryption software? A back up system? Stored in a secure location?

FINANCIAL ARRANGEMENTS

Clients need to know what to expect: Are you billing their insurance company for them or do they need to submit it to their insurance company? What amount of the co-insurance is required at each office visit? If it's private pay, is full payment due the day of service? When do you send out bills? And, what would put their account in an overdue status? There are many other expenses the client might need to be aware of, such as fees for telephone conversations, e-counseling, site visits, copying records, report writing and reading, consultations with other professionals, longer sessions, travel time by the counselor relevant to the client, etc.

FEE STRUCTURES

If a counselor is on an insurance panel as a preferred provider, the insurance company has established the maximum fees based on billing codes. Clients typically have a co-pay, plus an additional percent that will be their responsibility. Counselors who are preferred providers typically accept benefits and bill the insurance company for the client. Clients who carry insurance policies, that are outside a counselor's preferred provider network, typically pay their bill at the time of the visit and then the client submits their invoice to their insurance company for reimbursement. Clients who use insurance companies to pay their mental health services must be made aware that submitting a mental health invoice for reimbursement to an insurance company carries a certain amount of risk that their private health information could be requested by the insurance company for review. This is a limit of confidentiality and clearly needs to be made known to the client. When insurance is used by clients to pay a bill, a diagnosis must be given, and clients need to be made aware that their insurance company can request copies of their records.

There are many things to consider when setting prices.

If you are a "fee-for-service" (cash) practice, you need to structure fees that are fair, responsible, appropriate for the work done, and for the community you serve. Clients need to know how your policies. Most counselors in a cash practice request the full amount at the time of the visit, unless other arrangements are made in writing. If a client carries a balance, then counselors typically provide clients with a monthly invoice showing any unpaid balance, and typically request that the balance is due within the next 30 days.

The difference between private pay and insurance:
A diagnosis (DSM/ICD) is not required if the client is paying privately
DSM: Diagnostic and Statistical Manual; and, ICD: International Classifications of Diseases.

"Sliding scale fees" are typically based on annual income, and sometimes based on the size of the family in conjunction with annual income. For many individuals who suffer with mental health problems, the cost of receiving proper counseling prohibits them from seeking the help that they so greatly need. Most government-funded mental health centers, non-profit counseling centers, and some private counselors, offer sliding fee scales in order to make treatment more affordable for low-income individuals or those who have difficulty paying the full price of treatment due to other factors. Typically, to qualify for a lesser fee in treatment, a client would need to fill out a detailed questionnaire regarding their financial background and perhaps need to provide documents that support their claims (e.g., past tax returns).

RESEARCH
- Find a copy of a financial arrangement document being used by a colleague. (Ask for one or check the Internet) What would you change?
- Dentists typically have very detailed financial arrangement documents that require the patient to initial every line. Get three financial arrangement documents from a local dentist—*take note of how detailed their documents are. Would you incorporate any of their wording or style into your own document?*
- For a mental health organization that uses a sliding-fee scale. What would you change?

BARTERING

"Bartering" is the exchange of goods and services. It has been around since the beginning of time. In counseling, bartering is the acceptance of goods, services, or other non-monetary payments from clients in return for counseling services. In certain cultures and communities, bartering is a generally accepted norm and means of compensation or economic exchange. In these areas, bartering for counseling services is more common. However, it is also more common at times of economic depression. Another common scenario is a client who is established with a counselor, but loses their job and subsequently their insurance coverage. For counseling to continue in such a situation, bartering can become the bridge.

Bartering is an especially controversial issue among counselors, consumer protection agencies, licensing boards, ethics committees, and risk management experts. Bartering in mental health counseling is often frowned upon because experts believe that the "power differentiation" between counselor and client could lead to exploitation of the client by the counselor in the bartering arrangement. While bartering for services seems to be frowned upon by most experts. Bartering for goods seems more acceptable, because goods (a product) enables both the client and the counselor to place a dollar value on the item that is being bartered for the counseling services. The value of the item and the value of the counseling service should be as closely valued as equal, as possible.

The concern regarding bartering for services has to do with boundary crossing concerns that could lead to dual relationships. In fact, bartering for services constitutes dual relationships (additional contact with the client outside of the therapeutic relationship) while bartering for goods (a specific product) does not necessarily translate into a dual relationship. While all bartering can be viewed as a boundary crossing, it is not necessarily a boundary violation (harmful and exploitive behavior).

When a client barters artwork in exchange for therapy, most counselors agree that this does not create another relationship outside the therapy relationship. The artwork just replaces the cash payment. However, when a client pays for therapy by cleaning the counselor's home or repairing the counselor's car, this arrangement definitely constitutes a dual relationship because, in addition to the therapeutic relationship, there is now a relationship that exists outside of counseling.

Suggestion: Have the client propose the bartering arrangement to you in writing—why they are requesting to barter; what the bartering arrangement could be; the dollar values involved; and, then discuss the matter with the client. Note any changes to the initial proposal, and then accept the proposal or not. Make sure you keep a copy of this in the client's file. Remember that bartering arrangements, particularly those involving services, create the potential for conflicts of interest, exploitation, and inappropriate boundaries.

MOST ASSOCIATIONS' CODES OF ETHICS SAY SOMETHING LIKE THIS:
Counselors may participate in bartering only in very limited circumstances such as when it is an accepted practice among professionals in the local community, considered to be essential for the provision of services, negotiated without coercion, and entered into at the client's initiative and with the client's informed consent. Always check you state's licensing code of ethics regarding bartering.

RESEARCH
- Does your state licensing department allow counselors to barter? If not, why? If yes, are there any restrictions?
- What do each of the associations you belong to say about ethics and bartering?
- What circumstances would it take for you to consider bartering?

RECORD CUSTODIANS

If you work for someone else, the agency or organization is the custodian of the records. However, if you work for yourself (private practice) then you must name another licensed counselor who will become the custodian of your clients' charts upon your death. The record custodian does not have to see your clients, but they do take possession of the charts and notify your clients of your death. Record custodians would provide copies of a client's chart with appropriate authorization to do so by the client or in response to appropriate legal actions. They would retain your charts according to the required number of years for your state or insurance carrier.

It would be wise to have a backup record custodian named in your professional will. You would also need to note in your will instructions to your executor to contact the record custodian and accompany them to your office so they can secure your clients' files. Your executor should secure a signed document from your record custodian that your clients' charts are now in their possession. Typically, the record custodian also notifies current clients and the state licensing department of your death. Make sure the appointment book also is given to the record custodian and any other files that would have client contact information or confidential information.

MINORS AND ETHICS

The age of majority is not the age of maturity. The age of maturity is arbitrary—there are minors who are mature and adults who are not. Legislation is designed to protect minors from poor decisions. Maturity requires the assessment of a minor's capacity to understand the nature of their illness, treatment options, and potential risks.

RESEARCH
- The "age of majority" is typically 18, but some states differ. What is the age of majority for your state?

MATURE MINOR DOCTRINE

"Mature minors" are those who meet the conditions set forth by the mature minor rule, a legal doctrine that enables minors who are deemed mature (able to understand the nature and consequences of their medical concern and treatment) to consent to or refuse treatment. Determination of maturity requires an assessment of the minor's capacity to understand the concerns at hand. Usually this determination of maturity is left to physicians or judges. In some states, mature minor legislation extends to older minors (age 12-17) the authority to provide informed consent for medical treatment, but ages vary by state.

As mentioned in the previous paragraph, some states have legislation that defines specifically how old a minor needs to be to independently consent to certain types of health care: Contraceptive services; prenatal care; STD/HIV services; treatment for alcohol or drug abuse; and, outpatient mental health services.

RESEARCH
www.guttmacher.org
- Guttmacher is an organization that is involved with minors and their rights.
  - They move information around, so you'll need to explore their site for the information you're seeking.
- *They have information regarding minors for the various states.*
  (Continued on next page)

ETHICAL STANDARDS & CLINICAL FORMS

There's a lot of information on the Guttmacher website
(Continued from previous page)
- **Find your state. What age does the client need to be to receive state contraceptive services, prenatal care, STD/HIV services, treatment for alcohol or drug abuse, and outpatient mental health services?**
- **What other resource can you find on the Internet regarding minors and their rights to consent to health care for your state?**
  - **What state resource can you find for information about minors and the right to consent?**
- **Contact a mental health agency in your area that provides services to minors and see what information they will share.**

WHO'S THE CLIENT?

When a minor is old enough (per state legislation) to sign a consent form (without parental involvement) and the minor is paying for the care himself or herself, then confidentiality is owed to the minor—they are the client. However, in some states, they cannot use their parent's insurance or have their parents pay privately for the counseling and still be considered the sole client. In these states, if the parent is paying, but the minor is of consenting age per state laws, then parent(s) and minor both sign the consent form. If a minor is old enough to sign the consent then they are also old enough to refuse treatment (Patient's Rights Act). Counselors who work with minors have policies (or specific consent documents) that outline the counseling relationship between counselor, parents or legal guardians, and the minor. If you are in private practice and are thinking about working with minors, consult with colleagues who have provided services to minors. See what they are doing. Ask if they would share their consent form, policies, and procedures. If you are employed by an agency or organization that works with minors, follow the company's policies. Always follow your company's policies, as well as state laws and regulations.

RESEARCH
- **Find three counselors that work with minors...**
- **If the information is available on their website**—*read their consent and office policies, and any other policies regarding their work with minors*
- **If the information is NOT available on their website**—*stop by their office to see if they would share their paperwork or if they would briefly talk with you about their policies and procedures for working with minors and the minor's family.*

THE COUNSELOR

We are different professionals with different beliefs and different styles and different interventions, but we have common ethical guidelines. The commitment to the client's best interest is primary. Counselors do not impose their own values or beliefs. Styles and interventions should be client and condition appropriate. Counselors have an obligation to support and assist clients with their goals, only deviating from this when the law compels them to do so or when they are court ordered to deviate.

THERAPEUTIC INTERVENTIONS

There are hundreds of therapy approaches and therapy types. Some have been around for years; some are relatively new. Some have been grounded in research, while others in theory, and some rely on anecdotal evidence. Some are popularly accepted, others are cutting-edge, and some controversial. Please Note: I am not in the position to endorse or disapprove of any therapy types. My intention is to promote the awareness of the elements of therapy and the ethics of providing good care.

> **RESEARCH**
> - **Internet search using these words: "mental health therapy interventions" or maybe try "good therapy interventions"**
> - **Explore, research, and discover for yourself what kind of therapy might be a fit for you.**

THERAPEUTIC INTERVENTIONS ARE PURPOSEFUL

Effective therapeutic interventions are purposeful. What does this mean? It means that the counselor is knowledgeable, educated, trained, and that the interventions are based on the counselor's knowledge of the client. Counselors are to be competent using an intervention, and know which interventions might be effective with a particular client. Even a healthy model of therapy can be used in an unhealthy way. When you look at different therapy interventions, look at safety and effectiveness. If a therapy has not been tested for effectiveness, we don't know whether it delivers the result it claims.

It may have no effect at all (wasting the client's time and money), or it may be less effective than other available therapies. When considering effectiveness, the question *effective for what purpose?* should be considered. Every therapy intervention, either explicitly or implicitly, claims to be beneficial in one or more ways for one or more problems.

SO, WHEN EVALUATING EFFECTIVENESS, CONSIDER THREE THINGS:
- What condition does this therapy intervention claim to treat?
- What benefits does this therapy intervention claim to provide?
- Among a group of people with this condition, when the outcomes of clients treated with this therapy intervention are compared with control subjects, does this therapy show a statistically significant benefit in the way that it claims?

RESEARCH
- **Internet search using these key words: *"mental health interventions, treatment options, and/or therapeutic philosophies"***
  - Select three that interest you, and assess their effectiveness
- **Many therapy interventions and orientations claim to be useful for some purpose**
  - The questions to explore are:
    1) Has the therapy intervention been tested and found to be safe?
    2) Has the therapy intervention been tested and found to be effective?

COMPLEMENTARY AND ALTERNATIVE INTERVENTIONS

There are ways of treating mental health issues that have developed outside the mainstream of modern medicine. Many are remedies that have developed in different cultures over the centuries. Alternative treatments can be used on their own or with conventional treatments. Some of these treatments may work, but most have not been thoroughly tested; studies have often been too small to give a clear answer. Despite the lack of evidence, people all over the world are interested in or utilize complementary and alternative interventions. The term "complementary therapies" is generally used to indicate therapies that differ from orthodox Western psychology, ones used to complement, support, or replace traditional therapies.

The term "alternative therapy" is used for therapies that offer alternatives to orthodox Western psychology. A number of factors have contributed to a general rise in interest in complementary and alternative therapies. Continued dissatisfaction with psychiatric treatments among mental health service users has led to the search for safer and more effective alternatives. But a number of factors continue to limit the use of complementary and alternative therapies. These include a lack of resources and an absence of: 1) Adequate research evidence for their efficacy, 2) Formal training and certification programs, and 3) Quality supervision. There is a lot of research in the uses of complementary therapies for treating mental health problems. Acupuncture can have a positive effect on some people diagnosed with schizophrenia. Herbal medicines, for example St. John's Wort, have been linked to the relief of mild to moderate depression. Massage has been shown to reduce levels of anxiety, stress, and depression in some people. Reflexology has been shown to aid relaxation, relieve stress, and restore energy. Research in nutritional and dietary medicine has demonstrated that food sensitivities may cause psychiatric symptoms. Transcendental meditation, hypnotherapy, yoga, exercise, relaxation, massage, and aromatherapy have all been shown to have some effect in reducing stress, tension, and anxiety and in alleviating mental distress.

CATEGORIZING INTERVENTIONS

"Common or Majority interventions" are those therapies that are evidence-based, or commonly referred to as "best practices" or "model programs." These are the theories that have been around for a long time. If a type of therapeutic intervention is taught in a masters or doctorate program it typically falls under this common category. Examples: Acceptance and commitment therapy, Adlerian psychology/psychotherapy, emotion-focused therapy, family-attachment therapy, Gestalt therapy, humanistic psychology, internal family systems, mindfulness-based cognitive therapy, cognitive behavioral therapy, family systems therapy, psychoanalysis, positive psychotherapy, reality therapy, solution focused therapy to name a few. A common intervention does not mean that the counselor is competent to provide the intervention. When I was getting my masters in counseling psychology I took an elective sex therapy class. But after this class I never took any additional continuing education programs on the topic nor did I seek out any work or supervision in this field. Just because a class is offered in a masters or doctorate program on a particular therapeutic intervention, it does not mean that a counselor is competent to provide services utilizing the therapeutic intervention.

"Accepted or Respected interventions" are those therapies that counselors acquire skill training or certification typically after they have graduated from their masters or doctorate program. Certification is considered best practice before practicing a new psychotherapy technique whenever a certification program exists for that technique. Further, it is best to affiliate with other counselors who are practicing in the same type of intervention. A counselor can remain in standard of care without agreeing with the majority view. When using complementary therapies it is important to consider the nature of the client's condition and the probability of risks involved. Further consideration should include reasonably expected benefits and additional available options. Examples of accepted or respected therapies are: Art therapy, bio- and neuro-feedback, mind-body psychotherapy, dance-movement therapy, hypnosis, emotional transformation therapy, equine and animal assisted psychotherapies, eye movement and desensitization and reprocessing (EMDR), lifespan integration, music therapy, narrative therapy, neuro-linguistic programming (NLP), time line therapy, wilderness therapy, to name a few.

"Unproven or Developing in Nature interventions" (sometimes referred to as "Skeptical") are those therapies that have not yet fallen in the common or accepted areas. Most professional organizations do not officially sanction any specific interventions because of fierce controversy. Many counselors have been accustomed to providing therapeutic services to their clients based, not upon a body of scientific evidence in support of their particular approaches or techniques, but instead upon conventions derived from their professional interests and training, theoretical orientations, accumulated experience, clinical intuition, and/or personal preference.

We all recognize that counselors are credentialed through master or doctoral level training, plus professional licensure, because they provide professional services that require expertise beyond the facility of the general public. The professional's obligation to provide the most effective therapeutic intervention available would seem beyond controversy or dispute. Nevertheless, controversy, and dispute arises because counselors: 1) Believe and often proclaim that their services are the most effective among the available alternatives, and 2) Disagree with their colleagues about the treatment of choice for various psychological conditions or disorders based upon your training, orientation, experience, intuition, and/or preference.

It is important to understand that interventions once considered unproven or developing in nature (and sometimes referred to as skeptical) are now considered accepted or common. Many years ago a new therapy came along, in which you had clients move their eyes back and forth rapidly, ask questions, and help the client reprocess trauma. Eye Movement and Desensitization and Reprocessing (EMDR) sounded skeptical, but through a process of what is called "de-mystifying the mystical" the developers of EMDR continued researching, studying control groups, practicing the techniques; they wrote papers, formed an organization, developed training programs; they now issue certification, and provide supervision. Over time, what was considered skeptical, is now accepted.

But the skeptical debate continues. That's okay; there is a constant shift. Yet, as a licensed mental health counselor, be prudent when you choose the type of intervention and therapeutic work you do with your clients. If the type of work falls in the skeptical realm, you need to work diligently to ensure that you are remaining within the highest possible standard of care you can achieve while using that intervention.

When I travel from state to state and share this information, inevitably, at the end of the seminar someone tells me about the type of work they do. Let me share a few therapeutic interventions that have been shared with me, and you can make up your own mind as to whether or not they're skeptical or accepted.

A female counselor told me that her counseling was called "abracadabra." I asked her to explain the process. She explained that all you needed was a wand. When the client said something positive and self-affirming, she would tap them on the head with the wand and say, "Abracadabra." Basically, it's positive reinforcement. Is this really an intervention in and of itself? Or is it just a tool?

I have spoken with counselors who use aromatherapy, a form of alternative medicine that uses plant materials known as essential oils, and other aromatic compounds for the purpose of altering a person's mood, cognitive functions, or health. Two basic mechanisms are offered to explain the purported effects. One is the influence of aroma on the brain, especially the limbic system through the olfactory system. The other is the direct pharmacological effect of the essential oils.

The use of astrology as a therapeutic intervention is more common and more widely used than many realize. Psychological astrology, astrological psychology, or astro-psychology is the result of the cross-fertilization of the fields of astrology with psychology. The horoscope is analyzed through the archetypes within astrology to gain psychological insight into an individual's psyche. I am typically told that astrology brings transpersonal dimensions and spiritual notions to psychology by linking the psyche to the cosmos, and is used as a tool to help identify an individual's nature and potential for psycho-spiritual growth.

Let me continue sharing some of the other therapies that counselors have shared with me. I met a counselor who uses Bach Flower Therapy in her counseling practice. Bach flower remedies are homeopathic flower materials typically used by Naturopaths. The claim is the remedies contain the energetic or vibrational nature of the flower, and that this can be transmitted to the user. Edward Bach thought of illness as the result of "a contradiction between the purposes of the soul and the personality's point of view." This internal war leads to negative moods and energy blocking, which can further contribute to physical diseases. Prior to meeting this counselor, I had never heard of flower therapy being used in a psychology-only practice. Then there was crystal power therapy; the belief in the power of crystals to heal. This counselor incorporated the use of a large crystal in her counseling practice. I was able to meet with her in her office and see the crystal for myself. It was the purple and white crystal pattern in a half rock shell that stood three feet tall and two feet wide. It was an exceptional looking crystal! But how did she use it in her practice? She would see clients for one hour. The first ten minutes she called pre-briefing and she gathered information about how they are doing and what they wanted to focus on. The last ten minutes she called de-briefing where she gathered information about how the session went and where they wanted to go next. That left a forty-minute counseling session. The interesting thing about the session—the client was alone in the room with the crystal. (This was a private-pay practice because insurance companies would not pay for this; to be compensated by an insurance company, the counselor must be present in the room with the client)

Again, I had never heard of a counselor using a crystal in their counseling work but, after this, I did a web search using the words "crystal psychotherapy" and was surprised at how many counselors it yielded. Of course, the list I have accumulated is much larger than what I have shared, but this gives you an idea of some of the unproven or developing nature therapies. However, science is driven by and advances forwarded by skepticism.

A final thought on interventions: Culture can be an exception to skeptical. The subject of culture in psychotherapy is an ethical requirement for all counselors. Counselors working with specific cultures are ethically required to understand the culture-embedded indigenous healing practices, culture-influenced psychotherapies, cultural elements in mainstream therapies, the practice of psychotherapy in different societies, and intercultural psychotherapies. Cultural-relevant psychotherapy requires technical adjustment, theoretical modifications, and philosophical reconsideration.

RESEARCH
- Which of these (abracadabra, aromatherapy, astrology, aura therapy, Back Flower therapy, crystal therapy) do you think will move from skeptical to accepted? (Do you think one or more should already be considered accepted? Which one(s) and why?)
- Internet search the therapies I have referred to. Do you think they should be used in counseling psychology? If yes, why? If no, why not?
- Search these words: *"skeptical dictionary"* and check out the web site on new age psychotherapies. You'll be amazed...
- Web search these words: *"culture-embedded indigenous healing therapies"* and these words *"culture-influenced psychotherapies."* What did your search yield? Pick one culture: *If you worked with this specific culture, what would you do to incorporate that cultures beliefs into psychotherapy practice?*

THERE ARE HUNDREDS OF THERAPEUTIC ORIENTATIONS AND INTERVENTIONS

Consensus is hard to come by when there are hundreds of therapeutic orientations and interventions. Issues still remain with the treatment protocols that are called Empirically Supported Therapies (EST) or Evidence-based Therapies (EBT). Even these protocols have been criticized for lack of validity, narrow focus, and even for being biased and discriminatory against therapeutic orientations that cannot be standardized or easily quantified. When using complementary and alternative treatments and interventions, it is important that the counselor follow the standard of care doctrine.

ETHICAL STANDARDS & CLINICAL FORMS

Counselors should be aware of the contents in their professional associations' official publications, such as newsletters or journal articles, regarding interventions. Counselors are not required to follow the recommendations or guidelines in such publications, but they are expected to be aware of them and, when appropriate, consider them in their clinical and ethical decision-making processes. New psychotherapeutic techniques must be carefully, cautiously, and ethically employed.

COUNSELORS WHO USE ALTERNATIVE OR COMPLEMENTARY INTERVENTIONS SHOULD ALWAYS USE A CONSENT FORM THAT ADDRESSES THESE SIX KEY ISSUES:
1) The type of interventions to be used, 2) The nature of the client's condition, 3) The nature and probability of risks, 4) The benefits to be reasonably expected, 5) The inability of the counselor to predict results, and 6) The available alternatives.

RESEARCH
- Look up an intervention that falls, in what you believe to be, the accepted (or respected minority) intervention doctrine. Then find one that most likely would fall in the "developing in nature" or skeptical intervention doctrine
- Search for a sample informed consent for alternative or complementary mental health care and rewrite the consent for an intervention you've chosen.
  - Be sure to cover the six points listed above (*end of last paragraph*)

CLINICAL CARE SETTINGS

These days, many treatment options exist along a spectrum from less intensive to more intensive care.

"Outpatient care" is provided to a client who is not admitted to a facility. Outpatient care may be provided in an office, clinic, the client's home, or in a variety of therapeutic settings outside an office setting. Outpatient care remains the norm for most routine care.

"Home health care services" are rendered in the home to an individual who is confined to the home. Typically, these individuals do not need institutional care, but need services or therapy in their home setting.

In an "urgent care facility," treatment is provided for conditions requiring prompt medical attention, but those that are not emergencies. More acute injuries and illnesses need to be treated in hospital emergency rooms.

A "care center" provides a setting where a client can receive live-in care and more consistent treatment than can be provided in a clinical office.

"Residential treatment" provides a supportive place to live while receiving treatment-related to mental health, alcoholism or chemical dependency intervention.

"Outpatient hospitalization" takes advantage of hospital equipment and expertise but without the expense or life disruption of overnight stays. Partial hospitalization, sometimes called day programs, provides therapy and support.

"Inpatient care" is care given to clients admitted to a hospital, extended care facility, nursing home, or other facility.

RESEARCH
- What type of setting do you want to work in? Why?
- What type of setting would you avoid? Why?

CLINICIAN SELF-ASSESSMENT
EXPLORE YOUR VOCATION

PRACTICE WHERE YOUR BLISS IS...
- What are you very good at?
- Identify your gifts, talents and abilities at which you excel and were either born with or have acquired during your lifetime
- What are you not at all good at?
- Identify what you do not excel at and in general are not your gifts.
- What kinds of tasks or activities give you joy, delight, or pleasure?
- What do you like to do a lot?
- What would you do if you had all the money, time, health, and love you need?
- What kinds of tasks or activities deplete or bore you?
- What do you hate to do?
- What areas are you very disciplined at?
- Type of activities where you are consistent, methodical and do not procrastinate or regularly avoid.
- What activities do you regularly avoid, delay or procrastinate about?
- What areas are you not disciplined at?
- What, in your opinion, does the world, the region, the state, or your community need?
- What type of contribution does the world, the environment, people, children or animals need these days?
- What, in your opinion, does the world need less of these days?

SELF-ASSESSMENT OF YOUR AREAS OF STRENGTH

RATE YOURSELF in each of the following areas to determine your comfort zone for working with people with these issues.

Take into consideration:
1. Assessment of your own in-depth experience
2. Your capacity/skill to guide or facilitate others through their own journeys in these areas

Use a scale of 1-10:
1 = not comfortable/incapable of helping /consulting with people
10 = very comfortable/capable/expert in this area

Score Each 1-10 (per above)

_____Health/healing, psychological aspects of physical illness
_____Work and vocation or calling
_____Love/intimacy
_____Marriage, crises, affairs, communication, etc.
_____Parenting: babies/toddlers
_____Parenting: adolescents
_____Friendships/community
_____Spirituality and religion
_____Death, dying, conscious dying, grief and bereavement
_____Gender issues, men/women
_____Guilt, shame
_____Anxiety, depression
_____Creativity, play, blocks to creativity
_____Financial arrangements, trusts, wills, IRA's, 401K's
_____Mid-life transition and menopause, women
_____Mid-life transition, men
_____Retirement
_____Parenting one's parents, taking care of parents
_____Drug and alcohol addiction, AA, Alanon
_____Eating disorders
_____Food, medication, sex, gambling and other addictions
_____Ethics and moral issues in everyday life
_____Leisure, recreation
_____Solitude

ETHICAL STANDARDS & CLINICAL FORMS

____Meditation, relaxation, stress reduction
____Meaning in life
____Gay and lesbian issues
____Pre-nuptial counseling
____Conflict resolution, mediation
____Disabilities (e.g. deaf)
____Military psychology
____Forensic psychology (prisons, jails, insanity evaluations, etc.)
____Pain management, chronic pain
____ Chronic and terminal illness (e.g., MS, cancer)
____Aging: psychological/physiological
____Severe chronic mental illness (e.g., Schizophrenia, Bipolar)
____Personality disorders (e.g., Borderline)
____Other(s)

SELF-ASSESSMENT FOR CLINICAL SKILLS

CONSULTING AND CLINICAL SKILLS: Please rate yourself in each of the following areas/approaches, for your level of expertise or scope of practice. Expertise or scope of practice is determined by your education (courses, seminars, and reading), supervised experience, clinical experience, and your personal investment in the subject area.

Use a scale of 1-10:

1 = Not an expert in that approach

10 = Highest degree of expertise

Score Each 1-10 (per above)

_____Psychoanalytic
_____Psychodynamic
_____Cognitive
_____Behavioral
_____Existential
_____Family system
_____Humanistic
_____Intermittent long term
_____Organizational development
_____Crisis intervention
_____Body-mind approaches
_____Adult development and family life cycle
_____Mediation
_____Transpersonal
_____Philosophical counseling
_____Spiritual direction
_____Hospice/grief/bereavement counseling
_____Meditation
_____Psychopharmacology (psych-meds)
_____Cross cultural
_____Multi-Modality
_____Sand tray
_____Jungian
_____Gestalt
_____Forensic evaluations (e.g., Custody, Sanity)

*Vulnerable clients
plus
therapeutic
and
interpersonal challenges
equals
boundary concerns*

CLINICAL RELATIONSHIPS AND PROFESSIONAL BOUNDARIES

Our profession is a unique profession. Vulnerable clients plus therapeutic and interpersonal challenges equals boundary concerns.

FIVE COMMON BOUNDARY CROSSING OR BOUNDARY VIOLATION THEMES:
1) Intimate relationships, 2) Personal gain and benefit, 3) Emotional dependency needs, 4) Good intention gestures, and 5) Unanticipated circumstances.

It's not hard to understand why counselors find themselves in sticky situations, simple stumbles, and slippery slopes. Many things can trip us up: Mental mistakes, personal biases, limited perspectives, convincing rationalizations, accidental blunders, hidden agendas, blurred roles, conflictual relationships, difficult clinical settings, etc. Many ethical writings have a statement similar to this: The necessary intensity of a therapeutic relationship may tend to activate intense emotional, dependency, sexual, and other needs and fantasies on the part of both the client and the counselor, while weakening the objectivity necessary for good therapy. Clear expectations and boundaries, whenever possible, strengthen the therapeutic relationship. This is especially important in situations where out-of-therapy contact cannot be closely controlled. Obtaining informed consent, sticking to time limits, protecting confidentiality (and explaining its limits), and documenting case progress (including being explicit about any overlapping relationships) diminishes the risk of misunderstandings between client and counselor.

COUNSELOR'S PROFESSIONALISM

The dictionary defines "professionalism" as "the competence or skill expected of a professional in a profession." But what is true professionalism? We know it when we see it, and when we don't. It's easy to come up with a list of traits we consider unprofessional, but how do we capture the elements of what makes a true professional? No matter what business you're in, being a professional means that you are committed to a certain standard of behavior. This commitment must, at times, supersede our personal opinions and, indeed, should force us to rise above difficult obstacles—doing our job and not letting personal issues get in the way of doing what is right. We act in the client's best interests.

Our codes of ethics, and regulatory laws relevant to our profession, impose certain standards of behavior. But these alone are external guidelines; the real challenge is to be guided by our internal ethical standards.

The dictionary further defines professionalism as having to do with character, spirit, or methods—the standing, practice, or methods of a professional, as distinguished from an amateur. A professional has the ability to separate out the personal and remain focused on their fiduciary responsibility to act in the best interest of their client.

When a client needs help, clarification, changes, or alternatives, professionals accept this as a natural part of the process and they have the ability to shift gears, redo work, and not take criticisms as some kind of personal attack.

In the mental health care field, professional behavior is where your professional life dictates your professional actions rather than being superseded by your personal desires, compulsions, wishes, and habits. How can I sum this up: A counselor's professionalism is directly related to their adherence to appropriate ethical guidelines.

RESEARCH
- **Define who you are as a mental health professional**
  - I am a licensed... Who provides...
- **What qualities do you already possess?**
- **What qualities do you want to acquire?**
- **Professionalism, therefore, enables a person to carry out tasks that they may personally find unpalatable but which they recognize are essential for the success of their career.**
- **Do you agree or disagree with this statement? And Why?**

COUNSELOR'S PRESENCE

Theories of practice are numerous, but there's a humanness in therapy—the counselor. The ability to be compassionate with healthy boundaries is key. With compassion, counselors dethrone themselves as they put another foremost. In counseling, counselors are their own instrument—the "tool of their trade."

Research points to common factors that contribute to the success of counseling. These factors exist in all forms of therapy despite theoretical orientation (family, cognitive, behavioral), mode (individual, group, couples, family), duration (frequency of sessions), or specialty (problem type, professional discipline).

Factors are: 1) Structure, model, and/or technique, 2) Placebo, hope, and/or expectancy, 3) The therapeutic relationship which is a combination of counselor and client. What the client brings with them to therapy, such as their knowledge base, life experiences, strengths and abilities, and readiness to change combined with who the counselor is, their knowledge base, life experiences, strengths and abilities, and their professionalism.

The therapeutic relationship is the unsung hero of growth and recovery. When surveys are done that ask clients about what worked for them in counseling, consistently the number one answer is: "The relationship with my counselor." I don't think I've ever seen a survey in which a specific type of counseling—philosophical orientation or therapeutic intervention—took precedence.

RESEARCH
- **Web search for recent surveys on this topic... Use words like: "*What Works in Psychotherapy Surveys*"**
- **To have effective humanness in therapy you must know your weak spots...what hooks you...what words, people, and situations? What are your hooks?**
- **What are your vulnerabilities, biases, family of origin issues, or other personal limitations that could interfere with your work?**

An important element of counseling is the task of staying on task; staying focused— hearing what the client is saying; seeing what they are doing. Everyone takes mini mental vacations. But when a counselor takes (even of few) mini mental vacations—they could miss something important. What does this mean for counselors? It means counselors need to pay attention and remain consciously aware of what is being said and done. No time for mini mental vacations in a therapeutic session. It is important to give your mind a rest whenever you can, otherwise the negative effects of prolonged stress can increase your chances of compassion fatigue, burnout, or getting a stress-related illness.

ETHICAL STANDARDS & CLINICAL FORMS

Do you remember the story I told you about the very first counselor I went to see? The one who would not hug me. Well after that experience I decided I wanted to see another counselor, so I found a male counselor in his late thirties or possibly, his early forties. I'd seen him four or five times; he had me writing in a journal. I came in for my appointment and sat down on the couch. He asked me to read to him from my journal, so I began. After a few pages I looked up and what I saw was my counselor sleeping upright in his chair. At least I hoped he was sleeping, he was very still. I'm thinking, "My first counselor would not hug me, and my second counselor has fallen asleep." After a brief moment, I stood up, walked over and tapped him on the shoulder. He startled awake and said, "Did I fall asleep?" I'm thinking to myself, better than dead. So on this topic of counselor's presence, it's important that we stay awake. I saw a cartoon once that said I thought I understood everything and then I regained consciousness. For some reason, that always makes me think about this situation. Actually, this counselor is the counselor who inspired me to become a counselor; he was a wonderful man.

TRANSFERENCE

"Transference" describes the phenomenon in which the client ascribes both positive and negative feelings they have about others in the their past and present life onto the counselor. It is well documented in regards to the difficulty this presents for treating counselors: "The counselor must encourage clients to express their transferred feelings, while rejecting their angry, erotic, or irrational advances; at the same time, the counselor must explain to clients that their feelings are not really for the counselor, but that they are using the counselor in a symbolic role to react to some other significant person in their life."

In short, the counselor must both encourage transference and discourage certain aspects of it. This may be difficult to do and presents an occupational risk. The therapeutic alliance in this situation gives rise to a duty, imposed by professional standards of care as well as ethical standards of behavior, to refrain from a personal relationship with the client, whether during or outside therapy sessions. This is because personal relationship can infect the therapy treatment, rendering it ineffective and even harmful.

Freud first identified the psychological process of transference when he noticed that people had strong feelings and fantasies about him that had no basis in reality. Transference happens in life—not just counseling. During transference, people turn into a biological time machine when a nerve is struck, when someone says or does something that reminds them of their past. This creates an emotional time warp that transfers their emotional past and psychological needs into the present. Some counselors refer to transference as projection. Clients project their own feelings, emotions, or a motivation onto the counselor, without realizing their reaction is really more about them then it is about the other person. In a life filled with transference, a client may see their place of work as the very family reunion they are trying to avoid; yet, they are forced to go there each day. A client's new love may remind them of all the irritating things a parent did when they were growing up. Transference reactions are caused by unmet emotional needs, neglect, and other abuses that transpired early in life. In some forms of psychotherapy, a counselor will intentionally create or allow transference to form. When done properly, this helps the counselor to understand and find a connection between the client's past and how the client views their present.

Extreme forms of transference can become a full-blown obsession if not addressed. Transference meltdowns can result in accidents, dangerous choices, nightmares, fantasies, stalking someone, psychotic reactions, and sometimes violence.

COUNTER-TRANSFERENCE

"Counter-transference" is basically a counselor's emotional time warp around their client's transference. In other words, counter-transference is a counselor's counter-reaction. When a counselor takes into consideration their own personal historical issues, current life stressors, plus secondary traumas, such as a difficult client, lack of support, isolation, or impairment, then the chances of counter-transferring increases. I have been to seminars on ethics where instructors have stated that counter-transference is unethical and must be avoided. Counter-transference is not unethical; it's human. However, a counselor who counter-transfers and does nothing about it—just leaves it sitting in the room like the proverbial elephant—that is unethical, because counselors are to do no harm. And counter-transference can harm. Counselors need to model ownership and this includes ownership of their behavior, the things they say and the things they do. If counselors counter-transfer, they need to acknowledge it and bring it into the counseling session.

If you find that you have counter-transferred, and can see a look of confusion or shock or hurt on your client's face, then ask them how they felt when you said what you did. Make counter-transference a part of what can be talked about during the counseling session.

Transference and counter-transference can produce a powerful love or a destructive hatred based on a complete illusion. It can be a painful reality when people act on their transference reactions. Transference can be difficult to recognize, deal with, and understand. Working with transference, or creating transference in therapy must be done with good ethical boundaries. Counselors must encourage clients to deal with their transference issues as much as possible. Sometimes, a client is not able to deal with transference issues and they will terminate therapy; this is regrettable and potentially a lost opportunity, but clients have free will and a right to terminate therapy (unless court-ordered or otherwise mandated).

SELF-DISCLOSURE

Appropriate and clinically driven self-disclosures are sometimes carried out for the clinical benefit of the client. Self-disclosure can be viewed as boundary crossings, but not all boundary crossings are unethical. Inappropriate self-disclosures examples would include: 1) Self-disclosure that is done for the benefit of the counselor, 2) Clinically counter-indicated, 3) Burdens the client with unnecessary information, or 4) Creates a role reversal where the client, inappropriately, takes on the care of the counselor. All of these are considered boundary violations. The original Latin meaning of "client" means "one who depends" and "patient" means "one who suffers." Both words apply, in counseling we strive to assist those who are dependent and suffering without fostering dependency. Self-disclosure can serve a useful purpose, but only if done very judiciously and in limited ways. Therapy is demanding work, and privacy is essential. Not disclosing information about oneself is a key component for maintaining an appropriate influential position. It also gives the client more freedom to explore matters that they would be reluctant to explore with a person they are familiar with or in a relationship with defined by the word "friendly."

There are no absolute rules for when, or how much self-disclosure is appropriate; all clients are different. The key considerations are:
- Who the client is
- What their diagnosis is
- What their personality is like (shy and introverted, shrinking from knowing too much information or, inquisitive and extroverted, searching for too much information)

SELF-DISCLOSURE, THERE ARE TWO IMPORTANT GUIDELINES:
1) The client should not know more about the counselor then the counselor knows about the client, and 2) The counselor does not disclose anything they would not want to be public knowledge, since the client is not held to confidentiality. It would be an error in thinking to believe that self-disclosure is always therapeutic because it shows authenticity, transparency, and trust.

Skilled counselors frame their refusal to answer questions compassionately, in a way that clients can understand and accept the refusal as beneficial, even if they initially have negative feelings. For example, a client might even beg their counselor to give his or her relevant history to, or an opinion about, a situation or decision they are trying to make. Although the client may feel frustrated in the moment, the counselor can conveyed to them that their refusal is because they trust that the client will be able to make their own decisions—ultimately, validating the client's strengths.

TYPES OF SELF-DISCLOSURE

"Deliberate self-disclosure" refers to a counselor's intentional, verbal or non-verbal disclosure of personal information. It applies to verbal and also to other deliberate actions, such as placing a certain family photo in the office, your other office decor, or an empathetic gesture, such as a touch or a certain sound. There are two types of deliberate self-disclosure. The first one is self-revealing, which is the disclosure of information by counselors about themselves. The second type is often called self-involving, which involves a counselor's personal reactions to clients and to occurrences that take place during sessions.

"Unavoidable self-disclosure" might include an extremely wide range of possibilities, such as counselor's gender or age. It also includes disclosure through the appearance of your office decor, the tone of your voice, pregnancies, foreign or regional accent, stuttering, visible tattoos, obesity, and many forms of disabilities, such as paralysis, blindness, deafness, or an apparent limp. Counselors also reveal information about themselves through: Their dress, hairstyle, use of makeup, jewelry, perfume or aftershave, facial hair, wedding or engagement rings, or the wearing of a cross, Star of David, or any other symbol.

Non-verbal cues or body language are also sources of self-disclosure that are not always under the counselor's full control. Clients, like people in general, are often more attuned to non-verbal cues, then to verbal communication.

A counselor's announcement of an upcoming vacation, also is a self-disclosure. Self-disclosure could also be through: The car you drive as a symbol of economic status, information about your family and pets, information about hobbies, habits, neighbors, community, and much more. Counselors who practice in small communities or rural areas, on remote military bases or aircraft carriers, or those who work in institutional or faith-based settings, ethnic, underprivileged, disabled, or academic communities, must all contend with self-disclosure of their personal lives. In small communities and rural areas, a counselor's marital status, family details, religion or political affiliations, sexual orientation, and other personal information may be readily available to clients.

"Accidental self-disclosure" occurs when there are incidental or unplanned encounters outside the office, spontaneous verbal or non-verbal reactions, or other unplanned occurrences that happen to reveal a counselor's personal information to their clients.

CLIENT INITIATED COUNSELOR DISCLOSURE

"Client initiated" is not necessarily self-disclosure on the part of the counselor, because it is the client that is searching for the information. However, in this technological society of social interactive sites, counselors need to be cautious about what information they post and make available for others to see. A client's deliberate search activity is not unethical at all, but it can reveal personal information about their counselor.

Clients initiate inquiries about their counselor by conducting a simple web search. Such searches can reveal a wide range of professional and personal information, such as family history, criminal records, family tree, volunteer activity, community and recreational involvement, political affiliations, and much more.

Counselors do not always have control over what is posted online about them, which means they may not have control or even knowledge of what clients may know about them.

Clients should have access to a counselor's Professional Disclosure Statement— a counselor's biography or professional resume. *See "Professional Disclosure Statement" section for more details.*

Be aware of your "Digital Boundaries."
What can a client find out about you by searching the Internet?

> **RESEARCH**
> - If a client were to search for information on you, what would they discover? Web search yourself...

ATTITUDES TOWARD THERAPEUTIC SELF-DISCLOSURE

The attitude towards therapeutic self-disclosure is closely related to a counselor's primary theoretical orientation. Generally, counselors who disclose more view the focus of the psychotherapy process as an interconnection between the counselor and the client, where less disclosing counselors focus on working through clients' projections.

Different therapeutic orientations have different takes on self-disclosure.

Traditional psychoanalysis follows Freud's instructions to serve as a mirror or a blank screen for the client, freeing the client to project his or her own feelings and thoughts on to the rather neutral counselor. Self-disclosure, within the analytic tradition, is thought to result in gratification of clients' wishes rather than analysis of them. Humanistic psychotherapies have always emphasized the importance of self-disclosure and the counselor's transparency in enhancing authentic therapeutic alliance. They assert that self-disclosure allows clients to recognize commonalities. Behavioral, cognitive, and cognitive-behavioral therapies have emphasized the importance of modeling, reinforcement, and normalizing in therapy and views self-disclosure as an effective vehicle to enhance these techniques.

> **RESEARCH**
> - Look up these and ten other therapeutic orientations and explore their stance on counselor self-disclosure.

DIFFERENT RATIONALES FOR SELF-DISCLOSURE

Counselors working with different populations have different rationales for self-disclosure. Self-help and 12-step programs commonly use self-disclosure and counselor transparency to engage participation by attendees. Many of these self-help modalities have entered the therapeutic mainstream and include counselor-facilitated support groups for addiction, parenting, abuse, rape, domestic violence, grief and bereavement, divorce, etc. Additionally, children, and those with a diminished capacity for abstract thought, often benefit from more direct answers to questions requiring self-disclosure. Adolescents are often resistant to therapy as they frequently see adult counselors as authority figures and extensions of their parents. Self-disclosure is one way to make adolescent clients feel honored and respected, rather than judged and patronized. In religious and spiritual-based therapies, counselors are working psycho-therapeutically with clients who hold particular religious or spiritual beliefs. These clients often ask counselors questions about their spiritual orientations and values. Clients of various sexual orientations often want to know their counselor's sexual orientation. Counselors in this field agree that there is a high therapeutic value in the counselor's self-disclosure of sexual orientation as it increases trust, affiliation, and therapeutic alliance. Because of this, self-disclosure is often a necessity for counselors who want or choose to work with special populations.

RESEARCH
- **Identify five other client populations. Would counselor self-disclosure be beneficial?**

CONCERNS ASSOCIATED WITH SELF-DISCLOSURE

There are concerns that are associated with self-disclosure. The one most commonly-cited concern is when self-disclosure is not done for clinical or therapeutic purposes or for the client's benefit, but rather for the counselor's. So the intent of the counselor's self-disclosure is extremely important, because it should be focused firmly on the client's welfare and should not be done for the gratification of the counselor's needs or desires. Self-disclosure should never burden the client, nor be excessive. It should not create a situation where the client needs to care for the counselor. Categorically, ethicists agree that counselors should never share their sexual fantasies with their clients.

Self-disclosure is a boundary crossing (not a boundary violation, unless it is carried too far), and as with all boundary crossings the decision is based on the welfare of the client. The client's presenting problem, history, gender, culture, age, sexual orientation, mental ability, and other client factors should be considered before the counselor self-discloses beyond their Professional Disclosure Statement. A counselor's comfort zone with self-disclosure is often determined by culture, gender, and personality. It is the extent of self-disclosure that defines its inappropriateness.

HELPING CLIENTS

Therapy should make sense. Many psychological theories describe the dysfunctions that humans use to manage discomfort. These defense mechanism do offer partial protection from bad feelings, but they can also perpetuate and compound problems. Past experiences often lead to a style of life or to ways of interacting that strive to ensure survival in some sense, but largely at the cost of contentment. Love and warmth are often best relearned and recaptured through close present relationships. Therapy is a process of simultaneously increasing self-awareness, increasing direct self-expression, and increasing the capacity to have and hold strong feelings.

THERAPY IS MADE UP OF MANY FACTORS: 1) The structure, model, or technique, 2) The placebo, hope, or expectancy, 3) The clinical relationship, 4) The client's and the counselor's collective knowledge, life experiences, strengths, abilities, and readiness to explore and grow.

Is there a cure for mental health issues? Simply put, no, there is no "absolute cure" for mental health issues. The law does not hold mental health counselors to "a duty to cure." The word "cure" literally means, "recovery or relief from a disease." So when I say there are no absolute cures for mental health issues, I am not saying there is not recovery or relief. There are strategies that clients can learn to cope better with their symptoms. There are things that clients can learn to do that will lessen their symptoms. Expectations and goals for treatment are some of the first things to discuss with clients. For some clients, the idea that they will never achieve some idealistic state called "normal" is discouraging. For good therapy, counselors and clients have to agree on some tangible goals and temper unrealistic expectations. What is "normal" anyway? Is it being happy constantly, always having more than enough energy and motivation to get things done? Is it being outgoing and the life of the party?

Is having a great physique normal? Everyone's definition of normal is going to be different from everyone else's definition. Genes play a significant role; environment is another factor. Everyone is going to be up and down at certain times. For those that deal with depression, anxiety, anger, or stress, they might have more downs than ups. However, life's constant stressors can overwhelm anyone at times. Some people have better coping mechanisms to deal with these changes in life and others don't. The good thing is that coping strategies can be taught.

> **RESEARCH**
> - What are some of the best "coping strategies" that can be taught and learned?
> - DBT (Dialectical Behavior Therapy)—*what skills do they recommend?*
> - What would you want to help clients learn? *(List a least ten tools or skills and why they would be beneficial for life)*

Like all of us, clients have struggled with being invalidated—invalidation of their emotions and their personhood. So validation of a client's feelings, intuitions, and personhood is vital. Counseling can help clients clarify how they feel and why they feel that way; and, help clients have a sense of functionality in this world—to acquire a future-oriented life. Helping clients become more adaptable, flexible, and resilient is more than half the battle. Counselors want to ethically encourage experiences in the real world, because therapy should be an adjunct and not a substitution for life.

WITH PSYCHOTHERAPY, THE GOALS ARE:
- Decrease maladaptive behaviors
- Increase adaptive coping: Mindfulness, stress tolerance, emotional regulation, radical acceptance, and interpersonal relationship skills

> **RESEARCH**
> - Look up the adaptive coping skills listed above to get some information on each of them
> - What adaptive coping skills would you add to the list?
> - How many maladaptive behaviors can you list?

ASSESSMENT AND DIAGNOSING

"Treatment planning" requires good "assessment," ongoing assessment, and clear "diagnosis." Taking thorough social histories or compiling accurate background information helps counselors avoid errors. The diagnosis of a mental disorder should have clinical utility; it should help counselors to determine prognosis, treatment plans, and potential treatment outcomes for their clients. However, the diagnosis of a mental disorder is not equivalent to a need for treatment.

"Need for treatment" is a complex clinical decision that takes into consideration such factors as symptom severity, symptom salience (the presence of suicidal ideation), the client's distress (mental pain) associated with the symptom(s), disability related to the client's symptoms, and other factors (psychiatric symptoms complicating other illness). Counselors may thus encounter individuals who do not meet full criteria for a mental disorder, but who demonstrate a clear need for treatment or care. The fact that some individuals do not show all symptoms indicative of a diagnosis should not be used to justify limiting their access to appropriate care. Tests and measurements can never be the only source of diagnosis; they're combined with clinical perceptions.

RESEARCH
Diagnostic and Statistical Manual of Mental Disorders (DSM)
Go to www.dsm5.org and familiarize yourself with the site
- Research the history of the DSM: How was each different from the previous edition. [key words for searching]
  - DSM-I [Adolf Meyer; subjectivity]
  - DSM-II [Radical reaction to the DSM-I]
  - DSM-III [Striving for epidemiology accuracy]
  - DSM-III-R [Coding begins and Managed Care starts]
  - DSM-IV [Treatment outcome suggestions based on codes]
  - DSM-IV-TR [Responding to epidemiology; Culturally-bound Syndromes]
  - DSM5 [Process began in 1999]
- How has the DSM5 changed from the DSM-IV-TR?
  - What changes do you like? Why?
  - What changes do you not like? Why?

ENDING THERAPY DUE TO COUNSELOR VARIABLES

Counselors are to be objective. This can be a difficult task because counselors are people. The cornerstones of ethics: Do no harm, do not exploit clients, and do not continue counseling if your professional judgment is impaired, form the foundation of good therapeutic care. Impairment comes in many forms, such as a counselor's bias or judgmental attitude, or the misuse of prescription medications and/or abuse of other substances. Counselors can become impaired when their own life stressors are too great. Compassion fatigue and burnout can lead to impairment. When a counselor loses objectivity (for any of the above reasons, or others) and their integrity, they ethically need to consult with colleagues, seek self-care, and determine if they need to step away from counseling for a time.

A crucial element of being ethical is remaining objective and remaining non-judgmental. Counselors need to explore their judgments of clients, analyze them, and understand why they are critical. If a counselor is unable to get through certain feelings, they can express their concern(s) and give the client a choice about whether or not to continue therapy, or assist them in finding a new counselor. When a counselor, for whatever reason, cannot tolerate, accept, or remain objective regarding a client's behavior, it often is best to be open with the client about it (but choose your words carefully). Frame it as your problem, and then refer them to someone you believe can work with the issues better.

How should counselors deal with a client they don't like? Reframe the question, ask yourself: "Can I provide competent service? Can I overcome my opposition? Can I use my feelings to move therapy forward?"

And don't forget to consult with colleagues. If feelings toward a client are getting in the way of providing good treatment, seek help. If you are having a tough time with a client, consult with trusted colleagues.

RESEARCH

Consider these questions carefully...
- What if you have a client whose lifestyle opposes your significant personal beliefs, and that client is seeking validation from you? Or you have a client you don't like?
- What if you do not wish to work with clients who are involved in pornography, child abuse, or drug dealing?
- What is the role of the counselor? Is it to affirm a client's belief(s), or to offer support and guidance, even to clients that a counselor personally find distasteful or morally wrong?
- Is it unrealistic to suggest that counselors be unbiased? Is that the counselor's job—*to affirm any choice that a client makes?*
- Could referring a client be a lost opportunity for professional growth?
- How can a counselor's Professional Disclosure Statement help in heading off or avoiding some of the above issues?

TREATMENT PLANNING

"Treatment plans" are a negotiation between the counselor and the client, unless treatment has been court-ordered and a specific treatment compliance exists. Use the treatment plan as a roadmap for the clinical work and to assess progress toward the client's therapeutic goals. Treatment decisions are based on the severity and acuteness of the client's issues and the noted improvements with counseling.

Counselors should also take into consideration the invasiveness of the symptoms. No treatment decision and subsequent treatment action should be taken unless the counselor has the appropriate knowledge and competence. Review and update a treatment plan frequently. Counselors should make thoughtful adjustments to the plan based on the client's progress. Is the client moving toward treatment goals? Or, away from them? Either way, plans must be adjusted as needed.

ERRORS

Counselors have serious responsibilities to their clients, colleagues, and to the mental health profession. The focal point of these interrelated responsibilities is the fiduciary relationship in which the client has placed trust in the counselor with the expectation that the counselor is working in their best interest. This expectation is the foundation of a therapeutic relationship. Through this relationship, each party assumes separate and distinct roles. The counselor bears the burden of accountability within the relationship by assuming the expert role. Error definitions can be defined and governed by various entities, such as state legislation, mental health associations, and best practice policies, for the purpose of preserving the health, safety, and welfare of the clientele. A permanent loss of trust by a client can result from an error in assessment, diagnosis, and treatment planning. In the treatment planning process, counselors need to remain alert to the potential error risks. Whether the errors occur through direct or indirect client involvement, they can happen as a result of omission or commission acts. Omission acts represent negligence or omission of information.

Again, an error could be the failure of a planned intervention or the use of a wrong plan in the treatment process. While most errors are unintentional, some are, unfortunately, intentional. Negligence that causes harm, whether intentional or unintentional, is serious. Mental health counselors increase their odds of making mistakes when they are overly fatigued, in a hurry, inattentive and distracted; do not access and/or thoroughly review client records; do not document consistently and appropriately; and do not pay attention to laws and regulations regarding confidentiality and consent. The potential for error increases when counselors have habits of poor professional behavior, take work shortcuts, exhibits slow responses and follow-up with regard to clients' calls or crisis. Other factors may include imposing personal values, bias, or spiritual beliefs onto clients; inattention to, or minimization of client concerns; and poor communication with clients and their families or other treatment team members.

Intentional harm can be considered a crime when counselors mindfully become romantically and/or sexually involved with clients. Romantic or sexual innuendos are errors. Intentional harm can occur when counselors inappropriately assign a diagnosis in order to continue treatment and bill for more fees; knowingly or flagrantly over-charge a client or wrongly submit a bill to a client, insurance company, or other third-party payers. Failure to maintain billing records properly can be a criminal offense.

Errors also include ignoring proper consent protocol, failure to report child abuse, or make other appropriate reports to monitoring agencies as required by law. Abandoning clients, falsifying records, falsely claiming curative abilities, or administering inappropriate or grossly wrong methods of treatment all constitute errors.

WHAT ABOUT APOLOGIZING?

In the mental health and healthcare profession, there is a concern about apologizing to clients (or patients) for mistakes. Apologies can make someone feel vulnerable. What could happen? Will an apology be accepted or will it make things worse? Will the apology come back as an admission of guilt in a formal licensing complaint or lawsuit? Admitting mistakes can be difficult. However, it can come down to intention versus impact. If what you are apologizing for was intentional, then being fearful of an apology becoming an admission of guilt. But most of the time our actions, in words and deeds, are not done with the intention of harm, but rather impact others in a way we did not anticipate. Research and common sense suggest that an apology can help heal the effects of inadvertent or unintended mistakes. Many states have passed "I'm sorry" laws to encourage healthcare providers to promptly and fully inform clients of errors and to apologize when warranted, and other states are considering such laws. This law protects the apologizer from being held to an admission of guilt because of the apology. Research further suggests that ethical complaints, which were considered but never filed, were indeed not filed because an apology was made by the counselor to the client. As counselors in the mental health profession, we understand the healing power of words. Apologizing is a personal, intimate act that can calm hurt feelings, restore rapport, and open the possibility of honest dialogue. However, deciding whether or not to apologize requires careful consideration of many factors. I encourage all counselors to make the decision to do so thoughtfully, cautiously, and with the advice of legal consultation.

RESEARCH
- **Does your state have a health care related *"I'm Sorry"* law that was passed by your state's legislation?**

WORKING WITH OTHER PROFESSIONALS

Consultation with colleagues is ethically necessary, because it's a fundamental "reality check" for counselors and its helpful in the treatment process.

> **RESEARCH**
> - Select two separate codes of ethics. Look for information titled: *Responsibilities to Colleagues.*
>   - Is there a difference between the two samples? If yes, what?
>   - Do you believe the lists are comprehensive? If not, what would you add?
> - Now look for information on the ethical requirements for consultation between colleagues.
>   - Repeat the same steps as listed above.

WORKING WITH MORE THAN ONE PERSON IN THE ROOM

When there is more than one person in the room for a counseling session, confidentiality cannot be guaranteed. This limit of confidentiality must be explained to all parties present. It is important to be clear about who is the client and aware of potential conflicts of interest. Seek agreement from all parties to preserve confidentiality, but explain that there is no guarantee all parties will honor this. The counselor is the only one who has the obligation of confidentiality.

COUNSELING GROUPS, COUPLES, FAMILIES, AND MINORS: ETHICAL CONSIDERATIONS

With group work, counselors clearly explain the importance and parameters of confidentiality for the specific group.

In couples and family counseling, counselors clearly define who is considered "the client" and discuss expectations and limitations of confidentiality with all parties. Counselors need to seek agreement from all parties and document in writing such agreements among all involved parties having the capacity to give consent concerning their rights to confidentiality and any obligation to preserve the confidentiality of information shared.

When counseling minor clients, or adult clients who lack the capacity to give voluntary informed consent, counselors protect the confidentiality of the information received in the counseling relationship as specified by federal and state laws, written policies of the organization they work with, and all relevant ethical standards. Counselors inform parents and legal guardians about the role of the counselor and the confidential nature of the counseling relationship. Counselors are sensitive to the cultural diversity of families and respect the inherent rights and responsibilities of parents/guardians over the welfare of their children according to the law. Counselors are to establish, whenever appropriate, a collaborative relationship with parents/guardians to best serve clients. When working with minors it is important to understand who is the custodial parent(s). If a minor's parents are married, typically it only takes the signature of one of the parents to bring a minor child into mental health counseling. But, when a minor's parents are separated or divorced it is important for you, the counselor, to understand who has the authority to sign the minor child into mental health counseling. Ask for a copy of the parenting/custodial plan.

WHEN A CLIENT BRINGS A VISITOR TO SESSION CONJOINT SESSIONS

Clients often want to bring someone with them into a session for a variety of reasons. Sometimes this happens without pre-planning; a client shows up for their session with someone. There are a few things a counselor should consider before a conjoint session. First, speak with the client privately to make sure it is their wish and desire to have this person in the counseling session, since coercion could be a factor. Second, consider having a consent form that your client signs to allow a visitor in session.

SIMPLY PUT, THIS SHORT CONSENT FORM WOULD STATE:

- I, _____, understand that if I if I choose to invite a person or persons to be present during a session with my counselor that my confidentiality may be compromised by this person.
- This consent does not give permission to my counselor to discuss any confidential information with the visitor at any time after the visit.
- I have clarified to my counselor that the following topics should NOT be mentioned during the time that the visitor is in the session.

Finally, make sure you take the time to speak briefly with the visitor about the mandatory reporting requirements. Let them know that if they speak about abuse or neglect of children or vulnerable adult, or speak about harm to themselves or others, that they are placing you in a position of having to report or take other appropriate action according to the laws. Counselors are mandatory reporters and this can extends beyond just the clinical relationship, depending on your state's laws, especially with protective services.

CONFLICTS OF INTEREST

Rules of professional conduct require counselors to fully disclose "conflicts of interest" (or circumstances of dual relationships that create a conflict of interest) to the client and to secure the client's consent to continue providing care. If there is a conflict of interest that could potentially harm the client, exploit the client, or impair the counselor's judgment, then the counselor should withdraw. Anything that could interfere with the care and well-being of the clients—conflicts that could harm, exploit, or are "reasonably expected" to impair a counselor's judgment (diminish objectivity) are considered to be conflicts of interest. Take reasonable steps to clarify, modify (by defining the parameters), or withdraw.

Acknowledge conflicts of interest and attempt to harmonize conflicting interests while protecting the client's best interests. What can we do when a conflict of interest, or boundary crossing, gets complicated? We need to continue to carefully monitor the situation and consult with an experienced colleague. We need to listen carefully to client concerns and periodically assess our clinical relationships for the potential of conflicts of interest. Keep adequate, honest, and accurate records of situations as they involve. Our understanding of a conflict of interest may not be our client's understanding and vice versa. A situation that can be therapeutic for one client may not be therapeutic for another. Just because we don't see an issue, it doesn't mean there aren't any. Discuss situations with clients when needed and appropriate. Consult with colleagues to gain additional perspectives on various situations.

RESEARCH

- You have a client who is seeing you because they were raped, and then you get another client who confesses to you that they rape someone—*that "someone" is an established client. What would you do?*
- You are interested in politics in your community and decide to run for the school board. You find out a former client has also announced their candidacy—*do you campaign against your former client?*
- What if you are obligated to parties other than your client—*for example, an employer or another client.*
- You have an interest in your client that conflicts with clinical obligations—*for example, hidden sexual feelings.*
- There is a secondary agenda that interferes with treatment—*for example, using information the client has (e.g., stock tips)*

RESEARCH

What do these following statements mean to you?
Gather more information and form your own thoughts/opinions.

- "Conflicts of interest can wreak havoc in the therapy room. They can weaken therapeutic effectiveness by eroding trust—*the core of the therapeutic relationship.*"
- "They can also bring about allegations of ethical or legal impropriety. Counselors should always remain alert to and avoid conflicts of interest that interfere with the exercise of professional discretion and impartial judgment."

MULTIPLE RELATIONSHIPS

For many years the term "dual" was used in regard to relationships of concern in the mental health profession. More recently, the word "dual" has been replaced with "multiple" but both have to do with the breaking down of proper boundaries or any relationship outside the therapeutic relationship. When roles are mixed in a manner that can cause harm, exploitation, or impaired professional judgment, the potential for trouble exists. There can be violations of confidentiality, role confusion, impaired objectivity, and risk of exploitation.

If you are in a partnership, you can dissolve it. If you're In a committed relationship, you can break up and go your separate ways. Yet this question remains: "Does your client ever stop being your client, no matter how much time has elapsed since the end of treatment?" The issue here is whether or not the counselor-client relationship truly lasts in perpetuity. If, in fact, "once a client, always a client" then counselors will encounter many challenging situations with no simple solutions.

"Nonsexual overlapping relationships" are not a matter of "if" as much as they are a matter of "when" one (or more) will occur. A web search database turned up more than 2500 books and articles on the topic of boundaries, dual relationships, and multiple roles. There seems to be more written about dual relationships in the mental health profession than any other topic concerning ethical considerations. Associations are constantly looking at and reviewing their policies regarding dual/multiple relationships.

"Boundaries" help define the therapeutic relationship. These boundaries distinguish psychotherapy from other social, familial, sexual, and business types of relationships that we engage in every day.

We've talked about the difference between "boundary crossings" and "boundary violations." Boundary violations are very different from boundary crossings, since boundary violations can harm and exploit the client. Boundary crossings can be a purposeful part of a well-formulated treatment plan and the deviation from the traditional, office-only format. Boundary crossings are done for the benefit of the client.

ETHICAL STANDARDS & CLINICAL FORMS

Some counselors fly in an airplane with a client who suffers from a fear of flying; counselors have lunch or dinner with anorexic clients; counselors make home visits to bed-ridden clients; and, some counselors accompany their clients on walks to encourage exercise as a treatment for depression. Boundary crossings are not unethical and do not constitute a dual relationship in and of themselves, because the crossing is done for the benefit of the client. The boundary crossing has a therapeutic reason.

Legal authorities, associations, and others who study the intricacies of multiple relationships have expressed the concern that the prohibition of dual relationships may even be unconstitutional, as it may infringe on individual's constitutional rights of freedom of association. However, don't ignore the ethical warnings. Think about this: The prohibition of dual relationships leads to increased isolation for many counselors living in rural communities or small communities within large cities. And then, this isolation can increase the chance of exploitation of clients when isolation forces a counselor to rely on their clinical relationships to meet too many of their social needs. What are your thoughts about this?

RESEARCH
- Search the Internet using these key words: *"mental health care and multiple relationships"*
  - Select three, read, and take notes of key points that stand out (for you).
- Search the Internet using these key words: *"multiple relationships and boundary concerns"*
  - Repeat the steps listed above.

TYPES OF DUAL/MULTIPLE RELATIONSHIPS

- A "social" dual relationship is where the counselor and the client are also friends.
- A "professional" dual relationship is where the counselor and client are also professional colleagues in a work, academic, or institution setting. It could be that a client and a counselor are both presenters in a professional conference.
- A "business" dual relationship is where the counselor and the client are also business partners or have an employer–employee relationship.
- "Communal" dual relationships are where the counselor and client live in the same rural community or a small community within a larger one, belong to the same church or synagogue, or where the counselor shops in a store that is owned by the client or where the client works. These are just a few examples.
- "Institutional" dual relationships take place in the military, prisons, some police or fire department settings, and mental health hospitals where dual relationships are an inherent part of the institutional setting. Some institutions, such as state hospitals or detention facilities, mandate that counselors serve simultaneously or sequentially as the counselor and evaluator.
- "Forensic" dual relationships involve counselors who serve as treating counselors, and then as evaluators and/or witnesses in trials or hearings. Serving as the treating counselor as well as an expert witness, rather then a witness of fact, is considered a very complicated and often ill-advised dual relationship.

DUAL-CONCURRENT VS. SEQUENTIAL RELATIONSHIPS

Is there a difference? A "dual-concurrent relationship" is a relationship outside the therapeutic relationship that is not based on therapeutic necessity and it is occurring while the client is in therapy. Most counselors agree this is unethical. However, "sequential relationships" are relationships a counselor might have with a previous client. If one believes that clients grow mature and sometimes surpass their counselors in knowledge, wisdom, and power, then there is a significant difference between these two types.

RESEARCH
- Here's an example of a sequential relationship: *A previous client of yours continued on to college and eventually became a physician who specialize in a very narrow field of medicine in your community. You have been diagnosed with an illness that requires the specialized care of such a physician*
  - If it is an issue of power, who is in the position of power now?
- Is power in any relationship always static? Or, is it variable and subject to change based on the circumstances?
  - Think about this situation and draw your own conclusion.

OUR INFLUENTIAL POSITION AND MULTIPLE RELATIONSHIPS

Mental health counselors are aware of their influential position with regard to their clients. When a dual relationship cannot be avoided, counselors must take appropriate professional precautions. Multiple relationships involve the breaking down of proper clinical boundaries. Roles get mixed in a manner that can cause harm to the counseling relationship—a situation in which the very nature of the counseling relationship is potentially distorted. Non-sexual overlapping relationships are not a matter of "if" as much as "when" in the daily lives of counselors. Ethical codes and standards are necessary, but not sufficient and must be tempered by experience and context. Although it may seem obvious, knowledge of ethical codes and state laws is essential in framing the background for clinical relationships. And consultation with colleagues is helpful.

CONSULTATIONS AND MULTIPLE RELATIONSHIPS

Ongoing consultation and discussion of cases, especially those involving dual roles, provide a context for counselors to get additional perspectives and decrease the isolation that sometimes accompanies the mental health practice. Everyone has blind spots, so trusted colleagues, or a counselor of their own, can help counselors constructively examine their personal (and professional) blind spots.

AVOIDING MULTIPLE RELATIONSHIPS

Self-knowledge decreases the chance that counselors will use, even unknowingly, their clients for their own gratification. Counselors are ethically required to be aware of their influential position. They avoid exploiting the trust of their clients, and avoid fostering the dependency of their clients. Counselors make every effort to avoid dual relationships that could impair professional judgment or increase the risk of harm. Examples of such relationships may include, but are not limited to familial, social, financial, business, or close personal relationship.

Counselors are not to accept as clients individuals with whom they are involved in an administrative, supervisory, and in an evaluative nature. When a dual relationship cannot be avoided, counselors take appropriate professional precautions, such as consultation, supervision, and documentation to ensure that judgment is not impaired and no exploitation has occurred. In addition, mental health counselors always provide informed choice—any issues of unclear or overlapping boundaries must be discussed with the client.

> **RESEARCH**
> What do these statements mean to you? Gather more information and form your own thoughts/opinions.
> - "Different cultures have different expectations, customs, values and therefore judge the appropriateness of boundary crossings and multiple relationships differently."
> - "More communally-oriented settings such as military, universities and interdependent communities (e.g., deaf, ethnic, gays, etc.) judge the appropriateness of boundary crossings and multiple relationships differently."

ETHICAL STANDARDS & CLINICAL FORMS

RELATIONSHIPS OF CONCERN

Relationships that have a "special relationship perspective" or an "over-entitlement perspective" by either the client or counselor are considered to be "relationships of concern." There are special relationship issues and attitudes that can cause problems. Clients or counselors who yearn to be an "insider" or who feel that "someone owes them" are both examples of relationship perspectives that can be damaging to the therapeutic process. Black and white thinking, demanding to be believed, insatiable neediness, over-generalizations, over-dramatized responses, poor and confused boundaries, and diffused sexuality are all examples of relationships of concern. And, need to be addressed.

At the end of one of my counseling sessions, I said to my adult client, "We need to wrap things up, my next client will be here soon." We walked towards the door and I opened it. The client placed her hand on the door and shut it; she looked at me and said, "Do you like me more than the client that's coming?" Several things went through my mind, but the one dominant thought was do not answer that question. I looked at her and said, "That is an interesting question." She looked at me and explained that she really wanted to know. I found myself wondering if she knew who my next client was. I decided to turn her question—an expression of a special relationship perspective—into a homework assignment, so I said, "Here's what I'd like you to do; I want you to think about something. If I said 'yes' to your question, what would that mean to you? If I said 'no' to your question, what would that mean to you? I want you to think about this and we'll discuss it at your next session." At our next session, I was already to talk about her most interesting question. When I asked her what her thoughts were she leaned back and said, "It was a stupid question; I don't know why I asked it and I don't want to talk about it."

SPECIAL EXCEPTIONS

There might be a client that you like, connect with, and enjoy the therapeutic time with. But, what if you change the appointment time with this client to the end of the day so if sessions run a little longer it wouldn't be a problem? Think back to the word "justice" which is one of the moral principles. The formal meaning of justice is treating equals equally and unequals unequally, but in proportion to their relevant differences. In other words, if a counselor is to treat an individual differently, there should to be a reason for doing so that is based on a relevant difference.

When a special exception is made there are two questions that a counselor should ask themselves: 1) "Would I make this exception for all my clients?" 2) "Is this exception clinically relevant?" My colleague, who had changed the appointment time of his client to the end of the day, did so with the best intentions, but had not thought the situation through. By doing so he could create a perception, or the reality, of a special relationship perspective. When he mentioned this at a staff meeting he was able to see it through the eyes of his colleagues. Indeed, would he make this exception for all his clients and if not, why was he making it for this client? Was the exception clinically relevant? Is there justice in the decision? It's easier to see ethical boundary concerns in others, then it is to see them in ourselves, so input from trusted colleagues is vital.

MULTIPLE RELATIONSHIPS...INTENTIONAL... ACCIDENTAL... INCIDENTAL

The reality of overlapping social relationships, business or professional relationships, and professional roles with others service providers are ever present in the mental health profession. Working with more than one family member, working with others who have friendships with clients, and even overlapping relationships affecting members of the counselor's own family are all realities in mental health care. There are levels of involvement regarding dual or multiple relationships.

"Intentional" refers to an intense level of involvement. Intentional can be by the counselor's choice to have a dual relationship or it can refer to places of employment that often mandate a dual or multiple relationship because of the work setting. These work-setting-specific dual relationships often take place in the military, prisons, employee assistant settings, and in police department settings—to name a few. My colleague, who works and lives at a fire department, has an intentional, intense-level of involvement based on the setting of his practice.

"Incidental" refers to a medium level of involvement in which clients and counselors share occasional encounters. These dual relationships are often found in isolated rural areas, cultural groups, practice settings that provide services to specific groups, spiritual and faith-based communities, small communities within large city areas, and training institutions such as schools, colleges, and universities.

"Accidental" refers to a low-minimal level of involvement that includes accidental encounters between counselors and their clients. Even in large cities or metropolitan areas where there are many counselors, many places to shop, worship or recreate, we continually discover the small-world reality.

DUAL RELATIONSHIPS AND TREATMENT PLANS

Intervene with clients according to their needs. Some treatment plans demand a boundary crossing or dual relationship.

A colleague of mine was a mental health counselor at a local fire district. His work schedule was three days on and four days off. During the days on, he was at the fire station 24 hours a day; he lived with, ate with, exercised with, and worked with his clients. Because of this counseling setting, dual relationships were unavoidable. His ethical responsibility was the welfare of his clients, the effectiveness of treatment, the avoidance of harm and exploitation and conflicts of interest, and the impairment of his professinoal clinical judgment. All are paramount and appropriate concerns, which he managed well.

But boundary crossings that lead to dual relationships must not lead to boundary violations. Before entering complex dual relationships, consult with well-informed colleagues, consultants, and/or supervisors. When you consult with attorneys, ethics experts or licensing boards make sure you use the information gained to help educate and inform yourself. Examine your knowledge of laws and ethics from the necessity of providing appropriate care, intervention, and the effectiveness of the treatment you want to provide.

Discuss with clients the complexities, potential benefits, and potential negative consequences that encompasses a dual relationship. You are setting an example and modeling integrity. If you find yourself in a dual relationship that is not benefiting the client, causing harm to the client, or has created a conflict of interest, consult with colleagues and if necessary, step out of the clinical relationship, withdrawing as counselor, but do so in a way that preserves the client's welfare and best interest.

RESEARCH
Counselors need to self-assess professional boundaries by asking themselves questions:
- **With the absence of clinical relevance...**
  - Have you ever shared personal information with the client?
  - Kept a secret with the client?
  - Changed your style of dress for a client?
  - Bent the rules for our client?
  - Have you ever felt possessive about a client?
- **The key question to ask is this:** *Who's needs are being met?*
  - The answer should NOT be *"counselor"*

MYTHS AND MULTIPLE RELATIONSHIPS

THERE ARE SOME MYTHS REGARDING DUAL OR MULTIPLE RELATIONSHIPS:
1) "Dual relationships are always unethical"—this is not so, some intentional dual roles that are mandated by a specific work settings.
2) "There isn't always an inherent power differential between counselor and client"—not so, the counselor always has the influential position of power.

CONCLUDING THOUGHTS ON MULTIPLE RELATIONSHIPS

Most ethical codes and guidelines will have a statement similar to this paraphrasing: If multiple roles aren't reasonably expected to harm or exploit the client, or impair the counselor's judgment, then it's not necessarily unethical. The purpose of a statement like this is to acknowledge and allow clinically appropriate and/or non-harming or non-exploitive multiple roles.

Ethical codes are necessary, but they are not sufficient and do not answer or address all the complexities of counselor-client relationships. Ethical codes must be tempered by experience and context. Non-sexual boundary crossings can enrich therapy, serve the treatment plan, and strengthen the counselor-client's working relationship. They can also undermine the therapy, sever the counselor-client alliance, and cause immediate or long-term harm to the client.

Choices about whether to cross a boundary confront counselors daily; they are often subtle and complex, and can sometimes influence whether therapy progresses, stalls, or ends.

Counselors confront boundary issues on a daily basis: A client in crisis, should the session run over time? Best friend wants you to see their child in therapy. A client, who lost their job and their insurance, should the fee be waived? The counselor discovers that in a community fund raiser they've been paired them up with a client in the three-legged race, do you participate? Dual relationships with clients almost always involve experiences outside the office: The counselor and the client happen to attend the same church, or go to the same health club. They might play in the same sports league or their children are on the same soccer or baseball team. Counselors and client might be active members in local charities or at the Chamber of Commerce.

Dual relationships are common, inevitable, unavoidable, and a by-product of communal life in numerous settings. There must be safeguards that help minimize dual relationship risks. Clear expectations and boundaries, whenever possible, strengthen the therapeutic relationship. Clear expectations and appropriate boundaries should be discussed with clients, as needed, throughout the therapeutic relationship. Ongoing consultation and discussions of cases with appropriate colleagues helps counselors constructively examine their blind spots. Self-knowledge lessens the chances that counselors use, even unknowingly, their clients for their own self-benefit.

FACTOR TO ALWAYS CONSIDER BEFORE ESTABLISHING A DUAL OR MULTIPLE RELATIONSHIP:
- Passage of time since therapy ended
- Transference/counter-transference issues
- Length and nature of counseling
- Client's issues and diagnosis
- Client's ego strengths and mental wellness
- Feasibility of client returning to therapy
- Possibility of harm

LOCATION OF WORK: "OUT-OF-OFFICE" SETTINGS

Home visits to homebound or bed-ridden clients or home visits to clients who do not have the means to travel to an office are examples of out-of-office settings. Home visits can be a part of case management, child welfare, or child abuse prevention. Other therapeutic interventions are only possible outside the office space, such as adventure or outdoor therapy. Adventure or outdoor therapy is differentiated from other recreational or physical fitness programs in that it is geared specifically to elicit therapeutic change through individual and group goals, building trust, providing activities that challenge, involving activities that require problem-solving abilities, and incorporating other highly structured, carefully planned, challenging activities that are sequential, require commitment, tenacity, and resiliency; they help build character. With the proliferation of various rehabilitation programs, remotely located alternative boarding schools and therapeutic homes are also gaining popularity.

When there are clinical reasons to leave the office, therapy outside the office can provide special opportunities that cannot exist in office-based therapy. Benefits of clinical work outside an office are meeting important members of the family, friends, and seeing the community that a client lives in. In some cultures, the home is much more acceptable for mental health interventions than an office. So there are reasons to see clients outside an office setting. Sometimes, the home visit is the only option open for contact with the client. Home visits and other out-of-office interventions can be strategic clinical interventions. Crisis intervention, domestic violence, and culture can all be reasons for seeing clients outside an office.

There are many situations where interventions are only possible, and more likely effective, if they are done beyond the boundaries of an office: Treatment of phobias and systematic desensitization interventions; lunch or dinner with an anorexic client; an aerobic walk with the depressed client; sport psychologist who accompany their clients to the field in order to instruct, support, and observe; grief counselors accompanying a client to a cemetery or a funeral; street counselors working with the chronically mentally ill, sitting together on a bench in a nearby park; community counselors who meet on a basketball court and share the love of the game to help melt the reserve of young clients. Such interventions become a part of the treatment plan for certain clients under certain conditions and in certain contexts.

A counselor in my community for more than 30 years conducted his therapy practice outside office walls. He took his clients out walking. He worked with clients who struggled with depression, anxiety, and sleep disorders. The testimony of exercise as an effective therapeutic intervention is clear in the work that he did with his clients. Toward the latter years of his practice, and because of societal changes, he took precautions before going out on walks with clients. He required his clients to see their primary care physician and get a document signed that they were healthy enough to go on walks. He also included information in his consent form about what his counseling consisted of, along with its limits of confidentiality. Having practiced in a smaller community for many years he was well known as "the fitness counselor." In his consent form he stated, "I am well known in this community as the fitness mental health counselor. If you are seen walking with me in public, the assumption will be made that you are in therapy." This statement is an excellent example of clearly informed consent and a good explanation of additional confidentiality limitations. The various clinical reasons to interact with clients outside an office can be closely related to a counselor's theoretical orientation. Because there are many theoretical orientations, there can be much disagreement among counselors regarding the clinical significance and importance of out-of-office counseling. Counseling outside-the-office has been frowned upon by risk management advocates. Insurance companies, ethical committees, licensing boards, and attorneys advise counselors to conduct their practice defensively with a focus on reducing risks. Counseling outside the office has been associated with "slippery slope" issues that could snowball—the crossing of one boundary without negative consequences, leading to the crossing of the next boundary, and then the next, and the next, ultimately leading to the slippery slope that ends in ethical violations. The reality is many approaches to therapeutic interventions are best done outside an office. However, counseling that's offered outside the standard norm (an office setting) should always be clearly outlined and explained in an informed consent form, and discussed with clients, to ensure their understanding of the clinical relevance of such treatment.

RESEARCH

- **Look up some of the following theoretical orientations and determine their views on out-of-office counseling:** *analytical, humanistic, behavioral cognitive-behavioral, culture-sensitive, traditional psychoanalytical, expressive and art therapies, family systems and any others you'd like to add...*
    - **What are your views about out-of-office counseling?**
    - **Do your views reflect your theoretical orientation?**

MAKING BOUNDARY DECISIONS

When considering whether a specific boundary crossing is likely to be helpful or harmful, supportive or disruptive, consider the research and other published literature on boundary crossings. Be familiar with the information offered by professional guidelines, ethical codes, legislation, case law, and other resources such as colleagues. Imagine what might be the best and worst possible outcome from crossing a boundary or from not crossing a boundary. Is there significant risk of negative consequences or a real risk of serious harm for crossing? Pay attention to your own uneasy feelings; trust your intuition. If your intuition is leaning towards caution, don't dismiss it. If you have no clear sense of intuition, seek the advice of a trusted colleague. Boundary crossings can turn sour. Counselors who share their negative experiences have commonly expressed how they shrugged off or pushed aside their initial troubling thoughts and feelings. So, don't dismiss either.

Don't overlook the informed consent process for any planned boundary crossings or out-of-office therapeutic experiences. At the start of therapy, describe to the client exactly what kind of therapy you do. If the client appears to be uncomfortable, explore further their concern or refer the client to a colleague better suited for this person. Finally, keep careful notes on any planned boundary crossing, describing exactly the reason and its therapeutic relevance and explain why this will be helpful to the client. Just because we don't see any self-interest, problems, conflicts of interest, unintended consequences, major risks, or potential downsides to crossing a boundary, it doesn't mean they don't exist. With the defense mechanisms of rationalization and justification, we all share an amazing ability to deceive ourselves. When cases of merit are brought before ethics committees or tried in a court of law one wonders how highly educated individuals, professional licensed counselors with families and good careers, risk it all by violating ethical boundaries. Occasionally, there are counselors who step knowingly and boldly into boundary violations that disregard client safety, ethics, and common sense.

More commonly, cases reveal the slippery slope of tiny, sequential, rationalized steps that culminated in ethical violations. The importance of consistent, frequent, and honest consultation with trusted colleagues cannot be underscored. If a counselor is reluctant to let other trusted colleagues know about a potential or actual crossing, then that reluctance, in and of itself, is a red flag.

What can be done if a boundary crossing, one that was believed to be therapeutic, where the counselor acted in what was thought to be the client's best interests, manifests signs of trouble? The client may begin missing sessions or not paying; the rapport between counselor and client can begin to erode; things begin to feel "off." If this happens, the situation needs to be addressed. Boundary crossings can have negative results that were impossible to anticipate. We should never minimize the negative impact, nor leave it unexamined. Counselors need to model behavior for their clients. Part of this is taking ownership for decisions made. Avoid making assumptions about how the client is reacting to the boundary crossing or the negative consequences. These assumptions could be completely wrong. Ask the client and listen carefully. Counselors must try to see issues and concerns from the client's point of view. A client could experience a boundary crossing in a way that is completely opposite from what the counselor intended, anticipated, discussed with client, and agreed to (via informed consent).

SMALL TOWN OR SMALL COMMUNITIES

Familiarity with clients—it happens in rural communities or practice settings that are a type of community, such as military, universities, cultural or ethnic groups, or isolated businesses. Many times in these settings, clients choose counselors because of real, first-hand, personal knowledge of the counselor, their behavior, morals, ethics, and personality. In reality, selecting a counselor in this manner makes more sense than blind calling listings from the Yellow Pages or from an Internet search.

The fact that some clients may end up on a church field trip, or on a committee, or on the same soccer team as their counselor is a simple reality. Discussing these possibilities before hand can help reduce the chance of exploitation or ethical violations. Small town settings (or any settings where there is social overlapping) can present some interesting situations.

A client (perhaps one who is a plumber) could show up to repair your pipes after you've made a call for an emergency repair. You and your client might volunteer at the same civic organization. You could belong to the same health club. You could have common friends with your client, common friends who invite both of you to social gatherings. A client might buy the home that is for sale right next door to you.

All of these situations need to be managed and managed carefully. You need to refer back to the cornerstones of ethics: Do no harm, do not exploit, and do not continue counseling if your judgment is impair. You also have to take into consideration any conflicts of interest that might exist, and whether they are resolvable by clarifying or modifying, or whether you need to withdraw as their counselor.

SOCIAL INTERACTIONS

When it comes to invitations for social events, counselors again need to take into consideration the cornerstones of ethics and the issue of conflicts of interest. Sometimes, not attending could be more harmful to the client's well-being. Weddings, funerals, christenings, conformations, and bar mitzvahs have what is called "the formal function." You can attend the wedding, but not the reception; you can attend the funeral, but not the family gathering. Social events with formal functions give a counselor some cushion for anonymity, thus protecting the client's confidentiality.

Sometimes the decision to go to a social event that honors a client's accomplishment or represents a ritual or life transition can enhance therapeutic alliances and clinical outcomes. A counselor may accept invitations to attend significant life transitions and rituals or celebrations, as long as they have considered the client's best interest. Celebrating and affirming life accomplishments can be very important validation for many clients who often suffer from low self-esteem and have a long history of being invalidated. A counselor might be invited to a performance in the school play or the opening of a client's business—honoring client accomplishments can increase the effectiveness of therapy.

Counselors who work with different cultures inevitably will join their clients in celebrating special events: Native American clients and their sacred rituals; Catholic clients at confirmations; Latino clients in weddings (to name a few). Refusing to attend, in some cultures is likely to cause damage to the effectiveness of therapy.

Without exception, studies that look at what works in therapy arrive at the same conclusion: A positive and effective therapeutic relationship between a counselor and the client is one of the best predictors of positive and effective clinical outcomes.

RESEARCH

- Do you live in a small town or small community? Or work (or plan to work) in the military, at a university, college or school setting? Or with a specific cultural or ethnic group?
    - What other clinical settings would be similar to this example? (e.g., Native American [Indian] Reservation)
- What are the potential problems for such settings?
- What would you say to clients (or have written in your consent form) to help address and avert potential problems? (e.g., *"If we run in to each other in the community, I will not address you because I want to protect your privacy. If you address me, I, of course, will respond. But conversation between us in the community must be limited; we will not discuss aspects of your therapy"*, etc.)

GIFTS AND THE THERAPEUTIC RELATIONSHIP

If you work for an organization that has a strict "no gift" policy then you can lean on that. If a client brings a gift you can explain that it's against company policy for you to accept it. If you are in private practice, then you can establish your own policy. Some larger organizations have written into their consent form that they accept gifts up to a specific value (typically $50 or less), and only if the gift can be enjoyed by all care members (this is to avoid gifts for specific individuals). However, if you are self-employed and in private practice it would be unethical to write in your consent form that you accept gifts up to a specific value as long as "it can be enjoyed by me". Whatever your policy on gifts, make sure you discuss it with new clients.

But, in general, giving a gift is an ancient and universal way to express gratitude and appreciation. Exploring the meaning, intention, or patterns of a client's gift-giving in counseling can also enhance the clinical work and therapeutic outcomes. Rejecting appropriate gifts of small monetary value, but those of high symbolic or relational value, can be harmful to clients. A counselor's uneasiness or refusal to accept appropriate gifts can be experienced as rejection and invalidation.

My colleagues and I have tried a variety of methods to handle the gift-giving situation. We tried putting it in our consent form that no gifts were accepted and we explained why gifts were not necessary, but we still received gifts.

So the issue of gifts, typically, is handled client-by-client with a focus on the cornerstones of ethics and an avoidance of any conflicts of interest, perceptions of self-interest, or personal financial benefit at the client's expense.

RESEARCH
- **What boundaries do you have or plan to have around the issue of client gift giving?**
  - **What makes a gift appropriate?**
  - **When is a gift inappropriate?**
- **If you have been in practice, what gift situation do you recall?**
- **Is it ever appropriate for a counselor to give a gift to a client?**
  - **Give an example**

*Counselor impairment can
lead to boundary violations*

BOUNDARY VIOLATIONS AND ISSUES OF IMPAIRMENT

"Impairment" is a deterioration of a professional's abilities from a previous competency level. Impairment may manifest as a loss of empathy, respect, or correct attitudes regarding clients. A counselor's reactions to impairment can be a preoccupation with their own stress, escape behaviors, avoiding intimacy, control as a survival tool, justification and rationalization of behavior, compromising ethical boundaries, and even quitting the profession.

If impairment is a deterioration of abilities from a previous level of competency, then counselors need to continually measure their performance through the eyes of their loved ones and trusted colleagues. Counselors need to listen to the concerns of colleagues, family, and friends and conduct periodic self-assessments. They need to take their own "mental health days" where they can engage in activities that help reduce their own levels of stress. If counselors are overwhelmed by personal concerns, family issues, health illnesses, and/or addictive behaviors, then ethically they are not to continue counseling if their competency is diminished. They need to ask to be reassigned, or take a leave of absence, and/or seek appropriate help.

COMPASSION FATIGUE

"Compassion fatigue" and "professional burnout" (page 156) have to do with impairment concerns, but they have separate unique qualities. Compassion fatigue tends to come on quickly, but it diminishes quickly. Compassion is defined as: A sympathetic conscious awareness of another person's distress, combined with a desire to help.

> ***The work we do requires conscious caring and counselors can get caught up in and overwhelmed by the distresses of their clients.***

"Compassion fatigue" can be apparent after a difficult, long day at the office with some of your more challenging clients. By the end of the day you are fatigued and drained, but you can go home and relax, laugh, or exercise and get a good nights sleep. The next day you're ready to go back to work.

BURNOUT

"Burnout" is more serious than compassion fatigue; however, too much compassion fatigue can cause burnout. Burnout occurs over a longer period of time and requires more time to recover. Burnout is the breaking down of psychological defenses and coping skills are weakened. A fading sense of "self" makes it harder to mobilize effectively and a sense of helplessness breeds alienation and isolation.

The mental health profession has a "dangerousness" elements—it is the danger that counseling itself poses to the counselor. Counseling can be hazardous to our health. It can affect our emotional, physical, and spiritual well-being. Counselors notoriously focus on everyone else's problems and consistently fail to attend to their own needs. This self-neglect has led to an extremely high rate of alcoholism, depression, and suicide among helping professionals. Burned-out or impaired counselors cannot provide effective treatment. They put clients at risk for emotional damage and themselves at risk for legal or ethical liabilities.

Ethically, counselors are to refrain from taking on a professional role when personal, medical, professional, legal, financial, or other situations could reasonably be expected to impair their objectivity, competence, or effectiveness in performing their function as a counselor. Counselors should not allow their own personal problems, psychosocial distress, legal problems, substance abuse, or mental health difficulties to interfere with their professional judgment and performance or to jeopardize the best interests of the clients. Counselors with impairment issues, ethically, should seek immediate consultation and take appropriate remedial action by seeking professional help, making adjustments in workload, terminating practice, or taking any other steps necessary to protect the welfare and best interest of their clients.

IMPAIRMENT OF COLLEAGUES

Ethically, counselors are to expose persons or organizations, with whom they have a professional relationship, if and when there is impairment that could interfere with the best interest of those they serve. Counselors, who have direct knowledge of a colleague's impairment (that's a result of their personal problems, psychosocial distress, substance abuse, or mental health difficulties), and believe that the impairment interferes with practice effectiveness, talk with that colleague when feasible and assist that colleague in taking remedial action.

ETHICAL RESPONSIBILITIES TO COLLEAGUES

Counselors owe respect and confidentiality to their colleagues. They are not to take advantage of a dispute with a colleague to obtain a position or otherwise advance their own best interests. Counselors should seek the advice and counsel of colleagues whenever such consultation is in the best interests of clients, and should keep informed about colleagues' areas of expertise for the purpose of appropriate referrals. Counselors should refer clients to other professionals when the other professional has specialized knowledge or expertise that would best serve a client.

ENDURING PRINCIPLES OF COUNSELING

Enduring principles of counseling are our knowledge, our choice of treatments, our compassion, and our rapport with client.

"Knowledge" encompasses an understanding of the client as a person and a counselor's understanding of their our own limitations to best serve the client. It includes an understanding of the natural history of the mental disorder and the natural history of people with the condition. Despite all the new discoveries about how the brain works and acts and affects people, still the principal method for understanding those who struggle with thinking, emotions, perceptions, and behaviors is observation, assessment, and client history. An understanding of the client as a person, in the context of their life, past and present, is necessary. Necessary for effective treatment is the need to find out why the client has come into counseling and why at this particular time. Assessments are the beginning of a therapeutic partnership between the counselor and the client. There is an educational process in counseling.

When it comes to "choice of treatment," therapeutic interventions are purposeful and relevant to the client's condition. The counselor is knowledgeable, educated, trained, supervised and interventions are based on the counselor's knowledge of the client and what interventions might be effective with a particular client.

"Compassion" is kindness in action; empathy with muscle. The opposite of compassion is a failure to act on behalf of the client's best interest, whether that failure stems from lack of knowledge or personal biases. In the therapeutic relationship, loyalty is put to the test—loyalty to the process and the person. And boundaries are necessary to ensure appropriate and clinically relevant compassion.

Finally, a Counselor's "rapport" with the client has everything to do with therapeutic success. Without exception, studies that look at what works in therapy arrive at the same conclusion—the therapeutic relationship between a counselor and the client is one of the best predictors of positive and effective clinical outcomes.

THE A.R.T.ful COUNSELOR
Authenticity—Resiliency—Tenacity

Being an A.R.T.ful Counselor is to believe passionately in what you are doing, and never compromise your standards or values in the process of caring for your clients, interacting with your colleagues, and advancing your career.

When counselors are "authentic," they remain true to their personality, spirit, and character, despite encountering external forces, pressures, and influences.

"Resiliency" is the ability to recover from change, discouragement, and misfortune after being bent, stretched, or compressed.

"Tenacity" is the ability to keep a cohesive state adhering to and seeking what's valued. Persistence, doggedness, perseverance, and staying power are essential ingredients for success in most ventures.

HELPING CLIENTS UNDERSTAND WHAT TO EXPECT

The professional counselor takes reasonable steps to help clients understand the process of counseling and they always explain the limitations and the risks associated with counseling. Professional counselors remain aware of their influential position and strive to maintain high ethical standards.

Counselors rely on "external ethical guides" such as laws and codes of conduct as well as "internal ethical guides" through character and integrity. Ethics is the process of using legal and moral principles in the real world of mental health care and are the defining qualities that distinguished individuals as professionals. Subjectivity, bending the rules, and even stupidity are present in our daily lives, so awareness of and adherence to ethical guidelines is absolutely necessary in the mental health profession.

Ethical issues that violate ethical standards are not a dilemma, because that would be a "right vs. wrong" situation. A true ethical dilemma is a "right vs. right" situation, where there are two (or more) choices, each having merit.

Do you hug your client or not? Do you accept a gift or not? Do you go to a client's wedding or not? Do you counsel outside the office or not? These are the ethical dilemmas.

The ethical codes of various professional organizations offer a degree of guidance, but these guidelines do not deal with every situation nor do they answer every question. Sometimes, interpretation and application of a code of ethics in a specific case is difficult. So, counselors possess some freedom to exercise professional judgment as they act in the best interest of their clients.

…
THE A.B.C.s
OF GETTING HELP WITH ETHICAL DILEMMAS
Associations—Boards—Colleagues

Counselors can contact their associations, licensing boards, or consult with colleagues when faced with ethical dilemmas. Contact an ethics professor or read additional books on ethics. A multitude of information on mental health counseling ethics is available on the Internet. You can contact your insurance company and speak with somebody in their risk management department. If your policy allows, you can get access to an attorney who specializes in mental health law.

ETHICAL DECISION MAKING PRINCIPLES

The ability to reason with ethical principles and arrive at an ethical decision is part of the ethical decision-making process. You need to be willing to be accountable for the decision that you make, because in that final decision, it is yours alone.

THE ETHICAL DECISION MAKING MODEL:
1. Identify the problem
2. Apply your relevant code of ethics
3. Determine the nature and dimensions of the dilemma
4. Generate potential courses of action
5. Consider the potential consequences of all options
6. Choose a course of action
7. Evaluate the selected course of action
8. Implement the course of action

ETHICAL DECISION MAKING MODEL

IDENTIFY THE PROBLEM
- Ask yourself: Is it an ethical, legal, professional, or clinical problem? Is it a combination of more than one of these? If a legal question exists, seek legal advice.

OTHER QUESTIONS THAT MAY BE USEFUL. ASK YOURSELF...
- Is the issue related to me and what I am or am not doing?
- Is it related to a client and/or the client's significant others and what they are or are not doing?
- Is it related to the institution or agency and their policies and procedures?
- If the problem can be resolved by implementing a policy of an institution or agency, then look to the agency's guidelines.

It is good to remember that the dilemmas you face are often complex, so a useful guideline is to examine the problem from several perspectives and avoid searching for a simplistic solution.

APPLY YOUR RELEVANT CODE OF ETHICS: After you have clarified the problem, refer to relevant Codes of Ethics to see if the issue is addressed there. If there is an applicable standard or several standards and they are specific and clear, following the course of action indicated should lead to a resolution of the problem. If the problem is more complex and a resolution does not seem apparent, then you probably have a true ethical dilemma and need to proceed with further steps in the ethical decision-making process.

DETERMINE THE NATURE AND DIMENSIONS OF THE DILEMMA:
There are several avenues to follow in order to ensure that you have examined the problem in all its various dimensions.

- Consider the moral principles of autonomy, non-maleficence, beneficence, justice, and fidelity.
- Decide which principles apply to the specific situation, and determine which principle takes priority for you in this case. In theory, each principle is of equal value, which means that it is your challenge to determine the priorities when two or more of them are in conflict.
- Review the relevant professional literature to ensure that you are using the most current professional thinking in reaching a decision.
- Consult with experienced professional colleagues and/or supervisors. As they review with you the information you have gathered, they may see other issues that are relevant or provide a perspective you have not considered. They may also be able to identify aspects of the dilemma that you are not viewing objectively. Consult your state or national professional associations to see if they can provide help with the dilemma.
- Generate potential courses of action. Brainstorm as many possible courses of action as possible. Be creative and consider all options. If possible, enlist the assistance of at least one colleague to help you generate options.
- Consider the potential consequences of all options and determine a course of action. Considering the information you have gathered and the priorities you have set, evaluate each option and assess the potential consequences for all the parties involved.
- Eliminate the options that clearly do not give the desired results or cause even more problematic consequences. Review the remaining options to determine which option or combination of options best fits the situation and addresses the priorities you have identified.
- Evaluate the selected course of action. Review the selected course of action to see if it presents any new ethical considerations.

ETHICS

Codes of ethics are invaluable tools for guiding mental health counselors toward ethical practice and are used to help guide professionals in the ethical decision-making process. Rational, ethical decision making is supplemented by a person's intuition, and shaped by culture and profession. In an effort to maintain a rational, detached, and professional approach, counselors may ignore warning signals and gut instincts relevant to the situation. It is important to have safe, non-judgmental colleagues for open and regular discussions of ethical issues.

This is a unique profession. So many things can overwhelm, drain, distract, and seduce us into an "ethical sleep." Fatigue, endless paperwork, the urgency of our clients' needs, conflicts with managed care or the organizations or colleagues we work with, lack of adequate support, and mind-numbing routines can rob us of the alert and mindful awareness we need to maintain concerning the ethical implications of what we choose or choose not to do. Formal ethical codes and standards are important, but cannot take the place of thoughtful and creative approaches to our ethical responsibilities. Codes inform more than they determine ethical considerations. Each new client is unique. Each counselor is unique. Each situation is unique. Theoretical orientation, community, culture, and so many other elements influence the work we do, and every ethical decision must consider many contexts.

KEY ETHICAL CONSIDERATIONS

AUTONOMY: The duty to maximize the client's right to make their own decisions
DOING GOOD: The duty to do not harm
CONFIDENTIALITY: The duty to respect client's privacy; to protect their information
COMPETENCY: The duty to practice only within areas of expertise
FIDELITY: The duty to keep one's promise or word
JUSTICE: The duty to treat all fairly
RESPECT FOR OTHERS: The duty to honor others and respect their rights
UTILITY AND UNIVERSALITY: The duty to provide the greatest good, and least harm for the greatest number of people; actions that hold for all, regardless of time, place, and people involved
VERACITY: The duty to tell the truth

PART 2

ETHICAL STANDARDS: COMPETENCIES

*Competence,
within the field
of psychology,
is as important as
any other standard*

REQUIRED ETHICAL COMPETENCIES

Any one of us can make mistakes, because we might overlook something important or view a situation from a limited perspective. We could reach wrong conclusions as we hold too tightly to cherished beliefs or personal biases. An important part of the work we do in this unique profession is questioning ourselves. "Am I overlooking something? How can I understand the situation better? Are there other options?"

Human nature makes it easier to question the ethics of others than to question our own beliefs, biases, perspectives, assumptions, and actions. It is a red flag if we spend more time trying to point out the flaws, mistakes, and ethical blindness of others then we spend assessing our own choices and behaviors.

As we seek to help others who come to us because they are hurting, we also need to remain aware of a variety of issues, such as inadequate resources, conflicting responsibilities, frustrating limitations, and ethical struggles. Truly, this is a unique profession.

Competence, within the field of psychology, is as important as any other standard. Possibly, it is more important because the knowledge available to practicing counselors is constantly growing and continually changing. This makes competency a lifelong professional goal that is never quite satisfied. There is always more to learn.

Professional competency is not a static, fixed construct—either incompetent or competent.

Competency lies on a continuum.

RESEARCH
- **Research competence in mental health care.**
  - How is it measured? How do you think it should be measured?
- **What do the following two statements mean?**
  - *Competency is not a fixed construct*
  - *Competency lies on a continuum*

ETHICAL STANDARDS & CLINICAL FORMS

ETHICAL COMPETENCE

"Ethical competence" is based on ethical intelligence. Like emotional competence, ethical competence is difficult to measure, but its presence or absence in an individual, organization, or society is readily observable.

It is incumbent upon the counseling profession and each practicing counselor to examine how they are preparing for new skills and updating ongoing skills. Therefore, this information is to raise questions that encourage ethical thoughtfulness about issues related to competency and to suggest actions that can increase thoughts, reflections, and discussions about competence.

We have witnessed in recent years high profile examples of ethical incompetence. We begin to wonder whether there is not some way that we can set a standard of ethical competence that leads to practices that are teachable and able to be learned. Can there be standards that would raise the level of ethical competence at every level?

COMPETENCY OBLIGATIONS

- Familiarity with professional/scientific knowledge
- Acquiring professional skills
- Recognition of lack of expertise

DEFINING COMPETENCE

A standard dictionary will define "competency" generally along the lines of being "a sufficiency of qualification" or "fitness" or "legitimacy". In practice, there are two levels at which competency is determined. First, there is the "gateway" or generic level of qualification. However, there is also the "task-specific" level at which competency needs to be separately considered and confirmed.

DEFINING ETHICAL COMPETENCE: Ethical competence means understanding relevant laws and formal rules (codes) and applying them uniformly. It's challenging. And, relying on only "virtue ethics" makes the concept of ethical competence a bit unclear, except to force us into a "do good, be good" definition for such competence.

> **SELF-REFLECTION and/or GROUP DISCUSSION:**
> - When we speak of someone as a professional, generally we are referring to a person who is one of a group whose occupation and work requires extensive education or training and who have a special competency: A recognized high degree of particular skill and proven ability and competence in that particular field of work.
> - When we speak of someone's professionalism or professional standards, generally we are referring, not just to that person's competency, but also to an important additional dimension: A standard of "character" and "behavior'" in the way they practice their profession.
> - A standard dictionary will define performance generally along the lines of "the act, process or manner of performing" or "'he carrying out of a duty'" or "the accomplishment of any action or work."
>
> What do you look for in the professionals you refer to?

STANDARD OF CARE

"Standard of care" is a particularly difficult issue in counseling, as there are hundreds of different orientations and approaches to treatment. Each is based on different orientations, methodologies, and philosophies, belief systems, or even world views. Aside from the cornerstones of ethics (do no harm, do not exploit the client, and do not impair your professional judgment) and, beyond the obligations to honor the clients' rights; respect client's dignity, and privacy; work in a client's best interest, and work collaboratively with a client regarding therapy goals and treatment plans—there is no consensus on how to intervene, or help. For example, there is no one standard, or method, or way for the treatment of anxiety. Psychoanalysis, cognitive-behavioral, existential, biologically-based psychiatry, and faith-based counseling all define, explain, and treat the anxiety in very different terms.

STANDARD OF CARE IS...

1) A comparison between you an other "average" and "relatively prudent" professionals doing same/similar type of work, in same situations, same clientele base, similar educational backgrounds, licensing, etc.
2) A reference to best practices literature and practices, studies, outcomes.
3) A measure of competence.

FIDUCIARY RELATIONSHIP

A "fiduciary relationship" between a counselor and their client is based on the special knowledge and expertise of the professional and the facts that trust is an essential part of this relationship. Counselors should not take unfair advantage of any professional relationship or exploit others to further their personal, religious, political, or business interests. The primary responsibility of the mental health counselor is to respect the dignity and integrity of the client. Client growth and development are encouraged in ways that foster the client's best interest(s).

A VIRTUOUS PROFESSIONAL UPHOLDING A FIDUCIARY RELATIONSHIP WOULD:
- Be motivated to do what is good
- Possess a high degree of self-understanding and awareness
- Comprehend the "mores" (collective moralities) of their communities in relation to culture and client

DIAGNOSING CLIENTS' CONDITIONS

THE DIAGNOSIS OF A MENTAL DISORDER SHOULD HAVE CLINICAL UTILITY: It should help counselors to determine prognosis, treatment plans, and potential treatment outcomes for their clients.

However, the diagnosis of a mental disorder is not equivalent to a need for treatment. Need for treatment is a complex clinical decision that takes into consideration such factors as symptom severity, symptom salience (the presence of suicidal ideation), the patient's distress (mental pain) associated with the symptom(s), disability related to the patient's symptoms, and other factors (psychiatric symptoms complicating other illness).

Counselors may thus encounter individuals who do not meet full criteria for a mental disorder, but who demonstrate a clear need for treatment or care. The fact that some individuals do not show all symptoms indicative of a diagnosis in these individuals should not be used to justify limiting their access to appropriate care.

DOMAINS OF COMPETENCY

- The first domain is "foundational competencies." These are the knowledge, skills, attitudes, and values which underlie the function of counselors. (Page 173)
- The second encompasses "functional competencies" of a counselor, whether clinical, research, educational, or administrative in nature. (Page 189)
- The third is a "developmental competencies," advancing skills. (Page 195)

CAVEAT: Counselors should be aware of the contents in their professional associations' official publications, such as a newsletter or journal articles, regarding such various interventions. Counselors are not required to follow the recommendations or guidelines in such publications, but they are expected to be aware of them and, when appropriate, consider them in their clinical and ethical decision-making processes.

ETHICAL COMPETENCE FRAMEWORK

"To be competent" means having an ability in sufficient measure that one can perform at an acceptable standard. Ethical competence is closely associated with the concept of emotional competence, which determines how well we handle each other and ourselves. Emotional competence has been referred to as "a learned capability based on emotional intelligence that results in outstanding performance at work."

RELATIONSHIP TO EMOTIONAL COMPETENCE

Ground-breaking work was done in the 1990s by Daniel Goleman on promoting "emotional intelligence" as the new yardstick for measuring success at work. Though Goleman did not forge the link between ethics and emotions very forcefully, it is clear that a case can be made for a relationship between emotional intelligence and ethical competence.

Though difficult to measure, emotional intelligence is observable as the quality that distinguishes successful performance beyond just training or high cognitive intelligence.

RESEARCH
- Look up information about emotional intelligence
- How would being emotionally intelligent help with being ethically competent?

THREE DIMENSIONS OF COMPETENCE

Ethical Competence incorporates three dimensions of competence, beginning with personal, moving through social, and on to global competence.

SELF-REFLECTION and/or GROUP DISCUSSION:

ETHICAL COMPETENCY SCALE:

1) **PERSONAL ETHICAL COMPETENCE:** How we maintain our personal commitment to an ethical life; grounded in thought and action

2) **SOCIAL ETHICAL COMPETENCE:** How we handle relationships and strive to appreciate the worth of others; how we act to induce desirable, ethically grounded responses to others

3) **GLOBAL ETHICAL COMPETENCE:** How we see life as a web of delicate connections requiring stewardship for sustainability; how we act as part of a complex interconnected whole; how we act as responsible participants in creating a beneficial future

How do you define:
1) Trustworthiness, 2) Understanding others, and 3) Interdependence

FOUNDATIONAL COMPETENCIES
The Early Years...

STATES HAVE COMMON SPECIFIC LICENSING REQUIREMENTS

- Demonstrate Competence. The word "demonstrate" refers to measurable areas of competence such as graduation from a approved counseling program, completion of required internship hours with supervision, and the passing of a state examination
  - Counseling professionals are to comply with their state's applicable rules and regulations [codes of professional conduct/ethical codes].
  - Counselors do not use their professional relationships to further self-interests.
  - Counselors are of "good moral character."

Commonly, professions use various external measures for assuring competence. So, qualification for practice is assured by licensing laws and by professional standards. However, laws and standards are generally considered to uphold the lowest minimum standard for practice.

A standard dictionary will define the word "ethics" along the lines of "being the moral system of a particular writer or school of thought, or the rules of conduct recognized in certain limited departments of human life or even the science of human duty in its widest extent." In essence, ethics is about moral values. It is a moral philosophy or set of moral principles that are expressed in a formal way what "doing the right thing" means.

So when licensing requirements refer to "being of good moral character" what are they referring to? A good place to start is with the moral principles listed on the next page.

MORAL PRINCIPLES

- Autonomy: Professional counselors promote and encourage the client's independent decision-making; they respect clients' self-determination (only interfering with this independence when applicable reporting laws apply).
- Fidelity: Counselors strive to create and maintain a trusting therapeutic environment that includes confidentiality, and appropriate boundaries.
- Doing Good: Counselors foster the welfare and the growth of clients.
- Do No Harm: Counselors do not harm clients.
- Justice: Counselors conduct their professional relationships with fairness.

The formal meaning of justice is: Treating equals, equally; treating unequals, unequally, but in proportion to their relevant differences.

Here's an example of the formal meaning of justice applied to a counseling situation:

You see clients in an office. All your clients are able to come to your office. Some drive; some are driven; some take the bus. However your clients get there, they do. Now, you have a client who was in a serious accident and is back home, but bed-ridden. They want you to come to their home to continue counseling. If you do, there's a good reason for doing so—that's justice—a fairness given the circumstances.

FREEDOM OF INQUIRY

Mental health counselors accept the responsibility "freedom of inquiry" confers: Competence, objectivity in the application of skills, and concern for the best interest of clients, colleagues, and society in general.

Without freedom of inquiry, community members cannot search for new knowledge or challenge conventional wisdom. Freedom of expression and inquiry are not absolute.

The law, for example, provides that freedom of expression does not include the right to slander the reputation of another, to engage in specified forms of harassment, to threaten or obstruct a person who advances unwelcome ideas, or to incite another person to violence.

Scholarly inquiry also is limited by federal and state regulation, ethical tenets, and professional standards designed to protect human and animal subjects.

RESEARCH
- Do an Internet search for the phrase "freedom of inquiry"
- How does this concept apply to the counseling profession?

*It is vital for all counselors
to be familiar with
the codes of professional conduct
that are outlined by
their respective licensing*

COMPETENCIES AND CODES OF ETHICS

CAVEAT: There are many counseling associations, each with their own codes of ethics and competencies. It is necessary for all counselors to be familiar with the codes from the associations they belong to. It is vital that all counselors be familiar with the codes of professional conduct that are outlined by their respective licensing boards for the state in which they practice. The following is a summarized/condensed list adapted from the American Mental Health Counseling Association. Visit www.amhca.org for more information.

RESEARCH
- Research each of these principles LISTED BELOW and add your own ADDITIONAL KEY POINTS to each section.
  Use the code of ethics from your specific licensing.
  - Be sure to check out other associations
  - Use these key words: *"list of mental health counseling associations"* to find a listing and links to many associations

Principle of: Welfare of the Consumer

Primary Responsibility: The welfare of the client
ADDITIONAL KEY POINT(S): _____

Counseling Plans: Jointly devised by counselor and client
ADDITIONAL KEY POINT(S): _____

Freedom of Choice: Client's autonomy (unless the court system has intervened)
ADDITIONAL KEY POINT(S): _____

Clients Served by Others: secure consent/agreement to avoid confusion
ADDITIONAL KEY POINT(S): _____

Diversity: Counselors will actively attempt to understand the diverse cultural backgrounds of clients
ADDITIONAL KEY POINT(S): _____

ETHICAL STANDARDS & CLINICAL FORMS

Dual Relationships: Counselors are aware of their influential position; avoid exploiting trust; avoid dual relationships with clients that could impair professional judgment or increase the risk of harm
ADDITIONAL KEY POINT(S): _____

Sexual Relationships: Are strictly prohibited with current clients (States and Associations vary in regards to former clients)
ADDITIONAL KEY POINT(S): _____

Multiple Clients: Counselors clarify at the outset which person or persons are clients, and the nature of the relationship they will have with each involved person
ADDITIONAL KEY POINT(S): _____

Informed Consent: A clear description of what the client can expect in the way of tests, reports, billing, therapeutic regime and schedules, and the use of the mental health counselor's statement of professional disclosure
ADDITIONAL KEY POINT(S): _____

Conflict of Interest: Counselors clarify the nature of the conflict and inform all parties of the nature and direction of their loyalties and responsibilities, and keep all parties informed of their commitments
ADDITIONAL KEY POINT(S): _____

Fees and Bartering: Counselors clearly explain to clients all financial arrangements related to professional services, including the use of collection agencies or legal measures for nonpayment; Counselors ordinarily refrain from accepting goods or services from clients in return for counseling service because such arrangements create inherent potential for conflicts, exploitation and distortion of the professional relationship
ADDITIONAL KEY POINT(S): _____

Pro Bono Service: Counselors contribute to society by devoting a portion of their professional activity to services for which there is little or no financial return
ADDITIONAL KEY POINT(S): _____

Consulting: Counselors may choose to consult with any other professionally competent person about a client
ADDITIONALLY KEY POINT(S): _____

Group Work: Counselors screen prospective group counseling/therapy participants. Every effort is made to select members whose needs and goals are compatible with goals of the group
ADDITIONAL KEY POINT(S): _____

Termination and Referral: Counselors do not abandon or neglect their clients in counseling
ADDITIONAL KEY POINT(S): _____

Inability to assist clients: If services are not beneficial to the client, they avoid entering or terminate immediately a counseling relationship
ADDITIONAL KEY POINT(S): _____

Appropriate Termination: Counselors terminate a counseling relationship, securing a client's agreement when possible, when it is reasonably clear that the client is no longer benefiting, when services are no longer required, when counseling no longer serves the needs and interests of the client, when clients do not pay fees charged, or when agency or institution limits do not allow provision of further counseling services
ADDITIONAL KEY POINT(S): _____

Principle of: Clients' Rights

The following apply to all consumers of mental health services, including both in- and outpatients and all state, county, local, and private care mental health facilities, as well as clients of mental health practitioners in private practice.

The client has the right:
- To be treated with dignity, consideration and respect at all times...
- To expect quality service provided by concerned, trained, professional and competent staff...
- To expect complete confidentiality within the limits of the law...
- To a clear working contract in which business items are discussed...
- To a clear statement of the purposes, goals, techniques, rules of procedure and limitations...
- To appropriate information regarding the mental health counselor's education, training, skills, etc.
- To full, knowledgeable, and responsible participation in the ongoing treatment plan...

ETHICAL STANDARDS & CLINICAL FORMS

- To obtain information about their case record and to have this information explained clearly and directly…
- To request information and/or consultation regarding the conduct and progress of their therapy…
- To refuse any recommended services and to be advised of the consequences of this action…
- To a safe environment free of emotional, physical and sexual abuse…
- To a client grievance procedure…
- To a clearly defined ending process, and to discontinue therapy at any time…

ADDITIONALLY KEY POINT(S): _____

_____

Principle of: Confidentiality

Mental health counselors have a primary obligation to safeguard information about individuals obtained in the course of practice, teaching, or research. Personal information is communicated to others only with the person's written consent or in those circumstances where there is clear and imminent danger to the client, to others or to society. Disclosure of counseling information is restricted to what is necessary, relevant and verifiable.
ADDITIONAL KEY POINT(S): _____

_____

Utilization of Assessment Techniques
Test Selection
ADDITIONAL KEY POINT(S): _____

_____

Test Administration
ADDITIONAL KEY POINT(S): _____

_____

Test Interpretation
ADDITIONAL KEY POINT(S): _____

_____

Test Reporting
ADDITIONAL KEY POINT(S):: _____

_____

Principle of: Pursuit of Research Activities

Mental health counselors who conduct research must do so with regard to ethical principles. The decision to undertake research should rest upon a considered judgment by the individual counselor about how best to contribute to counseling and to human welfare. Mental health counselors carry out their investigations with respect for the people who participate and with concern for their dignity and welfare.
ADDITIONAL KEY POINT(S): _____

Principle of: Consulting

Mental health counselors acting as consultants must have a high degree of self-awareness of their own values, knowledge, skills and needs in entering a helping relationship that involves human and/or organizational change. The focus of the consulting relationship should be on the issues to be resolved and not on the personal characteristics of those presenting the consulting issues.
ADDITIONAL KEY POINT(S): _____

Principle of: Competence

The maintenance of high standards of professional competence is a responsibility shared by all mental health counselors in the best interests of the public and the profession. Mental health counselors recognize the boundaries of their particular competencies and the limitations of their expertise. Mental health counselors only provide those services and use only those techniques for which they are qualified by education, techniques or experience. Mental health counselors maintain knowledge of relevant scientific and professional information related to the services they render, and they recognize the need for on-going education.

Mental health counselors accurately represent their competence, education, training and experience.
ADDITIONAL KEY POINT(S): _____

As teaching professionals, mental health counselors perform their duties based on careful preparation in order that their instruction is accurate, up to date and educational.
ADDITIONAL KEY POINT(S): _____

ETHICAL STANDARDS & CLINICAL FORMS

Mental health counselors recognize the need for continued education and training in the area of cultural diversity and competency.
ADDITIONAL KEY POINT(S): _____

Mental health counselors are open to new procedures and sensitive to the diversity of varying populations and changes in expectations and values over time.
ADDITIONAL KEY POINT(S): _____

Mental health counselors and practitioners recognize that their effectiveness depends in part upon their ability to maintain sound and healthy interpersonal relationships. They are aware that any unhealthy activity would compromise sound professional judgment and competency. In the event that personal problems arise and are affecting professional services, they will seek competent professional assistance to determine whether they should limit, suspend or terminate services to their clients.
ADDITIONAL KEY POINT(S): _____

Mental health counselors have a responsibility both to the individual who is served and to the institution within which the service is performed to maintain high standards of professional conduct. Mental health counselors strive to maintain the highest level of professional services offered to the agency, organization or institution in providing the highest caliber of professional services. The acceptance of employment in an institution implies that the mental health counselor is in substantial agreement with the general policies and principles of the institution. If, despite concerted efforts, the member cannot reach an agreement with the employer as to acceptable standards of conduct that allows for changes in institutional policy conducive to the positive growth and development of counselors, then terminating the affiliation should be seriously considered.
ADDITIONAL KEY POINT(S): _____

Ethical behavior among professional associates, mental health counselors and non-mental health counselors is expected at all times. When information is possessed that raises serious doubts as to the ethical behavior of professional colleagues, whether association members or not, the mental health counselor is obligated to take action to attempt to rectify such a condition. Such action shall utilize the institution's channels first and then utilize procedures established by the state licensing board.
ADDITIONAL KEY POINT(S): _____

Mental health counselors are aware of the intimacy of the counseling relationship, maintain a healthy respect for the integrity of the client, and avoid engaging in activities that seek to meet the mental health counselor's personal needs at the expense of the client. Through awareness of the negative impact of both racial and sexual stereotyping and discrimination, the member strives to ensure the individual rights and personal dignity of the client in the counseling relationship.
ADDITIONAL KEY POINT(S): _____

Principle of: Professional Relationships
Mental health counselors act with due regard for the needs and feelings of their colleagues in counseling and other professions. Mental health counselors respect the prerogatives and obligations of the institutions or organizations with which they associate.
ADDITIONAL KEY POINT(S): _____

Principle of: Supervisee, Student and Employee Relationships
Mental health counselors have an ethical concern for the integrity and welfare of supervisees, students, and employees. They maintain these relationships on a professional and confidential basis. They recognize the influential position they have with regard to both current and former supervisees, students and employees. They avoid exploiting their trust and dependency.
ADDITIONAL KEY POINT(S): _____

Principle of: Moral and Legal Standards
Mental health counselors recognize that they have a moral, legal and ethical responsibility to the community and to the general public. Mental health counselors should be aware of the prevailing community standards and the impact of professional standards on the community.
ADDITIONAL KEY POINT(S): _____

Principle of: Professional Responsibility

In their commitment to the understanding of human behavior, mental health counselors value objectivity and integrity, and in providing services they maintain the highest standards. They accept responsibility for the consequences of their work and make every effort to ensure that their services are used appropriately.
ADDITIONAL INFORMATION: _____

_____

Principle of: Private Practice

A mental health counselor should assist, where permitted by legislation or judicial decision, the profession in fulfilling its duty to make counseling services available in private settings.
ADDITIONAL INFORMATION: _____

_____

In advertising services as a private practitioner, mental health counselors should advertise the services in such a manner so as to accurately inform the public as to services, expertise, profession, and techniques of counseling in a professional manner.
ADDITIONAL INFORMATION: _____

_____

Mental health counselors may join in partnership/corporation with other mental health counselors and/or other professionals provided that each mental health counselor of the partnership or corporation makes clear his/her separate specialties, buying name in compliance with the regulations of the locality.
ADDITIONAL INFORMATION: _____

_____

Principle of: Public Statements

Mental health counselors in their professional roles may be expected or required to make public statements providing counseling information or professional opinions; or supply information about the availability of counseling products and services.
In making such statements, mental health counselors take in to full account the limits and uncertainties of present counseling knowledge and techniques.
ADDITIONAL INFORMATION: _____

They represent, as accurately and objectively as possible, their professional qualifications, expertise, affiliations, and functions, as well as those of the institutions or organizations with which the statements may be associated.
ADDITIONAL INFORMATION: _____

All public statements, announcements of services, and promotional activities should serve the purpose of providing sufficient information to aid the consumer public in making informed judgments and choices on matters that concern it.
ADDITIONAL INFORMATION: _____

When announcing professional counseling services, mental health counselors may describe or explain those services offered but may not evaluate as to their quality or uniqueness and do not allow for testimonials by implication. All public statements should be otherwise consistent with this Code of Ethics.
ADDITIONAL INFORMATION: _____

Principle of: Internet On-Line Counseling

Mental health counselors engaged in delivery of services that involves the telephone, teleconferencing and the Internet in which these areas are generally recognized, standards for preparatory training do not yet exist. Mental health counselors take responsible steps to ensure the competence of their work and protect patients, clients, students, research participants and others from harm.

Counselors must take into consideration all of the following:
- Confidentiality Issues/Concerns
- Mental Health Counselor Identification
- Client Identification
- Client Waiver
- Electronic Transfer of Client Information
- Establishing the On-Line Counseling Relationship
- Legal Considerations

ADDITIONAL INFORMATION: _____

*Client familiarity
must be tempered
with wisdom*

THE VULNERABLE NATURE OF CLIENTS

Familiarity exists in counseling. There is a long continuum of what can and is considered "relational intimacy" or "familiarity." Familiarity must be tempered with wisdom and a counselor's empathy and warmth can be a potent medicine or an ethical concern.

Vulnerable Clients + Therapeutic Challenges
= Ethical Concerns

RESEARCH
- Look up in a dictionary the word "familiarity" and write the definitions down
- Look up the word "intimacy" and write the definitions down.
- What elements in the definitions are relevant to the work we do with our clients?

LABELING—THE CONCERN FOR CAUTION

It depends if the labeling is used for identifying or for oppressing, marginalizing, or prejudice. By understanding the characteristics of individuals and groups, the goal is to enable us to gain effective skills for dealing with many individuals.

"BAR CODING"
Bar coding refers to unearned privilege and/or unearned oppression.

RESEARCH
- See what you can find on the term "bar coding" and how it's used in the contexts of culture and ethnicity...
    - What about the term "code switching"?

OPPRESSION AND MARGINALIZATION

In mental health care, counselors must seriously consider the client's authorship of their own story. Counselors understand that oppressions and marginalization deeply influence clients' stories. Clients are both the author and the subject of their stories, thus the focus and agent of change. Oppression and marginalization specifically impacts client perceptions of their locus of control [power], and their access to inclusion [place].

A significant challenge in multicultural practice is facilitating a "balance" in client victimization and the ongoing realities of oppression and marginalization.

Labeling, oppressions, and marginalizations influence who we are and how we see ourselves. To be ethically competent, counselors must examine their own legacies, especially those that have influenced your ethical standards.

RESEARCH
- **Explore the concepts of oppression and marginalization**
  - Why are these terms and concepts important to the counseling profession?
- **Look up the term "microaggressions"**
  - What is important to understand about this concept?

SELF-REFLECTION and/or GROUP DISCUSSION:

DISCOVERING OUR ETHICAL LEGACY
- What are your ethical and moral touchstones?
- What are 6 principles your inner voice tells you to hold dear? (Write them down)
- Who are your top ethical role models? What principles do you think they hold or held dear?

WHAT HAS AFFECTED US: Our religious and cultural up-bringing and beliefs; then secular legacy (family, school, friends, community), third, our work legacy (work policies, corporate cultures, professional expectations).

FUNCTIONAL COMPETENCIES
The Practicing Years...

PROFESSIONAL ACTIVITIES (THE PRACTICING YEARS):
- Clinical
- Research
- Educational
- Administrative

The counselor's tasks are relatively simple to state and exceedingly challenging to accomplish. Counselors help clients to discern old patterns, become aware of issues, and help clients explore their feeling, thoughts, behaviors, and attitudes. Counseling provides therapeutic opportunities for change.

IN COUNSELING THE GOALS ARE TWOFOLD:
1) Decrease maladaptive behaviors
2) Increase adaptive coping: Mindfulness, stress tolerance, emotional regulation, radical acceptance, and interpersonal relationship skills

RESEARCH
- **Look up the adaptive coping skills listed above to get some information on each of them**
    - **What adaptive coping skills would you add to the list?**
    - **How many maladaptive behaviors can you list?**

COMPETENCY AND THE DSM
DIAGNOSTIC and STATISTICAL MANUAL OF MENTAL DISORDERS (DSM)

CURRENT DEFINITION OF MENTAL DISORDER
"Clinically significant behavioral or psychological or biological syndromes that are associated with present distress, disability, or significant impairment in important areas of functioning."
- The condition must draw concern from others in a relational, social, occupational, or vocational setting that requires a referral for treatment.
- The counselor must incorporate respect for age, gender, and culture-specific factors and sensitivity to conditions when making a diagnosis.

Refer to the most current DSM (Diagnostic and Statistical Manual of Mental Disorders); visit www.DSM5.org for current and/or additional information.

A "mental disorder" is a health condition characterized by significant dysfunction in an individual's cognitions, emotions, or behaviors that reflects a disturbance in the psychological, biological, or developmental processes underlying mental functioning. Some disorders may not be diagnosable until they have caused clinically significant distress or impairment of performance.

A "mental disorder" is not merely an expectable or culturally sanctioned response to a specific event such as the death of a loved one. Neither culturally deviant behavior (e.g., political, religious, or sexual) nor a conflict that is primarily between the individual and society is a mental disorder unless the deviance or conflict results from a dysfunction in the individual, as described above.

- Clinicians may thus encounter individuals who do not meet full criteria for a mental disorder, but who demonstrate a clear need for treatment or care. The fact that some individuals do not show all symptoms indicative of a diagnosis should not be used to justify limiting their access to appropriate care.

DIAGNOSTICS

"Diagnostics" are present in the therapy relationship, but we treat the person with the diagnosis, not the diagnosis.

THERAPY IS A PROCESS, NOT AN EVENT:
- Therapy is a relationship
- All relationships start with unknowns
- Relationships are about getting to know the person

CAVEAT: Tests and measurements can never be the only source of diagnosis. Tests and measurement tools must be combined with clinical perceptions. If legal action or litigation happens, diagnosis is where counsel will dig and try to prove incompetence. Follow DSM criteria.

ELEMENTS OF GOOD THERAPY

NON-PATHOLOGIZING: Viewing a client as greater than his or her problems is the hallmark of non-pathologizing therapy. It does not mean problems do not exist, it means not viewing the problems as the whole person or the whole person as the problems. Working non-pathologically does not negate pathology, it de-pathologizes it.

EMPOWERING: This maintains the belief that people can grow, heal, and transform. This hope is held no matter how intense a client's defenses and wounds are that they can heal; they can contribute to their own growth whatever is sufficient and necessary to that end.

ETHICAL STANDARDS & CLINICAL FORMS

APPROPRIATE BOUNDARY CROSSINGS

"Boundary crossings" are defined as non-exploitive deviations from standard practice. "Standard practice" [or the standard norm] is counseling in a confidential setting—one counselor and one client.

Boundary crossing occur when we deviate from standard norms, but we do so for the client's benefit; the boundary is changed to assist the client.

RESEARCH

- **Web search these key words:** *"mental health counseling and boundary crossings"*
- **Web search these key words:** *"mental health counseling and boundary violations"*
- **What is the difference? (Between "boundary crossings" and "boundary violations")**
  - Find ten examples of appropriate boundary crossings

SELF-REFLECTION and/or GROUP DISCUSSION:

BALANCING THE CORNERSTONES OF ETHICS:
Do no harm
Do not exploit
Do not continue counseling if your professional judgment is impaired

We are required to practice within appropriate boundaries...
Boundary Crossings: Deviation from "standard practice" that are beneficial for the client…

SO…
Is it possible to tell…
- Which boundary crossings are therapeutically helpful?
- Which are therapeutically contra-indicated as harmful?
- Which might be therapeutic useful in certain communities or cultures?

COMPETENCY OBLIGATIONS

On the competency continuum, counselors are to be familiar with professional and scientific knowledge, continually acquiring professional skills, and knowing when to refer and when not.

SELF-REFLECTION and/or GROUP DISCUSSION:

BALANCING THE CORNERSTONES OF ETHICS:

Do no harm

Do not exploit

Do not continue counseling if your professional judgment is impaired

We are required to practice within our competencies (areas of expertise)...

SO...

What are your options when a client presents a dilemma, issue, concern, condition outside your area of expertise?

- Can you continue working with the client?
- What would you need to do to remain ethical?
- When should you refer?
- How do you communicate that necessity for referral to the client?

*Understanding culture is critical
for mental health counselors
because both our cultural orientation
and our client's cultural orientation
is present in every interaction*

DEVELOPMENTAL COMPETENCIES
Continued Professional Growth...

COMPETENCY AND DIVERSITY: FOCUS ON CULTURAL SENSITIVITY

Since 2005, codes have been infused with multiculturalism, diversity concerns and ethical expectations.

ASSOCIATIONS HAVE HAD TO ASK THEMSELVES:
1) How do we need to rethink things in terms of changing population demographics and issues of multiculturalism?
2) What is missing from current codes that will make code revisions more culturally sensitive?

Sociologists and anthropologists have identified many basic elements that are present in cultural interactions. These elements interact with each other and result in patterns of behavior that are shared. Because these elements intersect with the experiences, the histories, and the psychological makeup of each individual, no one person can be pigeon holed by their race, ethnicity, gender or any other single feature.

It is in the mix of these features that each person develops individuality and group belonging in unexpected ways. Cultural, historical, experiential and psychological characteristics react with the contexts in which individuals find themselves, further complicating attempts to put people into specific boxes or categories.

Mental health professionals and service providers should be familiar with how all of these areas interact within, between and among individuals.

- Culture includes, but is not limited to, race, ethnicity, language, sexual orientation, gender, age, disability, class and socioeconomic status, education, religious and spiritual orientations.

ETHICAL STANDARDS & CLINICAL FORMS

CULTURAL COMPETENCE

- "Cultural competence" is the ability to relate effectively to individuals from various groups and backgrounds. Within the behavioral health system, cultural competence must be a guiding principle, so that services are culturally sensitive and provide culturally appropriate prevention, outreach, assessment and intervention.
- "Cultural competence" recognizes the broad scope of the dimensions that influence an individual's personal identity.

Understanding culture is critical for mental health counselors because both our cultural orientation and our client's cultural orientation are present in every interaction. Too often, assumptions about a person's beliefs or behaviors are made based on a single cultural indicator, particularly race or ethnicity. When in reality, cultural identities are a complex weave of all the cultural groups in which a person belongs to that influence their values, beliefs, and behaviors.

"Cultural identity" is constructed within the individual, but continually influenced by the interactions among and between people in society. Sociocultural and historical perspectives that interact with psychological and intrapersonal characteristics form cultural identity.

CULTURAL INTERVENTIONS

CULTURALLY COMPETENT INTERVENTIONS INCLUDE:
- Translated interventions
- Culturally-adapted interventions
- Culturally-specific interventions

RESEARCH
- **Look up each of these terms and write an explanation for each:**
    - **Translated Interventions...**
    - **Culturally Adapted Interventions...**
    - **Culturally Specific Interventions...**
- **Find two examples for each of the above approaches to interventions**

> **SELF-REFLECTION and/or GROUP DISCUSSION:**
> *BALANCING AWARENESS AND KNOWLEDGE AND TRANSLATING INTO SKILL*
> **We are required to be knowledgeable...**
> **SO...**
> - How do we go about gaining this knowledge?
> - What are best practice's resources, ideas, methods, etc, for acquiring knowledge?
>
> **THEN...**
> - How do we balance this knowledge against the unique experiences of each client's association with their culture—*sensitive to the clients' narratives*?

COMPETENCIES AND GROUP WORK

"Group work" includes the following: Principles of group dynamics, including group process components, developmental stage theories, group members' roles and behaviors, and therapeutic factors of group work.

Techniques should be congruent with the group's goals and purposes and group leaders must recognize their competencies and work only with groups they are trained and experienced to work with; collaborating with an experienced co-leader may reduce potential risks. Counselors must give potential group members enough information to make informed choices about participating in the group; this might include discussing the inclusion of emotionally disturbed individuals in the group. It is important to adequately screen, select, and prepare members for the group and keep specific treatment notes for each group member.

> **RESEARCH**
> - ***See what you can find on* group counseling methods, including group counselor orientations and behaviors, appropriate selection criteria and methods, and methods of evaluation of effectiveness.**
>   - **In work with groups, the rights of each group member should be safeguarded.** *The need for each member to respect the confidentiality of each other member of the group must be stressed.*

ETHICAL STANDARDS & CLINICAL FORMS

> **RESEARCH** *(for Group Therapy information on page 197)*
> - **Find an example of a group therapy consent form**
>   - **What would you change, or add, to the consent?**

COMPETENCIES AND FAITH-BASED COUNSELING

If you are providing a "faith-based" counseling service, be sure your informed consent provides information on the type of faith-based counseling provided.

Also, consider joining an association relevant to the type of faith-based counseling you provide.

> **RESEARCH**
> - **Take the time to explore faith-based association codes of ethics, if you are in this type of counseling**

COMPETENCIES AND EDUCATION

CAREER DEVELOPMENT INCLUDES THE FOLLOWING:

Various career development theories and decision-making models; career development program planning, organization, implementation, administration, and evaluations. Additionally, interrelationships among and between work, family, and other life roles and factors, including the role of multicultural issues in career development; career and educational planning, assessment instruments and techniques relevant to career planning and decision making; and career counseling processes, techniques, and resources.

COMPETENCIES AND ASSESSMENTS

ASSESSMENT REQUIRES KNOWLEDGE:
- Understands various models and approaches to clinical evaluation for disorders and their appropriate uses, including screening and assessment for addiction, diagnostic interviews, mental status examination, symptom inventories, and psycho-educational and personality assessments.
- Counselors must know specific assessment approaches for determining the appropriate level of care for disorders and related problems.
- Counselors need to understand the assessment of bio/psychosocial and spiritual histories, and understand basic classifications, indications, and contradictions of commonly prescribed psychopharmacological medications so that appropriate referrals can be made for medication evaluations, and so side effects of such medications can be identified.

ASSESSMENT REQUIRES SKILLS:
- Counselors select appropriate comprehensive assessment interventions to assist in diagnosis and treatment planning, with an awareness of cultural bias in the implementation and interpretation of assessment protocols.
- Counselors must demonstrate skills in conducting an intake interview, a mental status evaluation, a bio/psychosocial history, a mental health history, a psychological assessment for treatment planning and case management and a cultural formation interview.
- Screens for psychoactive substance toxicity, intoxication, and withdrawal symptoms; aggression or danger to others; potential for self-inflicted harm or suicide; and co-occurring mental and/or addictive disorders.
- Help clients identify the effects of addiction on life problems and the effects of continued harmful use or abuse.
- Apply the assessments of clients' addictive disorders to the stages of dependence, change, or recovery to determine the appropriate treatment modality and placement criteria in the continuum of care.

ASSESSMENTS INCLUDE THE FOLLOWING INFORMATION:

Historical perspectives; basic concepts of standardized and non-standardized testing and other assessment techniques, including norm-referenced and criterion-referenced assessment, environmental assessment, performance assessment, individual and group test methods, psychological testing, and behavioral observations; statistical concepts, including scales of measurement, measures of central tendency; social and cultural factors related to the assessment and evaluation of individuals, groups, and specific populations; and ethical techniques in counseling.

COMPETENCIES AND RESEARCH

RESEARCH AND EVALUATION REQUIRES KNOWLEDGE:
- Counselors need to understand how to critically evaluate research relevant to the practice of counseling.

RESEARCH AND EVALUATION REQUIRES SKILLS:
- Counselors apply relevant research findings to inform the practice of counseling.
- Counselors develop measurable outcomes, interventions, and treatments and they analyzes and use data to increase the effectiveness of counseling programs.

RESEARCH AND EVALUATIONS INCLUDE THE FOLLOWING:
Qualitative, quantitative, single-case designs, action research, and outcome-based research; statistical methods used in conducting research and program evaluation; principles, models, and applications of needs assessment, program evaluation, and how the use of research findings affects program modifications; the use of research to identify evidence-based practice; and ethical and culturally relevant strategies for interpreting and reporting the results of research and/or program evaluation studies.

COMPETENCIES AND DIAGNOSIS

DIAGNOSIS REQUIRES KNOWLEDGE:
- Counselors know the principles of the diagnostic process, including differential diagnosis, and the use of current diagnostic tools, such as the Diagnostic and Statistical Manual of Mental Disorders (DSM).
- Counselors know the impact of co-occurring addictive disorders on medical and psychological disorders.
- Counselors understand the relevance and potential cultural biases of commonly used diagnostic tools as related to clients with disorders in multicultural populations.
- Counselors are clear about current definitions for mental disorders.

DIAGNOSIS REQUIRES SKILLS:
- Counselors demonstrate the appropriate use of diagnostic tools, including the current edition of the DSM, to describe the symptoms and clinical presentation of clients with disorders and mental and emotional impairments.
- Counselors are able to conceptualize an accurate diagnosis of disorders presented by clients and communicate the diagnosis with collaborating professionals.

COMPETENCIES AND CONSULTATIONS

- Counselors must be a part of and utilize consultation with colleagues .
- Identify who you consult with in your consent form.
- Get authorization to consult (if in private practice and/or you haven't identified a consultation group in the consent.
- Reluctance to consult with colleagues can be a warning sign of impairment or boundary violations.
- Don't limit consultation to colleagues who you think will agree with you.
- On-line consultation groups are now available.
- Consultation provides feedback on your thinking: What are you not considering? Are you missing something?
- Document all consultations as it documents your efforts to adhere to standard of care and best practices.

Counselors provide services and represent themselves as competent within the boundaries of their education, training, license, certification(s), consultation(s) received, supervised experience(s), or other relevant professional experience

RETAINING COMPETENCY
Throughout the years...

MAINTAINING CLINICAL COMPETENCE
- Education and Continuing Education
- Advanced Training and Clinical Supervision
- Clinical experience... the learning curve
- Commitment to your Ethical Standards

COMPETENCE IN PROVIDING SERVICES
- Counselors should provide services and represent themselves as competent within the boundaries of their education, training, license, certification, consultation received, supervised experience, or other relevant professional experience.

COMPETENCE IN ACCEPTING EMPLOYMENT
- Counselors should accept responsibility or employment only on the basis of existing competence or the intention to acquire the necessary competence.

RETAINING COMPETENCY: GUIDING PRINCIPLES

MENTAL HEALTH PROFESSIONALS...

- Promote optimal quality of life for people with mental health problems and mental disorders.
- Focus on clients and the achievement of positive outcomes for them.
- Recognize clients', family members' and/or care-givers' unique physical, emotional, social, cultural and spiritual dimensions and work with them to develop their own supports in the community.
- Learn about and value the lived experiences of clients, family members and/or care-givers.
- Recognize and value the healing potential in the relationship between clients and service providers and care-givers and service providers.
- Recognize the human rights of people with mental health problems and mental disorders as proclaimed by the United Nations Principles on the Protection of People with a Mental Illness.
- Wherever possible, ensure equitable access to appropriate mental health services when and where they are needed and notify service managers of any gaps in service delivery.
- Encourage decision-making by clients about their treatment and care.
- Maintain an in-depth knowledge of support services in the community and develop partnerships with other organizations and service providers to ensure continuity of care.
- Involve clients, family members, care-givers and the local community in mental health service planning, development, implementation and evaluation.
- Are aware of, and implement best practice and continual quality improvement processes.
- Ensure clinical practice is driven by the evidence base where this exists.
- Provide comprehensive, coordinated and individualized care that considers all aspects of a client's recovery.
- Participate in professional development activities and reflect acquired learning(s) in practice.

RESEARCH
- **What is your plan for maintaining professional competencies?**
- **What could you add to this list?**

WARNING SIGNS of QUESTIONABLE THERAPY AND UNETHICAL COUNSELING

THESE ARE RED FLAGS, VIOLATIONS OF STATE REGULATIONS, ETHICAL TENETS, AND PROFESSIONAL STANDARDS DESIGNED TO PROTECT CLIENTS:

- Counselor does not have sufficient and specific training to address client issues and/or attempts to treat problems outside the scope of their practice.
- Counselor is not interested in the changes client wants to make and their goals for therapy.
- Counselor cannot or does not clearly define how they can help a client solve whatever issue or concern they have brought to therapy.
- Counselor provides no explanation of how to identify when therapy is complete.
- Counselor does not seek consultation with other counselors.
- Counselor makes guarantees and/or promises.
- Counselor does not provide client with information about their rights as a client, confidentiality, office policies, and fees so they can fairly consent to your treatment.
- Counselor is judgmental or critical of clients' behaviors, lifestyles, or problems.
- Counselor knowingly or unknowingly gets his/her own psychological needs met at the expense of the client.
- Counselor tries to be a client's friend.
- Counselor initiates touch without consent.
- Counselor attempts to have a sexual or romantic relationship with client.
- Counselor talks excessively about himself and/or self-discloses often without any therapeutic purpose.
- Counselor tries to enlist client's help with something not related to therapy.
- Counselor discloses client identifying information without authorization or mandate.
- Counselor tells the identities of his or her other clients.
- Counselor cannot accept feedback or admit mistakes.
- Counselor often speaks in complex "psychobabble" which leaves client confused.
- Counselor acts as if he or she has the answers or solutions to everything and spends time telling the client how to best fix or change things.

- Counselor encourages client dependency by allowing them to get their emotional needs meet from the counselor.
- Counselor seems overwhelmed with the client's problems.
- Counselor believes that only their counseling approach works and ridicules other approaches to therapy.
- Counselor is not sensitive to client culture/religion.
- Counselor denies or ignores the importance of client's spirituality.
- Counselor seems over-emotional, affected, or triggered by client's feelings or issues.
- Counselor does not ask client's permission to use various psychotherapeutic techniques.

RESEARCH
- **The above list is comprehensive; however, can you think of anything to add?**
- **Would this list be a good tool for self-assessing competencies?**

THERAPY ERRORS: GOOD THERAPY IS IMPERFECT

The phrase "good therapy" encourages a misconception—the idea that there is such a thing as pure good therapy, a process exempt of any problems or issues. In the same way, a good relationship is not one without problems, but rather one that works through problems. No counselor is perfect and no therapy can be provided perfectly, no matter how ideal a therapy may be in theory. Even those counselors who do the best they can to be conscious of their inner world and attuned to the therapeutic process, have aspects they are unaware of, pieces of themselves unhealed.

Therapy is the sum of all the experiences, internal and external, occurring as a result of the imperfect counseling process. What a blessing it is that even the best therapy can be lined with areas of unawareness, mistakes, challenges to the therapeutic relationship, and yet, so often, it still turns out well.

SOMETIMES WE CAN'T HELP

Never give up hope that a person can heal, but also recognize that you may not be the one to help, that the time may not be right, the client not ready, and that, for whatever reason, the client may never do the work envisioned. So a better concept of good therapy means letting go of pre-conceived outcomes, rigid expectations for ourselves and for the clients we work with, all without giving up hope.

Counselors greet clients with great hope. Counselors have spent countless hours studying the trade, doing their own inner work, mastering techniques, and learning to "be" with the client. But, can counselors work with anyone who walks into their offices?

The responsibility that counselors carry as healers requires each to seek not just consultation, but their own therapy, especially when working with someone who is provoking something significant within them. The danger lies in situations in which counselors are unaware they are unaware, or unaware they are defending against something inside themselves. And because most harbor pockets of unawareness which impact a capacity to remain calm, curious, compassionate, and connected, aspects of "healthy" therapy and "not so healthy" therapy exist together in counseling work. Again, good therapy is a process, not a state, and it is filled with good stuff and, unfortunately, sometimes the not-so good-stuff.

COUNSELING ERRORS

Understanding "therapeutic errors" can improve future performance through the refinement of counseling strategies. Counselors grow by demonstrating what works and by identifying what does not work. Lapses in judgment, mistakes in timing and pace, and misuse of techniques and interventions are instructive because they are fundamental errors suggesting the need to utilize different strategies. A good indication of therapy failure is "when both parties agree there has been no apparent change."

LEARNING FROM THERAPY FAILURE

Rarely does one specific reason explain unsuccessful therapy. Causes of failure are difficult to identify because clients may not know why they felt dissatisfied, or even given such awareness, they often keep silent about the reason for leaving treatment.

The many complexities of the therapeutic encounter itself imply that a number of variables are involved, rather than just one factor.

THE MOST PERVASIVE VARIABLES IN THERAPY FAILURE, WHETHER ALONE OR IN COMBINATION, ARE CATEGORIZED AS:
- Client's behavior
- Therapist's behavior
- Interactive effects between counselor and client
- Sabotaging influences outside of therapy

SELF-REFLECTION and/or GROUP DISCUSSION:
COUNSELOR CAN ASK THEMSELVES THE FOLLOWING QUESTIONS TO HONESTLY ASSESS THEIR WORK:
- What are my expectations of the client? Of myself?
- What does the client expect of me? Of him-or herself?
- Are my expectations congruent with client's expectations?
- What is my investment in this case?
- What do I need from the client?
- How aware am I of timing necessary for process to unfold?
- What reaction is triggered in me by this client?
- What am I doing that is helpful?
- What am I doing that is not helpful?
- How may I be getting in the client's way?
- What changes can I make?
- What outside resources can I tap? Colleagues? Experts? Literature?

Examining clinical work by asking such questions can engender greater receptiveness to new information and discovery.

COMPETENCY PROFILES
Building your Competency Profile...

Building a competency profile, but not identifying how you'll assess a competency like integrity (or any other competency for that matter) is like buying a map to plan your next trip without deciding how you will get there. Without some mode of transportation, the vacation will never begin. So while it might be easy to put pen to paper and list the competencies you want, actually obtaining them is a different story.

ETHICS AND THE REAL WORLD
Creating a Personal Code to Guide Decisions in Work (and Life)

FIRST: Recognize a common human flaw; for love, money, or other "good" reasons, people do violate ethics. Common ethical temptations are to lie, deceive, steal, or harm.

SECOND: Learn the distinctions necessary to reason ethically.
- Prudential (What is prudent or NOT)
- Legal (What is legal or NOT)
- Ethical (What is ethical or NOT)

THIRD: Become aware of the ethical principles you have acquired from your childhoods, cultures, communities, etc.

SELF-REFLECTION and/or GROUP DISCUSSION:
ETHICS AND THE REAL WORLD
A Moment of Remorse... (You will not be asked to share)
Recall an ethical decision in your life that still bothers you or an episode or interaction that sits uncomfortably in your memory.
What was the category of wrong-doing? (Lie, deceive, steal, harm or other)

> **SELF-REFLECTION and/or GROUP DISCUSSION:**
> Choose a current topic/event/counseling situation that addresses an ethically sensitive situation.
> - What combination of prudential, legal, and ethical issues exist?
> - Any apparent rationalizations?
>
> *Rationalizations blur right and wrong actions; devising deceptively attractive and self-satisfying reasons for acting.*

ETHICS AND MENTAL HEALTH CARE

Indeed, professional codes of ethics are fundamental for ethical practice; however, simply knowing these codes is just the beginning. The ability to think critically and apply general ethical principles to specific situations is vital.

PART 3

ETHICAL STANDARDS: MULTICULTURALISM

*Since individuals are a complex weave of
many cultural influences,
it is impossible to define any person
by a single cultural label*

CULTURAL DIVERSITY AND ETHICAL STANDARDS: A MULTICULTURAL APPROACH FOR YOUR PRACTICE

Understanding culture is critical for counselors, because every counselor's, and every client's, individual cultural orientations are both present in every counseling interaction.

The purpose of this information is to define and understand the different factors that impact our cultural identity development; gain a perspective on the ways that others may differ; and, understand difference as something to celebrate and learn about rather than to reject.

By becoming culturally responsive, counselors strive to understand culture, not as a static element, but as an ongoing evolution. Culture affects everyone; because, everyone is "of culture."

SELF-REFLECTION and/or GROUP DISCUSSION:
DIVERSITY QUESTIONS
- In a few words, what does "diversity education" mean to you?
- What are your thoughts as they apply to male/female diversity?
- What are your thoughts as they apply to cultural/ethnic diversity?
- What are your thoughts as they apply to the term "oppression"?

Since individuals are a complex weave of many cultural influences, it is impossible to define any person by a single cultural label.

COMPETENCY AND MULTICULTURALISM

Since 2005, ethical codes have been infused with multiculturalism, diversity concerns, and ethical expectations. Associations had to ask themselves: "How do we need to rethink things in terms of changing population demographics and issues of multiculturalism?" And, "What is missing from current codes that will make code revisions more culturally sensitive?"

ETHICAL STANDARDS & CLINICAL FORMS

Sociologists and anthropologists have identified many basic elements that are present in our cultural interactions. These elements interact with each other and result in patterns of behavior that are shared. Because these elements intersect with the experiences, the histories, and the psychological makeup of each individual, no one person can be pigeon holed by their race, ethnicity, gender or any other single feature. It is in the mix of these features that each person develops individuality and group belonging in unexpected ways. Cultural, historical, experiential and psychological characteristics react with the contexts in which individuals find themselves, further complicating attempts to put people into specific boxes or categories.

TERMS

"Multicultural Counseling" refers to preparation and practices that integrate multicultural and culture-specific awareness, knowledge and skills into counseling interactions. In the context of ethnicity, here are the five major cultural groups in the United States and its territories: African/Black, Asian, Caucasian/European, Hispanic/Latino and Native American or indigenous groups who have historically resided in the Continental USA and its territories. All persons can point to one or more of these macro-level, cultural groups as sources of their cultural heritage. For the aforementioned groups named, ethnicity, and race, are identifiers although oftentimes the terms are interchanged with culture, introducing confusion. But a distinction is made between the terms ethnicity/race and diversity.

"Diversity" refers to other individual differences including age, gender, sexual orientation, religion, physical ability or disability and other characteristics by which someone may prefer to self-define. The term diversity emerged in the mid to late 1980s. The term demographic diversity became shortened to diversity. The problem with the term diversity is that it has been overused, confused with everything from Affirmative Action to political correctness.

"Oppression" is a term that is used to characterizes destructive, difference-driven interactions; an active, vertically oriented, exclusionary process.

"Microaggressions" are the brief and commonplace daily, verbal, behavioral and environmental indignities, whether intentional or unintentional, that communicates hostile, derogatory, or negative (trait driven) slights or insults to the target person or group. While any one microaggression may seem inconsequential, the continuous, accumulating nature of these unpredictable indignities damages health. Microaggressions degrade self-esteem, alter perceptions of reality, affect relationships, and the capacity to trust, as well as, the "willingness to try." Because microaggressions are often perpetrated unconsciously and unintentionally, and are thus "invisible" in the experience of the offender, the recipient's experience most often goes unaddressed, and therefore unresolved.

"Marginalization" is the process of being relegated to the "sidelines" of society—excluded—as a function of individual or group traits that are targets of oppression. Marginalization reflects the active combination of oppressions and exclusion. It reflects dominant "class codes" for inclusion/exclusion, superiority/inferiority, normality/abnormality, and desirability/undesirability.

DEBATES WITHIN MULTICULTURALISM: DIVERSITY AND ETHICS

The complexity of defining multiculturalism and diversity is influenced by the tremendous differences "within a group" in addition to the differences "between groups." Most certainly, religions, nationalities, disabilities, socioeconomic status, education, political affiliations, and even choice of friends and recreational choices—all can contribute to "within-group" diversity. It is the individual's identification with their culture that should be the focus, and understanding the individual and how they have been impacted by that group membership, as well as understanding how that group membership has affected their life choices.

ETHICAL STANDARDS & CLINICAL FORMS

> **RESEARCH**
> - **Gather for yourself additional information on the terms** *(pages 214-215)*
> - **Find two examples for each of these:** *oppression, microaggressions, and marginalization*
>   - **Why are these concepts important in the counseling process?**

PREJUDICE: "PRE-JUDGMENT"

Prejudice refers to the maintenance of a prior attitude irrespective of new or contradictory information. The more perspectives on an issue that one can consider, the more possibilities exist for solutions. The point is not to look at only one or two different perspectives, but to capture and explore as many different ones as possible. Prejudices interfere with this ability.

OPPRESSION: CLOSED MINDEDNESS

Everyone wants to view themselves as fair, open minded, and responsive to sensible or constructive suggestions. However, the behaviors of most people in stressful situations tend to display high levels of rigidity, narrow-mindedness, and one-sided thinking. It's during these times that defense mechanisms (projection, rationalization, etc.) come into play.

Mental health counselors and service providers must be aware of how stereotypes and stigma influence, not only their clients, but also their own thoughts and views of others.

DISCRIMINATION

FORMS OF DISCRIMINATION INCLUDE:
- Racism
- Ageism
- Sexism
- Heterosexism
- Homophobia
- Classism
- Religious intolerance

> **RESEARCH**
> - Look up the definition for each of the above terms...
> - Are there any others?

GENDER AND SEXUAL IDENTITY

Ideas about gender are impacted as we develop understandings of these roles, along with the values and beliefs associated with gender. Ideas of gender are complex and interdependent upon our membership in cultural groups; many groups have well defined gender roles; others may be less obvious. "Gender roles" reflect one area in which people do change identity over time. A child may be raised in a household that had very defined gender roles, but then leave home and experience a greater flexibility of roles.

SEX DIFFERENCES

In all cultures and ethnic groups, gender boils down to male and female (e.g., the XY (m) XX (f) chromosomes). But there is also "intersex," which is a general term used for a variety of conditions in which a person doesn't seem to fit the typical definitions of female or male. Although, intersex differs from sexual identity, gender identity, and transgender. Counselors should understand that culture affects differences in gender; culture affects sexuality; and culture affects equality and inequality between the sexes.

RESEARCH
Select two or three different cultures...
- **How are women and men valued differently in these different cultures?**
  - **In different aspects of the same culture?**
- **How do the different values placed on women and men affect their lives?**

Our views of ourselves in relation to our personal interests and memberships in social groups can often form the core of our individual cultural identity. Chosen affiliations or hobbies, such as athlete, outdoorsman, cowboy, biker, artist, or environmentalist, can influence our cultural identity development.

Personal interests and memberships in social groups can often form the core of one's individual cultural identity. They develop their individual and cultural identity as they define themselves in relation to their environments, in their relationships with others, and in their participation in groups.

SELF-REFLECTION and/or GROUP DISCUSSION:

CULTURAL BIASES AND STEREOTYPES

In general, discrimination refers to the hostile or negative feelings towards one group from people of another. Stereotyping can cause bias in service provision and can prevent people from seeking help.

Cultural competency must address the biases and stereotypes that are associated with an individual's culture and various identities.

Forms of discrimination include... [What are your thoughts?]

The more perspectives on an issue that one can consider, the more possibilities exist for solutions.

PRINCIPLES RELEVANT TO MULTICULTURALISM

KEY PRINCIPLES:
- There is no checklist of behaviors or beliefs that describes a particular culture.
- Every person should be understood from his/her unique frame of reference.
- All individuals are a dynamic blend of multiple roles and self-identified cultural groups.

"Cultural identity" is constructed within the individual, but continually influenced by the interaction among people in society. Sociocultural and historical perspectives that interact with psychological and intrapersonal characteristics form cultural identity. Culture is a combination of thoughts, feelings, attitudes, beliefs, values, and behavior patterns that are shared by racial, ethnic, religious, or social groups of people. Culture refers not only to the aspects we are born into (racial or ethnic groups), but also those that we choose, such as religious or social groups.

Culture is not static; it is dynamic. We often move between cultures. A person may grow up on a farm, but choose to live in an urban environment. Similarly, one might grow up in a poor family, but become more affluent as an adult. Another cultural shift occurs when children grow up in families in which gender roles are pre-determined, but enter the workforce and adjust their ideas about what acceptable roles for men and women. These are only some examples of the many cultural shifts that occur. These shifts are notable because the contexts in which people find themselves create the opportunity for changes in values, feelings, beliefs, and behaviors.

Individuals who shift cultures often find themselves adopting new customs while retaining elements of their previous cultural experiences. Culture is broader than race and ethnicity. Gender, class, physical and mental abilities, religious and spiritual beliefs, sexual orientation, age and many other factors influence our cultural orientations.

BENEFITS OF BECOMING CULTURALLY RESPONSIVE

THE FOLLOWING BENEFITS ARE COMMON:
- Increased level of comfort with members of different cultures
- Increased knowledge of own culture
- Increased freedom to explore other ways of being
- Increased passions and interests that complement current interests
- Increased capacity to counsel members of diverse cultures
- Increased resources and knowledge

Understanding culture is critical for counselors, because individual cultural orientations (the counselor's/the client's/the family's) are present in every clinical interaction. Too often, assumptions about a person's beliefs or behaviors are based on a single cultural indicator, particularly race or ethnicity, when in reality, cultural identities are a complex weave of all the cultural groups in which a person belongs to that influence their values, beliefs, and behaviors. Cultural identity development is an ongoing process, as people are exposed to more and different sets of beliefs and values, they may choose to adopt ones that were not part of their original upbringing.

RESEARCH

What do these statements mean to you? Gather more information and form your own thoughts/opinions.

- *Usually, when people talk about culture, there is an assumption that they are talking about: African American, Native American, Asian American, and Hispanic/Latino American, and rarely Caucasian/European, but we ALL are members of cultural group combinations, and develop cultural identities based on group memberships and influences.*
- *Cultural identity development is an ongoing process, as we are exposed to more and different sets of beliefs and values, and may choose to adopt ones that were not part of our original upbringing.*

Cultural identity is constructed within the individual, but continually influenced by the interactions among and between people in society; it is formed by sociocultural and historical perspectives that interact with psychological and intrapersonal characteristics.

COMMON ERRORS IN DEMONSTRATING CULTURAL COMPETENCE

Demonstrating ethical behavior in cultural competency can be somewhat challenging and, at times, confusing for mental health counselors, depending on their regional, cultural, and linguistic orientation, and those of the clients they serve.

COMMON ERRORS DEMONSTRATED BY OFTEN WELL MEANING COUNSELORS INCLUDE:
- Miscommunication
- Lack of personal awareness
- Insensitivity to nonverbal cues
- Gender bias
- Overemphasis of cultural explanations for psychological difficulties
- Lapse in including appropriate questions within the cultural context when acquiring background information
- Non-participation in multicultural activities that facilitate cultural awareness that would include inactions among people of similar and different identities
- Inability to identify multiple hypotheses and integrate this information in a culturally competent manner into a client's presenting problem

BECOME CULTURALLY COMPETENT...
- Develop cultural self-awareness
- Appreciate the value of diverse views
- Avoid imposing your own values
- Resist stereotyping

Culture is not static; it is dynamic.
We often move between cultures.

The development of "checklists" that attempt to describe how a particulargroup of people will act, or what they believe, has value for assessments, but not absolution.

RESEARCH

- **Develop cultural self-awareness:** Think about the different factors that have influenced your own cultural identity development. Be aware of cultural values that you hold and understand that others may hold different values.
  - How have cultural factors influenced your beliefs and values?
  - Have your beliefs and values changed over time? Why and how?
- **Appreciate the value of diverse views:** Think about friends or acquaintances that have different values than yours.
  - Can you understand their point of view?
  - Can you accept that their values are different from yours without judging them to be wrong?
  - Think of a specific belief that you hold, then list what other perspectives of that belief might be.
  - Can you identify advantages to holding another perspective?
- **Avoid imposing your own values:** As you become familiar with the values that you hold, and identify the differences in values that others hold, think about how the choices you make are based in your values and beliefs.
  - When observing or interacting with others, and something makes you uncomfortable, resist the urge to make a judgment about the person or behavior; instead, make a conscious effort to understand the perspective they may be coming from.
  - Can you recall a situation that reflects opposing values?
- **Resist stereotyping:** List as many stereotypes as you can think of, including both "positive" and "negative" examples. (Asians are good at math, gay men have an eye for fashion, blondes are dumb, Blacks are natural athletes, women are emotional).
  - Think about people you know who fall in these groups.
  - Consider the accuracy of these statements.
  - Identify groups that you belong to.
- Do stereotypes accurately reflect the way you see yourself?

CULTURE IN THERAPY PRACTICE

Cultural competence is a construct to help counselors improve service delivery by increasing their understanding of "cultural factors." However, what it means to be culturally competent and how to acquire this competence can be confusing, unclear and often elicits conflicting perspectives.

"Negative stereotyping" too often assumes that members of a racial or ethnic group hold a static set of beliefs and values. As an example, many people believe that African-Americans are a distinct racial and cultural group that all hold similar values and have common characteristics. Yet reality illustrates the importance that other influences, beyond racial group membership, also have an impact.

CULTURAL IDENTITY

"Cultural identity" is an individual's focus on their primary influencer. Remember these principles: There is no checklist of behaviors or beliefs that describes a particular culture; every person should be understood from his/her unique frame of reference; and, all individuals are a dynamic blend of multiple roles and identified cultural groups. The development of checklists that attempt to describe how an individual or a group of people will act or what they will value has assessment value, but not absolution.

CULTURAL COMPETENCE

"Cultural competence" is the ability to relate effectively to individuals from various groups and backgrounds. Within the behavioral health system, cultural competence must be a guiding principle, so that services are culturally sensitive and provide culturally appropriate prevention, outreach, assessment and intervention. Cultural competence recognizes the broad scope of the dimensions that influence an individual's personal identity. Mental health counselors should be familiar with how these dimensions interact within, between and among individuals. These dimensions include: Race, ethnicity, language, sexual orientation, gender, age, disability, class and socioeconomic status, education, religious, and spiritual orientation.

Understanding culture is critical for mental health professionals, because everyone's individual cultural orientation is present in every interaction.

As mentioned previously, assumptions about a person's beliefs or behaviors are often made based on a single cultural indicator, particularly race or ethnicity, when in reality, cultural identities are a complex weave of many things that influence their values, beliefs, and behaviors. Cultural identity is constructed within the individual, but continually influenced by the interactions among and between people in society. Sociocultural and historical perspectives that interact with psychological and intrapersonal characteristics form cultural identity. Since individuals are a complex weave of many cultural influences, it is impossible to define any person by a single cultural label. Also, "within group differences" are as significant as "between group differences" in individual cultural identity development. Further, cultural histories are filtered by experience and psychological characteristics, making people unique. Unless we make a conscious effort to learn about and understand the idea of culture and cultural influences on identity development we may assume that our own beliefs and values are normal, privileging our own cultural identities at the expense of those who hold different beliefs or values.

CULTURAL COMPETENCY: AWARENESS, KNOWLEDGE, AND SKILLS

AWARENESS: Counselors are to organize and explore influences of age and generation, developmental or acquired disability, religion and spirituality, ethnicity, socioeconomic status, sexual orientation, indigenous heritage, national origin, and gender. Awareness also includes counselor self-awareness.

KNOWLEDGE: Counselors are encouraged to ask clients directly about their experience of their culture while being careful to consider the balance between the individual and group-based experiences.

SKILLS: Counselors are encouraged to examine cultural influences on the interpersonal interactions between the counselor and client. Counselors are required to use interventions and tools that are culturally competent: Translated interventions, culturally adapted interventions, and culturally specific interventions.

RESEARCH
- Look up the terms (listed below) and write an explanation for each.
  - Translated Interventions...
  - Culturally Adapted Interventions...
  - Culturally Specific Interventions...

- Find two examples for each of the above approaches to interventions.

MULTICULTURAL COUNSELING COMPETENCIES

OPERATIONALIZATION OF THE MULTICULTURAL COUNSELING COMPETENCIES
The Association for Multicultural Counseling and Development (AMCD)
The following information is reprinted with permission.

PERSONAL DIMENSIONS OF IDENTITY

For the past 20 years, the Association for Multicultural Counseling and Development (AMCD) has provided leadership for the American counseling profession, in major sociocultural and sociopolitical domains. Through their vision of the centrality of culture and multiculturalism to the counseling profession, they have created new directions and paradigms for change. One of the major contributions has been the development of the Multicultural Counseling Competencies.

The Dimensions of Personal Identity (A-B-C Dimensions) model can be utilized as a paradigm to see people more completely, as well as an educational tool. It provides a reference point for recognizing the complexity of all persons. The model highlights the different identity-based affiliations, memberships and sub-cultures and, therefore, complements the discussion of multiculturalism.

A DIMENSION

The A Dimension is a listing of characteristics that serve as a profile for the majority of the dimensions we are born with or into, making most "fixed" and less changeable. For example, our age, gender, culture, ethnicity, race and language are pre-determined. We have no control over these when we are born and there is very little we can do to change most of these dimensions. Some research suggests that sexual orientation is biologically based while other data promote a sociocultural explanation. In the model, sexual orientation appears as an A Dimension characteristic. For some individuals, it has been possible to transcend pre-determined roots. Social class status, however, may persist for generations based on one's culture or society. One artifact of social class status is the social register, which accords a listing for some at the time of birth. For better or worse, attributions and judgments are made about all of us based on our social status. At times, this is less visible or known. However, appearances are often used to make assessments of an individual's value. How someone dresses, their "attractiveness" in terms of height, weight, and other physical criteria also interact with A Dimensions.

RESEARCH
For discussion:
- **Would a counselor respond similarly to an overweight, white woman as he/she would to a slim, black woman? How might his/her previous experiences, or lack thereof, with these type of women affect his/her assumptions, comfort and behavior in a counseling encounter?**

Note that the A Dimensions also holds "protected class" status based on government classifications and Equal Employment Opportunity (EEO) and Title VII of the Civil Rights Act of 1964.

The other noteworthy feature of the A Dimension list is that these are the characteristics that most readily engender stereotypes, assumptions, and judgments, both positively and negatively. If placed on a continuum, all of the A Dimensions can bring positive and negative reactions. Because they tend to be more visible, they invite feedback; both wanted and unwanted, from others, thus contributing to clients' self-concepts and self-esteems.

It is the A Dimensions that invites and challenges counselors to operate from a framework of multiculturalism and cultural competence.

In the context of counseling preparation and application, here are the five major cultural groups in the United States and its territories: African/Black, Asian, Caucasian/European, Hispanic/Latino and Native American or indigenous groups who have historically resided in the Continental USA and its territories. All persons can point to one or more of these macro-level, cultural groups as sources of their cultural heritage. For the aforementioned groups named, race and ethnicity are further identifiers although oftentimes the terms are interchanged with culture, introducing confusion.

Because individuals embody all of the A Dimensions, to be culturally effective, counselors need to see individuals holistically, not in terms of color, ethnicity, culture or accent alone. We are complete packages, as will be described with the B and C Dimensions.

C DIMENSION
(B DIMENSION INFORMATION WILL FOLLOW)

The C Dimension is discussed because it encompasses universal and important phenomena. This Dimension indicates first of all, that all individuals must be seen in a context; we do not exist in a vacuum. The C Dimension grounds us in historical, political, sociocultural and economic contexts indicating that events of a sociopolitical, global and environmental form have a way of impacting one's personal culture and life experiences.

Reflecting on the questions and the data that emerge from C Dimension exploration provides individuals with a landscape of their personal history. The time at which one was born also indicates the significant political and environmental incidents that may also affect personal identity. The C Dimension suggests that there are many factors that surround us over which we have no control as individuals, but which will affect us both positively and negatively. These contextual factors, though not seemingly to have a direct impact, do affect the way people are treated and perceived and how they treat others. The C Dimension also invites exploration of institutional oppression and how it continues to occur in contemporary society and counseling sites.

ETHICAL STANDARDS & CLINICAL FORMS

> ### SELF-REFLECTION and/or GROUP DISCUSSION:
>
> Multiculturalism and diversity impacts every area of our life and our practice. It affects our sensitivity toward the people we serve. Sociologists and anthropologists have identified many basic human needs—*to be needed, valued, loved.*
>
> **Norms** (standards for accepted and expected behavior) are prevalent in every culture, and many norms are static across cultural boundaries.
> **What are some of these norms?**
>
> Dimensions intersect with experiences, histories, and the psychological makeup of each individual, no one person can be pigeon holed by their race, ethnicity, gender or any other single feature. It is in the mix of these features that each person develops individuality and group belonging in unexpected ways.
>
> *The time one is born is an historical moment that will never happen again. Be encouraged to think about the following:*
> 1) How was your family life at the time of your birth?
> 2) What was taking place in the local community or in your home country?
> 3) What was going on in the world? (Reflecting on this questions and the data that emerges provides individuals with a landscape of their personal history.)

B DIMENSION

The B Dimension is discussed last because theoretically it may represent the "consequences" of the A and C Dimensions. What occurs to individuals relative to their B Dimension is influenced by some of the immutable characteristics of the A Dimension and the major historical, political, sociocultural, and economic legacies of the C Dimension. The B Dimension also represents possible shared experiences (who we identify with) that might not be observable by stopping with the A Dimension. The B Dimension can be a point of connection. People from the same organization are invariably surprised when they learn that others attended the same university, were also in the military, or have children under five. There are ways that categories (B Dimensions) can actually foster rapport-building between client and counselor than seems apparent. This may depend, however, on the counselor's position of self-disclosure.

A, B, AND C DIMENSIONS SUMMARY

The purpose of this model is to demonstrate the complexity and holism of individuals. It suggests that in spite of the categories we may all fit into or that are assigned to us, the combination of these affiliations is what makes everyone unique. Personal culture is comprised of these different dimensions of identity. By definition and in reality everyone is a "multicultural person."

It is important (not just an ethical requirement or competencies) to understand and appreciate the cultural context of a client. Commonalities result in patterns of behavior that are shared.

Cultural similarities are prevalent in every culture, and many norms are static across cultural boundaries.
- *FRIENDSHIP: People in every culture share some universal norms for friendship.*
- *TRAITS: Around the world, people use similar traits to describe others. People in every culture are described in terms of how outgoing they are, whether they are stable, and if they are open, agreeable, etc.*

RESEARCH
- What other norms are common among various cultures?

Cultural, historical, experiential and psychological characteristics react with the contexts in which an individual finds themselves, further complicating our attempts to put people into specific boxes or categories.

> **OPERATIONALIZATION OF THE MULTICULTURAL COUNSELING COMPETENCIES**
> The Association for Multicultural Counseling and Development (AMCD)
> The following information is reprinted with permission.

COMPETENCY EXPECTATIONS

I. Counselor AWARENESS OF OWN CULTURAL VALUES AND BIASES: ATTITUDES AND BELIEFS

Culturally skilled counselors believe that cultural self-awareness and sensitivity to one's own cultural heritage is essential.

Explanatory Statements

a. Can identify the culture(s) to which they belong and the significance of that membership including the relationship of individuals in that group with individuals from other groups, institutionally, historically, educationally, etc. (Includes A, B, and C Dimensions as do the other suggestions in this section).

b. Can identify the specific cultural group(s) from which counselor derives fundamental cultural heritage and the significant beliefs and attitudes held by those cultures that are assimilated into their own attitudes and beliefs.

c. Can recognize the impact of those beliefs on their ability to respect others different from themselves.

d. Can identify specific attitudes, beliefs and values from their own heritage and cultural learning, which support behaviors that demonstrate respect, and valuing of differences and those that impede or hinder respect and valuing of differences.

Culturally skilled counselors are aware of how their own cultural background and experiences have influenced attitudes, values, and biases about psychological processes.

Explanatory Statements

a. Can identify the history of their culture in relation to educational opportunities and its impact on their current worldview (includes A and some B Dimensions).

b. Can identify at least five personal, relevant cultural traits and can explain how each has influenced cultural values of the counselor.

c. Can identify social and cultural influences on their cognitive development and current information processing styles and can contrast that with those of others (Includes A, B, and C Dimensions).

d. Can identify specific social and cultural factors and events in their history that influence their view and use of social belonging, interpretations of behavior, motivation, problem solving and decision methods, thoughts and behaviors (Including subconscious) in relation to authority and other institutions and can contrast these with the perspectives of others. (A and B Dimensions)

e. Can articulate the beliefs of their own cultural and religious groups around differences, such as sexual orientation, and the impact of these beliefs in a counseling relationship.

Culturally skilled counselors are able to recognize the limits of their multicultural competency and expertise.
Explanatory Statements
a. Can recognize in a counseling or teaching relationship, when and how their attitudes, beliefs and values are interfering with providing the best service to clients. (Primarily A and B Dimensions).
b. Can give real examples of cultural situations in which they recognize their limitations and referred the client to more appropriate resources.

Culturally skilled counselors recognize their sources of discomfort with differences that exist between themselves and clients in terms of race, ethnicity and culture.
Explanatory Statements
a. Able to recognize their sources of comfort/discomfort with respect to differences in terms of race, ethnicity and culture.
b. Can identify at least five specific cultural differences, the needs of culturally different clients, and how these differences are handled in the counseling relationship.

I. Counselor AWARENESS OF OWN CULTURAL VALUES AND BIASES: KNOWLEDGE

Culturally skilled counselors have specific knowledge about their own racial and cultural heritage and how it personally and professionally affects their definitions and biases of normality/abnormality and the process of counseling.
Explanatory Statements
a. Have knowledge regarding their heritage, for example: A Dimensions in terms of ethnicity, language, and so forth, and C Dimensions in terms of knowledge regarding the context of the time period in which their ancestors entered the established United States and/or North American continent.
b. Can recognize and discuss their family and culture's perspectives of acceptable (normal) codes of conduct and what are unacceptable (abnormal) and how this may or may not vary from those of other cultures and families.
c. Can identify at least five specific features of culture-of-origin and explain how those features impact the relationship with culturally different clients.

Culturally skilled counselors possess knowledge and understanding about how oppression, racism, discrimination, and stereotyping affect them personally and in their work. This allows individuals to acknowledge their own racist attitudes, beliefs, and feelings. Although this standard applies to all groups, for White counselors it may mean that they understand how they may have directly or indirectly benefited from individual, institutional, and cultural racism as outlined in White identity development models.

Explanatory Statements

a. Can specifically identify, name, and discuss privileges that they personally receive in society due to their race, socioeconomic background, gender, physical abilities, sexual orientation, and so forth.
b. Specifically referring to White counselors, can discuss White identity development models and how they relate to one's personal experiences.
c. Can provide a reasonably specific definition of racism, prejudice, discrimination and stereotype. Can describe a situation in which they have been judged on something other than merit. Can describe a situation in which they have judged someone on something other than merit.

Culturally skilled counselors possess knowledge about their social impact upon others. They are knowledgeable about communication style differences, how styles may clash with or foster the counseling process with persons of color or others different from themselves based on the A, B and C Dimensions, and how to anticipate the impact it may have on others.

Explanatory Statements

a. Can describe the A and B Dimensions of Personal Identity with which they most strongly identify.
b. Can behaviorally define their communication style and describe both their verbal and nonverbal behaviors, interpretations of others behaviors, and expectations.
c. Recognize the cultural bases (A Dimension) of their communication style and the differences between their style and the styles of those people different from themselves.
d. Can describe the behavioral impact and reaction of their communication style on clients different from themselves.
e. Can give examples of an incident where communication broke down with a client of color and hypothesize about the causes.
f. Can give 3-5 concrete examples of situations in which they modified their communication style to compliment that of a culturally different client, how they decided on the modification, and the result of that modification.

I. Counselor AWARENESS OF OWN CULTURAL VALUES AND BIASES: SKILLS

Culturally skilled counselors seek out educational, consultative, and training experiences to improve their understanding and effectiveness in working with culturally different populations. Being able to recognize the limits of their competencies, they (a) seek consultation, (b) seek further training or education, (c) refer out to more qualified individuals or resources, or (d) engage in a combination of these.

Explanatory Statements
a. Maintain an active referral list and continuously seek new referrals relevant to different needs of clients along A and B Dimensions.
b. Understand and communicate to the client that the referral is being made because of the counselor's limitations rather than communicating that it is caused by the client.
c. Actively consult regularly with other professionals regarding issues of culture in order to receive feedback about issues and situations and whether or where referral may be necessary.

Culturally skilled counselors are constantly seeking to understand themselves as racial and cultural beings and are actively seeking a non-racist identity.

Explanatory Statements
a. When receiving feedback the counselor demonstrates a receptivity and willingness to learn.

> **SELF-REFLECTION and/or GROUP DISCUSSION:**
> **BALANCING THE CORNERSTONES OF ETHICS:**
> Do no harm; Do not exploit; Do not impair your judgment
> We must be self-aware (we are not immune from the culture in which we were raised)...
> **SO...**
> What are the options when a client presents a dilemma, issue, concern, condition that triggers unexpected counselor biases?
> - When should you refer?
> - How do you communicate that necessity for referral to the client?
>
> *We do not rely on clients for our cultural education; however, we do rely on clients for their cultural experience*

COMPETENCY EXPECTATIONS

II. Counselor AWARENESS OF CLIENT'S WORLDVIEW ATTITUDES AND BELIEFS

Culturally skilled counselors are aware of their negative and positive emotional reactions toward other racial and ethnic groups that may prove detrimental to the counseling relationship. They are willing to contrast their own beliefs and attitudes with those of their culturally different clients in a non-judgmental fashion.

Explanatory Statements

a. Identify their common emotional reactions about individuals and groups different from themselves and observe their own reactions in encounters.

b. Can articulate how their personal reactions and assumptions are different from those who identify with that group (e.g., if the reaction upon approaching three young African American males is fear, what is the reaction of a young African American male or female in the same situation? What might the reaction be of an African American female approaching a group of White young men?).

c. Can describe at least two distinct examples of cultural conflict between self and culturally different clients, including how these conflicts were used as "content" for counseling.

Culturally skilled counselors are aware of their stereotypes and preconceived notions that they may hold toward other racial and ethnic minority groups.
Explanatory Statements
a. Recognize their stereotyped reactions to people different than themselves. (e.g., silently articulating their awareness of a negative stereotypical reaction).
b. Can give specific examples of how their stereotypes (including "positive" ones).
c. Recognize assumptions of those in a similar cultural group but who may differ based on A or B Dimension.

II. Counselor AWARENESS OF CLIENT'S WORLDVIEW
KNOWLEDGE

Culturally skilled counselors possess specific knowledge and information about the particular group with which they are working. They are aware of the life experiences, cultural heritage, and historical background of their culturally different clients. This particular competency is strongly linked to the "minority identity development models" available in the literature.
Explanatory Statements
a. Can articulate (objectively) differences in nonverbal and verbal behavior of the five major different cultural groups most frequently seen in their experience of counseling.
b. Can describe at least two different models of "minority identity development" and their implications for counseling with persons of color or others who experience oppression or marginalization.
c. Can identify within-group differences and assess various aspects of individual clients to determine individual differences as well as cultural differences.
d. Can discuss viewpoints of other cultural groups regarding issues such as sexual orientation, physical ability/disability, gender, and aging.

Culturally skilled counselors understand how race, culture, ethnicity, and so forth may affect personality formation, vocational choices, and manifestation of psychological disorders, help seeking behavior, and the appropriateness or inappropriateness of counseling approaches.

Explanatory Statements

a. Can distinguish cultural differences and expectations regarding role and responsibility in family, participation of family in career decision making, appropriate family members to be involved when seeking help, culturally acceptable means of expressing emotion and anxiety, and so forth. (Primarily along A Dimension and portions of B Dimension).

b. Based on literature about A Dimensions, can describe and give examples of how a counseling approach may or may not be appropriate for a specific group of people based primarily upon an A Dimension.

c. Understand and can explain the historical point of contact with dominant society for various ethnic groups and the impact of the type of contact (enslaved, refugee, seeking economic opportunities, conquest, etc.) on potential relationships and trust when seeking help from dominant culture institutions.

d. Can describe one system of personality development, the populations(s) on which the theory was developed, and how this system relates or does not relate to at least two culturally different populations.

e. Can identify the role of gender, socioeconomic status, and physical disability as they interact with personality formation across cultural groups.

Culturally skilled counselors understand and have knowledge about sociopolitical influences that impinge upon the life of racial and ethnic minorities. Immigration issues, poverty, racism, stereotyping, and powerlessness may impact self-esteem and self-concept in the counseling process.

Explanatory Statements

a. Can identify implications of concepts such as internalized oppression, institutional racism, privilege, and the historical and current political climate regarding immigration, poverty, and welfare (public assistance).

b. Understand the economic benefits and contributions gained by the work of various groups, including migrant farm workers, to the daily life of the counselor and the country at large.

c. Can communicate an understanding of the unique position, constraints and needs of those clients who experience oppression based on an A or B dimension alone (and families of clients) who share this history.

d. Can identify current issues (social climates) that impact groups of people (A and B Dimensions) to whom the counselor may be providing services.

e. Are aware of legal legislation issues and legal rights that impact various communities and populations
f. Counselors are aware of how documents such as the book, The Bell Curve, and affirmative action legislation impact society's perception of different cultural groups.

II. Counselor AWARENESS OF CLIENT'S WORLDVIEW
SKILLS

Culturally skilled counselors should familiarize themselves with relevant research and the latest findings regarding mental health and mental disorders that affect various ethnic and racial groups. They should actively seek out educational experiences that enrich their knowledge, understanding, and cross-cultural skills for more effective counseling behavior.

Explanatory Statements
a. Can identify at least five multicultural experiences in which counselor has participated within past three years.
b. Can identify professional growth activities and information, which is presented by professionals respected and seen as credible by members of the communities being studied.

Culturally skilled counselors become actively involved with minority individuals outside the counseling setting (e.g., community events, social and political functions, celebrations, friendships, neighborhood groups, and so forth) so that their perspective of minorities is more than an academic or helping exercise.

Explanatory Statements
a. Actively plan experiences and activities that will contradict negative stereotypes and preconceived notions they may hold.

ETHICAL STANDARDS & CLINICAL FORMS

COMPETENCY EXPECTATIONS

III. Culturally APPROPRIATE <u>INTERVENTION STRATEGIES</u>
BELIEFS AND ATTITUDES

Culturally skilled counselors respect clients' religious and/ or spiritual beliefs and values, including attributions and taboos, because they affect worldview, psychosocial functioning, and expressions of distress.

Explanatory Statements

a. Can identify the positive aspects of spirituality (in general) in terms of wellness and healing aspects.
b. Can identify in a variety of religious and spiritual communities the recognized form of leadership and guidance and their client's relationship (if existent) with that organization and entity.

Culturally skilled counselors respect indigenous helping practices and respect help-giving networks among communities of color.

Explanatory Statements

a. Can describe concrete examples of how they may integrate and cooperate with indigenous helpers when appropriate.

Culturally skilled counselors value bilingualism and do not view another language as an impediment to counseling (monolingualism may be the culprit).

Explanatory Statements

a. Communicate to clients and colleagues values and assets of bilingualism (if client is bilingual).

III. Culturally APPROPRIATE INTERVENTION STRATEGIES
KNOWLEDGE

Culturally skilled counselors have a clear and explicit knowledge and understanding of the generic characteristics of counseling and therapy (culture bound, class bound, and monolingual) and how they may clash with the cultural values of various cultural groups.

Explanatory Statements

a. Can identify, within various theories, the cultural values, beliefs and assumptions made about individuals and contrast these with values, beliefs, and assumptions of different racial and cultural groups.

b. Can identify and describe primary indigenous helping practices in terms of positive and effective role.

Culturally skilled counselors are aware of institutional barriers that prevent minorities from using mental health services.
Explanatory Statements
a. Can describe concrete examples of institutional barriers within their organization that prevent minorities from using mental health services and share those examples with colleagues and decision-making bodies within the institution.
b. Can identify and communicate possible alternatives that would reduce or eliminate existing barriers.

Culturally skilled counselors have knowledge of the potential bias in assessment instruments and use procedures and interpret findings keeping in mind the cultural and linguistic characteristics of the clients.
Explanatory Statements
a. Demonstrate ability to interpret assessment results including implications of dominant cultural values affecting assessment/interpretation, interaction of cultures for those who are bicultural, and impact of historical institutional oppression.
b. Can discuss information regarding cultural, racial, gender profile of normative group used for validity and reliability on any assessment used by counselor.
c. Use assessment instruments appropriately with clients having limited English skills.

Culturally skilled counselors have knowledge of family structures, hierarchies, values, and beliefs from various cultural perspectives. They are knowledgeable about the community where a particular cultural group may reside
and the resources in the community.
Explanatory Statements
a. Are aware of legal issues that impact various communities and populations.

ETHICAL STANDARDS & CLINICAL FORMS

III. Culturally APPROPRIATE INTERVENTION STRATEGIES
SKILLS

Culturally skilled counselors are able to engage in a variety of verbal and nonverbal helping responses. They are able to send and receive both verbal and nonverbal messages accurately and appropriately. They are not tied down to only one method or approach to helping, but recognize that helping styles and approaches may be culture bound. When they sense that their helping style is limited and potentially inappropriate, they can anticipate and modify it.

Explanatory Statements

a. Can articulate what, when, why and how they apply different verbal and nonverbal helping responses based on A and B Dimensions.
b. Can identify and describe techniques in which they have expertise for providing service that may require minimal English language skills (e.g., expressive therapy).
c. Can discuss with the client aspects of their religious/spiritual beliefs that have been helpful to the client in the past.

Culturally skilled counselors are able to exercise institutional intervention skills on behalf of their clients. They can help clients determine whether a "problem" stems from racism or bias in others (the concept of healthy paranoia) so that clients do not inappropriately personalize problems.

Explanatory Statements

a. Can recognize and discuss examples in which racism or bias may actually be imbedded in an institutional system or society.
b. Communicate to clients an understanding of the necessary coping skills and behaviors viewed by dominant society as dysfunctional that they may need to keep intact.
c. Can describe concrete examples of situations in which it is appropriate and possibly necessary for a counselor to exercise institutional intervention skills on behalf of a client.

Culturally skilled counselors are not averse to seeking consultation with traditional healers or religious and spiritual leaders and practitioners in the treatment of culturally different clients when appropriate.

Explanatory Statements

a. Participate or gather adequate information regarding indigenous or community helping resources to make appropriate referrals (e. g., be familiar with the American Indian community enough to recognize when, how and to whom it may be appropriate to refer a client to indigenous healers).

Culturally skilled counselors take responsibility for interacting in the language requested by the client and, if not feasible, make appropriate referrals. A serious problem arises when the linguistic skills of the counselor do not match the language of the client. This being the case, counselors should (a) seek a translator with cultural knowledge and appropriate professional background or (b) refer to a knowledgeable and competent bilingual counselor.

Explanatory Statements

a. Are familiar with resources that provide services in languages appropriate to clients.
b. Will seek out, whenever necessary, services or translators to ensure that language needs are met.
c. If working within an organization, actively advocate for the hiring of bilingual counselors relevant to client population.

Culturally skilled counselors have training and expertise in the use of traditional assessment and testing instruments. They not only understand the technical aspects of the instruments but also are aware of the cultural limitations. This allows them to use test instruments for the welfare of culturally different clients.

Explanatory Statements

a. Demonstrate ability to interpret assessment results including implications of dominant cultural values affecting assessment/interpretation, interaction of cultures for those who are bicultural, and the impact of historical institutional oppression.
b. Understand that although an assessment instrument may be translated into another language, the translation may be literal without an accurate contextual translation including culturally relevant connotations and idioms.

Culturally skilled counselors should attend to as well as work to eliminate biases, prejudices, and discriminatory contexts in conducting evaluations and providing interventions, and should develop sensitivity to issues of oppression, sexism, heterosexism, elitism and racism.

Explanatory Statements

a. Recognize incidents in which clients, students and others are being treated unfairly based on race, ethnicity, and physical disability, and take action by directly addressing the incident or perpetrator, filing informal complaint, filing formal complaint, and so forth.

ETHICAL STANDARDS & CLINICAL FORMS

Culturally skilled counselors take responsibility for educating their clients to the processes of psychological intervention, such as goals, expectations, legal rights, and the orientation.
Explanatory Statements
a. Assess the client's understanding and familiarity with counseling and mental health services and provides accurate information regarding the process, limitations, and function of the services into which the client is entering.
b. Ensure that the client understands client rights, issues and definitions of confidentiality, and expectations placed upon that client. In this educational process, counselors adapt information to ensure that all concepts are clearly understood by client. This may include defining and discussing these concepts.

RESEARCH
What do these statements mean to you? Gather more information and form your own thoughts/opinions.
- **The subject of culture in counseling is an ethical requirement for all counselors. Counselors working with specific cultures are ethically required to understand the culture-embedded indigenous healing practices, culture-influenced psychotherapies, cultural elements in mainstream therapies, the practice of counseling in different societies, and intercultural psychotherapies. Cultural-relevant counseling requires technical adjustment, theoretical modifications, and philosophical reconsideration is.**
- **Counselors should be aware of the contents in their professional associations' official publications, such as a newsletter or journal articles, regarding such interventions. Counselors are not required to follow the recommendations or guidelines in such publications, but they are expected to be aware of them and, when appropriate, consider them in their clinical and ethical decision-making processes.**

FAMILY STORIES-LEGACIES

For better or worse, we are shaped by our family's notion(s) of our identity. The image that our family mirrors back to us exists earlier and is often more substantial than our own. Family is our first effort to enter into a group (our family), and absorb without resisting. Our next effort, often years later, is to distinguish ourselves from the family.

We can never be entirely self-inventive. But we can reach independently for what is at hand—to discover who we are as separate, as well as who we are in our connectedness.

"Family stories" are monuments of history or slices of sociology. In counseling, helping a client discover who they are can often begin with an exploration of family stories. Family stories offer starting points for individual discoveries.

FAMILIAL ROLES

Beliefs vary between cultures—beliefs about providing for oneself, the young, the old; who protects whom; and, the age at which a person is expected to become autonomous. Different standards also exist, such as perspectives on caring for elderly family members. There are limitless family types in which individuals may be raised: Traditional (biological mom, dad, and kids), single parent, stepparent (blended), foster, grandparent, adoption, same sex. What constitutes "family" is ever-evolving.

LIFE CYCLES

The age at which children are seen to be mature enough to handle adult responsibilities varies significantly across cultural groups. In many cultures, young adolescents are seen as old enough to be responsible for themselves, and even for other members of the family.

STATUS OF AGE

Some cultural groups will show a general respect for all members of that culture, regardless of age. Others treat respect in a more hierarchical fashion: younger members given less respect; plder embers are greatly respected.

SELF-REFLECTION and/or GROUP DISCUSSION:

Stories are there within all of us and within our clients and they mean something, but they acquire an additional dimension once we ask the question to which of these stories do I agree with; which are part of who I am.

FAMILY TIES
How a person sees themselves in the context of family; who is considered part of the family, roles within the family, responsibility towards family members. How did you feel tied to and into your family of origin?

FAMILY STATUS
Family status has a significant impact on individual cultural identity development. How and why?

TABOOS
Attitudes and beliefs about doing things against culturally accepted patterns. Discussions about politics, religion, sexuality, or family issues may be taboo. What was taboo in your family of origin?

While some groups value the individual achievement of members, others value the collective actions of the family or group. Group members may feel obligated to place the needs of family or community above their own personal needs or goals.

RESEARCH
What does this statement mean to you? Gather more information and form your own thoughts/opinions.
- **Family is our first effort to enter into a group (our family), and absorb without resisting. Our next effort, often years later, is to distinguish ourselves from the family's myths and ideas. To reach independently for what is at hand—*to reach independently to discover who we are as separate.***

SPIRITUALITY

Adequacy of a counselor's understanding regarding the scope of spiritual concerns and client's cultural differences is now required. Every counselor needs to ask himself or herself if they lack a conceptual and professional awareness of cultures (which includes spirituality), an awareness and knowledge that would provide a critical link to effective responsiveness to clients.

> *The United States was founded on the idea that individual choice*
> *and expression of religious belief are inalienable rights,*
> *which contribute significantly to our cultural identity.*

Given that culture is a combination of beliefs, values, attitudes, and behavior patterns, and that for many, religion/faith is a primary source of guidelines, it seems logical that beliefs play an important role in an individual's conception of themselves as cultural beings.

A critical variable for men and women is reflected in their relatedness to spirituality or religious practices. When spirituality/religion are a significant part of one's cultural surroundings, it informs meaning, value, and direction for their issues.

RESEARCH

What do these statements mean to you? Gather more information and form your own thoughts/opinions.

- The United States was founded on the idea that individual choice and expression of religious beliefs is an unalienable right; these beliefs and practice contribute significantly to our cultural identity. Given that culture is a combination of beliefs, values, attitudes, and behavior patterns, and that for many, religion is the primary source of these...it seems that religion must play an important role in our individual conception of ourselves as cultural beings.
- A critical variable for many men and women is reflected in their relatedness to spirituality or religious practices. Spirituality/religion is a part of one's cultural surroundings and informs meaning, value and direction of human issues.

Standard of care is a particularly difficult issue in psychotherapy, as there are hundreds of different orientations and approaches to treatment

CULTURE AND THERAPEUTIC INTERVENTIONS

Consensus is hard to come by when there are hundreds of "therapeutic orientations and interventions." There still remains issues/debates in regards to the identification of treatment protocols that have been called Empirically Supported Therapies (EST) or Evidence-based Therapies (EBT). Even these protocols have been criticized for their lack of validity, narrow focus, and even for being biased and discriminatory against therapeutic orientations that have not be standardized or cannot be easily quantified.

Counselors should be aware of the contents in their professional associations' official publications, such as website-provided information, newsletters, or journal articles, regarding various interventions. Counselors are not required to follow the recommendations or guidelines in such publications, but they are expected to be aware of them and, when appropriate, consider them in their clinical and ethical decision-making processes.

"Standard of care" is a particularly difficult issue in counseling, as there are hundreds of different orientations and approaches to treatment. Each approach is based on different orientations, methodologies, philosophies, belief systems, and even world views. Beyond these things: 1) The cornerstones of ethics: Do no harm, do not exploit the client, and do not continue counseling if your professional judgment is impaired; and, 2) The client's rights that counselors honor, such as respect clients' dignity, and privacy; and, work in the client's best interest, there is no consensus on how to intervene, or help. For example, there is no one standard, or method, or specific approach for the treatment of anxiety. There are best practices, but psychoanalysis, cognitive-behavioral, existential, biologically-based psychiatry, and faith-based counseling all define, explain, and treat anxiety in very different terms.

> *In addition to all of this, counselors must consider cultural orientations and provide culturally appropriate interventions.*

The subject of culture in counseling is an ethical requirement for all counselors. Counselors working with specific cultures are ethically required to understand the culture-embedded indigenous healing practices, culture-influenced psychotherapies, cultural elements in mainstream therapies, the practice of counseling in different societies, and intercultural psychotherapies. Cultural-relevant counseling requires technical adjustment, theoretical modifications, and philosophical reconsiderations.

SELF-REFLECTION and/or GROUP DISCUSSION:

Three broad approaches to the development of culturally sensitive therapy programs:
- Rendering western traditional treatments more accessible to other cultural groups.
- Selecting available therapeutic modalities according to the features of a culture.
- Extracting elements from a culture to modify traditional treatments or to use them as an innovative treatment tool.

Fundamental approach to exploring interventions and cultures:
How is the relationship between culture and therapy conceived by clinical practitioners and how should interventions be adapted/developed for specific cultures?

Question for discussion:
- Must the content of all culturally sensitive therapies stand in mirror-like relationship to the client's culture?

THE CULTURAL FORMULATION INTERVIEW (CFI)
For this assessment tool and many others: www.psychiatry.org/dsm5

The Cultural Formation Interview is a set of questions that counselors may use to obtain information during a mental health assessment about the impact of a client's culture on key aspects of care.

In the CFI, culture refers primarily to the values, orientations, and assumptions that individuals derive from membership in diverse social groups (e.g., ethnic groups, the military, faith communities), that which they may conform to or differ from.

The term culture also refers to aspects of a person's background that may affect his or her perspective, such as ethnicity, race, language, or religion.

The CFI focuses on the client's perspectives on the problem, the role of others in influencing the course of the problem, the impact of the client's cultural background, the client's help-seeking experiences, and current expectations about treatment and other forms of care.

The CFI follows a person-centered approach to cultural assessment by asking the client to address these topics based on his or her own views, rather than inquiring about the views of the person's cultural group(s) of origin. This is intended to avoid stereotyping, as individuals vary substantially in how they combine and interpret cultural information and perspectives.

Since the CFI is about the client's views, there are no right or wrong answers to a cultural formation interview.

THE CULTURAL FORMATION INTERVIEW: FOUR AREAS OF FOCUS

1) CULTURAL DEFINITION OF THE PROBLEM: The presenting issues that led to the current illness episode, cast within the client's worldview. In this section, the patient describes the problem and focuses on its most troubling aspects. This information starts to address what is most at stake for the patient with respect to the current presentation, including non-medical aspects.

2) CULTURAL PERCEPTIONS OF CAUSE, CONTEXT, AND SUPPORT: The client's explanations for the circumstances of illness, including the cause of the problem. The client also clarifies factors that improve or worsen the problem, with particular attention to the role of family, friends, and cultural background. The counselor seeks to obtain a holistic picture of the client in his or her social environment with emphasis on how cultural elements affect the presentation.

3) CULTURAL FACTORS AFFECTING SELF COPING AND PAST HELP SEEKING: The strategies employed by the client to improve the situation, including those that have been most and least helpful. The client also identifies past barriers to care. This information helps clarify the client's perspective on the nature of the problem, his or her mental health treatment expectations as opposed to other forms of help, and current resources to address the situation.

4) CURRENT HELP SEEKING: The client's perception of the relationship with the counselor, current potential treatment barriers, and preferences for care. In this section, the client specifies how the counselor may facilitate current treatment and what may interfere with the clinical relationship. Treatment preferences are elicited that may be incorporated into the treatment plan.

This interview process and the information it elicits are expected to enhance the cultural validity of the diagnostic assessment, facilitate treatment planning, and promote patient engagement and satisfaction.

RESEARCH
- Go to: *www.psychiatry.org/dsm5* **for a copy of the Cultural Formation Interview (CFI) ©** *www.APA.org* **(American Psychological Association)**

OVERALL STRATEGIES FOR ACHIEVING CULTURAL COMPETENCIES

- Learn a second or third language relevant to clients.
- Communicate to conference organizers and workshop providers that you will attend only if the activity addresses cross cultural aspects of the topic
- Actively communicate in your organization the need for education in cross-cultural training relevant to that organization.
- Speak up in your organization when you observe that clients, students, etc. are being treated unfairly based on race, ethnicity, physical ableness, etc.
- Become a member of a culture-focused organization and/or a state or local organization that provides cross-cultural exchanges.

SELF-REFLECTION and/or GROUP DISCUSSION:

BALANCING AWARENESS AND KNOWLEDGE AND TRANSLATING INTO SKILL

We are required to be knowledgeable about cultures.

SO...
- How do we go about gaining this knowledge?
- What are best practice's resources, ideas, methods, etc., for acquiring this knowledge?

THEN...
- How do we balance this knowledge against the unique experiences of each client's association with their culture—*sensitive to the clients' narratives*?

We do not rely on clients for our cultural education; however, we do rely on clients for their cultural experience.

HOW DO COUNSELORS BECOME CULTURALLY RESPONSIVE?

INDICATORS OF CULTURAL RESPONSIVENESS:
- Awareness of and sensitivity to personal cultural heritage.
- Value and respect for differences between cultures.
- Awareness of the role of cultural background and experiences, attitudes, and values in creating unconscious and conscious bias that influence communication and connection with others.
- Acknowledgement of personal competency and expertise.
- Comfort with differences that exist between self and students in terms of race, ethnicity, culture, and beliefs.
- Sensitivity towards potential negative emotional reactions toward others that may cloud interpersonal connections.
- Willingness to contrast own beliefs and attitudes with those of culturally different people in a non-judgmental fashion.
- Awareness of personal stereotypes and preconceived notions about individuals with differing experiences, cultural orientations, language and abilities.

BUILD ON CLIENTS' STRENGTHS:
- Instead of focusing on what clients aren't doing or don't know, identify a few strengths for a couple of your clients.
- Think about how you could use those strengths to increase their success
- Discover your clients' primary cultural roles and incorporate their culture.
- Learn what you can from others by visiting their celebrations, reading information about other cultures, talking with members of that culture.
- Attend cultural events in your community.
- Contact local culturally based organizations.

Look in your local Yellow Pages or on the Internet for organizations with a specific focus on culture or diversity. Call them. They may have activities that are ongoing; they may be able to set up a presentation for you and your colleagues about their organization.

RESOURCES TO INCREASE YOUR KNOWLEDGE OF OTHER CULTURES

Visit your local library or bookstore: Browse through the children's book section and look for stories from other cultures. Ask your librarian or bookstore owner for recommendations of authors in your favorite genre that are from other cultural backgrounds than yours. Check out the biographies and autobiographies of people from different cultural backgrounds. Look for novels that explore the difficulties of moving from one country to another, of overcoming hardships, of growing up in non-traditional families.

EXPLORE THE INTERNET: Research cultural topics. Look for websites that contain information about different cultures, or those that focus on cultural education. Search for websites about identity development and learning styles. Find websites that offer information and activities designed to explore culture and discover student strengths.

Attend local cultural celebrations: In your hometown, or while traveling, seek out opportunities to explore your own and other cultures by participating in street fairs, festivals, or other cultural celebrations. Enjoy the art, demonstrations, and foods. Read about the traditions depicted in various scenes. Ask questions about the history of the celebration. Observe people.

CULTURAL COMPETENCE: SELF-ASSESSMENTS

MENTAL HEALTH PRACTITIONERS SHOULD UNDERSTAND FIVE ELEMENTS OF CULTURAL COMPETENCE THAT INCLUDE:

1) Valuing diversity cross-culturally in behaviors, practices, policies, attitudes and structures
2) Conducting cultural self-assessment to assess for personal and professional proficiency in cultural competence
3) Managing the dynamics of difference within natural, formal or informal support and helping networks within clinical settings
4) Acquiring and integrating cultural knowledge by seeking out information and consultation and practice application
5) Adapting to diversity and cultural contexts that include policies, structures, values, and services

LET'S FOCUS ON ITEM #2 ABOVE:
Counselors should conduct cultural self-assessments, so here are some tools...

COUNSELOR SELF-ASSESSMENT

- What experiences of your own cultural history influence your work as a mental health professional?
- To what extent does cultural sensitivity influence the consciousness of your work as a mental health professional in the following areas:
    1) Assessment and diagnostics
    2) Treatment planning and implementation
    3) Support system development
    4) Outcome assessment
    5) After care support
    6) Community outreach and advocacy
- List examples of your observations of the interaction between cultural diversities and mental health symptoms. How often, rarely-moderately-frequently, does your professional practice include such observations?
- Have you considered client experiences of oppression and marginalization impacting your client's health status?
- Discuss the extent to which your clients consciously connect their experiences of emotional/mental distress and experiences of their surrounding culture. How are these connections expressed?

- To what extent do your clients report experiences of oppression and marginalization as factors impacting their mental health?
- To what extent do the extended family and community support players associate cultural dynamics with the mental health status of your clients?
- To what extent do extended family and community support players observe oppression and marginalization at work in the disease/recovery status of your clients?
- To what extent do you perceive community/organizational demonstration of awareness and inclusion of diversity beyond what is legislated? Are these relevant to the clients your serve? Please provide examples.
- What role do you observe mental health professionals serving, or that you believe ought to be served, in advancing community level change in support of mental health and oppressions and marginalization?
- Beyond traditional mental health focuses, to what components of community and social structure do you believe mental health professionals can contribute wisdom and understanding regarding oppression and marginalization? In what ways?

SELF-REFLECTION: YOUR OWN IDENTITY—DESCRIBE YOURSELF...

Examine your own identity
- Age, gender, birth order, educational level, profession, socioeconomic level, and ethnic background...
- Describe your personality: typical thoughts, emotions, and behaviors.
- How did the relationships with your family members affect your gender identity?
- How have your relationships with your peers affected it?
- Who is your reference group and what are their norms?
- How have the communities you have lived in affected it?
- How has your society and culture affected your identity?
- What is your ethnic identity?
- What locality or community did you grow up in?
- How did your family see itself as like or different from families of other ethnic groups?
- What are your earliest images/remembrances of ethnic differences?
- How has the historical era in which you have lived affect you?
- When did you graduated from high school?
- How much did a house cost in your hometown to be considered middle-class?
- What were the fads?
- Who were the heroes?
- What were the morality trends at the time regarding sex, drugs, marriage, etc.?
- What were the political issues?

Sex Role Analysis:
- Beginning with early childhood to present day, write down the dominant messages you have received about how you should or should not be because of your sex.

SELF-REFLECTION: GENDER AND ETHNICITY

Answer questions on issues of gender and ethnicity.
Complete the following sentence stems at least ten times.
- A good mother (or significant female caregiver) should be...
- A good daughter should be...
- List 10 words to describe your mother...
- Describe your relationship with your mother...
- How are you similar?
- What gifts have you received?
- What shackles?

- Describe your mother's relationship with her husband and how does it influence her relationships with men.
- How did it influence you?
- What did your mother teach you about intimate relationships, either overtly or covertly? What have you incorporated? What did you reject?
- Name the significant female role models ('Great Mothers') in your life and describe their characteristics, especially those you have decided to incorporate into your own identity.
- List your heroines, either known or idolized from afar or imagined. Describe their characteristics, especially those you would like to incorporate into your own identity.
- Write a new positive myth for women.

Complete the following sentence stems at least ten times.
- A good father (or significant male caregiver) should be...
- A good son should be...
- List 10 words to describe your father...
- Describe your relationship with your father...
- Write a dialogue between you and your father about your relationship.
- What did your father teach you about sexuality?
- Name the significant positive male role models 'Sacred Warriors' in your life and describe their characteristics, especially those you have decided to incorporate into your own identity.
- List your heroes either known, or idolized from afar or imagines. Describe their characteristics, especially those you would like to incorporate into your own identity.
- Write a new, positive myth for men.

Other Family Members
- How have your relationships with other family members affected the development of your gender identity?

Peers and Reference Groups
- How have your relationships with your peers affected the development of your gender identity?
- Describe your reference groups and their norms and values. How has being a member, or not being a member, of these groups impacted the development of your gender identity?
- Which other social relationships have had the most impact on you and why?
- Which people have been pivotal in the direction your life has taken?

Teachers and the Educational System
- How have your relationships with your teachers and your experience in the educational system affected the development of your gender identity?

Work/Career and Organizational Systems
- What work organizations have affected the development of your gender identity? How have they affected you?
- How might you, your gender identity and your life have been different without the influence of these organizations?

Your Community
- Describe the communities in which you have lived.
- How have these communities affected the development of your gender identity?

History, Society and Culture
- How have your society and culture affected the development of your gender identity?

PART 4

SAMPLE CLINICAL FORMS

CONTENT

CLINICAL FORMS

> Academic Settings: 263
> Administrators: 268
> Assessing Yourself: 270
> Assessments: 275
> Attorney (Working with): 293
> Authorizations for Disclosures: 294
> Bartering: 297
> Bill of Rights: 300
> Breaches of Confidentiality: 302
> Business Associate Agreement: 305
> Clinical Records: 311
> Clinical Relationships: 321
> Coaching: 341
> Complementary (Alternative) Treatments: 345
> Confidentiality Statements: 347
> Conflicts between Laws/Codes: 348
> Consultation: 349
> Counselor Impairment: 353
> Couples (And Families): 357
> Cultural Competencies: 365
> Diagnosing: 367
> E-counseling: 369
> E-mail (Texting/Phones): 373
> Financial Records: 377
> Forensic Psychology: 385
> Group Therapy: 391
> Informed Consent: 397
> Intake: 426
> Interval History Form: 427

CLINICAL FORMS (Continued)

    Limited Access to Records: 428
    Mandatory Reporting: 429
    Minors: 431
    No Charge Initial Session: 445
    Non-Subpoena Contract: 446
    Notice of Privacy Practice: 447
    Patient's Rights Act: 449
    Professional Disclosure Statement: 451
    Professional Will: 455
    Psychotherapy Notes: 457
    Records Custodian: 459
    Record Retention: 461
    Record Summaries 462
    Recordings (Audio/Video): 463
    Release of Information: 465
    Research: 466
    Responding to a Subpoena: 467
    Session Notes: 469
    Suicide Safety Plan: 473
    Supervision: 475
    Technology: 483
    Termination (and Referrals): 493
    Touch in Therapy: 505
    Transfer Plans: 509
    Treatment Planning: 511
    Visitor to Session: 526

Navigate "Best Practice" Paperwork

ACADEMIC SETTINGS
Confidentiality for Academic Settings

CAVEAT: Know your state's policies and laws; following employer guidelines, policies and procedures.

KEY PRINCIPLE
- Each person has the right to privacy and thereby the right to expect the counselor-student relationship to comply with all laws, policies and ethical standards pertaining to confidentiality in the school setting.

CONFIDENTIALITY
Students should be informed of the purposes, goals, techniques and rules of procedure under which they may receive counseling. This should be done at or before the counseling relationship begins. A disclosure notice includes the limits of confidentiality such as the possible necessity for consulting with other professionals, privileged communication, and legal or authoritative restraints. The meaning and limits of confidentiality are defined in developmentally appropriate terms to students.

- Protects the confidentiality of students' records and releases personal data in accordance with prescribed laws and school policies. Student information stored and transmitted electronically is treated with the same care as traditional student records.
- Protects the confidentiality of information received in the counseling relationship as specified by federal and state laws, written policies and applicable ethical standards. Such information is only to be revealed to others with the informed consent of the student, consistent with the counselor's ethical obligation.
- Recognizes his/her primary obligation for confidentiality is to the student but balances that obligation with an understanding of the legal and inherent rights of parents/guardians to be the guiding voice in their children's lives.

LIMITS OF CONFIDENTIALITY

Keeps information confidential unless disclosure is required to prevent clear and imminent danger to the student or others or when legal requirements demand that confidential information be revealed, such as with child and vulnerable adult protective services. Make sure students understand these limits of confidentiality. In the absence of state legislation expressly forbidding the following disclosure, considers the ethical responsibility to provide information to an identified third party who, by his/her relationship with the student, is at high risk of contracting a disease that is commonly known to be communicable and fatal. Disclosure requires satisfaction of all of the following conditions: 1) Student identifies partner or the partner is highly identifiable, 2) Counselor recommends the student notify partner and refrain from further high-risk behavior, 3) Student refuses, 4) Counselor informs the student of the intent to notify the partner, 5) Counselor seeks legal consultation as to the legalities of informing the partner, and/or 6) Requests of the court that disclosure not be required when the release of confidential information may potentially harm a student or the counseling relationship.

> **CAVEAT: Counselors must consult with appropriate professionals when in doubt as to the validity of an exception to confidentiality. Follow established policies and procedures according to your employment, varying only if you are being asked to do something illegal or unethical. Seek legal advice when needed.**

RESEARCH Assessing Your Program *(Below)*
- Ask yourself the following questions listed below...
    - Assessing these questions can be done individually or within a group setting (with appropriate personnel)

ASSESSING YOUR PROGRAM
Mission/Purpose
- What is the career center's unique mission? What is the counseling center's unique mission?
- How are the center's services distinct from other counseling services? How do they overlap, if at all?

- What is the nature of the collaborative arrangements (if any) between student services that are involved in the provision of these services?
- What are the views of higher-level administrators regarding how career and mental health counseling services are provided?

Facilities
- How will facilities be designed/accommodated to provide services?
- Does the space provide for videotaping, supervisor observation?
- Will students (or community clients) seeking counseling be waiting in the same area as individuals needing a resume critique?

Service Delivery
- To what extent do intake procedures "screen" for mental health issues?
- How is readiness for various types of services assessed?
- How are career and mental health issues reflected in the theories and models that guide practice in the setting?
- To what extent is the mental health aspect of a career services unit promoted to target audiences? For example, career services may want to avoid appearing too "clinical."

Records
- Record keeping/confidentiality-Types of records, forms (e.g., confidentiality agreement, release of information, no-suicide contract, etc.) are needed when services are offered that combine career and mental issues.
- Would different kinds of records be needed for mental health versus career counseling, or the same for both? Attention to HIPAA?

Assessments/Resources
- What kinds of materials and assessments are needed in a center providing career and mental health services.
- Beyond standard career assessments/inventories, will career assessments be used that incorporate mental health issues?
- To what extent are more "clinical" assessments used?
- What types of forms are maintained (suicide contract, confidentiality agreement, release of information)?

Staff
- Does staff have professional identities in psychology, mental health counseling, professional counseling, social work, other fields, or all of the above? Are these identities compatible or reconcilable?
- How will accrediting agencies view the staffing patterns in organizations that combine career and mental health counseling?

ETHICAL STANDARDS & CLINICAL FORMS

- Use of student paraprofessionals—is there a role for such staff in career centers that include mental health counseling services?
- Is professional development and training provided in both mental health and career counseling for all staff and all graduate students? Does career staff supervise mental health personnel, and vice versa?
- Does such staff have all the credentials needed (e.g., licensure, certification) to supervise staff?
- Are staff properly insured, credentialed, and prepared to provide services in both areas and where they overlap? Or if a career services program opts to integrate mental health and career counseling, is the pattern for some staff to be proficient in both areas and other staff to proficient in only one?
- What are the costs to providing expanded delivery? (e.g., licensed professionals, consulting, continuing education, facilities, accreditation, and professional memberships, insurance)

ACADEMIC SETTINGS: INFORMED CONSENT
SAMPLE STUDENT INFORMED CONSENT

CAVEAT: You must modify the forms so they comply with your state laws, professional organizations' codes of ethics and your State Licensing Board's guidelines.

SAMPLE STUDENT INFORMED CONSENT

[Student/client name]

I understand that as a subscriber to the [name of school and program], I am eligible to receive a range of services. The type and extent of services that I will receive will be determined following an initial assessment and thorough discussion with me. The goal of the assessment process is to determine the best course of treatment for me. Typically, treatment is provided over the course of several weeks. I understand that all information shared with the counselors at [name of school] is confidential and no information will be released without my consent. However, during the course of treatment, it may be necessary for my counselor to communicate with other providers employed by [school/university/college]. While written authorization will not be requested, prior to any discussion with these other providers, I understand that my counselor will discuss such communications with me. In all other circumstances, consent to release information is given through written authorization. Verbal consent for limited release of information may be necessary in special circumstances.

I further understand that there are specific and limited exceptions to this confidentiality which include the following:
- When there is risk of imminent danger to myself or to another person, the counselor is ethically bound to take necessary steps to prevent such danger.
- When there is suspicion that a child or elder is being sexually or physically abused or is at risk of such abuse, the counselor is legally required to take steps to protect the child, and to inform the proper authorities.
- When a valid court order is issued for medical records, the counselor and the agency are bound by law to comply with such requests.
- I understand that a range of mental health professionals, some of whom are in training, provides counseling services. All professionals-in-training are supervised by licensed staff.
- I understand that while psychotherapy and/or medication, may provide significant benefits, it may also pose risks. Psychotherapy may elicit uncomfortable thoughts and feelings, or may lead to the recall of troubling memories. Medications may have unwanted side effects.

If I have any questions regarding this consent form or about the services offered, I may discuss them with my counselor. I have read and understand the above. I consent to participate in the evaluation and treatment offered to me. I understand that I may stop treatment at any time.

REMEMBER TO: Include appropriate lines for signature and date; Keep a copy of any document that was signed by a client in the client's file (hardcopy or electronic); Copy to client optional, unless they request a copy.

RESEARCH
Sample Student (Academic Settings) Informed Consent
- **What would you change? Delete? Add?**
- **What sample text in the above consent do you strongly agree with? Why?**
  - **What sample text do you strongly disagree with? Why?**

ETHICAL STANDARDS & CLINICAL FORMS

ADMINISTRATORS: ETHICAL RESPONSIBILITIES

ADMINISTRATION'S DUE CARE IS IMPORTANT...

- Administrators should advocate within and outside their agencies for adequate resources to meet clients' needs.
- They should advocate for resource allocation procedures that are open and fair. When all clients' needs cannot be met, an allocation procedure should be developed that is nondiscriminatory and based on appropriate and consistently applied principles.
- They should take reasonable steps to ensure that adequate agency or organizational resources are available to provide appropriate staff supervision.
- In addition, supervisor/administrators should also take reasonable steps to ensure that the working environment for which they are responsible is consistent with and encourages compliance with all appropriate Codes of Ethics and take reasonable steps to eliminate any conditions in their organizations that violate, interfere with, or discourage compliance with these Codes.
- Finally, administrators and supervisors should take reasonable steps to provide or arrange for continuing education and staff development.

RESEARCH
- **What else can you add that's taken from your company's polices and procedures?**
- **What else can you add that's taken from your ethical codes?**

ADMINISTRATORS: THE APPRAISAL PROCESS

One of the most important and demanding responsibilities facing a supervisor is evaluating the performance of employees. It is a continuous day-to-day activity. Without appraisals a supervisor cannot make sound decisions regarding promotion, transfer, counseling, discharge, etc.

PRINCIPLES:
- An appraisal system that satisfies everyone is unknown
- Always seek objective appraisal processes
- There is no substitute for merit
- Uniformity is essential in rating
- Employee development must be universal
- All development is ultimately self-development
- Avoid inconsistencies, common errors: halo effect, leniency, over-emphasizing recent events

Components of Effective Performance Appraisals: Planning and Execution
- The appraisal interview can do more harm than good if handled improperly
- Control the discussion tactfully
- Direct criticism at job performance (not at the employee personally)
- Use active listening skills when it's the employee's turn to talk
- Comment on improvements
- Do not compare one employee to another
- Employee's strengths should be emphasized

Subjective vs. Objective Appraisals
- Subjective = ratings are a matter of personal opinions and feelings
- Objective = ratings can be counted and verified

Rating systems can be placed in one of two categories:
- Person-to-person (person-centered; person-focused performance)
- Person-to-category (work-focused; task-focused performance)

Uniformity is essential in the rating process—common errors are:
- Halo: Most recent performance determines overall ratings
- Leniency: Not wanting to give low ratings

Principles of Employee Development
- Development is an individual matter
- All development is self-development
- Development is mostly a result of the day-to-day job
- Opportunity for development must be universal

RESEARCH
- **Looking at your current employee appraisal process…**
  - Are you satisfied? Any changes you'd like to see?

ASSESSING YOURSELF

In counseling...we are our own instrument, or tool of our trade.
- Our ability to be compassionate with healthy boundaries is key
- With compassion we dethrone ourselves as we put another foremost
- Compassion is linked to emotion/empathy and followed by behavior/action

FOLLOW YOUR PAST INTO YOUR FUTURE: Many individuals enter counseling because they were sensitized to people's sufferings because of their own struggles.

GOOD WORK COMES FROM: Personal energies—positive and negative.

Positive energies come from where we have been blessed (healed). We all leave childhood with blessings—talents, that were developed or came naturally. There are incidences of good luck (being in the right place at the right time) that individuals experience. There were people who believed in you, encouraged you, or told you were good at something or that you could do something.

Negative energies come from where we have be cursed (wounded). We all leave childhood with wounds, frustrations and disappointments. The problems that stained our psyche may become the great source of our ability to help others. The injuries we have suffered can invite us to healing and being healed—for ourselves and others.

RESEARCH
- **Who has taken a special interest in you and encouraged you?**
  - Who believes or believed in you?
  - Who has been or is your mentor?
  - Who has been your inspirational model?
  - How were you blessed? Remember, blessings often come from adversities.
- **Where have you been wounded?**
  - Where have you been cursed?
  - What would you like to change about other people or the world?
  - If given one hour on prime time TV to influence the nation—*what would you talk about?*
  - How can you turn this wound or disrespect or curse into a blessing and a contribution?

EXPLORE YOUR VOCATION
- What are you very good at?
- What are your gifts, talents and abilities at which you excel, whether you were born with them or have acquired them during your lifetime?
- What are you not at all good at?
- What kinds of tasks or activities give you joy, delight, or pleasure?
- What do you like to do a lot?
- What would you do if you had all the money, time, health, and love you need?
- What kinds of tasks or activities deplete or bore you?
- What do you hate to do?
- What areas are you very disciplined at?
- What type of activities are you consistent, methodical with and do not procrastinate or regularly avoid?
- What activities do you regularly avoid, delay or procrastinate about?
- What areas are you not disciplined at?
- What, in your opinion, does the world, the region, the state, or your community need?
- What type of contribution does the world, the environment, people, children or animals need these days?
- What, in your opinion, does the world need less of these days?

COUNSELOR SELF-ASSESSMENT FOR TREATMENT FOCI

Rate yourself in each of the following areas to determine your comfort zone for working with people with these issues. Take into consideration: an assessment of your own in-depth experience, exploration and investment in each of these areas and your capacity/skill to guide or facilitate others through their journeys in these areas.

Use a scale of 1-10:

1 = not comfortable/incapable of helping or consulting with people

10 = very comfortable/capable/expert in this area

Score

_____Health/healing, psychological aspects of physical illness
_____Work and vocation or calling
_____Love/intimacy
_____Marriage, crises, affairs, communication, etc.
_____Parenting: babies/toddlers
_____Parenting: adolescents
_____Friendships/community

- _____Spirituality and religion
- _____Death, dying, conscious dying, grief and bereavement
- _____Gender issues, men/women
- _____Guilt, shame
- _____Anxiety, depression
- _____Creativity, play, blocks to creativity
- _____Mid-life transition and menopause, women
- _____Mid-life transition, men
- _____Retirement
- _____Parenting one's parents, taking care of parents
- _____Drug and alcohol addiction, AA, Alanon
- _____Eating disorders
- _____Food, medication, sex, gambling and other addictions
- _____Ethics and moral issues in everyday life
- _____Leisure, recreation
- _____Solitude
- _____Meditation, relaxation, stress reduction
- _____Meaning in life
- _____Gay and lesbian issues
- _____Pre-nuptial counseling
- _____Conflict resolution, mediation
- _____Disabilities (e.g., deaf)
- _____Military psychology
- _____Forensic psychology
- _____Pain management, chronic pain
- _____Chronic and terminal illness (e.g., MS, cancer)
- _____Aging: psychological/physiological
- _____Severe chronic mental illness (e.g., Schizophrenia, Bipolar)
- _____Personality disorders (e.g., Borderline)
- _____Other(s)

COUNSELOR SELF-ASSESSMENT FOR CLINICAL SKILLS

Consulting and clinical skills: Please rate yourself in each of the following areas or approaches, for your level of expertise or scope of practice. Your expertise or scope of practice is determined by your education (courses, seminars, and reading), supervised experience, and most importantly your personal investment in the subject area as well as clinical experience.

Use a scale of 1-10:
Not an expert in that approach
10 - Highest degree of expertise
Score
_____Psychoanalytic
_____Psychodynamic
_____Cognitive
_____Behavioral
_____Existential
_____Family system
_____Humanistic
_____Intermittent long term
_____Organizational development
_____Crisis intervention
_____Body-mind approaches
_____Adult development and family life cycle
_____Mediation
_____Transpersonal
_____Philosophical counseling
_____Spiritual direction
_____Hospice/grief/bereavement counseling
_____Meditation
_____Psychopharmacology (psych-meds)
_____Cross cultural
_____Multi-Modality
_____Sand tray
_____Jungian
_____Gestalt
_____Forensic evaluations (e.g., Custody, Sanity)
Others....

*"What treatment, and by whom, would be
most effective for this individual,
with this specific problem,
and under these circumstances?"*

ASSESSMENTS

PRINCIPLES

ASSESSMENT REQUIRES KNOWLEDGE:

Counselors need to understand various models and approaches to clinical evaluation for disorders and their appropriate uses, including screening and assessment for addiction, diagnostic interviews, mental status examination, symptom inventories, and psycho-educational and personality assessments. Counselors must know specific assessment approaches for determining the appropriate level of care for addictive disorders and related problems.

Counselors need to understand the assessment of biopsychosocial and spiritual history, and understand basic classifications, indications, and contra-indications of commonly prescribed psychopharmacological medications so that appropriate referrals can be made for medication evaluations and so that the side effects of such medications can be identified.

ASSESSMENT REQUIRES SKILLS AND PRACTICES:

Counselors select appropriate comprehensive assessment interventions to assist in diagnosis and treatment planning, with an awareness of cultural bias in the implementation and interpretation of assessment protocols. Counselors must demonstrate skills in conducting an intake interview, a mental status evaluation, a biopsychosocial history, a mental health history, a psychological assessment for treatment planning and case management and a cultural formation interview.

ASSESSMENTS AND ADDICTIONS:

Counselors screen for psychoactive substance toxicity, intoxication, and withdrawal symptoms; aggression or danger to others; potential for self-inflicted harm or suicide; and co-occurring mental and/or addictive disorders. Help clients identify the effects of addiction on life problems and the effects of continued harmful use or abuse.

Counselors apply assessment of clients' addictive disorders to the stages of dependence, change, or recovery to determine the appropriate treatment modality and placement criteria in the continuum of care.

Assessments includes all of the following... (But are not limited to)

ASSESSMENTS of CLIENT FACTORS:
- Biological factors: genetic, potential predisposition's, biochemical agents
- Development factors: physical development, psychosocial development, cognitive development and psychogenetic predisposition's
- Social-interactive factors: culture, family or system, parent/child relationship, family attitudes, socioeconomic and community

ASSESSMENT of CLIENT STRESSES:
- Psychological vulnerabilities: person response to stress, arousal rate, intensity, temperaments and cognitions
- Socioenvironmental stresses: status of current primary relationships, use of substances, socioeconomic status and changes

ASK YOURSELF: "What treatment, and by whom, would be most effective for this individual, with this specific problem, and under these circumstances?"

ASSESSMENT INTRODUCTION: (Sample Text)
"I would like to understand the problems that bring you here so that I can help you more effectively. I want to know about your experiences and ideas. I will ask some questions about what is going on and how you are dealing with it. There are no right or wrong answers. I just want to know your views and those of other important people in your life."

ETHICAL ASSESSMENTS:
- Assessment is ongoing and forms the basis of an integrated treatment plan
- Be culturally sensitive when assessing

Assess multiple facets including development, behavior, mental, and physical health:
- Explore infancy and early childhood experiences
- Explore strengths and resources
- Explore self-management skills
- Explore communication skills
- Explore interpersonal skills
- Explore task skills
- Explore personal behaviors
- Explore awareness of emotional and environmental triggers

- Explore parenting attitudes and competencies
- Explore family backgrounds explore marital relationships
- Explore sibling relationships
- Explore current support systems
- Explore stressors and stress management
- Explore rules, roles, and boundaries

Look at your information from a variety of paradigms: psychodynamic, family systems, developmental, attachment, and cognitive.

ASSESSMENTS AND TESTING:
- Counselor must administer test under the same conditions that were established in their standardization
- Counselor does not permit unsupervised or inadequately supervised use of tests or assessments unless the test or assessments are designed, intended and validated for self-administering and/or scoring
- Counselor recognizes the effect of age, color, race, culture, disability, ethnic group, religion, sexual orientation and socioeconomic status on test administration and interpretation and place test results in proper perspective with other relevant factors
- Counselor indicates any reservations that exist regarding the validity of a test in norms for the person being tested

ASSESSMENT CONSIDERATION OF...
MARGINALIZATION: The process of being relegated to the "sidelines" of society- excluded- as a function of individual or group traits that are targets of oppression.
- Marginalization reflects the active combination of oppressions and exclusion
- Marginalization reflects dominant class "codes" for inclusion/exclusion, superiority/inferiority, normality/abnormality and desirability/undesirability
- Marginalization results in decreased access to meaningful participation in the larger community: its history, its norms, its resources and its services
- Marginalization results in increased, or at least protected, access for the dominant (aka: privileged) class
- Marginalization assures increased exposure to social injustice
- Marginalization results from oppressive processes, particularly in the form of microaggressions

RESEARCH
- In what ways are your mental health clients marginalized? Consider multiple societal levels: family, peers, neighborhood, community, educational system, health care system, governance, religious practice, etc.
- Who, or what organizations, are the primary perpetrators of this marginalization?
- What steps can you, as a counselor, take to address the marginalization of your client(s)?
- Where is your compassion for your client's marginalized experience most important? How are you able to express your compassion for their exclusion?
- What therapeutic strategies can you afford your client specific to their marginalized experience(s)?

MICROAGGRESSIONS: These are the brief and commonplace daily, verbal, behavioral and environmental indignities, whether intentional or unintentional, that communicate hostile, derogatory, or negative (trait driven) slights or insults to the target person or group. While any one microaggression may seem inconsequential, the continuous, accumulating nature of these unpredictable indignities damages health. The combination of uncertainties, helplessness and the "catch-22" entrapment degrades self-esteem, perceptions of reality, relationship styles, capacity to trust and often, the "willingness to try." Because microaggressions are often perpetrated unconsciously and unintentionally, and are thus "invisible" in the experience of the offender, recipient experience most often goes unaddressed, and therefore unresolved.

- Microaggressions convey the "active manifestation" of oppressive cultural views that create and sustain marginalization
- Microaggressions enforce marginalization through processes of imposition and deprivation: imposition of false beliefs and abusive messages and deprivation of access to resources and opportunities
- Microaggressions create the interminable quality of marginalized existence.
- Microaggressions can be experienced at the individual, community and organizational levels.
- Microaggressions permeate community "knowledge" of groups and thus impose expectations and limitations on individuals.

> **RESEARCH**
> - What microaggressions are most significant in the marginalization process?
> - Should individuality, autonomy, self-examination and self-efficacy be emphasized in all mental health treatment?
> - Do you use your own history of experiencing oppression and marginality as the framework for interacting with clients about their life experiences?
> - Is it possible ,with hard work and persistence, to break through cultural barriers equally for everyone?

ASSESSMENT AND SUICIDE RISK
There is no pure legal duty to prevent suicide—the duty is to intervene appropriately. The law recognizes limits in the ability to stop a determined person from suicide.

The duty to intervene is judged according to the degree of suicidal risk exhibited by a client and the counselor's ability to accurately assess and control that risk. The counselor's liability increases as the risk of suicide increases and the counselor is able to foresee and control the client's actions. Since the counselor in an inpatient facility can control the patient's behavior more than in an outpatient setting, liability is greater when suicide occurs in a hospital, day treatment, or residential care facility.

LAWS AND ETHICS IN SUICIDE INTERVENTION
Suicide is not only one of the riskiest cases for a counselor clinically and spiritually, but legally as well.

Professional counselors are increasingly at legal risk for the suicide of their clients and patients. Indeed, the counselors working in an inpatient or restrictive treatment setting has a strong duty to intervene in the life of someone judged to be a substantial risk for suicide.

In contrast, a pastor in a church setting may be ethically and morally, but not legally, bound to a duty of suicide intervention.

SUICIDE ASSESSMENT

Assessment of suicidal risk involves gathering information from multiple sources across a number of key variables. The essential two-part question of suicide assessment is: Is this person at risk for committing suicide, and If so, how serious is the risk?

The competent counselor will assess this risk according to history, trait, mood, personality, and situational factors. Begin counseling with assessment of suicide risk. The easiest way to get information about suicide risk is to ask questions at the beginning of counseling. Structuring assessment this way and addressing these questions on initial interview puts clients more at ease as they see it as part of the routine we follow with all new clients.

Evaluate suicide risk across key variables...
RISK FOR SUICIDE INCREASES ACCORDING TO:
- Past suicide attempts and their seriousness
- Communication of intent/denial of intent
- Assessing the violent-angry-impulsive person
- Professional counselor liability for suicide cuts across two issues:
- The setting in which the crisis arises and the nature of the alleged harm
- Whether it involved failure to take preventive action to avoid suicide or whether the clinical behavior caused the suicide

SUICIDE RISK ASSESSMENTS

A selection of sample content to help assess suicide risk...
- Past suicide attempts
- Age (risk increases with age)
- Expression of wish to die
- Means, availability, access to means of guns, pills, knives, etc.
- Suicidal thoughts, feelings, plan of action
- Past suicide attempts or suicides by family members or close friends
- Level of depression (hopelessness, helplessness, sleep/eating patterns)
- Recent loss of a loved one (especially loss of a child or elderly spouse)
- Major psychiatric disorders (other than depression)
- Major recent physical illness, recent accident/crisis, chronic illness
- Past bouts with depression or hospitalizations, etc.
- Financial problems
- Recent or chronic stressors (e.g., loss, separation, illness, life transition)

- Marital status (increased risk with single)
- Level of social support (increased risk with isolation)
- Sleep patterns (increased risk with too much or too little sleep)
- General level of impulse control
- Volatility of mood
- Drug and alcohol use/abuse/dependency
- Physical or sexual abuse in the family
- Sexual orientation (regarding comfort or discomfort level)
- Sense of humor, or ability to reflect cognitively on one's situation
- Level of cooperation with treatment
- Recent involvement in risky activities
- Excessively dependent on others
- Inability to take care of self or others

Summary of client's suicide risk (circle one): High / Medium / Low / None

Plan of action (see also treatment plan and/or suicide safety plan)
- No action required
- Suicide "Safety Plan"
- Frequency of contact: sessions, phone, etc.
- Voluntary hospitalization
- Involuntary hospitalization
- Further evaluation
- Medication, medication evaluation
- Obtain other medical or psychological records (with client authorization)
- Consultation with _____
- Other

RESEARCH
Sample Suicide Risk Assessment
- **What would you delete from the list and why?**
- **What would you add to the list and why?**

SAMPLE TEXT: SUICIDE SAFETY AGREEMENT

CAVEAT: No suicide document is a substitute to thorough clinical assessment, referrals, consultations, etc. Counselors must continue to monitor the situation and evaluate options even when client sign a safety plan. NOTE: The below paragraph is considered the minimum agreement. It is best to complete a "suicide safety plan" instead.

I, _____ agree that I will keep myself from harm. If I feel an impulse to hurt myself, I will call _____ or 911, or the crisis hot line at _____. I am aware that [counselor] may not be able to respond to a call right away and will utilize the other resources if needed. I have also read, signed, and have had explained to me the limits of confidentiality outlined in the consent form, especially in regard to clients who pose a danger to themselves or others.

REMEMBER TO: Include appropriate lines for signature and date; Keep a copy of any document that was signed by a client in the client's file (hardcopy or electronic); Copy to client optional, unless they request a copy.

RESEARCH
Sample Suicide Safety Agreement
- **What would you change? Delete? Add?**
- **What sample text in the above consent do you strongly agree with? Why?**
- **What sample text do you strongly disagree with? Why?**

SAMPLE TEXT: SUICIDE SAFETY PLAN

A suicide safety plan is written sets of instructions as a contingency plan should client begin to experience thoughts about harming themselves. It contains a series of gradually escalating steps that can be followed, proceeding from one step to the next, until they are safe.

Suicide safety plan should include the following elements, in the same order as presented below:
- **When the Plan Should be Used:** *This step will involve making yourself familiar with what types of situations, images, thoughts, feelings and behaviors might precede or accompany suicidal urges for you.*
- **What I Can do to Calm/Comfort Myself if I am Feeling Suicidal:** *Create a list for yourself of activities that are soothing to you when you are upset.*
- **What Are my Reasons for Living?** *Create a list that will help client refocus on the reasons to keep going*
- **Who Can I Talk to?** *Keep a list of contacts you can talk to if you are unable to distract yourself with self-help*
- **Who Can I Talk to If I Need Professional Assistance?** *Create a list of all professional resources available*
- **How Can I Make My Environment Safe?** *Plan what steps you can take to make yourself safe. (e.g., Going to another location until the urges have passed or getting another person involved to help you)*
- **What to Do if I Am Still Not Feeling Safe:** *If all other steps have failed to keep you feeling safe, go to your nearest hospital emergency room and ask for assistance*

REMEMBER TO:
Include appropriate lines for signature and date; Keep a copy of any document that was signed by a client in the client's file (hardcopy or electronic); Copy to client optional, unless they request a copy.

RESEARCH
Sample Suicide Safety Plan
- **Search the Internet for two samples of "Suicide Safety Plans."**
- **Put yourself in the client's position; write out two sample answers for each of the above questions**
- **Why do you think this is recommended that clients write out the plan in their own handwriting?**

ASSESSMENTS: HOMICIDE RISK

Since it is impossible to predict with 100% accuracy dangerousness ahead of time, violation of a client's confidentiality must be undertaken with great care and in consultation with others.

The art of counseling involves learning to discern what a client is really saying. When someone says, "I wish I (or someone else) was dead" are they talking suicide or homicide or just expressing frustration with their current stress levels or relationship difficulties?

How do we distinguish between the client who vents in scary ways and those who may carry out their threatening words?

THE BEST PREDICTOR OF FUTURE VIOLENCE IS A HISTORY OR PATTERN OF PAST VIOLENCE.

- Good documentation is essential in every case, but with dangerous and threatening clients, it's critical
- Make sure you have a treatment plan and you update and date it regularly
- In your case notes record specifically what a client said, your assessment of the threat, what you did, and why you decided to do it

THE VIOLENT-ANGRY-IMPULSIVE PERSON WILL…

- Shows a history of violent behavior, such as assaults, hitting and injuring others, destroying or damaging property, and injury to self for such action
- Reveals impulsive anger or rage that is explosively triggered by various people or events. The person quickly gets out-of-control and becomes destructive to things or people and relationships
- Shows a tendency to hurt others and vengefully reacts when angry using cutting, harmful words, hiding or destroying things special to the person who is the focus of one's anger
- Projects blame onto others and is critical and condemning of others, while being unable to receive any criticism from others
- Justifies anger and harmful expressions, unable to forgive, tending to hold grudges and resentments over a long period of time
- Suppresses anger and denies anger in the face of obvious evidence
- Physical responses: flushed face, clenched teeth and muscles, harsh and loud tone of voice, threatening posture

- Represses anger and denies anger problems (contrary to history) without obvious anger signals. They are passive-aggressive, aloof, sarcasm-cynicism, conflict-avoidant
- Shows associated physical complaints and symptoms such as gastric-intestinal distress, ulcers, spastic colon, headache, hypertension, and cardiac irregularities

FEATURES of DANGEROUS
- Dangerous is defined as "attended with risk; perilous; hazardous; unsafe"
- Danger is defined as "jeopardy; exposure to loss or injury; peril"
- Violent ideation: thoughts, fantasies, and dreams of violent acts; delusions or hallucinations commanding violent acts
- Violent affect: person manifests intense, overwhelming rage, destructive impulses, drivenness, or fear of inability to control violent impulses
- Violent behavior: physical agitation, accompanying psychosis, intoxication, or delirium; explosive rage; or domestic violence

IMMEDIATE DANGER SIGNS OF IMMINENT VIOLENCE:
- Motor activity is irritable with an inability to be calmed
- Verbal indicators such as threats when stated loudly, defamatory statements, and sexual verbal aggression
- Nonverbal indicators include glaring eyes, demanding demeanor, tense, forward-leaning posture, and a hyper-alert state

RESEARCH
Use the Internet or the DSM...
- **What is the psychological profile of a dangerous person?**
- **What are the biological components of dangerousness?**
- **Sociocultural features of dangerousness?**
- **Developmental profiles of dangerousness?**

WORKPLACE VIOLENCE

Workplace violence is any act or threat of physical violence, harassment, intimidation, or other threatening disruptive behavior that occurs at the work site. It ranges from threats and verbal abuse to physical assaults and even homicide. It can affect and involve employees, clients, customers and visitors.

In most workplaces where risk factors can be identified, the risk of assault can be prevented or minimized if employers take appropriate precautions. One of the best protections employers can offer their workers is to establish a zero-tolerance policy toward workplace violence. This policy should cover all workers, patients, clients, visitors, contractors, and anyone else who may come in contact with company personnel.

PROTOCOL FOR DEALING WITH A DANGEROUS PERSON:
- Try not to be alone
- Employ active listening
- Express concern; exploring alternative to violence
- Check for the here-and-now transference
- Perform a mental status exam
- Take a careful history
- Inform about legal realities
- Refer for psychiatric consultation; hospitalization; or call authorities

SAMPLE ASSESSMENT TEXT

CAVEAT: For use in your own setting, forms must be personalized to reflect your state's relevant laws, ethical requirements for your licensing, and your own actual policies.

CHECKLIST for MENTAL STATUS...
MENTAL FUNCTIONING PRESENTATION:
Appearance: Well Groomed / Unkempt / Unusual / Bizarre
Mood: Normal / Depressed / Anxious / Euphoric
Attitude: Cooperative / Friendly / Guarded / Exaggerates / Minimizes / Suspicious / Hostile / Uncooperative
Affect: Appropriate / Expansive / Constricted / Flat
Speech: Normal / Slow / Detailed / Slurred / Incoherent
Motor Activity: Relaxed / Calm / Restless / Agitated / Tense / Tremors / Tics
Orientation: Fully Oriented / Person Oriented / Place Oriented / Disoriented
Simple Calculations: Accurate / Mostly Accurate / Inaccurate / Mostly Inaccurate
Immediate Memory: Intact / Impaired, Partially or Mostly or Severely
Remote Memory: Intact / Impaired, Partially or Mostly or Severely
General Knowledge: Accurate / Mostly Accurate / Inaccurate / Mostly Inaccurate

HIGHER ORDER ABILITIES:
Judgment: Intact / Impulsive / Immature / Minimally Impaired / Moderately Impaired / Severely Impaired
Insight: Intact / Limited / Very Limited / None
Intelligence: High / Average / Low / Retarded
Thought Form/Content
Thought Process: Logical / Organized / Loose Association / Disorganized / Flight of Ideas/ Mental Blocking / Obsessive
Delusions: None Evident / Persecutory / Actions Controlled / Thought Controlled / Grandiosity / Bizarre / Somatic / Infidelity Delusions
Hallucinations: None Evident / Auditory / Visual / Olfactory

RISK ASSESSMENT:
Suicide Risk: None / Slight / Moderate / Significant / Extreme
Violence Risk: None / Slight / Moderate / Significant / Extreme
Child Abuse Risk: None / Slight / Moderate / Significant / Extreme

SUICIDE RISKS:
- **Suicide Ideation:** Two months or more; there are psychiatric, psychological, or physical pain so severe it defines the person's capacity to cope. Client views death as a remedy.
- **Chronic Suicide Ideation:** For over one year in duration. *NOTE: Could be coupled with secondary gain: retaining a relationship; continue in counseling; getting Social Security disability benefits .*
- **Suicide Attempts:** Lethal actions with intent to die. Assess if the act was accidental, how they were rescued or if client misjudged lethality.

EGO-SYNTONIC or EGO-DYSTONIC:
- **Ego-Syntonic:** Emotionally responsive to surroundings describes somebody who is emotionally attuned to his or her environment. According to beliefs in ego psychology, it is used to describe behavior that does not conflict with somebody's basic attitudes and beliefs and, therefore, is not anxiety provoking.
- **Ego-Dystonic:** Denoting aspects of a person's thoughts, impulses, and behavior that are felt to be repugnant, distressing, unacceptable, or inconsistent with the self-conception, or inconsistent with the rest of the personality. Describing elements of a person's behavior, thoughts, impulses, drives, and attitudes that are unacceptable to him or her and cause anxiety.
  - *This assessment allows for client's attitude considerations—their eagerness and motivation for therapy and the client's awareness of a problem. Kids are, by nature, ego-syntonic until they reach adolescence when they become more ego-dystonic. Avoid anthologizing ego-syntonic and ego-dystonic; all behavior is purposeful.*

CLIENT INSIGHT RATINGS:
- **Good/Fair Insight** = ego-dystonic; client knows they have a problem and have insight regarding their problem(s); the "loci" of the client's pain; the client is in the "contemplation stage of change."
- **Poor Insight** = ambivalence; they know others are concerned but they are not. They see there's a problem because others have a problem with them. Reluctant to change.
- **Absent Insight** = ego-syntonic; client does not see the problem or any problem at all. Resistant to therapy; no motivation to change.

ASSESSMENTS of CLIENT FACTORS:
- **Biological factors:** genetic, potential predisposition's, biochemical agents.
- **Development factors:** physical development, psychosocial development, cognitive development and psychogenetic predispositions.
- **Social-interactive factors:** culture, family or system, parent/child relationship, family attitudes, socioeconomic and community.

ASSESSMENT of CLIENT STRESSES:
- **Psychological vulnerabilities:** person response to stress, arousal rate, intensity, temperaments and cognitions.
- **Socioenvironmental stresses:** status of current primary relationships, use of substances, socioeconomic status and changes.

ASSESSMENT of CLIENT HISTORY: DATA BASES...
- **Cross-sectional items:** (a point in time) are presenting complaints, relevant history and mental status (consciousness, attentions span, orientation, memory, concentration and judgment).
- **Longitudinal items:** (over a lifetime) include family constellation and history, psychosocial history, educational history, employment history, legal problems, drug and alcohol history and medical history.

GENOGRAMS: A pictorial display of a person's relationships
- Family
- Emotional
- Relational

Search www.wikipedia.org for "genograms"
You will find detailed information and examples of all the various symbols used in genograms.

ETHICAL STANDARDS & CLINICAL FORMS

ASSESSMENT OF CLIENT'S PERCEPTION OF INFLUENCE:
- To what extent do you feel your opinion, creativity and capabilities have influence in your_____? (a) Home (b) School (c) Work place (d) Place of worship (e) Neighborhood (f) Community (g) Social circles
  - For each area above, describe how your access (or lack of access) to influence happens?
- How do you feel about these experiences when they happen and after they have happened?
- Over time, what decisions have you made about your place and importance within your _____? (a) Home (b) School (c) Work place (d) Place of worship (e) Neighborhood (f) Community (g) Social circles
- How do you cope with, or try to change, your place and importance in these areas of your life?
- Please check any of the following personal traits that you believe determine your access to influence

ASSESSING CLIENT STRENGTHS:
- What kinds of things do you do well?
- Tell me about some of your satisfactions and successes?
- What are things you enjoy doing well?
- What have you noticed that you do in the past that helps you?
- Which of your jobs lasted the longest? Did you do anything to help this happen?
- What is keeping you, right now, from doing worse than you are?
- Which of your good points about yourself do you forget most often?

ASSESSMENTS MUST SHOW RESPECT FOR AGE, GENDER, AND CULTURE:
Diagnoses must be respectful of cultural idiosyncratic behaviors. Culturally sanctioned behavior or cultural idiosyncratic behaviors are to be considered. Also, we must consider behaviors that are an expected response to a particular situation/event such as depression in response to grief is not necessarily a mental disorder. Further consideration needs to be given to the fact that behaviors may, or may not, be medical or biological illness in an effort to reduce pharmacological treatment, especially with children.

ASSESSMENT QUESTIONNAIRE: GETTING TO KNOW YOUR CLIENT...

- What problems or concerns bring you to the clinic? (If patient only mentions symptoms, probe: *"Anything else?"*)
- What troubles you most about your problem?
- How would you describe your problem to someone else?
- Is there a specific term or expression that describes your problem?
- Why do you think this is happening to you?
- What do you think are the particular causes of your [PROBLEM]?
- What, if anything, makes your [PROBLEM] worse, or makes it harder to cope with?
- What have your family, friends, and other people in your life done that may have made your [PROBLEM] worse?
- What, if anything, makes your [PROBLEM] better, or helps you cope with it more easily?
- What have your family, friends, and other people in your life done that may have made your [PROBLEM] better?
- Is there anything about your background, for example your culture, race, ethnicity, religion or geographical origin that is causing problems for you in your current life situation?
- On the other hand, is there anything about your background that helps you to cope with your current life situation?
- Sometimes people consider various ways of making themselves feel better. What have you done on your own to cope with your [PROBLEM]?
- Often, people also look for help from other individuals, groups, or institutions to help them feel better. In the past, what kind of treatment or help from other sources have you sought for your [PROBLEM]?
- What type of help or treatment was most useful? Why? How?
- What type of help or treatment was not useful? Why? How?
- Has anything prevented you from getting the help you need, for example, cost or lack of insurance coverage, getting time off work or family responsibilities, concern about stigma or discrimination, or lack of services that understand your language or culture?
- Is there anything about my own background that might make it difficult for me to understand or help you with your [PROBLEM]?
- How can I, and others at our clinic, be most helpful for you?
- What kind of help would you like from us now, as specialists in mental health?

RESEARCH
Sample Assessment Text (pages 287-291)
- **Take all the sample assessment text suggestions into consideration, and create your ultimate assessment form**
- **Remember to add anything that personalizes it to your practice**

TESTS AND MEASUREMENTS
- Counselor must administer test under the same conditions that were established in their standardization.
- Counselor does not permit unsupervised or inadequately supervised use of tests or assessments unless the test or assessments are designed, intended and validated for self-administering and/or scoring.
- Counselor recognizes the effect of age, color, race, culture, disability, ethnic group, religion, sexual orientation and socioeconomic status on test administration and interpretation and place test results in proper perspective with other relevant factors.
- Counselor indicates any reservations that exist regarding the validity of a test in norms for the person being tested.

ATTORNEYS: WORKING WITH AN ATTORNEY

Decide now what you'll fight for later.
THREE CATEGORIES:
- Willing to litigate at all costs
- Willing to settle on favorable terms
- Those to be managed by a case-by-case basis

Know when to call your attorney. Discuss with your attorney about when you need to call him/her. What decisions need legal counsel? What information needs to be provided? What events, circumstances, or situations would your attorney want to hear about?

KEY POINTS
- Partner with your attorney (especially in larger firms)
- Be wary of an attorney that is dismissive of your questions
- Insist on thoughtful advice
- You need clear answers to your questions

HELP YOUR ATTORNEY UNDERSTAND YOUR PROBLEM(S) QUICKLY
- Make sure your attorney sees relevant documents in the same way other parties would have seen them
- Provide complete but concise documents

SELECTING AN ATTORNEY
SAMPLE QUESTIONS
First, describe your problem as concisely as possible: (use less than 200 words)
Then ask your attorney:
- What will you be able to do to help me with this situation?
- Have you handled this type of situation before? What was the outcome?
- What is your fee? How often would we need to meet?
- What documents would you need from me?
- If you are going to work with the attorney, then ask:
  - What should I do next?
  - What should I not do?
  - What laws, statutes, or regulations are relevant to my situation? (Then do some research on these for yourself)

ETHICAL STANDARDS & CLINICAL FORMS

AUTHORIZATION FOR DISCLOSURE

The following is a sample of the typical elements of an authorization for the disclosure of private health information.

SAMPLE HIPAA Privacy Authorization Form

CAVEAT: For use in your own setting, forms must be personalized to reflect your state's relevant laws, ethical requirements for your licensing, and your own actual policies.

Authorization for Use or Disclosure of Protected Health Information

1. Authorization

I authorize _____ (healthcare provider) to use and disclose the protected health information described below to _____ _____ (individual seeking the information).

2. Effective Period

This authorization for release of information covers the period of
[ ] 90 days
[ ] From: _____ to _____.
[ ] Other: _____.

3. Extent of Authorization

[ ] I authorize the release of my complete health record (including records relating to mental health care, communicable diseases, HIV or AIDS, and treatment of alcohol or drug abuse).

[ ] I authorize the release of my complete health record with the exception of the following information:
- Mental health records
- Communicable diseases (including HIV and AIDS)
- Alcohol/drug abuse treatment
- Other (please specify): _____

4. This medical information may be used by the person I authorize to receive this information for medical treatment or consultation, billing or claims payment, or other purposes as I may direct.

5. This authorization shall be in force and effective until _____ (date or event), at which time this authorization expires.

6. I understand that I have the right to revoke this authorization, in writing, at any time. I understand that a revocation is not effective to the extent that any person or entity has already acted in reliance on my authorization or if my authorization was obtained as a condition of obtaining insurance coverage and the insurer has a legal right to contest a claim.

7. I understand that my treatment, payment, enrollment, or eligibility for benefits will not be conditioned on whether I sign this authorization.

8. I understand that information used or disclosed pursuant to this authorization may be disclosed by the recipient and may no longer be protected by federal or state law.

REMEMBER TO:
Include appropriate lines for signature and date; Keep a copy of any document that was signed by a client in the client's file (hardcopy or electronic); Copy to client optional, unless they request a copy.

RESEARCH
Sample Authorization for Disclosure
- **This document is required by HIPAA Act, 45 C.F.R. Parts 160 and 164**
  - **Internet search for the above and take the time to read it**

See the "Release of Information" section for additional information.

*Records do more than
support good client care;
they are essential to it!*

BARTERING

> **CAVEAT:** Always check with your state's licensing board for their official position on bartering. Almost all ethical guidelines do not mandate a blanket avoidance of bartering. However, all ethical guidelines prohibit exploitation of clients. Bartering arrangements also have tax implications. Consult your tax preparer and make informed decisions regarding your legal, civic and professional responsibilities.

WHAT IS BARTERING?
Barter is the acceptance of services, goods or other non-monetary remuneration from clients in return for psychological services. It is not inherently unethical, illegal or counter-clinical.

BARTERING ARRANGEMENTS
Bartering is common with poor clients who seek or need therapy, but do not have the money to pay for it. It is also very common in cultures and communities where bartering is an accepted norm for compensation and exchange.

In some circumstances, bartering that could benefit the client might become a part of a clinical intervention that is negotiated with the client and articulated in the treatment plan.

BARTER FOR GOODS OR SERVICES OR BOTH?
Bartering can be of goods (product) or of services. Bartering has often been equated, mistakenly, with dual relationships and boundary violation. While bartering of services is, indeed, dual relationships, bartering of goods is generally not.

All bartering is considered a boundary crossing, but it's not necessarily a (harmful) boundary violation.

See the "Clinical Relationships" section, boundaries, for more details.

CLINICAL AND ETHICAL CONSIDERATIONS

- Make sure that the client involved in the negotiation fully understands and consents, in writing, to the agreement.
  - Suggestion: Have the client propose the bartering to you, in writing, including the proposed terms and conditions of the bartering arrangement. If you, the counselor, decides to barter after discussing the bartering terms with the client, then place the letter in the client's file and note the discussion in the clinical records.
- The bartering arrangement must be well documented in the clinical notes. Consult with clinical, ethical or legal experts in complex cases and document the consultations in your clinical notes. Keep excellent written records throughout treatment if or when problems and complications arise with regard to the bartering agreement.
- Make sure that the bartering agreement is consistent with and is not in conflict with the treatment plan.
- Evaluate the effectiveness and appropriateness of the bartering arrangement regularly and change it if necessary through discussion with and, hopefully, consent from your client.
- If complications, negative feelings or disagreement arise due to the bartering agreement, discuss it with your client, get consultations and change it in a way that will be most helpful to the client and conducive to therapy.

CAVEAT: It is important to realize that bartering can be counter-clinical in some situations such as with certain clients who see themselves primarily as victims. Most analytically oriented counselors, consumer protection agencies and risk management experts frown upon bartering, because the traditional analysts view bartering as interfering in transference analysis. Licensing boards, ethics committees and risk management experts often view bartering as potentially exploitative and damaging to the therapeutic work. In planning on entering into a bartering agreement, counselors must take into consideration the welfare of the client, his/her culture, gender, history, condition, wishes, economic status, type of treatment, avoidance of harm and exploitation, conflicts of interest and the impairment of clinical judgment. These are the paramount and appropriate concerns.

SAMPLE TEXT FOR A BARTER AGREEMENT

CAVEAT: For use in your own setting, forms must be personalized to reflect your state's relevant laws, ethical requirements for your licensing, and your own actual policies.

Text could include:

[Counselor] and [Client] have agreed to continue counseling under a barter agreement. In exchange for a [minute] counseling session, client will give to counselor _____ (describe the product). Client understands that bartering has often been equated, mistakenly, with dual relationships and boundary violation. Bartering is a boundary crossing but not a (harmful) boundary violation. Counselor has explained to client how this bartering agreement is consistent with, and is not in conflict with, the treatment goals. Counselor has explained that together we will evaluate the effectiveness and appropriateness of the bartering arrangement regularly and change it if necessary through discussion and consent from the client. As the client, I understand that If complications, negative feelings or disagreement arise due to this bartering agreement, I will discuss it with my counselor. If counselor believes there are complications he/she will get consultations and change it in a way that will be most helpful to the client and conducive to therapy.

REMEMBER TO:
Include appropriate lines for signature and date; Keep a copy of any document that was signed by a client in the client's file (hardcopy or electronic); Copy to client optional, unless they request a copy.

RESEARCH
Sample Barter Agreement
- **What statements would you change?**
- **What additional statements would you add?**

BILL OF RIGHTS

A client's Bill of Rights is a list of guarantees for those receiving medical care. It may take the form of a law or a non-binding declaration. Typically, a client's bill of rights explains the client's right to information, fair treatment, and autonomy over medical decisions.

SAMPLE CLIENT BILL OF RIGHTS AND RESPONSIBILITIES

CAVEAT: For use in your own setting, forms must be personalized to reflect your state's relevant laws, ethical requirements for your licensing, and your own actual policies.

CLIENT BILL OF RIGHTS AND RESPONSIBILITIES

As an individual receiving counseling services from [name of business or counselor], let it be known and understood that you have the following rights and responsibilities.

RIGHTS

- To select those who provide your care
- To receive the services in a professional manner without discrimination relative to your age, gender, race, religion, ethnic origin, sexual preference, or physical or mental disability
- To be dealt with and treated with friendliness, courtesy, and respect by each and every individual representing
 our company who provides services for you, and to be free from neglect or abuse be it physical or mental.
- To assist in the development and planning of your healthcare program that is designed to satisfy, as best as possible, your current needs
- To be provided with adequate information from which you can give your informed consent for the commencement of service, the continuation of service, the transfer of service to another healthcare provider, or the termination of service
- To request and receive complete and up-to-date information relative to the services you are receiving
- To receive treatment and services within the scope of your healthcare plan, promptly and professionally, while being fully informed as to our policies, procedures, and charges

- To refuse treatment, within the boundaries set by law, and be informed of the consequences of such refusal
- To request and receive information regarding treatment, services, or costs privately and with confidentiality
- To request and receive the opportunity to examine or review your medical records
- To express concerns or grievances or recommend modification to your services without fear of discrimination or reprisal
- To request and receive a copy of our Notice of Privacy Practice

RESPONSIBILITIES
- To provide a complete and accurate medical history
- To let it be known whether you comprehend a contemplated course of action and what you are expected to do
- To provide information about unexpected complications that arise in an expected course of treatment
- To provide timely and accurate information concerning your sources of payment and ability to meet financial obligations

REMEMBER TO:
Include appropriate lines for signature and date; Keep a copy of any document that was signed by a client in the client's file (hardcopy or electronic); Copy to client optional, unless they request a copy.

RESEARCH
Sample Bill of Rights
- **Find three additional examples of this document from local hospitals or clinics...**
- **Read and compare**
  - **What statements would you change?**
  - **What additional statements would you add?**

ETHICAL STANDARDS & CLINICAL FORMS

BREACH OF CONFIDENTIALITY

When a mobile device, that contains private health information or client information, has been stolen or lost the counselor must contact clients in a timely manner. This is imperative from both a legal and ethical perspective. It is equally important that a report be filed with law enforcement as soon as one learns their mobile device has been lost or stolen.

> **CAVEAT:** The professional codes of ethics do not and should not deal with specific pieces of technology. Maintaining confidentiality and protecting client privacy is foundational to psychotherapy, and the potential risks to confidentiality associated with lost or stolen laptops, flash drives, and cell phones are well known. Just as ignorance is not a defense against violations of a law, carelessness and laziness are not an excuse for violating professional ethics and responsibility. Should a counselor's laptop or cell phone be lost or stolen and a client's confidentiality violated, the counselor must be able to demonstrate they did everything reasonably possible to secure the device and the information therein in order to minimize liability.

SAMPLE BREACH OF CONFIDENTIALITY NOTIFICATION

CAVEAT: For use in your own setting, forms must be personalized to reflect your state's relevant laws, ethical requirements for your licensing, and your own actual policies.

Recently, a _____ was stolen from _____ that may have contained the names and confidential information of some clients or former clients of _____. On _____ (date), we sent out personal notices, by first class mail, to each of the individuals who may have been impacted, for whom we were able to locate a current address. There were some individuals whose current addresses we were unable to obtain.

We have no reason to believe that the person who stole the laptop targeted personal information, nor do we believe there is any significant probability that personal harm will result from this breach.

OPTIONAL AND ONLY USE IF RELEVANT: The _____ (device) did not contain _____ that is typically used to perpetrate identity theft or financial fraud.

The information stolen contained the following data: _____.
[Counselor or business name] takes computer and data security seriously and we continue to provide strong protection for our systems and work computers and other mobile devices. As a result of this incident, an investigation is underway looking into this incident, including an audit of the security of client records and we will be taking appropriate responsive action.

A police report has been filed.
If you have any questions or would like to verify whether your information may have been involved, please contact us at _____ or send an e-mail message to _____.

REMEMBER TO:
Include appropriate lines for signature and date; Keep a copy of any document that was signed by a client in the client's file (hardcopy or electronic); Copy to client optional, unless they request a copy.

RESEARCH
Sample Breach of Confidentiality Notification
- **Research the Internet for information related to "breaches of security" for "mental health care clients"**
  - **Can you find any other sample letters notifying clients of a breach of security?**
- **If your office was broken into, or your computer stolen, how would you notify your clients?**

*Records help counselors
store a chronological account
of clinical situations*

BUSINESS ASSOCIATE AGREEMENT

CAVEAT: If you work for someone else, the agency/company either pays internal employees to handle these various clerical, professional or technical business related activities OR the agency/company's human resource/legal department executes needed Business Associate Agreements. IF you are self-employed [private practice], then you are responsible for completing this document.

You complete one of these when you use a third-party billing agencies, attorneys, agencies involved in the care of the client; cleaning services; computer technicians; collection agencies—any entity that could gain access to your clients protected health information.

BUSINESS ASSOCIATE DEFINED: In general, a business associate is a person or organization, other than a member of a covered entity's workforce, which performs certain functions or activities on behalf of, or provides certain services to, a covered entity that involves the use or disclosure of individually identifiable health information. Business associate functions or activities on behalf of a covered entity include claims processing, data analysis, utilization review, and billing.

Business associate services to a covered entity are limited to legal, accounting, consulting, data aggregation, management, administrative, accreditation, or financial services.

However, persons or organizations are not considered business associates if their functions or services do not involve the use or disclosure of protected health information, and where any access to protected health information by such persons would be incidental, if at all.

A covered entity can be the business associate of another covered entity.

SAMPLE BUSINESS ASSOCIATE AGREEMENT

CAVEAT: *For use in your own setting, forms must be personalized to reflect your state's relevant laws, ethical requirements for your licensing, and your own actual policies.*

BUSINESS ASSOCIATE AGREEMENT

This agreement is being entered into by and between the Healthcare Provider _____ and Business Associate _____ _____ to set forth the terms and conditions under which "protected health information" (PHI), as defined by the Health Insurance Portability and Accountability Act of 1996 (HIPAA) and Regulations enacted hereunder, created or received by ("Business Associate") on behalf of Healthcare Provider may be used or disclosed.

This Agreement shall commence on (Date) and the obligations herein shall continue in effect so long as Business Associate uses, discloses, creates or otherwise possesses any protected health information created or received on behalf of Health

Care Provider and until all protected health information created or received by Business Associate on behalf of Healthcare Provider is destroyed or returned to Healthcare Provider.

Healthcare Provider and Business Associate hereby agree that Business Associate shall be permitted to use and/or disclose protected health information created or received on behalf of Healthcare Provider for the following purposes:
- Completing and submitting healthcare claims to health plans or other third-party payers
- Collection of fees for Healthcare Provider
- Establishing, maintaining or repairing business management programs for Healthcare Provider
- Introducing, maintaining, and programming Electronic Medical Records Systems for Healthcare Provider.
- Other:
- Other:

It is to be understood by all parties that the permitted uses and disclosures must by within the scope of and necessary to achieve, the obligations and responsibilities of Business Associate in performing on behalf of, or providing services to, the Healthcare Provider.

Business Associate may use and disclose protected health information created or received by Business Associate on behalf of Healthcare Provider if necessary for the proper management and administration of Business Associate or to carry out legal responsibilities, provided that any disclosure is: Required by law, or Business Associate obtains reasonable assurances from the person to whom the protected health information is disclosed that (i) the protected health information will be held confidentially and used or further disclosed only as required by law or for the purpose for which it was disclosed to the person; and (ii) Business Associate will be notified of any instances of which the person is aware in which the confidentiality of the information is breached.

Business Associate hereby agrees to maintain the security and privacy of all protected health information in a manner consistent with XYZ State and Federal laws and regulations, including the Health insurance Portability and Accountability Act of 1996 ("HIPAA") and regulations hereunder, and all other applicable law. Business Associate further agrees not to use or disclose protected health information except as expressly permitted by this Agreement, applicable law, or for the purpose of managing Business.

Business Associate shall not disclose protected health information to any member of its workforce unless Business Associate has advised such person (employee) of Business Associate privacy and security obligations and policies under this Agreement, including the consequences for violation of such obligations. Business Associate shall take appropriate disciplinary action against any member of its workforce who uses or discloses protected health information in violations of this Agreement and applicable law.

Business Associate shall not disclose protected health information created or received by Business Associate on behalf of Healthcare Provider to a person, including any agent or subcontractor of Business Associate but not including a member of XYZ's workforce, until such person agrees in writing to be bound by the provisions of the Agreement and applicable [state] or Federal law.

Business Associate agrees to use appropriate safeguards to prevent use or disclosure of protected health information not permitted by this Agreement or applicable law.

Business Associate agrees to maintain a record of all disclosures of protected health information, including disclosures not made for the purposes of this Agreement. Such record shall include the date of the disclosure, the name and, if known, the address of the recipient of the protected health information, the name of the individual who is the subject of the protected health information, a brief description of the protected health information disclosed, and the purpose of the disclosure.

Business Associate agrees to report to Healthcare Provider any unauthorized use or disclosure of protected health information by Business Associate or its workforce or subcontractors and the remedial action taken or proposed to be taken with respect to such use or disclosure.

Business Associate agrees to make its internal practices, books, and records relating to the use and disclosure of protected health information received from Healthcare Provider or created or received by Business Associate on behalf of Healthcare Provider, available to the Secretary of the United States Department of Health and Human Services, for purposes of determining the Covered Entity's compliance with HIPAA.

Within thirty (30) days of a written request by Healthcare Provider, Business Associate shall allow a person who is the subject of protected health information, such person's legal representative, or Healthcare Provider to have access to and to copy such person's protected health information in the format requested by such person, legal representative, or practitioner unless it is not readily producible in such format, in which case it shall be produced in standard hard copy format.

Business Associate agrees to amend, pursuant to a request by Healthcare Provider, protected health information maintained and created or received by Business Associate, on behalf of the Practitioner. Business Associate further agrees to complete such amendment within thirty (30) days of a written request by Healthcare Provider, and to make such amendment as directed by Healthcare Provider. In the event Business Associate fails to perform the obligations under this Agreement, Healthcare Provider may, at its option: Require Business Associate to submit to a plan of compliance, including monitoring by Healthcare Provider and reporting by Business Associate, as Healthcare Provider, in its sole discretion, determines necessary to maintain compliance with this Agreement and applicable law. Such plan shall be incorporated into this Agreement by amendment hereto and Require Business Associate to mitigate any loss occasioned by the unauthorized disclosure or use of protected health information. Immediately discontinue providing protected health information to Business Associate with or without written notice to Business Associate.

Healthcare Provider may immediately terminate this Agreement and related agreements if Healthcare Provider determines that Business Associate has breached a material term of this Agreement. Alternatively, Healthcare Provider may choose to (i) provide Business Associate with ten (10) days written notice of the existence of an alleged material breach; and (ii) afford Business Associate an opportunity to cure said alleged material breach to the satisfaction of Healthcare Provider within (10) days. Business Associate's failure to cure shall be grounds for immediate termination of this agreement. Healthcare Provider's remedies under this Agreement are cumulative, and the exercise of any remedy shall not preclude the exercise of any other.

Upon termination of this Agreement, [business name] shall return or destroy all protected health information received from Healthcare Provider, or created or received by Business Associate on behalf of Healthcare Provider and that Business Associate maintains in any form, and shall retain no copies of such information. If the parties mutually agree that return or destruction of protected health information is not feasible, Business Associate shall continue to maintain the security and privacy of such protected health information in a manner consistent with the obligations of this Agreement and as required by applicable law, and shall limit further use of the information to those purposes that make the return or destruction of the information infeasible. The duties hereunder to maintain the security and privacy of protected health information shall survive the discontinuance of this Agreement.

Healthcare Provider may amend this Agreement by providing ten (10) days prior written notice to Business Associate in order to maintain compliance with XYZ State or Federal law. Such amendment shall be binding upon Business Associate at the end of the ten (10) day period and shall not require the consent of Business Associate Business Associate may elect to discontinue the Agreement within the ten (10) day period, but Business Associate duties hereunder to maintain the security and privacy of PROTECTED HEALTH INFORMATION shall survive such discontinuance. Healthcare Provider and Business Associate may otherwise amend this Agreement by mutual written agreement.

ETHICAL STANDARDS & CLINICAL FORMS

Business Associate shall, to the fullest extent permitted by law, protect, defend, indemnify and hold harmless Healthcare Provider and his/her respective employees, directors, and agents ("Indemnities") from and against any and all losses, costs, claims, penalties, fines, demands, liabilities, legal actions, judgments, and expenses of every kind (including reasonable attorneys fees, including at trial and on appeal) asserted or imposed against any Indemnities arising out of the acts or omissions of Business Associate or any of Business Associate's employees, directors, or agents related to the performance or nonperformance of this Agreement.

REMEMBER TO:
Include appropriate lines for signature and date.

RESEARCH
- **Search the Internet for "HIPAA Business Associate Agreements"**
  - Read the HIPAA text regarding these agreements
- **Find two more samples:**
  - How are they different from this sample? (Remember they can be tailored)
- **When, in your practice, would you need to use a Business Associate Agreement?**
- **If you are already using one or more, who is the agreement between?**

CLINICAL RECORDS

CAVEAT: States vary in laws, statutes, and state boards' ethical codes—*readers should know their state's health and safety codes, as well as the laws and statutes relevant to: Minors' Rights, Protective services, Mandatory Reporting, Licensing Board's Ethical Guidelines, and record requirements.*

DISCLAIMER: All samples & sample texts are intended as a guideline only. For use in your own setting, forms must be personalized to reflect your state's relevant laws and your own actual policies. Sample forms are designed for training purposes. Modify sample forms or sample text according your state's requirements and to the client, setting, and context of the work you do. Sample Forms and Sample Text ideas are provided "as is," without warranty of any kind; they are not intended to be a substitute for legal, ethical, or clinical advice or consultation.

CLINICAL RECORDS OVERVIEW

ETHICALLY YOU ARE REQUIRED TO MAINTAIN THE FOLLOWING INFORMATION ON A CLIENT:
- Client name and relevant information
- Consent/Patient Rights and Responsibilities' form—signed
- Dates seen
- Presenting problems
- Diagnosis (required if services are being paid by a third-party)
- Clinical encounters (with session notes)
- Document special occurrences: 1) important telephone calls, 2) emergencies, 3) dangerousness, 4) mandated and other reporting, 5) consultations, 6) testing, 7) referrals, 8) contact with family members
- Fee arrangement document and record of payments

CLINICAL NOTES REFLECT SERVICES
CLINICAL ASSESSMENTS SUPPORT A DIAGNOSIS
A DIAGNOSIS SHOULD SUPPORTS THE TREATMENT PLAN

ETHICAL STANDARDS & CLINICAL FORMS

RECORD KEEPING GUIDELINES
Records should reflect a counselor's competence, and their...
- Decision-making ability
- Capacity to weigh available options
- Rationale for treatment selection
- Knowledge of clinically, ethically and legally relevant matters

THE MAIN REASONS TO KEEP RECORDS ARE:
- Records help counselors provide quality care by providing counselors with continuity where they do not need to rely on their memory to recall details of their patients' lives and the treatment provided
- Not keeping any records is below the standard of care, is unethical and, in many states, illegal

CLIENT RECORDS
Maintaining records of service and storing them is not always easy.
Aside from the potential negative legal fallout of not doing so, there are good reasons for keeping records, including:
- Assisting both the practitioner and client in monitoring service progress and effectiveness
- Ensuring continuity of care should the client transfer to another worker or service
- Assisting clients in qualifying for benefits and other services
- Ensuring continuity of care should the client return
- To facilitate the delivery and continuity of services the counselor, with respect to documentation and client records must ensure that:
- Records are accurate and reflect the services provided:
    - Documentation is sufficient and completed in a timely manner
    - Documentation reflects only information relevant to service delivery
    - Client privacy is maintained to the extent possible and appropriate
    - Records are stored for a sufficient period after termination

RECORD RETENTION
State statutes, contracts with state agencies, accreditation bodies and other relevant stakeholders prescribe the minimum number of years records should be kept.

RECORD RETENTION (Continued)
- Typically it is seven years from the last time you saw a client [and seven years after a client turns 18] for mental health records. You can only destroy records by burning or shredding. Electronic records are typically stored forever.
- Many insurance companies are requiring preferred providers to keep records for 10 years from the last time they saw a client or 10 years from when a minor client turns 18.
- Records retention can vary depending on practice setting.
- If you work for an organization then adhere to their record retention policies.

CAVEAT: Counselors that are primary custodians of client records should refer to additional legal requirements, such as those established by state licensing boards and state laws regarding record retention and the care for client records in the event they retire and/or close their business or practice.

RESEARCH
- States vary regarding record retention
  - Contact your State's association or licensing board for requirements
- Internet search for record retention laws/record disclosure laws

MAINTAIN PROPER RECORDS

General guidelines recommend that records be accurate, current and relevant to the services provided.

Records are defined as any information, including information stored in a computer, that may be used to document the nature, delivery, progress, or results of psychological services.

MINIMUM STANDARDS FOR MAINTAINING PROPER RECORDS:

- Keep notes and assessment forms current. It is not uncommon to read a file with contradictory and confusing background information. Unless charts are shared, medical and mental health professionals can work at cross-purposes. As a counselor it is typically important to obtain releases and contact the other treating individuals. It is important to record a lack of response after the query.
- Review forms, especially consents and treatment interventions verbally with clients. Forms must be individualized to meet the needs of each client.
- Record client information changes in file and this includes basic contact information, as well as medication alterations.
- Include client's response to changes in medications or mental health treatment.
- Note changes in client compliance.
- Note other practitioner advice or treatment.
- Maintain neat and orderly files.
- Maintain client files for the legally required period. The length of time varies from state to state.
- Keep files in a secure location and all information confidential. It is not uncommon for clients to request their records several years after completing treatment.
- Counselors should protect the confidentiality of deceased clients consistent with the state standards.
- Counselors should take reasonable precautions to protect client confidentiality in the event of the counselor's termination of practice, incapacitation, or death.
- Counselors should transfer or dispose of clients' records in a manner that protects clients' confidentiality and is consistent with state statutes governing records and counseling licensure.
- Counselors should take precautions to ensure and maintain the confidentiality of information transmitted to other parties through the use of computers, electronic mail, facsimile machines, telephones and telephone answering machines, and other electronic or computer technology. Disclosure of identifying information should be avoided whenever possible.

CLIENT'S RIGHT TO...
REQUEST TO INSPECT, COPY, AND AMEND MEDICAL RECORDS

Clients have the right to review their medical records and to receive a copy of their medical records, but HIPAA takes the client's rights a step further. Clients have the right to request to amend their medical record, but they cannot automatically amend it. The following process must be followed.

THE STANDARD: An individual has a right to request to inspect, copy, and amend their medical record in most circumstances. Exceptions to this are specified below.

THE PURPOSE: Information is the rightful property of the individual whom the information is about; thus, individuals have a right to request to inspect, copy, and amend their medical records. Healthcare providers must act on the individual's request for inspection within 30 days for on site records and 60 days for off site records, and amendment requests within 60 days. The client's request can be denied with a valid explanation.

> **CAVEAT: HIPAA has determined these time frames. It is the reader's responsibility to ensure the current correct time frames as HIPAA could amend these at some point in time.**

PROCEDURE: An individual has a right to request to inspect, copy, and amend their medical record except for the following situations:
- Psychotherapy notes
- Information to be used in legal proceedings, civil, criminal, or administrative
- Information in regards to forensic purposes
- Information regarding research on testing human specimens
- If the requestor is an inmate whose knowledge of the information could cause harm or put in jeopardy, the individual, another inmate, other's involved in the criminal activity and case, or correction personnel
- Individuals participating in research studies cannot have access to the notes on the research while the research is ongoing

The individual accepting the request must verify the identification of the individual making the request. The identification verification method must be documented (e.g., checked driver's license). The healthcare provider typically has 30 days for on site record inspection and 60 days for off site record inspection and 60 days for amendment to be in compliance with the request. If more time is need, the provider must give to the requestor a written statement as to why the request is not completed within the 60 days. At this point, a one-time 30-day extension can be granted.

> **CAVEAT: HIPAA has determined these time frames. It is the reader's responsibility to ensure the current correct time frames as HIPAA could amend these at some point in time.**

IF THE REQUEST TO AMEND THE RECORD IS GRANTED, THE FOLLOWING OCCURS:
- Inform the requestor that the amendment was granted
- Insert the amended language at the point of the amendment or provide a note or symbol as to where the amendment is to be found
- Obtain from the requestor their consent [in writing] to share the amended information with relevant parties (e.g., consulting physician)

IF THE REQUEST TO AMEND THE RECORD IS DENIED, THE FOLLOWING OCCURS:
- A written statement in laymen's term of the reason for denial is given to the requestor
- The requestor has the right to submit in writing a statement of disagreement of which the facility can limit its length
- The healthcare provider can submit in writing a rebuttal, in laymen's terms, and a copy must be given to the requestor of the amendment
- The healthcare provider must make known to the requestor that they can follow-up with the Secretary of Health and Human Services
- The healthcare provider must include the denied request with any future disclosures of the client's health information

There is no limit as to how many times a request for amendment can be made.

REQUESTING AN AMENDMENT

CAVEAT: If the requesting client asks for assistance in completing a request, the healthcare provider must comply with the request. Two copies are to be made. The original is to go into the requestor's chart; the first copy is given to the requestor; and the second copy is given to the healthcare provider who is being asked to amend the record. (If multiple healthcare providers signed the record, such as a doctor, psychologist, and/or a physical counselor, then additional copy(ies) are made to satisfy the number of parties involved).

SAMPLE REQUEST FOR AMENDMENT

CAVEAT: For use in your own setting, forms must be personalized to reflect your state's relevant laws, ethical requirements for your licensing, and your own actual policies.

TO BE COMPLETED BY THE HEALTHCARE FACILITY:

Date original request was received on _____ by _____
Client's name _____Birthdate _____
Client's identification Verification _____[driver's license, passport]
Request for amendment has been (Circle one)   ACCEPTED   DENIED
If DENIED, check reason:
[ ] Information was not created by this facility
[ ] Information is not required by law to be inspected
[ ] Information is not part of the designated record set
[ ] Information is certified accurate and complete
Additional explanation, if needed: _____

REMEMBER TO: Include appropriate lines for signature(s) and date.

RESEARCH
Find another sample of a "request for amendment." Ask larger clinics if they would share. Always follow the policies and procedures of the organization you work for regarding this matter.

ETHICAL STANDARDS & CLINICAL FORMS

SUGGESTED DOCUMENTS
- Administrative and Intake Forms
- HIPAA Compliance
- Assessment Forms
- Psychological Evaluations
- Treatment Planning Forms and Procedures
- Progress Notes
- Other Forms Used During the Course of Treatment
- Chart Review and Outcomes Documentation
- Termination and Aftercare
- Essential Initial Forms
- Informed Consent
- Intake Information
- Financial Arrangements
- Biographical Questionnaire
- Assessments
- Essential Documents
- HIPAA Disclosure Document regarding PHI [Protected Health Information]
- Consent to Release Information (FOLLOW HIPAA GUIDELINES)
- Authorization to Release Information (FOLLOW HIPAA GUIDELINES)
- Billing
- Financial Arrangements
- Overdue Payment Letter
- Consents and Authorizations
- Consent for Treatment (Tailored to your practice)
- Professional Disclosure Statement
- Session Related Documents
- Treatment Plan
- Progress Notes
- Suicide Check List/Suicide Safety Plan
- Misc. Documents
- FAX cover sheet and e-mail statement regarding confidentiality
- Responding to a Subpoena
- Professional Will
- Directive to Protect Mental Health Information
- Termination Forms and Letters
- Termination Summary
- Termination Letters

THREE KEY FORMS:
1) Notice of Privacy Practices (page 319)
2) Authorization Forms (page 319)
3) Client Consent Forms (page 320)

1) NOTICE OF PRIVACY PRACTICES
Organizations considered covered entities under HIPAA are mandated to inform clients of the new privacy rights and their privacy policies and procedures. To comply, you'll need to develop a Notice of Privacy Practices and provide it to your patients at the first office visit. HIPAA also requires you to obtain the client's written acknowledgement that the notice has been received and file the acknowledgement in the client's record. A client's refusal to sign the acknowledgement should be documented and filed in the client record.

RESEARCH
Key word Internet searches for:
- **HIPAA and covered entities; HIPAA and Notice of Privacy Practice document; HIPAA and HITECH Privacy Requirements; Health Information Technology and HIPAA; Electronic Health Records (EHR); Conversion to electronic health records; Summary of HIPAA Privacy Rule; *www.HHS.gov* and HIPAA; Patient access to electronic health records; Securing electronics health records; HHS rules for electronic health records**
  - **These are all documents that you should be familiar with.**

2) AUTHORIZATION FORM
To comply, you'll need to identify situations in your practice where special authorization is needed and develop an authorization form for clients to sign. Forms should be adapted for use in your practice. A signed copy or documentation of the client's refusal to sign should be retained in the client record.

RESEARCH
Key word Internet searches for:
- **Sample HIPAA authorization form**
  - **Also see the "Authorization for Disclosure" section.**

3) CLIENT CONSENT FORM

Informed consent is a legal procedure to ensure that a patient, client, and research participants are aware of all the potential risks and costs involved in a treatment or procedure. Providing professional disclosure statements and financial arrangement is also considered elements of informed consent. Informed consent includes informing the client of the nature of the treatment, possible alternative treatments, and the potential risks and benefits of the treatment.

The principles of informed consent revolve around: protection, autonomy, the prevention of abusive conduct, trust, self-ownership, non-domination, and personal integrity.

> **RESEARCH**
> Key word Internet searches for:
> - Informed consent form templates for counseling

See the "Informed Consent" section for more details.

CLINICAL RELATIONSHIPS
CLINICAL RELATIONSHIPS AND CLIENT SELF-DETERMINATION

A standard that strongly reflects the mental health counselor's commitment to a client is that of client self-determination.

Counselors have an obligation to support and assist clients in accomplishing their goals, only deviating from this when a client's goal puts them or others imminently at risk. Defining risk can be difficult—mental health counselors cannot argue that suicide or homicide presents a clear risk to the client or to others. Other client choices, such as staying in an abusive relationship or living in squalor or on the streets may challenge a counselor's personal values and sincere desire to protect; also known as "professional paternalism." However, in the absence of clear and present harm, the client has a right to choose his or her own path and make his or her own decisions, whether we agree or disagree.

RESEARCH
- Look up "professional paternalism." Make note of key points.
  - Aside from the examples listed above, what other situations can you think of that are harmful behaviors? (Those that fall outside the mandatory duty of intervening/reporting, such as suicide, homicide; the intention of harm to self or others)
  - To get you started: severe eating disorders, fire-starting, driving under the influence of drugs or alcohol...
- How would you address these concerns with your client?
  - Would the use of a specific treatment plan with a compliance element be helpful? If the client agreed to the plan and the compliance...
- Do you think they would tell you if they were out of compliance?
  - If they told you, what would you do?

CLINICAL RELATIONSHIPS: THE THERAPEUTIC RELATIONSHIP

The Therapeutic Relationship: Assisting or attempting to assist an individual with emotional, behavioral, or mental issues.

SAMPLE IDEAS / SAMPLE TEXT TO EXPLAIN COUNSELING IN GENERAL AND THE CLINICAL RELATIONSHIP:
- Counseling, as in the context of a therapeutic relationship, does not guarantee saved marriages, continued employment, social acceptance, or elimination of presenting symptoms. Nor, is it a guarantee that symptoms won't worsen.
- Many clients remain "stuck" due to external influences beyond the therapeutic relationship or lack of commitment to explore options and try alternatives.
- You, as the client, are ultimately responsible for change or non-change.
- Everyone has periods of time in their life of difficulty, change and transition, when personal issues affect their work and relationships. Issues such as family, marital, career, financial, physical, abuse of alcohol/drugs, or a variety of mental issues.
- Counseling can help with incongruent thoughts, difficult relationships, career issues, over-whelming emotions, fears, disturbing memories, bad habits, confusion, chemical dependencies, violence and anger issues, adjustment issues and depression.
- It is a multi-level process that requires you to have the ability, desire and willingness to see yourself objectively.
- Drugs and alcohol create false realities and self-images, interfering with the underlying issues and the ability to gain deeper insights. Individuals actively using drugs or alcohol must go through assessment and be referred to a recovery program, or Chemical Dependency Counselor, first.
- Mental struggles can be physical, psychological, emotional, intellectual or cultural. There are no discrimination barriers to private pain.
- Counseling provides options for change. Change can be the catalyst for growth and personal maximization.
- You will benefit the most from counseling if you explore options and pursue solutions to your hopes and aspirations.
- The input and active participation from you, the client, is essential in order to ensure your individuality and personal style.

RESEARCH
- **Being able to explain to a client, in a few words, what counseling is; what counseling is about, is needed.**
  - **Add as many other general statements about counseling as you can to the above list.**
- **What would your "90 second" explanation be? Write it down.**

CLINICAL RELATIONSHIPS: BUILDING TRUST WITH CLIENTS

TO HELP BUILD A TRUSTING THERAPEUTIC RELATIONSHIP, DISCUSS WITH YOUR CLIENT:
- The guidelines for counselor/client affiliation, such as professional practice boundaries and client rights
- Review fees for professional service
- Discuss mental health treatment protocols
- Share under what circumstances confidentiality can legally be breached, such as reporting child abuse
- Building trust:
  - Avoid intimidation or abusing professional authority
  - Work at partnering with clients
  - Be consistently on time, returning phone calls and responding to other communication
  - Be authentic about advocating on behalf of client
  - Encourage clients to ask questions and seek out answers regarding their medical treatment as an active member of their healthcare team
  - Teach assertiveness and encourage questions, and model behavior
  - Understand your professional limitations and make referrals whenever necessary
  - Check in frequently with client about their perceptions of treatment progress

CLINICAL RELATIONSHIPS AND FAITH BASED COUNSELING

There are many associations and articles on the Internet regarding religious and faith-based counseling.

Faith-based counseling is an approach to therapy that includes insights of theology and spirituality, which are integrated with the principles of psychology to help individuals, couples, families, and groups.

Different from other forms of counseling, faith-based counseling is guided by the conviction that emotional illnesses are best healed by taking into consideration both the wisdom of spiritual teachings and the knowledge of human psychology.

CAVEAT: If you are a faith-based counselor, offering counseling that incorporates a specific faith, make sure your consent form includes this information.

RESEARCH
- Research two associations that are relevant to the type of faith-based practice you offer.
  - Explore their code of ethics. Training programs. Philosophy.
- Web search these key words: faith-based [insert specific faith] counseling consent form sample.

CLINICAL RELATIONSHIPS: HUMOR AND THERAPY

The goal of counseling is to help clients feel better and act differently. All models of counseling attempt to reach this goal by creating interventions that focuses on one of four areas: feelings, behaviors, thinking, and/or biochemistry. Humor can effect changes in all four areas.

THE USE OF HUMOR IN COUNSELING REQUIRES THE COUNSELOR TO:
- Have humor in their repertoire and be willing to risk using the humor
- Have the ability to assess a client's level of humor; their openness to it
- Be prepared to respond to a client's negative reaction to humor

> **CAVEAT: The counselor must avoid gratifying his or her own need to be humorous and focus on how humor will be helpful to the client. As with all therapeutic interventions the counselor must ask, "How will this humor help my client?" Use humor, which is genuine and natural, congruent with who the counselor is as a person.**

- Many counselors argue that to be effective, humor must be spontaneous. Humor indeed must be spontaneous; however, it can be "planned spontaneity."
- Effective therapeutic interventions are planned in that the counselor is trained to offer facilitative responses to the client. At any moment during treatment the counselor selects a particular response based on his or her knowledge of the client and what interventions might be effective with a particular client.
- The above concept applies to the use of therapeutic humor. However, the way in which "humor" tools are utilized to intervene therapeutically with a particular client is based on the counselor's understanding of the client and the timing of the intervention.

RESEARCH
- **The use of humor in therapy would depend on the type of counseling, the setting, the diagnosis, theoretical orientations, and counselor's personality?**
  - **Which would be conducive to humor; which would not?**
  - **Do you think humor can be planned? (Planned spontaneity)**

CLINICAL RELATIONSHIPS AND CONFIDENTIALITY: KEY POINTS

CAVEAT: there are many more ethical points on confidentiality, but here are some of the key points. It is the reader's responsibility to know all ethical and legal guidelines regarding confidentiality.

Confidentiality is an ethical concept, and simply put, means that what is shared within the therapeutic relationship will not be voluntarily disclosed by the counselor. Confidentiality is essential because it fosters trust, which is the bedrock of the therapeutic alliance. Privilege is distinguished from confidentiality in that disclosure is typically involuntary. In other words, confidentiality "binds" the counselor not to reveal client material even if the counselor feels "inclined" to do so. Privilege protects client information from inappropriate disclosure when pressed by legal authorities.

- Counselors should not discuss confidential information in any setting unless privacy can be ensured. Counselors should not discuss confidential information in public or semi public areas such as hallways, waiting rooms, elevators, and restaurants.
- Counselors should protect the confidentiality of clients during legal proceedings to the extent permitted by law. When a court of law or other legally authorized body orders counselors to disclose confidential or privileged information without a client's consent and such disclosure could cause harm to the client, they should request that the court withdraw the order or limit the order as narrowly as possible or maintain the records under seal, unavailable for public inspection.
- Counselors should discuss with clients and other interested parties the nature of confidentiality and limitations of clients' right to confidentiality. Counselors should review with client's circumstances where confidential information may be requested and where disclosure of confidential information may be legally required. This discussion should occur as soon as possible in the counselor-client relationship and as needed throughout the course of the relationship.

BASIC CONFIDENTIALITY POLICIES
- Counselors should respect clients' right to privacy. They should not solicit private information from clients unless it is essential to providing services or conducting counseling evaluation or research. Once private information is shared, standards of confidentiality apply.
- Counselors may disclose confidential information when appropriate with valid consent from a client or a person legally authorized to consent on behalf of a client.
- Counselors should protect the confidentiality of all information obtained in the course of professional service, except for compelling professional reasons, such as mandatory reporting (to prevent harm to a client/other).
- In all instances, counselors should disclose the least amount of confidential information necessary to achieve the desired purpose; only information that is directly relevant to the purpose for which the disclosure is made.
- Counselors should inform clients, to the extent possible, about the disclosure of confidential information and the potential consequences, when feasible before the disclosure is made.

CONFIDENTIALITY AND INSURANCE COMPANIES
- Counselors should not disclose confidential information to third-party payers unless clients have authorized such disclosure.
- Counselors should protect the confidentiality of clients when responding to requests from members of the media.
- Counselors should protect the confidentiality of clients' written and electronic records and other sensitive information. Counselors should take reasonable steps to ensure that clients' records are stored in a secure location and that clients' records are not available to others who are not authorized to have access.
- Counselors should not disclose identifying information when discussing clients with consultants unless the client has consented to disclosure of confidential information or there is a compelling need for such disclosure.

RESEARCH
- **Web search with these key words: Mental health confidentiality case examples**
    - Take the time to read a few of these examples. Personally reflect on or discuss with colleagues.

CLINICAL RELATIONSHIPS AND PROFESSIONAL BOUNDARIES

Our profession is a unique profession, as we have previously discussed. Vulnerable clients plus therapeutic and interpersonal challenges equals boundary issues. There are five common boundary crossing or boundary violation themes: Intimate relationships, personal gain and benefit, emotional dependency needs, good intention gestures, and unanticipated circumstances.

It's not hard to understand why counselors can find themselves in sticky situations, simple stumbles, and slippery slopes. Many things can trip us up: mental mistakes, personal biases, limited perspectives, convincing rationalizations, accidental blunders, the client's diagnosis, hidden agendas, blurred roles, conflictual relationships, difficult clinical settings, etc. The necessary intensity of a therapeutic relationship may tend to activate intense emotions, dependency, sexual and other needs, and fantasies on the part of both the client and the counselor, while weakening the objectivity necessary for good therapy.

CLINICAL RELATIONSHIPS AND BOUNDARY VIOLATIONS

Boundary violations are the wrong, unethical, and possibly illegal behaviors between a counselor and the client. Self-interest or personal gain by the counselor is present in boundary crossings. This self-interest has nothing to do with being paid for services rendered, nor the personal satisfaction a counselor can feel from doing their job well; these are exploitive. Boundary violations are reflected in self-interest(s) gained by a counselor at the expense of their client. There is exploitation.

CAVEAT: A client's consent is never a defense with boundary violations, because of the respective roles. The counselor has the fiduciary responsibility to act in the best interests of the client and boundary violations reflect self-interests. When a counselor exploits a client it is universally regarded as unethical, is considered in every jurisdiction to constitute malpractice, and in some states certain types of boundary violations are a criminal offense. Clients are harmed by boundary violations. Injuries include sexual dysfunction, anxiety disorders, psychiatric hospitalizations, increased risk of suicide, depression, dissociative behavior, internalized feelings of guilt, shame, anger, confusion, hatred, inability to trust and feelings of worthlessness and humiliation. Clients are harmed by boundary violations.

CLINICAL RELATIONSHIPS AND BOUNDARY CROSSINGS

Boundary crossings are defined as non-exploitive deviations from standard practice. What is "standard practice" or counseling norm? It is counseling a client in an office; counselor and client working together in a private setting. Boundary crossings may encompass benign and beneficial departures from established counseling norms. There is a virtual explosion of healthy controversy and thoughtful writings on the issue. Is it possible to tell which boundary crossings are therapeutically helpful; which are therapeutically contra-indicated as harmful; which might be common or even unavoidable in certain communities, settings, or cultures? The meaning of boundaries and their appropriate application can only be understood and assessed within the context of therapy.

THE CONTEXT OF THERAPY CONSISTS OF FOUR MAIN COMPONENTS: CLIENT, SETTING, THERAPY, AND COUNSELOR.

CLIENT FACTORS: Culture and history, such as: history of trauma, sexual and/or physical abuse, age, gender, presenting problem, mental state, and type and severity of mental disturbances, socioeconomic class, personality type and/or personality disorder, sexual orientation, social support, religious and/or spiritual beliefs and practices, physical health, prior experience with therapy and counselors, etc.

SETTING FACTORS: Outpatient versus inpatient; solo-practice versus group-practice; office in medical building versus private setting versus home office; freestanding clinic versus hospital-based clinic; privately owned clinic versus publicly run agency, as well as the presence or proximity of a receptionist, staff, or other professionals. It also includes locality: large, metropolitan area versus small, rural town; affluent, suburban setting versus poor neighborhood; or university, school or other academic settings; culturally-bound settings, major urban settings, remote military bases, prisons, or police department settings.

THERAPY FACTORS:
- Modality: individual versus couple versus family versus group therapy; short-term versus long-term versus intermittent therapy.
- Intensity: therapy sessions several times a week versus once a month; population: child versus adolescent versus adults.
- Therapeutic orientation: psychoanalysis versus humanistic versus group therapy versus psychotherapy versus eclectic therapy

- In addition, there are therapeutic relationship factors such as the quality and nature of the therapeutic alliance (secure, trusting, tentative, fearful, or safe connection). Intense and involved versus neutral or casual relationships; length of counseling, long term relationship versus the beginning of therapy versus middle of therapy versus towards termination of therapy. Other relationship factors include idealized or transference relationship issues, familiarity or distanced, presence or absence of dual relationships and type of dual relationships, if applicable.

COUNSELOR FACTORS: culture, age, gender, philosophy, therapeutic orientation, faith and belief issues, scope of practice (training and experience).

CLINICAL RELATIONSHIPS:
BOUNDARIES AND DUAL RELATIONSHIPS...

The prohibition against dual relationships, originates from two sources: 1) Appropriate concerns with the power differential between counselors and clients along with the appropriate attempt to protect clients from harm or exploitation. 2) Traditional counseling emphasis on neutrality and transference work and the concern for the impairment of a counselor's judgment. Many sources warn counselors about the dangers of dual relationships: Professional organizations, consumer protection agency (state licensing boards), and, in some states, legislative laws, agree completely with counselor-client prohibitions of sexual relationships due to exploitation and client harm as the basis for all these protective policies and guidelines. As mention previously, boundary crossings occur when we deviate from standard norms, but we do so for the client's benefit—the boundary is changed to assist the client. Such crossings have the potential for creating a dual relationship, but it is not a dual relationship "in and of itself" because the purpose of the boundary crossing is therapeutic. The purpose is relevant to theory orientations and the boundary crossing is discussed with the client and informed consent obtain.

RESEARCH
- **Is it possible to tell which boundary crossings are therapeutically helpful?**
  - **Which are therapeutically contra-indicated as harmful?**
  - **Which might be common or even unavoidable in certain communities or cultures?**

CLINICAL RELATIONSHIPS AND BOUNDARY CROSSING PLAN

You can create a boundary-crossing plan (not unlike a suicide safety plan) or an addendum to your consent regarding planned boundary crossings. Clear expectations and boundaries, whenever possible, strengthen the therapeutic relationship. This is especially important in situations where out-of-therapy contact cannot be closely controlled. Obtaining informed consent, sticking to time limits, protecting confidentiality (and explaining its limits), and documenting case progress (including being explicit about any overlapping relationships) diminishes the risk of misunderstandings between client and counselor

---

SAMPLE TEXT FOR A BOUNDARY CROSSING AGREEMENT

CAVEAT: For use in your own setting, forms must be personalized to reflect your state's relevant laws, ethical requirements for your licensing, and your own actual policies.

[Counselor] and [Client] have agreed to an intervention that will occur [state the location] for the purpose of helping the client with [state the condition]. Counseling outside the office is not a dual relationship nor is it unethical. This type of counseling can enhance trust and therapeutic effectiveness, but can also detract from it and often it is impossible to know that ahead of time. It is the client's responsibility to communicate to [counselor] if this intervention, done in the above stated location, becomes uncomfortable for you in any way. [Counselor] will always listen carefully and respond accordingly to your feedback; take appropriate steps to clarify, modify or withdraw from any situation that might be interfering with the effectiveness of the therapy or the welfare of the client, and, of course, you can do the same at any time.

REMEMBER TO: Include appropriate lines for signature and date; Keep a copy of any document that was signed by a client in the client's file (hardcopy or electronic); Copy to client optional, unless they request a copy.

RESEARCH
Sample Boundary Crossing Agreement
- **What statements would you change?**
- **What additional statements would you add?**

CLINICAL RELATIONSHIPS: NON-SEXUAL DUAL (MULTIPLE) RELATIONSHIPS

Non-sexual dual relationships are not necessarily unethical or illegal. Only sexual dual relationships with current clients are always unethical and illegal. Non-sexual dual relationships do not necessarily lead to exploitation, sex, or harm. Almost all ethical guidelines do not mandate a blanket avoidance of dual relationships; however, all guidelines do prohibit exploitation and harm of clients.

GUIDELINES FOR NON-SEXUAL DUAL RELATIONSHIPS IN PSYCHOTHERAPY

- Develop a clear treatment plan for clinical interventions, which are based on the context of therapy (the type of therapy intervention) and intervene with clients according to their needs
- Always take into consideration the welfare of the client, effectiveness of treatment, avoidance of harm and exploitation, conflicts of interest, and the impairment of clinical judgment. These are the paramount and appropriate concerns
- Remember that treatment planning is an essential and irreplaceable part of your clinical records and your first line of defense
- Consult with clinical, ethical or legal experts in very complex cases and document the consultations well
- Attend to and be aware of your own needs through personal therapy, consultations with colleagues, supervision or self-analysis
- Discuss with your clients the complexity, richness, potential benefits, drawbacks and likely risks that may arise due to dual relationships
- Make sure that your treatment plan include the risks and benefits of dual relationships and that they are fully explained, read and signed by your clients before you implement them
- Make sure your clinical records document clearly all consultations

RESEARCH

- **Which therapeutic orientations might utilize dual relationships as an element of therapeutic care?**
  - Internet search for information about "community assertiveness programs" and "social clubs." What do you think? Can you come up with other examples like these?
- **What client conditions would make a non-sexual dual relationship therapeutically contra-indicated as harmful?**
- **Which might be common or even unavoidable in certain communities or cultures?**

SAMPLE TEXT FOR DUAL RELATIONSHIP CONSENT

CAVEAT: For use in your own setting, forms must be personalized to reflect your state's relevant laws, ethical requirements for your licensing, and your own actual policies

- Not all dual or multiple relationships are unethical or avoidable
- Therapy never involves sexual or any other dual relationship
- [Counselor] has assessed carefully before entering into a non-sexual and non-exploitative dual relationship with [client's name]
- [Name of community/town] is a small community and many clients know each other and [counselor] from the community
- [Counselor] will never acknowledge working with anyone without his/her written permission.
- Many clients choose to see [counselor] as their counselor because they know him/her from the community or from other clients
- [Counselor] has discussed with client the potential benefits and difficulties that may be involved in dual or multiple relationships
- Dual or multiple relationships can enhance trust and therapeutic effectiveness, but can also detract from it and often it is impossible to know that ahead of time
- It is the client's responsibility to communicate to [counselor] if the dual or multiple relationship becomes uncomfortable in any way
- [Counselor] will always listen carefully and respond accordingly to your feedback
- [Counselor] will take appropriate steps to clarify, modify or withdraw from any situation that might be interfering with the effectiveness of the therapy or the welfare of the client, and, of course, you can do the same at any time

RESEARCH
Sample Dual Relationship Consent
- **What would you change?**
  - Delete? Add?
- **What sample text in the above consent do you strongly agree with? Why?**
- **What sample text do you strongly disagree with? Why?**

CLINICAL RELATIONSHIPS:
CLIENT ATTITUDES THAT CAN CAUSE PROBLEMS...
- Yearning to be an "insider"
- Feeling "someone owes me"
- Black and white view of things
- Demanding to be believed
- Insatiable neediness
- Over-generalizations
- Over-dramatized responses
- Poor and confused boundaries
- Diffused sexuality

CLINICAL RELATIONSHIPS AND SUICIDE RISK
- Laws and Ethics in Suicide Intervention: Suicide is not only one of the riskiest cases for a counselor clinically and spiritually, but legally as well. Professional counselors are increasingly at legal risk for the suicide of their clients and patients.
- Indeed, the counselor working in an inpatient or restrictive treatment setting has a strong duty to intervene in the life of someone judged to be a substantial risk for suicide.
- In contrast, a pastor in a church setting may be ethically and morally, but not legally, bound to a duty of suicide intervention.

CLINICAL RELATIONSHIPS AND HOMICIDE RISK
- Since it is impossible to predict with 100% accuracy dangerousness ahead of time, violation of a client's confidentiality must be undertaken with great care and in consultation with others.
- The art of counseling involves learning to discern what a client is really saying.
- When someone says, "I wish I (or someone else) was dead" are they talking suicide or homicide or just expressing frustration with their current stress levels or relationship difficulties?

RESEARCH
- **How do we distinguish between the client who vents in scary ways and those who may carry out their threatening words?**
- **How would you assess the difference?**

CLINICAL RELATIONSHIP
FEATURES of DANGEROUS...
- Immediate danger signs of imminent violence:
  - Motor activity is irritable with an inability to be calmed
  - Verbal indicators such as threats when stated loudly, defamatory statements, and sexual verbal aggression
  - Nonverbal indicators include glaring eyes, demanding demeanor, tense, forward-leaning posture, and a hyper-alert state

NOTE: See the "assessment" section for more detailed information on assessing suicidal, homicidal behaviors and issues of dangerousness.

CLINICAL RELATIONSHIPS
CONFRONTING THERAPY IMPASSE...
The counselor's best understanding of the situation suggests a course of action. However unclear that initial understanding is action needs to be taken to confront therapy impasses. Not doing so may close the door to the counselor's own creativity, intuition, and ability to help; and, to refrain from discussing impasses may interfere with the client's progress and recovery.

When an impasse is reach, it is helpful to consider these options:
Carefully review your work with a client, this can help in finding a way beyond an impasse. ASK YOURSELF THESE QUESTIONS:
- Was there something the client said or did that didn't seem make sense?
- Is there an issue that needs to be clarified with the client?
- Has the client said or done something that cast confusion and diminishes understanding of what is going on?

REGARDING AN IMPASSE: Counselors should ask themselves if the contemplated action is consistent with the welfare of the client?

> **CAVEAT:** Complex legal issues may make this consideration more difficult. In some instances, a counselor may take an action that may not be construed by all concerned as clearly consistent with the welfare of the patient. A counselor may be legally required to report that the client has engaged in child abuse or has threatened to kill a third party, even though some counselors may believe that such reports are not consistent with the welfare of the client.

WHEN AN IMPASSE IS REACHED, IT IS HELPFUL TO CONSIDER:
- Is the contemplated action consistent with the basic informed consent of the client? (All action by the counselor must be carefully considered in light of its consistency with the client's autonomy)

SEE THE IMPASSE THROUGH THE CLIENT'S EYES:
- Empathize imaginatively with the client
- Regardless of the theoretical soundness, intended outcome, or intervention sophistication, consider how the client might understand or view the situation
- Consult with colleagues and talk with the client

CAVEAT: Counselors-in-training may cling to theory, intention, and technique as a way of coping with the anxieties and combat the overwhelming responsibilities of the therapeutic venture. Seasoned counselors may rely almost exclusively on theory, intention, and technique out of learned reflex, habit, and the sheer weariness that approaches burnout. There is always risk that the counselor will fall back on repetitive and reflexive responses that verge on stereotype. One way to help avoid responses that are driven more by anxiety, fatigue, or similar factors is to consider carefully how you, the counselor, would think, feel, and react if you were the client.

CLINICAL RELATIONSHIPS AND ERRORS
DEFINITION OF AN ERROR
"Medical Error" definitions can be defined and governed by various entities such as state legislatures, mental health associations, and best practice institutions; for the purpose of preserving the health, safety and welfare of the public.

"Medical errors" can occur at any point in treatment, even in preventive care and are not limited to patient/client injury or death

As more and more mental health clients are being treated for complex physical and mental co-occurring conditions, mental health counselors often work with teams of intervention specialists. Also, counselors are increasingly in contact with mental health clients who are following medication protocols and other medical therapies; many of which are potentially lethal when taken improperly.

Medical Error (Harm) includes:
- Permanent loss of trust by client/patient

As a result of medical error, mental health clients can:
- Lose trust that their personal information will be properly shared
- Lose trust in the psychological or medical community due to the medical team's inability to share information pertinent only to specific team members

A medical error is, not necessarily the failure of a planned intervention, but it is the use of a wrong plan that causes an adverse event or near miss that is preventable under the current state of knowledge. Counselors have serious responsibilities to their clients, colleagues, and to the mental health profession. The focal point of these inter-related responsibilities is a fiduciary relationship in which the client places trust in the counselor with the expectation that the counselor is working in the client's best interest. This expectation is the foundation of a therapeutic relationship. Through the therapeutic relationship each party assumes separate and distinct roles. The counselor bears the burden of accountability within the relationship because they assume the expert role; this creates a power differential within the relationship. By virtue of expertise through education, degree, license, skills, and experience, counselors have the positional power setting the stage for potential misuse of power. With any position of power comes the risk for abuse that can range from minor improprieties to gross misconduct and crime.

GREATEST RISK FOR COMMITTING MEDICAL ERROR OCCURS THROUGH:
- Multiple professional involvements
- Misdiagnosis
- Over treatment
- Lack of involvement

WHEN COUNSELORS DO NOT MAINTAIN APPROPRIATE BOUNDARIES, THE FOLLOWING COMMON MEDICAL ERRORS CAN OCCUR:
- Inappropriately shares or distorts information
- Attempts to treat out of their realm of expertise
- Does not consult with medical professionals
- Does not thoroughly collect background histories
- Does not thoroughly complete assessments
- Assigns an incorrect, or false diagnosis
- Recommend inappropriate or dangerous treatment protocol

NEGLIGENCE CAN OCCUR WHEN THE COUNSELORS IS:
- Overly fatigued; In a hurry; or, Inattentive and distracted
- Does not access and/or thoroughly review client records
- Negligent in not writing, recording, reading or sharing critical reports, reviews or correspondence
- Not paying attention to laws and regulations regarding confidentiality and consent
- Counselor is physically or mentally ill
- Not providing an adequate physical professional environment
- Imposing religious or spiritual beliefs on to clients
- Lacking in follow-up; or, Habituated Behavior
- Negligent in gaining correct medication information
- Slow response and follow up with regard to client or calls or crisis
- A lack of concern for the client's well being
- Inattention to, or minimization of client concerns and self-reporting
- Poor communication with clients, their families or other treatment team members
- Disregard for professional boundaries
- Lack of Knowledge

INTENTIONAL HARM
Intentional harm can be considered a crime when counselors mindfully...
- Become romantically and/or sexually involved with clients
- Romantic or sexual innuendos are medical errors
- Falsely bill and/or charge fees to clients or insurance
- Administer inappropriate or grossly wrong methods of treatment
- Fail to contact medical personnel or law enforcement when clients threaten to, and/or actually harm themselves or others
- Fail to report child abuse or make other appropriate reports to monitoring agencies or personnel
- Prescribe medications without sufficient licensing or expertise
- Abandon Clients. It is imperative that mental health professionals do not abandon their clients due to failure to pay or incompatibility; it is the professional's job to transition clients and pursue alternative treatment avenues before closing a case
- Falsify records; or, Breach confidentiality
- Falsely claim curative abilities

CLINICAL RELATIONSHIPS: AVOIDING ERRORS
COMPETENT COUNSELORS FOLLOW THESE GUIDELINES...

- Best practice knowledge: It is important that licensed mental health practitioners, through various ways, stay current in their counseling practice.
- Professional development: Professional development includes but is not limited to on-going consultation and supervision, peer review, course work, certification training, seeking additional schooling through graduate degree work or academic participation, professional membership and periodical reading.
- Current laws and regulations: Regulations regarding the practice of psychotherapy change. It is best to keep abreast of these changes through legislation and association participation. Every state has a state website that provides information on proposed laws.
- Necessary certification training: Certification is usually required before practicing a new psychotherapeutic technique. It is always best to affiliate with other practitioners who are participating in the same type of protocol.
- Thorough client social histories or background information: Medical error occurs when medical or mental health practitioners do not diagnosis and treat from the same back ground information.
- Consultation with colleagues/experts: Consultations with colleagues and experts provide fundamental reality checks for mental health practitioners.

WHAT ABOUT APOLOGIZING?

In the mental health and healthcare professions, there is a concern about apologizing to clients (or patients) for mistakes. Apologies can make someone feel vulnerable. Will the apology be accepted or will it make things worse? Will the apology come back to hurt me as an admission of guilt in a formal licensing complaint or lawsuit? Admitting mistakes can be difficult. However, it can come down to intention versus impact. If what you are apologizing for was intentional then being fearful of apologizing as an admission of guilt has merit. But most of the time our actions, in words and deeds, are not done with the intention of harm, but rather impact others in a way we did not anticipate. Research, and common sense, suggests that an apology can help heal the effects of inadvertent or unintended mistakes. Many states have passed "I'm sorry" laws to encourage healthcare providers to promptly and fully inform clients and patients of errors and to apologize when warranted, and other states are considering such laws.

This law protects apologizer from being held to an admission of guilt because of the apology. Research further suggest that ethical complaints, that were considered, but never filed, were indeed not filed because an apology was made. As counselors in the mental health profession, we understand the healing power of words. Apologizing is a personal, intimate act that can calm hurt feelings, restore rapport, and opens the possibility of honest dialogue. However, deciding whether or not to apologize requires careful consideration of many factors. The decision to do so should be considered thoughtfully, cautiously, and with the advice of consultation.

RESEARCH
- **Does your state have healthcare related "I'm Sorry" laws and legislation?**

CLINICAL RELATIONSHIPS: BOUNDARIES SELF-ASSESSMENT
Below are red flags that professional boundaries may be compromised.
- Have you ever kept a secret with a client?
- Have you ever adjusted your dress for a client?
- Has a client ever changed a style of dress for you?
- Have you ever received a gift from a client?
- Have you shared personal information with a client? (information that has no therapeutic relevance)
- Have you ever bent the rules for a client?
- Have you ever given a client a gift?
- Do you think you could ever become over-involved with a client?
- Have you ever felt possessive about a client?
-

RESEARCH
- **Answer the above questions.**
- **What other questions can you come up with?**
- **Think of a difficult counseling situation (or find a case example on the Internet regarding boundaries/clinical relationships)**
  - Explore all the ways you can think of that would make the situation worst.
  - Explore all the best practice approaches to the same situation.

COACHING

Coaching, as a modality for mental health care, is a personal alliance designed to uncover and amplify the personal strengths of clients to achieve their health, sports, business and life goals. It is typically an active approach using powerful questions and processes to resolve limiting beliefs and promote new effective strategies for thinking and acting.

Counselors who use this approach to counseling typically help clients develop a personal "map" of health and excellence. The client's unique map isn't just about what behaviors would be helpful, but it includes their beliefs and values, strategies, and their sense of self and purpose in the world. With a coaching approach, counselors help clients rapidly resolve barriers to change and maximize their focus and motivation.

SAMPLE COACHING CONSENT

CAVEAT: For use in your own setting, forms must be personalized to reflect your state's relevant laws, ethical requirements for your licensing, and your own actual policies.

Coaching and Psychotherapy

Explain your education and experience: In addition to being a coach, I am also a licensed [type] in [name of state(s)] with training and experience in diagnosing and treating emotional problems. While there are some similarities between coaching and psychotherapy, they are very different activities and it is important that you understand the differences between them.

Psychotherapy is a healthcare service and is usually reimbursable through health insurance policies. This is not true for coaching. Both coaching and psychotherapy utilize knowledge of human behavior, motivation and behavioral change, and interactive counseling techniques. The major differences are in the goals and focus.

The focus of coaching is development and the implementation of strategies to reach client-identified goals of enhanced performance and personal satisfaction. Coaching may address specific personal projects, life balance, job performance and satisfaction, or general conditions in the client's life, business, or profession. Coaching utilizes personal strategic planning, values clarification, brainstorming, motivational counseling, and other counseling techniques.

The primary foci of psychotherapy are identification, diagnosis, and treatment of mental and nervous disorders. The goals of psychotherapy include alleviating symptoms, understanding the underlying dynamics which create symptoms, changing dysfunctional behaviors which are the result of various disorders, and developing new strategies for successfully coping with the psychological challenges which many face.

Most research on psychotherapy outcomes indicates that the quality of the therapeutic relationship is most closely correlated with therapeutic progress. Psychotherapy clients are often emotionally vulnerable. This vulnerability is increased by the expectation that they will discuss very intimate personal data and expose feelings about themselves, which are sensitive. The past life experiences of psychotherapy clients have often made trust difficult to achieve. These factors give counselors greatly disproportionate power that creates a fiduciary responsibility to protect the safety of their clients and to "above all else, do no harm."

The relationship between the coach and client is specifically designed to avoid the power differentials that occur in the psychotherapy relationship. The client sets the agenda and the success of the enterprise depends on the client's willingness to take risks and try new approaches. The relationship is designed to be more direct and challenging. You can count on your coach to be honest and straightforward, asking powerful questions and using challenging techniques to move you forward. You are expected to evaluate progress. When coaching is not working as you wish, you should immediately inform me so we can both take steps to correct the problem.

Because of these differences, the roles of coach and counselor are often in potential conflict and I believe that, under most circumstances, it is ethically inappropriate for one to play both roles with a client, whether concurrently or sequentially. Positive change is difficult enough without having to worry about role confusion. This means that if either of us recognizes that you have a problem that would benefit from psychotherapeutic intervention, I will refer you to appropriate resources. In some situations, I may insist that you initiate psychotherapy and that I have access to your counselor as a condition of my continuing as your coach. It is also important to understand that coaching is a professional relationship.

While it may often feel like a close personal relationship, it is not one that can extend beyond professional boundaries both during and after our work together. Considerable experience shows that when boundaries blur, the hard won benefits gained from the coaching relationship are endangered.

> **CAVEAT: You must also include regular consent information, especially information regarding the limits of confidentiality.**

REMEMBER TO:
Include appropriate lines for signature and date; Keep a copy of any document that was signed by a client in the client's file (hardcopy or electronic); Copy to client optional, unless they request a copy.

RESEARCH
Sample Coaching Consent
- **What would you change? Delete? Add?**
- **What sample text in the above consent do you strongly agree with? Why?**
- **What sample text do you strongly disagree with? Why?**

*Records provide analysis
of clinical work and
of your interactions with clients*

COMPLEMENTARY AND ALTERNATIVE THERAPIES

Many Americans use "Complementary and Alternative Medicine" (CAM) in pursuit of health and well-being.

- Defining CAM is difficult; the field is very broad and constantly changing.
- CAM practices are often grouped in broad categories, such as natural products, mind and body medicine, and manipulative and body-based practices.

SAMPLE CAM CONSENT

CAVEAT: For use in your own setting, forms must be personalized to reflect your state's relevant laws, ethical requirements for your licensing, and your own actual policies.

By signing this form, I, _____ [name of client], agree that [name of counselor] has disclosed to me sufficient information, including the risks and benefits, to enable me to decide to undergo (or forgo) [name of therapy or course of treatment] for [name of client's condition].

Our discussion has included:
    1) The nature of my condition
    2) The nature and probability of risks
    3) The benefits to be reasonably expected
    4) The inability of the practitioner to predict results
    5) The available alternatives

I have elected to use the following Complementary and Alternative therapy(ies): [list therapies]. My consent to this course of treatment is given voluntarily, without coercion, and may be withdrawn, and I am competent and able to understand the nature and consequences of the proposed treatment or procedure. I have carefully read this form and acknowledge that I understand it.

I have read, understand, and agree to the above stated policies.
Include appropriate signature lines...

ETHICAL STANDARDS & CLINICAL FORMS

CAVEAT: You must also include regular consent information, especially information regarding the limits of confidentiality.

REMEMBER TO:
Include appropriate lines for signature and date; Keep a copy of any document that was signed by a client in the client's file (hardcopy or electronic); Copy to client optional, unless they request a copy.

RESEARCH
Sample CAM Consent
- **What would you change? Delete? Add?**
- **What sample text in the above consent do you strongly agree with? Why?**
- **What sample text do you strongly disagree with? Why?**

CONFIDENTIALITY STATEMENT FOR ELECTRONIC TRANSMISSIONS

When sending a fax or an e-mail that has to do with private health information, the following statement needs to be included.
- For a fax, the statement should be on the cover page
- For an e-mail, the statement should follow your signature line

SAMPLE CONFIDENTIALITY STATEMENT

CAVEAT: For use in your own setting, forms must be personalized to reflect your state's relevant laws, ethical requirements for your licensing, and your own actual policies. Always check for the latest requirements.

E-mail or Fax Cover Page Confidentiality Statement:

This message and accompanying documents are covered by the Electronic Communications Privacy Act, 18 U.S.C. 2510-2521, and contain information intended for the specified individual(s) only. This information is confidential. If you are not the intended recipient or an agent responsible for delivering it to the intended recipient, you are hereby notified that you have received this document in error and that any review, dissemination, copying, or taking of any action based on the contents of this information is strictly prohibited. If you have received this communication in error, please notify us immediately by _____, and delete the original message.

RESEARCH
- **Periodically, you must check to see if the above text has had any content change(s)**
- **If you work for an agency or organization, follow their policy**
- **Internet search for the "Electronic Communication Privacy Act, 18 U.S.C. 2510-2521"**
    - Take the time to read it

ETHICAL STANDARDS & CLINICAL FORMS

CONFLICTS BETWEEN CODES OF ETHICS AND LAWS

CONFLICTS BETWEEN ETHICS AND LAW, REGULATIONS, OR OTHER GOVERNING LEGAL AUTHORITY:
- If counselor's ethical responsibilities conflict with law, regulations, or other governing legal authority, psychologists make known their commitment to the Ethics Code and take steps to resolve the conflict
- If the conflict is unresolvable via such means, counselor may adhere to the requirements of the law, regulations, or other governing legal authorities

CONFLICTS BETWEEN ETHICS AND ORGANIZATIONAL DEMANDS
- If the demands of an organization with which counselors are affiliated or for whom they are working, conflict with their ethical codes, counselors clarify the nature of the conflict, make known their commitment to the ethical code and, to the extent feasible, resolve the conflict in a way that permits adherence to the ethical code.

RESEARCH
- **Think of a situation from your past or conceptualize one that's an example of an organization asking a counselor to do something unethical. (You can also web search these key words: conflicts between counselors and organizations case example)**
  - **If you were the counselor in the situation, how would you approach your supervisor?**
  - **What if it was your supervisor that was asking you to do something unethical?**
- **What would you do if the situation was unable to be resolved?**

CONSULTATION

Making use of consultation as a regular component of clinical activities, rather than, as a resource used only on atypical occasions, is one way to extend the learning process as a focus of exploration and discovery.

- Consultation with a variety of colleagues on a frequent basis can strengthen the sense of community in which counselors work
- It can provide a safety net, helping counselors to ensure that their work does not fall into needless errors, unintentional malpractice, or harmful actions that are due to lack of knowledge, guidance, perspective, challenge, or support
- It can create a sense of cooperative venture in which the process of professional development, exploration, and discovery continue
- Consultation with colleagues reflects a counselor's competence
- Consultation is an element of remaining in "standard of care" (what other mental health professionals would reasonable do)

One red flag to the possibility that a course of action is inappropriate is the counselor's reluctance to disclose it or talk about it with colleagues.

COMPETENT COUNSELORS FOLLOW THESE GUIDELINES:
- Best practice knowledge: It is important that licensed mental health practitioners, through various ways, stay current in their counseling practice.
- Professional development: Professional development includes but is not limited to on-going consultation and supervision, peer review, course work, certification training, seeking additional schooling through graduate degree work or academic participation, professional membership and periodical reading.
- Current laws and regulations: Regulations regarding the practice of psychotherapy change. It is best to keep abreast of these changes through legislation and association participation. Every state has a state website that provides information on proposed laws.
- Necessary certification training: Certification is usually required before practicing a new psychotherapeutic technique. It is always best to affiliate with other practitioners who are participating in the same type of protocol.

- Thorough client social histories or background information:
  Medical error occurs when medical or mental health practitioners do not diagnosis and treat from the same background information. Obtaining releases of information is essential when providing and coordinating appropriate client service.
- Consultation with colleagues/experts: Experts are fundamental reality checks for mental health practitioners.

CAVEAT: To remain ethical, counselor must consult with colleagues on a regular basis. Counselors, who work in an organization, have, at their disposal, colleagues, consultation groups and supervisors to consult with. Counselors in private practice must connect with other counselor and form a consultation group. Ethical codes refer to the necessity for consultation throughout the sections.

RESEARCH
- If a counselor does not choose to consult, then reflect on this question.
    - Is there a compelling reason for not discussing the contemplated action with a colleague, consultant, or supervisor?
    - What could some compelling reasons be? Are they ethical reasons? Or unethical?
- Think of a situation where consultation would be ethically appropriate (or find a case example on the Internet)
    - One question a counselor may ask about any proposed action is this: If I took this action, would I have any reluctance for all of my professional colleagues to know that I had taken it?
- If discussion with a colleague has not helped to clarify the issues, consultation with additional professionals, each of whom may provide different perspectives and suggestions, may be needed.

SAMPLE INFORMED CONSENT FOR CLINICAL CONSULTATION
(CONSULTANT-CONSULTEE CONTRACT)

CAVEAT: *For use in your own setting, forms must be personalized to reflect your state's relevant laws, ethical requirements for your licensing, and your own actual policies.*

I wish to receive consultation services from _____ [*list colleague's name and credentials*]. I understand that these consultations do not constitute clinical supervision and that I remain completely responsible, ethically and legally, for the decisions I make in my own clinical case situations. My consultant will provide me with an opportunity to discuss clinical cases and issues about which my consultant may have some expertise, and he/she may help me consider options for responding, but the comments made for my consideration are not supervisional mandates. I also understand that although we may sometimes need to discuss personal issues that may be relevant to my clinical work, these consultation services do not constitute psychotherapy. I understand the potential limits of the confidentiality of this relationship. To the extent possible, my case presentations will provide no identifiable patient information. However, I understand that if I provide identifiable information about a situation regarding which my consultant has an ethical or legal obligation to report confidential information, my consultant will inform me at the time and will give me the opportunity to make the report myself. I understand that if my consultant becomes aware that she/he knows or has a prior relationship with the presented client(s), or if she believes she has a potential conflict of interest in her relationship with me, she will notify me of that fact immediately and will cooperate in helping me find a different consultant. I agree to the fee of $_____ per one-hour consultation session, payable at each meeting.

REMEMBER TO: *Include appropriate lines for signature and date.*

RESEARCH
Sample Consultation Consent
- **What would you change? Delete? Add?**
- **What sample text in the above consent do you strongly agree with? Why?**
- **What sample text do you strongly disagree with? Why?**

Counselors refrain from initiating an activity when they know or should know that there is a substantial likelihood that their personal problems will prevent them from performing their work-related activities in a competent manner

COUNSELOR IMPAIRMENT

BURNOUT

An area receiving increasing attention is that of burnout and compassion fatigue. The consequences of burnout and compassion fatigue (or any other form of professional impairment) include the risk of malpractice action. Results from the effects of day-to-day annoyances, overburdened workloads, crisis, and other stressors in the work place; burnout and compassion fatigue can be serious and considered similar in many ways to acute stress and post-traumatic stress.

BURNOUT: It is a "breakdown of psychological defenses that workers use to adapt and cope with intense job-related stressors and syndrome in which a worker feels emotionally exhausted or fatigued, withdrawn emotionally from clients, and where there is a perception of diminishment of achievements or accomplishments." Burnout occurs when gradual exposure to job strain leads to an erosion of idealism with little hope of resolving a situation.

WHEN MENTAL HEALTH COUNSELORS EXPERIENCE BURNOUT:
- Their coping skills are weakened
- They are emotionally and physically drained
- They feel that what they do does not matter anymore
- They feel a loss of control
- They are overwhelmed

COMPASSION FATIGUE

A newer definition of worker fatigue was introduced late in the last century by social researchers who studied workers who helped trauma survivors. This type of worker fatigue became known as Compassion Fatigue or Secondary Traumatic Stress (STS). Mental health practitioners acquire Compassion Fatigue or STS as a result of helping or wanting to help a suffering person in crisis.
- "Burnout" is gradually acquired over time and recovery can be somewhat gradual.
- "Compassion Fatigue" surfaces rapidly and diminishes more quickly. Both conditions can share symptoms such as emotional exhaustion, sleep disturbance, or irritability.

DEALING WITH BURNOUT AND COMPASSION FATIGUE

A professional mental health counselor can take steps to increase her or his ability to cope and achieve balance in life. Maintaining a healthy lifestyle balance and recognizing the signs of burnout and compassion fatigue are one thing: the responsible mental health counselor will also take action, such as a vacation break or change in schedule or job duties. Counselors also need to not only be aware of the signs and symptoms of burnout and compassion fatigue, but more importantly the situations that may set the stage for their occurrence.

MEASURES TO HELP PREVENT BURNOUT OR COMPASSION FATIGUE:

- Listen to the concerns of colleagues, family, and friends
- Conduct periodic self-assessments
- Take needed "mental health days" and use stress-reduction techniques
- Arrange for reassignment at work, take leave, and seek appropriate professional help as needed

COUNSELOR IMPAIRMENT

Counselors should not allow their own personal problems, psychosocial distress, legal problems, substance abuse, or mental health difficulties to interfere with their professional judgment and performance or to jeopardize the best interests of people for whom they have a professional responsibility.

Counselors whose personal problems, psychosocial distress, legal problems, substance abuse, or mental health difficulties interfere with their professional judgment and performance should immediately seek consultation and take appropriate remedial action by seeking professional help, making adjustments in workload, terminating practice, or taking any other steps necessary to protect clients (patients) and others.

PERSONAL PROBLEMS AND CONFLICTS:

- Counselors refrain from initiating an activity when they know or should know that there is a substantial likelihood that their personal problems will prevent them from performing their work-related activities in a competent manner.

COUNSELOR IMPAIRMENT:
IMPAIRMENT OF COLLEAGUES...
- Counselors who have direct knowledge of a counseling colleague's impairment that is due to personal problems, psychosocial distress, substance abuse, or mental health difficulties and that interferes with practice's effectiveness should consult with that colleague when feasible and assist the colleague in taking remedial action.
- Counselors who believe that a counseling colleague's impairment interferes with practice effectiveness and that the colleague has not taken adequate steps to address the impairment should take action through appropriate channels established by employers, agencies, licensing and regulatory bodies, and other professional organizations.

CAVEAT: Generally, each state has an oversight or governing agency where counselors can make reports and/or access complaint forms. They can differ in complaint procedure and action. Nationally, The Joint Commission on Accreditation of Healthcare Organizations (JCAHO) conducts investigations. Professional associations monitor membership and usually have established protocols to investigate complaints as well. These oversight or governing entities gather and analyze complaints, and determine probable cause and disciplinary action. If a complaint is determined to be a possible violation of law it will be investigated by a legal designate.

RESEARCH
- Think of a situation from your past or conceptualize one that's an example of colleague impairment? (You can also web search these key words: counselor impairment case example)
  - If you were the counselor in the situation, how would you approach your colleague?
  - What would you do if the situation were unable to be resolved?

ETHICAL STANDARDS & CLINICAL FORMS

In work with families,
the rights of each family member
should be safeguarded

COUPLES AND FAMILIES
COUNSELING COUPLES AND FAMILIES
TREATMENT WITH COUPLES OR FAMILIES
Providing services to several persons who have a relationship (such as spouses, significant others, or parents and children):
- Counselors should seek agreement among the parties involved concerning each individual's right to confidentiality and obligation to preserve the confidentiality of information shared by others.
- Counselors should inform participants in couples and family counseling that counselors cannot guarantee that all participants will honor such agreements.

Confidentiality is weakened whenever there are more than two people (counselor and client) in the room. In couple's counseling, the courts say that either one can compel the release of the records.

ETHICAL GUIDELINES FOR COUPLES AND FAMILY WORK:
- When counselors provide services to two or more people who have a relationship with each other (for example, couples, family members), they should clarify with all parties which individuals will be considered the client(s) and the nature of counselors' professional obligations to the various individuals who are receiving services.
- Counselors who anticipate a conflict of interest among the individuals receiving services or who anticipate having to perform in potentially conflicting roles should clarify their role with the parties involved and take appropriate action to minimize any conflict of interest.
- In work with families, the rights of each family member should be safeguarded. The provider of service also has the responsibility to discuss the contents of the record with the parent and/or child, as appropriate, and to keep separate those parts, which should remain the property of each family member.
- Where a child or adolescent is the primary client, or the client is not competent to give consent, the interests of the minor or the incompetent client shall be paramount. Where appropriate, a parent(s) or guardian(s) may be included in the counseling process. The mental health counselor must still take measures to safeguard the client's confidentiality.

ETHICAL STANDARDS & CLINICAL FORMS

> **CAVEAT:** When counseling couples and families (minors) specific consent forms addressing the special circumstances (relationship of parties involved to the counselors and the counselors responsibilities to those involved) are developed, explained and used. Careful consideration about what information has to be shared, and shared with whom, should be addressed and documented.

COUPLES AND FAMILY TREATMENT

Change happens within the context of the relationship(s) and the community systems through increasing healthy relationships and healthy environments.

- With couples and In families, all members interact with and affect each other in continuing patterns that can be understood as a dance
- There is a process of change that can be taught and learned
- Attachment theory involves skill building for all members
- Self-soothing and self-regulation for children and caregivers are essential

COUNSELING COUPLES AND FAMILIES
KEY POINTS FOR COUNSELORS:

- Stay for the long haul
- Stay calm
- Understand where behavior is coming from
- Reframe, reframe, reframe
- Use love, boundaries, and humor
- Caregivers need respite because this is exhausting work

THE PROCESS OF CHANGE:

- You can help with change, but you cannot make a client change. It must be a cooperative process
- Change is easiest when done with the support of the entire family
- Motivation (and supportive relationships) is the primary vehicle for change
- Change is not a straight path. It is up and down
- Hope and a picture of the destination are essential for success

FAMILY SYSTEMS
Systems are made up of many interactive parts and the whole is more than the sum of its parts.
- Every part of a system can change and this will affect another part of the system
- A well functioning system will gather information from other systems and grow and learn from the interactions fairly easily and tend to be healthy
- Closed systems will reject information and relationships from the outside and are more likely to be unhealthy

REDUCING AND MANAGING FAMILY CONFLICTS:
- Reframe a perception to help family members see it in another light and react differently

COUPLES OR FAMILY MEETINGS:
- Set aside one night each week for family discussion and have an agenda
- Let every family member sign up for a topic
- Practice good problem solving skills
- Practice "I statements" and active listening
- Manage emotions effectively

CAVEAT: Counselors should inform clients involved in couples or families counseling concerning the counselor's disclosure of confidential information among the parties involved in the counseling.

RESEARCH
- Working with more than one client requires... (List what as many things as you can think of)
- For a counselor leading a group, what specific skills would best serve them?
  - Search the Internet: How many established groups (e.g., AA) programs can you find?
  - What do you think would be the most difficult part of leading a group?

ETHICAL STANDARDS & CLINICAL FORMS

COUPLES AND FAMILY COUNSELING
AVOIDING THE SECRET KEEPER ROLE, DISCUSS WITH COUPLES:
- Whether you also see each party individually or only as a couple.
- The reality that you are not the "secret keeper." Explain that what's discussed individually [if relevant to the relationship] needs be discussed at the next couple's session. (See CAVEAT below)
- Both parties' signatures will be required to release copies of the file to either party individually.

CAVEAT: When counseling minors, families, couples, or groups some counselors choose to include the following statement in a consent document: "The counselor remains the arbitrator as to what information shared individually need to be shared jointly." WHY? Such a statement enables counselors to remove themselves from a "secret keeper" position. Certainly counselors take into consideration all information shared individually and its relevance and necessity of being shared jointly, before doing so.

SAMPLE COUPLES AND FAMILY COUNSELING RECORD RELEASE AGREEMENT

CAVEAT: For use in your own setting, forms must be personalized to reflect your state's relevant laws, ethical requirements for your licensing, and your own actual policies.

When there is more than one person in the room with the healthcare professional there is a "limit of confidentiality." Anyone in the room could choose to speak about the session to outsiders. Although all parties should treat information shared as confidential, it is equally important that all parties involved know that confidentiality is limited. Further, if any one of the parities requests copies of the chart it will require the signature of all parties that signed the original "Consent of Treatment" before any information will be released.

REMEMBER TO:
Include appropriate lines for signature and date.

COUPLES AND FAMILIES
SAMPLE CONFIDENTIALITY CONTRACT

CAVEAT: For use in your own setting, forms must be personalized to reflect your state's relevant laws, ethical requirements for your licensing, and your own actual policies.

This contract is an agreement between the interested parties that neither party shall for any reason attempt to subpoena my testimony or my records to be presented in a deposition or court hearing of any kind for any reason, such as a divorce case. Both parties acknowledge that the goal of psychotherapy, either individual or marital or couples therapy, is for the sole purpose of the amelioration of psychological distress and that the process of psychotherapy depends on trust and openness during the therapy sessions. Therefore it is understood by both parties that if they request my services as a counselor, they are expected not to use information given to me during the therapy process against the other party in a judicial setting of any kind, be it civil, criminal, or circuit.

REMEMBER TO:
Include appropriate lines for signature and date; Keep a copy of any document that was signed by a client in the client's file (hardcopy or electronic); Copy to client optional, unless they request a copy.

RESEARCH
Samples: Record Release Agreement AND Confidentiality Contract for Couple and Families
- **What would you change? Delete? Add?**
- **What sample text in the above two consent samples do you strongly agree with? Why?**
- **What sample text do you strongly disagree with? Why?**

SAMPLE COUPLES AND FAMILY COUNSELING
COLLABORATIVE COUNSELING

CAVEAT: For use in your own setting, forms must be personalized to reflect your state's relevant laws, ethical requirements for your licensing, and your own actual policies.

LITIGATION LIMITATION

[Counselor] has explained the "collaborative" nature of the therapeutic process they provide in working with couples and/or families. The goal of therapy is to seek resolution for the issues that brought you to therapy. This process may result in decisions about changing behaviors, employment, or relationships (to name a few). Another family member may view a decision that is positive for one family member as negative. Change sometimes can be easy and quick, but more often it will be slow and frustrating. There is no guarantee that psychotherapy will yield the positive or intended results.

Working with couples and/or families often involves making a full disclosure with regard to many matters which may be of a confidential nature, so all parties involved agree that if legal proceedings (such as, but not limited to divorce and custody disputes, injuries, lawsuits, etc.) occur in the future, all parties involved in psychotherapy with [counselor] agree to not call on [counselor] to testify in court or at any other proceeding. Further, the psychotherapy records will not be requested and/or disclosed unless otherwise agreed to by all parties involved. [Counselor] provides neither custody evaluation recommendation; medication or prescription recommendation; nor, legal advice, as these activities do not fall within [counselor's] scope of practice.

REMEMBER TO:
Include appropriate lines for signature and date; Keep a copy of any document that was signed by a client in the client's file (hardcopy or electronic); Copy to client optional, unless they request a copy.

RESEARCH
Sample Collaborative Counseling for Couple and Families
- What would you change? Delete? Add?
- What sample text in the above consent do you strongly agree with? Why?
- What sample text do you strongly disagree with? Why?

CAVEAT: Please note that there is some controversy over this type of document. If a client(s) signs this, it does not guarantee you'll never be court ordered to appear in court, However, it does help establish up front the nature of collaborative counseling. Further, attorneys use such an agreement with clients seeking a divorce— *"collaborative divorce" counsel, which basically states that as long as the couple is working together corroboratively the attorney will work with them.* However, if the couple cannot continue to work together corroboratively, then they will need to find new attorneys.

***Both the counselor's
and the client's culture
is present in each
interaction***

CULTURAL COMPETENCIES

CULTURAL COMPETENCE AND SOCIAL DIVERSITY
Cultural competence and social diversity in mental health practice recognizes that mental health professionals provide services that are sensitive to each client's culture.

DEMONSTRATING ETHICAL CULTURAL COMPETENCE INCLUDES:
- Being knowledgeable about culture and its impact on human behavior
- Recognizing and appreciating the strengths found in cultures
- Considering the nature of social diversity and oppression

CULTURAL COMPETENCE, IN GENERAL, IS DEFINED AS: The ability of individuals and systems to respond respectfully and effectively to people of all cultures, classes, races, ethnic backgrounds, sexual orientations, and faiths or religions in a manner that recognizes, affirms, and values the worth of individuals, families, tribes and communities, and protects and preserves the dignity of each.

LINGUISTIC COMPETENCE IS DEFINED AS: The capacity of a mental health professional to communicate effectively and convey information in a manner that is easily understood by diverse audiences including persons of limited English proficiency, those who are not literate or have low literacy skills, and even individuals with disabilities.

IMPROVING CULTURAL COMPETENCIES:
Mental health professionals and service providers can improve their cultural competence by taking the following steps:
- Use open-ended questions to identify each person's unique cultural outlook
- Re-evaluate intake and assessment documentation, as well as policies and procedures, to be more inclusive
- Employ qualified mental health workers who are fluent in the languages of the groups being served
- Understand the cultural biases of staff and provide training to address educational needs
- Understand the cultural biases in program design
- Identify resources, such as natural supports, within the community that will help an individual recover

ETHICAL STANDARDS & CLINICAL FORMS

- Design and implement culturally sensitive treatment plans
- Evaluate procedures and programs for cultural sensitivity and effectiveness
- Survey clients and colleagues to elicit their understanding of cultural competence and culturally competent practice

The Association for Multicultural Counseling and Development (AMCD) outlines the need and rationale for A MULTICULTURAL PERSPECTIVE IN COUNSELING. Visit: multiculturalcounseling.org for more information.

RESEARCH
- **The "Cultural Formation Interview"**
  - Go to *www.psychiatry.org/dsm5* for this assessment (and others)

INDICATORS OF CULTURAL RESPONSIVENESS:
- Awareness of and sensitivity to personal cultural heritage(s)
- Value and respect for differences between cultures
- Awareness of the role of cultural background and experiences, attitudes, and values
- Acknowledgement of personal competency and expertise
- Sensitivity towards potential negative emotional reactions toward others that may cloud interpersonal connections
- Willingness to contrast own beliefs and attitudes with those of culturally different people in a non-judgmental fashion

RESEARCH
- **What are resources that you can use to increase your knowledge of other cultures?**
- **Visit your local library or bookstore:** Browse through the children's book section and look for stories from other cultures. Check out the biographies and autobiographies of people from different cultural backgrounds.
- **Explore the Internet:** Do searches on topics of interest to you.
- **Attend local cultural celebrations:** street fairs, festivals, or other cultural celebrations.

DIAGNOSING

Diagnosing requires knowldge, skills, practice.

> and CAVEAT: If legal action or litigation is brought against a counselor the diagnosis they've given to a client is where apposing counsel will dig and try to prove incompetence. We need to follow DSM criteria. As a counselor you must be familiar with the current version of the DSM and competent in its use. If at all possible, take your time when it comes to a diagnosis. Therapy is a relationship. All relationships start with unknowns. Relationships are about getting to know the person. Diagnostics are present in the therapy relationship, but we treat the person with the diagnosis, not the diagnosis. Therapy is a process, not an event. And, test and measurements can never be the source of diagnosis; it must be combined with clinical perceptions.

DIAGNOSING REQUIRES KNOWLEDGE

Counselors know the principles of the diagnostic process, including differential diagnosis, and the use of current diagnostic tools, such as the Diagnostic and Statistical Manual of Mental Disorders (DSM). They know the impact of co-occurring addictive disorders on medical and psychological disorders. Counselors understand the relevance and potential cultural biases of commonly used diagnostic tools as related to clients with disorders in multicultural populations. They are clear about current definitions for mental disorders.

DIAGNOSING REQUIRES SKILLS AND PRACTICE

Counselors demonstrate the appropriate use of diagnostic tools, including the current edition of the DSM, to describe the symptoms and clinical presentation of clients with disorders and mental and emotional impairments. They are able to conceptualize an accurate diagnosis of disorders presented by clients and communicate the diagnosis with collaborating professionals.

MISDIAGNOSIS

When a counselor fails to diagnosis a condition accurately, or at all, it can be malpractice when the failure occurs by virtue of providing care below generally accepted professional standards, pursuant to which the client was injured.

REASONS FOR DIAGNOSIS ERRORS:
- Clients with the same diagnosis do not necessarily function at similar levels. Therefore, much more than a diagnosis should be documented.
- A diagnosis, in itself, does not imply the level of care needed. Therefore, specific client needs must be considered and documented.
- If medical necessity is not documented the client may be denied services by a third-party payer. Therefore, specific problems in functional impairment must be documented.
- Although counseling may be helpful, it does not imply medical necessity. Therefore, it is important to explain to the client that services are not necessarily covered by a third-party.

REASON THAT THE SAME CLIENT RECEIVES DIFFERENT DIAGNOSES:
- Multiple disorders, but not all initially detected.
- Incorrect, incomplete, or conflicting previous or current information obtained
- Discrepant cyclical behaviors that are observed at different points in the cycle by different counselors
- Effects of using (or abstaining from) alcohol or drugs
- Medications: effects, level of compliance, changes, interactions, side effects
- Changes in levels and types of environmental stressors that lead to different reactions
- Organic or physical factors affecting psychological conditions
- Counselor's expertise, experience, and theoretical stance
- Level of client's insights, exaggerations, or denial
- Malingering or secondary gain
- Actual changes in diagnosis

RESEARCH
- **The DSM has been criticized for pathologizing bias against women, lower socioeconomic class, geriatric population, ethnic groups, and other populations:**
  - What other populations can you add?
  - Give examples of how each of these groups might be diagnosed incorrectly...

E-COUNSELING

IMPORTANT ISSUES REGARDING E-COUNSELING
Clients should be informed about...
- Confidentiality: Mental health counselors ensure that clients are provided sufficient information to adequately address and explain the limitations of computer technology in the counseling process in general and the difficulties of ensuring complete client confidentiality of information transmitted through electronic communications over the Internet through on-line counseling. Professional counselors inform clients of the limitations of confidentiality and identify foreseeable situations in which confidentiality must be breached in light of the law in both the state in which the client is located and the state in which the professional counselor is licensed.
- Mental Health Counselor Identification: Counselors provide professional disclosure statements that include information regarding their education, licensing and certification, and practice information.
- Client Identification: Professional counselors identify clients, verify identities of clients, and obtain alternative methods of contacting clients in emergency situations.
- Electronic Transfer of Client Information: informed written consent of the client, acknowledging the limits of confidentiality, has been obtained.

OBTAIN A CLIENT WAIVER: Mental health counselors require clients to execute client waiver agreements stating that the client acknowledges the limitations inherent in ensuring client confidentiality of information transmitted through on-line counseling and acknowledge the limitations that are inherent in a counseling process that is not provided face-to-face.

ESTABLISHING THE ON-LINE COUNSELING RELATIONSHIP:
- Appropriateness of On-line Counseling: Mental health counselors ensure that clients are intellectually, emotionally, and physically capable of using on-line counseling services, and of understanding the potential risks and/or limitations of such services.
- Counseling Plans: Mental health counselors develop individual on-line counseling plans that are consistent with both the client's individual circumstances and the limitations of on-line counseling.

ETHICAL STANDARDS & CLINICAL FORMS

- Mental health counselors who determine that on-line counseling is inappropriate for the client should avoid entering into or immediately terminate the on-line counseling relationship and encourage the client to continue the counseling relationship through a traditional alternative method of counseling.
- Boundaries of Competence: Mental health counselors provide on-line counseling services only in practice areas within their expertise. Mental health counselors do not provide services to clients in states where doing so would violate local licensing laws or regulations.

LEGAL CONSIDERATIONS

Mental health counselors confirm that the provision of on-line services are not prohibited by or otherwise violate any applicable state or local statutes, rules, regulations or ordinances, codes of professional membership organizations and certifying boards, and/or codes of state licensing boards. Treating clients exclusively via technology puts counselors at a disadvantage because they cannot detect nonverbal cues, may not be aware of the resources available locally, and may not be able to intervene as effectively as necessary in emergency situations. Acute crises and severe psychological disturbances, such as schizophrenia, bipolar or some types of personality disorders may not be effectively handled via phone, e-mail or other web-based communications.

CAVEAT: Make sure you operate within your scope of practice and be very careful about practicing across state lines or with clients who are in danger to themselves or others or suffer from significant mental impairments.

SAMPLE E-COUNSELING CONSENT

CAVEAT: For use in your own setting, forms must be personalized to reflect your state's relevant laws and your own actual policies.

CAVEAT: You must also include regular consent information, especially information regarding the limits of confidentiality.

E-COUNSELING
- I hereby consent to engage in e-counseling (using the Internet for counseling) with [counselor] as the main venue for my psychotherapy treatment

- I understand the laws that protect the confidentiality of my medical information also apply to e-counseling; however, there are both mandatory exceptions to confidentiality including, but not limited to: *reporting child, elder, and dependent adult abuse; expressed threats of violence as outlined in my main consent form, which you have signed*
- I understand that there are risks with e-counseling. These may include, but are not limited to, the possibility, despite reasonable efforts on the part of my counselor, that the transmission of medical information could be disrupted or distorted by technical failures; interrupted by unauthorized persons; or, medical information could be accessed by unauthorized persons. Further, miscommunication or misunderstandings in dialog can more easily occur due to the lack of face-to-face counseling
- Additionally, e-counseling services may not produce the same results nor be as effective as face-to-face counseling. I also understand that if my counselor believes I would be better served by another form of psychotherapeutic service (e.g., face-to-face therapy), I will be referred to a counselor in my area who can provide such service
- Finally, I understand that there are potential risks and benefits associated with any form of psychotherapy, and that despite my efforts and the efforts of my counselor, my condition may not improve and in some cases may even get worse. I will openly and honestly discuss any concerns with my counselor on a regular basis
- Some benefits of e-counseling may include, but are not limited to: *finding a greater ability to express thoughts and emotions; transportation and travel difficulties are avoided; time constraints are minimized; and there may be a greater opportunity to prepare in advance for therapy sessions*

REMEMBER TO: Include appropriate lines for signature and date.

RESEARCH
Sample E-Counseling Consent
- **What would you change? Delete? Add?**
- **What sample text in the above consent do you strongly agree with? Why?**
- **What sample text do you strongly disagree with? Why?**

*Modern digital technologies
have raised many complex,
ethical and legal issues*

E-MAILS-TEXTING-PHONE USE IN COUNSELING

Modern digital technologies have raised many complex clinical, ethical and legal issues.

- Are phone messages, e-mails and texting a part of the clinical record?
  - If the correspondence has clinical or other counseling significant relevance then it should be considered part of the clinical records.
  - If the correspondence is simply about appointment scheduling or cancelling an appointment or other issues with little or no clinical significance then it does not need to be included in the clinical record.
- Additionally, if a counselor receives unwanted, excessive, harassing, stalking, or threatening communication from a client in any form, it should be kept as a part of the clinical record.

ARCHIVING OPTIONS:

- How do you archive phone messages? You can play the message and record it into a small handheld digital recorder that has a USB flash drive. You can then transfer the voice recording to your computer.

- How do you archive e-mails? Easiest is to print them out a place them in the client's file or scan them into an electronic client record.

- How do you archive text messages? You can forward the text message to your business e-mail. There are services (e.g., Google Voice) that can record and save phone text messages. Some services (e.g., Missing Sync) connect your phone to your computer and backs up text messages. Security concerns must be thought through before using such services.

CAVEAT: Therapists who communicate with their clients via e-mail and store clinical records digitally must assure that their computers have password, firewall, virus protection, logs, backup systems, encryption when necessary, and other computer safety measures.

ETHICAL STANDARDS & CLINICAL FORMS

PHONE THERAPY
- Consulting with clients exclusively over the phone rather than in person in the counselor's office brings up additional complexities and potential disadvantages to the therapeutic process.
- Phone counseling works best with established in-office clients as a supplemental means of contact.
- Phone counseling is typically private pay, as most insurance companies do not pay for this format.

PHONE COUNSELING INFORMED CONSENT CONSIDERATIONS
Use a simple informed consent explaining under what circumstances you will provide phone counseling to established clients. Explain the limits of confidentiality. Counselors should encourage clients to phone counsel only when they are in a private area and can speak freely with out others listening. Explain fees.

SAMPLE CONSENT: THE USE OF E-MAIL OR TEXTING

CAVEAT: For use in your own setting, forms must be personalized to reflect your state's relevant laws and your own actual policies.

IMPORTANT: In a medical emergency do not use e-mail or texting.

Risks of using e-mail or texting
Transmitting client information by e-mail or texting has a number of risks that clients should consider before using e-mail or text. These include, but are not limited to:
- E-mail/Texting can be circulated, forwarded, and stored in numerous paper and electronic files
- E-mail/Texting can be immediately broadcast worldwide and be received by many intended and unintended recipients
- E-mail/Texting senders can easily miss address and e-mail
- E-mail/Texting is easier to falsify than hand written or signed documents
- E-mail/Texting creates back up copies that exist after the sender or the recipient has deleted his or her copy
- E-mail/Texting can be intercepted, altered, forwarded, and used without authorization or detection

- E-mail/Texting can be used to introduce viruses into computer systems
- E-mail/Texting can be used as evidence in court

Conditions for the use of e-mail or texting
- (Company name/Counselor) will use reasonable means to protect the security and confidentiality of the e-mail or texted information sent and received. However, because of the risks outlined above, I/we cannot guarantee the security and confidentiality of e-mail or texted communication.
- Clients must consent to the use of e-mail or texts. Consent to the use of e-mail or text includes agreement with the following conditions;
- Company/Counselor may forward e-mails or text messages internally to staff and agents necessary for diagnosis, treatment, reimbursement, and other handling. Company/Counselor will not, however, forward e-mails to independent third-parties without the clients prior written consent, except as authorized or required by law.
- Although Company/Counselor will endeavor to read and respond promptly to an e-mail or text from a client, I/we cannot guarantee that any particular e-mail or text will be read and responded to within any particular period of time. Thus the client shall not use e-mail or texting for medical emergencies or other time sensitive matters.
- If the client's e-mail or text message requires or invites a response from Company/Counselor, and the client has not received a response within a reasonable time period, it is the client's responsibility to follow up to determine whether the intended recipient will respond.
- The client should not use e-mail or text messages for communication regarding sensitive medical information, such as sexually transmitted diseases, mental health, developmental disability, or substance abuse.
- The client is responsible for informing Company/Counselor of any types of information the client does not want to be sent by e-mail or text message, in addition to sensitive material previously described.
- The client is responsible for protecting their password or other means of access to e-mail or text messages. Company is not liable for breaches of confidentiality caused by the client or any third-party.
- It is the client's responsibility to follow up and/or schedule an appointment if warranted.
- The client or clients designated caregiver must be 18 years or older before company can respond to an e-mail or text message about the client.

Instructions
To communicate by e-mail or texting, the client shall:
- Inform Company/Counselor of changes in their e-mail address or cell phone number
- Include the client's name in the body of the e-mail or text message
- Review the e-mail or text to make sure it is clear and that all relevant information is provided before sending
- Take precautions to preserve the confidentiality of your e-mail or text message
- Withdraw consent to use e-mail or texting only by written communication to Company/Counselor

Client acknowledgment and agreement:
I acknowledge that I have read and fully understand this consent form. I understand the risks associated with the communication of e-mail and texting between Company/Counselor and me, and consent to the conditions here in. In addition, I agree to the instructions outlined here in, as well as any other instructions that Company/Counselor may impose to communicate with clients by e-mail or texting.

Agreement to Participate in E-mail or Texting:
If you have any questions, please feel free to discuss them with me/us prior to signing this form. Your signature indicates that you have read, understand, and agree with our policies in accordance with our terms and conditions.

This authorization constitutes informed consent without exception.

REMEMBER TO: Include appropriate lines for signature and date; Keep a copy of any document that was signed by a client in the client's file (hardcopy or electronic); Copy to client optional, unless they request a copy.

RESEARCH
Sample Use of E-mail or Texting Document
- **What would you change? Delete? Add?**
- **What sample text in the above consent do you strongly agree with? Why?**
- **What sample text do you strongly disagree with? Why?**

FINANCIAL RECORDS

FINANCIAL ARRANGEMENTS
PAYMENT OF SERVICES:
- With regard to payment of services it is most helpful to refer to your particular professional association's financial arrangement ethical standards.
- Professional association ethical guidelines, in general, call for fair and reasonable fees for services, prohibition or no prohibition of solicitation of fees for services entitled and rendered through the workers' employer, and avoidance of bartering arrangements.
- Other guidelines include no acceptance or offering of kickbacks, rebates, bonuses, or other remuneration for referrals.
- Clear disclosure and explanation of financial arrangements, reasonable notice to clients for intention to seek payment collection, third-party payer fact disclosure, and no withholding of records because payment has not been received for past services, except otherwise provided by-law, are also examples of ethical financial guidelines.

FEE TYPES: Counselors should try to come to an agreement as soon as possible with their clients on the fee structure. Some of the most common options are:
- Full fee
- Sliding scale
- No fee
- Third-party payment
- Bartering for goods
- Bartering for services
- Fluctuating fees

FULL FEE: This is probably the simplest and clearest arrangement for fees in therapy. The counselor is paid his or her full fee, as stated in the Office Policies.

SLIDING SCALE: Sliding scale is a very common fee arrangement. It allows clients to pay what they can afford in a flexible individually tailored way. Some agencies (especially public and/or tax dollar supported) provide a standard chart where clients insert their income and expenses and that helps calculate the fee. The concern with sliding scale is that it can put counselors and clients in a conflict of interest where clients may have an investment in presenting a scaled down financial picture in order to obtain a lower rate. This can undermine the therapeutic relationship.

NO FEE (PRO BONO): Many ethicists, and counseling associations have advocated that counselors devote part of their practices to a no or very low fee client.

THIRD-PARTY PAYMENT: Third-party payments most often represent partial payment for counselors who agree to serve on insurance or managed care panels as preferred providers in exchange for lowering their fees. Most insurance and managed care companies require some amount of co-pay, where clients must pay directly to the counselor a fixed amount which is in addition to the payment receive directly from the insurance company.

BARTERING: All bartering arrangements are boundary crossings. While bartering for services is always dual relationships, bartering for goods is mostly only a boundary crossing. Bartering for goods is often viewed as less complicated than bartering for services, which create dual relationship situations that can be complicated if the clients did less than a satisfying job. See "bartering" section for more details.

FLUCTUATING FEES: Sometimes clients lose their jobs and health insurance, get sick or are faced with unexpected financial burdens. It is important that counselors are open and flexible to adjusting the fee arrangements to accommodate changes in clients' lives.

FEES AND OVER DUE AMOUNTS
SOLUTION OPTIONS:
- Counselor and client agree on realistic and affordable payment plans
- Counselor and client negotiate an ethical and appropriate bartering arrangement
- Counselor may consider forgiving part of or the whole debt
- Considering continuing counseling Pro Bono

CAVEAT: Counselors must be careful when considering forgiving debt as many insurance companies frown upon this because it may constitute fraud or violation of the contract the counselor has with the insurance agency. In these situations, counselors must comply with the contract, make good faith efforts to collect the co-payment or deductible and, if allowed, forgive it under extraordinary reasons of hardship.

COLLECTION AGENCIES

Turning client debt over to a collection agency is not recommended unless this has been fully explained to the client at the onset of counseling via informed consent/financial arrangement documents. It must be explained to the client that the counselor may use a collection service as a last resort if clients do not pay their balance and that the collection agency will receive only basic information, such as the client's name, contact information and total money owed.

SMALL CLAIMS COURT

Filing with small claim court or initiating a lawsuit is not recommended.

RESEARCH
- Would you use a collection agency? Why or why not?
- Why do you think using a small claim's court or lawsuit for the collection of fees is not recommended?

SAMPLE EXPLANATION OF FEES: FINANCIAL ARRANGEMENTS

CAVEAT: For use in your own setting, forms must be personalized to reflect your state's relevant laws, ethical requirements for your licensing, and your own actual policies.

EXPLANATION OF FEES
Fees
Initial Evaluation $_____ for _____ minutes
Subsequent Treatment Sessions $_____ for _____ minutes
Telephone Calls $_____ for _____ minutes
Testing, Interpretation, & Report* $_____ for _____ minutes

*This can vary depending on whether it is being done by a psychologist, licensed counselor or technician (fee for each should be listed if this applies). Testing is charged at the hourly rate for administration, scoring, and report writing. In the case of extensive neuropsychological evaluations, additional charges for chart review may be applied. We will attempt to discuss these charges with you in advance.

ETHICAL STANDARDS & CLINICAL FORMS

Misc. Fees: Additional fees may be applied for extended psychotherapy sessions, reports, photocopies of records, and review of records. Patients will also incur charges for letters, reports, or telephone calls made on their behalf to attorneys, doctors, agencies, employers, school personnel, etc.

Fees regarding testimony include:

Conference/Legal Records Review	$_____ per _____ hour		
Telephone Conference	$_____ per _____ hour		
Arbitration	$_____ per _____ hour		
Deposition	$_____ per _____ hour		
Travel Time	$_____ per _____ hour		
Court Testimony	$_____ per _____ hour 1st hour		
and	$_____ per _____ for each additional hour		

Financial Responsibility: Payments for services provided to you are expected at the time they are delivered. Many, though not all, insurance companies do cover a portion of the cost of psychological services. We will assist you in the proper billing of your insurance company. However, in all cases, YOU, not your insurance company, ARE RESPONSIBLE that your account is paid in full. We strongly recommend that you check with your insurance company to see if you are entitled to receive benefits for counseling services. Payments returned from your bank due to non-sufficient funds will be subject to a returned check fee of $_____. For your convenience we accept Visa and Mastercard [list others]. (if applicable)

Overdue Accounts: You are responsible for your account and are expected to pay for all services that you receive. Overdue accounts may be charged interest or a minimum late payment fee on a monthly basis. Accounts overdue 90 days or more may be turned over to a collection agency or an attorney. We reserve the right to pursue all legal means necessary to secure our interests in being paid for treatment services provided to you. You will be responsible for legal fees and/or collection agency fees in the event that your account becomes delinquent.

Understanding Managed Care for Mental Health: Managed care involves cooperation between the client, provider, and the insurance company to provide services efficiently as possible.

Case Reviews: This practice reviews client cases for quality assurance. A utilization review/quality assurance group set up by the insurance company or members of this practice may review your case.

Your contract with your health insurance company may state that your mental health coverage is limited to:
- Services that are determined to be "medically necessary."
- Medically necessary may be defined as presentation of a covered DSM diagnosis.

You will need to discuss with your counselor the nature of your presenting complaints and set a specific goal for treatment that falls within treatment guidelines. Your insurance will then cover a limited number of office sessions requiring you and the counselor to work on your problems as intensely as possible with the focus of eliminating acute symptoms. We will work with you to accomplish the identified goals in a cost effective manner. [If applicable] Counselors in this practice have entered into an agreement with the following insurance company to provide services within the above-mentioned conditions. **INCLUDE: THE LIST OF INSURANCE COMPANIES OR EMPLOYEE ASSISTANCE REFERRAL PROGRAMS THAT COUNSELOR IS A PREFERRED PROVIDER WITH.**

Some conditions are not covered by insurances: Sometimes people enter treatment with a number of problems. Some problems may meet the conditions of your insurance coverage while others (individual growth, long term personality issues, etc.) will not. Should you desire to continue treatment for a non-covered condition, your counselor will discuss your options with you.

REMEMBER TO:
Include appropriate lines for signature and date; Keep a copy of any document that was signed by a client in the client's file (hardcopy or electronic); Copy to client optional, unless they request a copy.

RESEARCH
Sample Explanation of Fees: Financial Arrangements
- **What would you change? Delete? Add?**
- **What sample text in the above consent do you strongly agree with? Why?**
- **What sample text do you strongly disagree with? Why?**

SAMPLE BILLING AND PAYMENT RESPONSIBILITY FINANCIAL ARRANGEMENTS

CAVEAT: For use in your own setting, forms must be personalized to reflect your state's relevant laws, ethical requirements for your licensing, and your own actual policies.

BILLING AND PAYMENT RESPONSIBILITY
Client's Name _____ BD_____ Date_____
Consent to Release Medical Information
I authorize, (1) release of any medical information necessary to process my insurance claim(s) and request payment of medical benefits directly to my physicians (radiologists); (2) that use of a photocopy in place of this original form will cover all medical services rendered until such authorization is revoked by me. _____(initials)
Patient Financial Responsibility
I understand I have authorized treatment for the person named above and I am responsible for any balance owed. The balance can be the entire charge for the exams performed or the coinsurance and/or deductible after my insurance company has paid. I understand that [name of business] does not allow delay of payment or wait for legal settlement. I am expected to pay the account balance within 30 days from receipt of a statement or based on the agreement I signed. If this agreement is not met and I default on payment of the balance my account can be assigned to a collection agency. The collection agency has the authority to report the debt to a credit bureau. _____(initials)

In the event legal action should become necessary to collect any unpaid balance due for medical services rendered to me or my family. I / we agree to pay reasonable attorney fees or other such costs as the court determines proper. I agree that the venue for any legal action shall be _____ County. _____(initials)

It is agreed that payment will not be delayed or withheld because any insurance coverage or pendency of claims action thereon, all proceeds of insurance are assigned to this office where applicable, but without their assuming responsibility for the collection thereof. _____(initials)

I authorize [name of business] to bill my insurance company and that the payment will be sent to the provider of service. I verify that the above is correct and complete. _____(initials)

REMEMBER TO:
Include appropriate lines for signature and date; Keep a copy of any document that was signed by a client in the client's file (hardcopy or electronic); Copy to client optional, unless they request a copy.

> **RESEARCH**
> **Sample Billing and Payment Responsibility**
> - **What would you change? Delete? Add?**
> - **What sample text in the above consent do you strongly agree with? Why?**
> - **What sample text do you strongly disagree with? Why?**

SAMPLE PAYMENTS and INSURANCE REIMBURSEMENT FINANCIAL ARRANGEMENTS

CAVEAT: For use in your own setting, forms must be personalized to reflect your state's relevant laws, ethical requirements for your licensing, and your own actual policies.

PAYMENTS AND INSURANCE REIMBURSEMENT

For your convenience, your primary insurance company can be billed for you. In this case you will only be required to pay your cost share and unmet deductibles at the time of service. Secondary insurances are not billed for you.

Clients are expected to pay the standard fee of $_____ per ___ minute or $_____ per hour session at the [ ] end of each session; at the [ ] end of the month, unless other arrangements have been made. Telephone conversations, site visits, report writing and reading, consultation with other professionals, release of information, reading records, longer sessions, travel time, etc., will be charged at the same rate, unless indicated and agreed in writing upon otherwise. Please notify [counselor] if any problems arise during the course of therapy regarding your ability to make timely payments. Clients, who carry insurance outside the [counselor's] network as a preferred provider, should remember that professional services are rendered and charged to the clients and not to the insurance companies. Unless agreed upon differently, [counselor] will provide you with a copy of your receipt on a monthly

ETHICAL STANDARDS & CLINICAL FORMS

basis, which you can then submit to your insurance company for reimbursement if you so choose. As was indicated in the consent form, you must be aware that submitting a mental health invoice for reimbursement by your insurance company carries a certain amount of risk. Insurance companies do not reimburse all issues/conditions/problems, which are dealt with in psychotherapy. It is your responsibility to verify the specifics of your coverage. If your account is overdue (unpaid) and there is no written agreement on a payment plan, [counselor] can use legal or other means (courts, collection agencies, etc.) to obtain payment.

Authorization and Release
I authorize [your name/company] to bill my primary insurance company. I authorize payment of medical, government, or employee assistance program benefits to be paid directly to [your name/company]. I understand that my insurance carrier may pay less than the actual bill for services. I agree to be responsible for payments of all services rendered on my behalf or my dependents. I authorize [your name/company] to release my information necessary to process my insurance claim for mental health counseling.
There will be a $_____ fee for any returned or insufficient checks.

Divorced Parents: It is the policy of this counselor that the parent accompanying the minor child for treatment is responsible for payment; billing of the other parent is not done by counselor.

REMEMBER TO:
Include appropriate lines for signature and date; Keep a copy of any document that was signed by a client in the client's file (hardcopy or electronic); Copy to client optional, unless they request a copy.

RESEARCH
Sample Payments and Insurance Reimbursement
- **What would you change? Delete? Add?**
- **What sample text in the above consent do you strongly agree with? Why?**
- **What sample text do you strongly disagree with? Why?**

FORENSIC PSYCHOLOGY

> **CAVEAT:** Clinical psychologists, schools psychologists, neurologists or counselors who lend their psychological expertise to provide testimony, analysis or recommendations in legal or criminal cases are working in the forensic/psychology field. The use of the word "counselor" in the following refers to all the above.

Forensic psychology is typically defined as an intersection of psychology and the law. There are many roles that forensic counselors can perform so definitions of forensic work can vary. Forensic psychologists are often called as expert witness to give testimony in court. In these situations, forensic counselors can face a great deal of confrontation and attempts to disprove their testimony; it is important that they remain calm, collected and professional.

A LIST OF SOME OF THE FUNCTIONS THAT ARE TYPICALLY PERFORMED WITHIN FORENSIC PSYCHOLOGY:
- Competency evaluations
- Sentencing recommendations
- Evaluations for the risk of re-offending
- Testimony as an expert witness
- Child custody evaluations

DUTIES OF A FORENSIC COUNSELOR
The duties of a forensic counselor are fairly limited in terms of scope and duration. They are asked to perform a very specific duty in each individual case, such as determining if a suspect is mentally competent to face charges. Unlike the typical clinical setting where a client voluntarily seeks assistance or evaluation, forensic work deals with clients who are present against their own free will.

STATE AND FEDERAL LAWS
Jurisdictions differ with respect to the many issues regarding forensic work. Some state laws do not specify that any entity other than the examinee is the client, whereas others acknowledge that psychological services may be retained by an entity other than the examinee. State and federal laws provide guidelines for the maintenance and dissemination of records and raw test data and must be considered primary when determining how to respond to requests for records.

OBJECTIVITY: A primary responsibility of counselors performing independent forensic examinations is to strive to examine status objectively. Interpretation of results should ideally be made without preconceived ideas about the examinee and with proper attention to the potential effects of bias. Attempts to satisfy the examinee or align with the retaining third party have the potential to bias conclusions and recommendations. Care should be taken to consider potential biases and take action to guard against them.

ALL OF THE FOLLOWING INFORMATION SHOULD BE LAID OUT CLEAR AND CONCISE FOR INDEPENDENT AND COURT-ORDERED FORENSIC EXAMINATIONS:
- Purpose, The counselor/retaining party relationship, The counselor/client relationship, The importance of objectivity, Limits of confidentiality, Informed consent and disclosure of potential conflicts of interest, Third-party observers, Examination procedures, Scope of interpretation, Presentation of findings, Revising reports, Release of raw data, Termination of the relationship with the retaining party, Licensing board and ethics committee complaints, and relevant State and federal laws.

RESEARCH
Consider these questions to determine if you are suited for forensic psychology:
- Can you cope with emotionally stressful situations?
- Do you enjoy learning about the law and criminal justice system?
- Are you able to communicate well with others, able to consult with law enforcement, lawyers, judges and other psychologists?
- Can you remain calm in the face of a crisis situation?
- Would you be able to give testimony or act as an expert witness in a civil or criminal trial?
- Would you enjoy assessing suspects to determine their competency to stand trial?
- Are you prepared to deal with tedious tasks such as compiling case notes, reading reports and documents on cases, learning about the laws and legal procedures, practicing testimony repeatedly and interviewing numerous people in order to compile a full report on a specific case?

SAMPLE FORENSIC CONSENT

CAVEAT: For use in your own setting, forms must be personalized to reflect your state's relevant laws, ethical requirements for your licensing, and your own actual policies.

FORENSIC INFORMED CONSENT CONTRACT
This Forensic Psychological Evaluation is being conducted at the request of [Insert name of attorney, presiding court listing, name of insurance company, etc.] and is therefore somewhat different than other psychological services.

It is important for you to understand how a forensic evaluation differs from more tradition psychological evaluations. While the results of this evaluation may or may not be helpful to you personally, the goal of this evaluation is to provide information about how you are functioning psychologically to the individual or agency requesting the evaluation. In most cases, this evaluation is intended for use in some type of a legal proceeding.

As such, the confidentiality of the evaluation and the results is determined by the rules of that legal system. If your attorney has requested this evaluation, he/she will receive a copy of my report and will control how it is to be used and who has access to it.

Normally, the results of this evaluation are protected by the attorney-client privilege. Exceptions to this might include a determination on my part that you are dangerous to another person or if you reveal information that a minor child has been abused.

I would also have to release this information if a court orders me to do so. There may be other examples where the laws require me to release the information obtained during the evaluation. We will discuss these situations on a case-by-case basis.

Once a decision has been made to use the report in a legal proceeding, the report and any information pertaining to it will probably be admissible into evidence as well as any other information that was provided concerning your mental health and functioning. If you have any concerns about the use or distribution of my report, you should discuss these issues carefully with your attorney.

ETHICAL STANDARDS & CLINICAL FORMS

In addition, because the evaluation was requested by another party, and is not for the purpose of treatment or counseling, the confidentiality may have fewer legal protections. I will not release the information unless instructed to do so by the person or entity that hired me or when I am legally required to do so. Your participation in this evaluation is voluntary. I will not conduct the evaluation without your signature on this document. You also have the right to stop the evaluation at any time. There may be legal consequences if you stop the evaluation; therefore, it would be in your best interest to consult with an attorney before doing so.

In addition, if appointments are not kept or are cancelled within 48 hours of the appointment time, the person requesting the evaluation will incur charges for the unused time that has been set aside for these services. The evaluation itself consists of two separate parts: *an oral interview and psychological testing*. In addition, it may be necessary for me to review other related materials such as court records, depositions, transcripts, medical records, etc. **If you use audio or video recordings, insert a sentence like this in to your consent form:** *The interview and testing will be [audio or video] recorded in order to preserve an accurate record of the evaluation.*

If, at any time, you have a question about any aspect of the evaluation or these procedures, pleased feel free to ask me. In addition, if at any time you need a break from the evaluation, please let me know and we will stop. Once the evaluation is completed, and with the permission of the requesting party, I may be able to have a meeting with you to explain the results and answer any questions you might have.

REMEMBER TO:
Include appropriate lines for signature and date; Keep a copy of any document that was signed by a client in the client's file (hardcopy or electronic); Copy to client optional, unless they request a copy.

RESEARCH
Sample Forensic Consent
- **What would you change? Delete? Add?**
- **What sample text in the above consent do you strongly agree with? Why?**
- **What sample text do you strongly disagree with? Why?**

FORENSIC ASSESSMENTS

SAMPLE FORENSIC PSYCHOLOGICAL ASSESSMENT CONSENT

CAVEAT: For use in your own setting, forms must be personalized to reflect your state's relevant laws, ethical requirements for your licensing, and your own actual policies.

Approach to Assessment
The assessment process is designed to help the counselor answer questions about the possible causes of problems or distress that the client may be currently experiencing. It is not meant to be psychotherapy, and will be brief and focused on the legal questions raised by the attorney who made this referral.

The assessment process usually has two parts that require your participation:
1) A structured interview, which normally takes between __ to __ hours, and
2) The administration of psychological testing, which normally takes from __ to __ hours. The times vary depending on how much information you have to share with me, and the complexity of the issues being assessed. I will also probably be reviewing your medical and psychological records, and other written materials relevant to your case. I may also ask you for permission to speak to other people who have known you well who may help me to understand you. I am conducting this assessment process because you are, or are planning to become a party in a legal matter. If that is the case, I will be consulting with the attorney who referred you to me regarding my findings. Your consent to this evaluation includes a consent to release information to that attorney and/or their agents (for example, their paralegal). If I am called upon to testify in a deposition or courtroom proceedings, the findings of this evaluation and all supporting materials can be subpoenaed for examination by the opposing attorney, and it is very likely that this will happen. When you raise the issue of your mental status in a legal case, you may have waived your right to confidentiality of these records. In addition, if the opposing attorney deposes me, I will be required to respond to questions regarding my evaluation of you and my findings. I will take all possible steps to protect your privacy at any time when I am not required to render opinions or share information. It is important that you be as candid and open with me as you can possibly be during this assessment. Information that is concealed from me is potentially far more damaging than if it is revealed here so that I can integrate it into the complete findings of my evaluation.

ETHICAL STANDARDS & CLINICAL FORMS

I may be asked to write a report of my findings. If so, you will receive a copy of a draft of that report to check for factual accuracy. If you find that what I say misrepresents you or the facts in some way, you may request that I make changes so as to more accurately reflect your perceptions. However, I retain my right to include those of my professional opinions and observations that I believe to best represent my findings in your case. You are not obligated to use any report that I write.

I will be audio-recording all of our meetings. This is standard practice in a forensic evaluation and preserves an absolutely accurate record of what you say to me. You have the right to request that I turn off the tape recorder at any time. However, I cannot be responsible for the accuracy of my reporting of any information that you give me when the tape recorder is not running.

If during our evaluation you report information to me that causes me to suspect child abuse or vulnerable adult abuse, I must by law report my findings to the appropriate state agencies. I would inform you if I planned to take this step. If I learned that you were likely to harm another person, I must by law inform that person and the authorities. I would inform you if I took that step. Then include the following items: *fees and complaints, including what and where the client can go if they feel the counselor has acted in an unethical or unprofessional manner.* Also add a paragraph stating that the client has read and understands the terms, etc.

REMEMBER TO:
Include appropriate lines for signature and date; Keep a copy of any document that was signed by a client in the client's file (hardcopy or electronic); Copy to client optional, unless they request a copy.

RESEARCH
Sample Forensic Psychological Assessment Consent
- **What would you change? Delete? Add?**
- **What sample text in the above consent do you strongly agree with? Why?**
- **What sample text do you strongly disagree with? Why?**

GROUP THERAPY

ETHICAL CONSIDERATIONS:
- Techniques should be congruent with the group's goals and purposes and group leaders must recognize their competencies and work only with groups they are trained and experienced to work with; collaborating with an experienced co-leader may reduce potential risks.
- Counselors must give potential group members enough information to make informed choices about participating in the group; this might include discussing the inclusion of emotionally disturbed individuals in the group. It is important to adequately screen, select, and prepare members for the group and keep specific treatment notes for each group member.

GROUP THERAPY:
- Group counseling, like individual counseling, is intended to help people who would like to improve their ability to cope with difficulties and problems in their lives.
- The aim of group counseling is to help with solving emotional difficulties and to encourage the personal development of the participants in the group.
- The counselor (called conductor, leader or facilitator) chooses as candidates for the group people who can benefit from this kind of therapy and those who may have a useful influence on other members in the group.
- There are many kinds of groups in the group-counseling field. With psychotherapy groups—process is emphasized; with psychoeducational groups—education is emphasized.

GROUP WORK INCLUDES ALL OF THE FOLLOWING:
- Principles of group dynamics
- Developmental stage theories
- Group members' roles and behaviors
- Therapeutic factors of group work
- Group leadership or facilitation styles and approaches
- Theories of group counseling
- Pertinent research and literature
- Group counseling methods
- Appropriate selection criteria and methods
- Methods of evaluation of effectiveness

GROUP WORK AND CONFIDENTIALITY

When working with groups, the rights of each group member should be safeguarded. The provider of service also has the responsibility to discuss the need for each member to respect the confidentiality of each other member of the group. He must also remind the group of the limits on and risk to confidentiality inherent in the group process. Confidentiality is weakened whenever there are more than two people (counselor and client) in the room.

GROUP THERAPY
CONSENT CONSIDERATIONS...

- Counselors should seek agreement among the parties involved concerning each individual's right to confidentiality and obligation to preserve the confidentiality of information shared by others.
- Counselors should inform participants attending group counseling that counselor cannot guarantee that all participants will honor confidentiality agreements.
- Counselors should inform clients, involved with group counseling, about mandatory reporting requirements.
- Counselors who anticipate a conflict of interest among the individuals receiving services or who anticipate having to perform in potentially conflicting roles should clarify their role with the parties involved and take appropriate action to minimize any conflict of interest.

CAVEAT: When counseling groups, specific consent forms addressing the special circumstances (relationship of parties involved to the counselors and the counselors responsibilities to those involved) are developed, explained and used. Careful consideration about what information has to be shared, and shared with whom, should be addressed and documented.

SAMPLE GROUP THERAPY CONSENT

CAVEAT: For use in your own setting, forms must be personalized to reflect your state's relevant laws, ethical requirements for your licensing, and your own actual policies.

GROUP THERAPY
Group counseling can be a powerful and valuable venue for healing and growth. It is the desire of your group facilitator(s) that you reap all the benefits group has to offer. To help this occur, groups are structured to include the following elements:
- A safe environment in which you are able to feel respected and valued as you work
- An understanding of group goals and group norms
- Investment by both your facilitator(s) and members to produce a consistent group experience
- Your group facilitator(s) will monitor discussions and maintain an environment to keep safety and trust a priority

A SAFE ENVIRONMENT
A safe environment is created and maintained by both the facilitator(s) of a group and its members. Mutual respect and the opportunity to cultivate trust are vital. Another important element for creating a safe environment has to do with confidentiality. Your group facilitator(s) are bound by law to maintain confidentiality; however, group members are not bound by law, but rather are bound by honor to keep what is said in the group in the group. We realize that you may want to share what you are learning about yourself in group with a significant other. If you share, do not use names nor specific about how the session unfolded.

LIMITS OF CONFIDENTIALITY
- If you are a threat to yourself or others (showing suicidal or homicidal intent), your facilitator(s) may need to report your statements and/or behaviors to family, your counselor, or other appropriate mental health or law enforcement professionals in order to keep you and others safe.
- There is wide variety of events that are reportable under child protection statues. Physical or sexual abuse of a child will be reported to Child Protective Services. When the victim of child abuse is over age 18, reporting is not mandatory unless there are other minors still living with the abuser. Elder abuse must also be reported to appropriate authorities.

- If a court of law orders a subpoena of case records or testimony, your facilitator(s) will first assert "privilege" (which is your right to deny the release of your records although this is not available in all states for group discussions). Your facilitator(s) will release records if a court denies the assertion of privilege and orders the release of records.
- Records may also be released with your written permission. The facilitator(s) of your group will ask you to sign a release form so that they can talk with your individual counselor. This is a safeguard for you which allows consultation between group leaders and your individual counselor should the need arise. This also provides you with extra support should a difficult issue come up in group that may need more individual attention.
- Records will include only your personal progress in group—*not information about other group members.* Facilitators may consult with other professionals regarding group interactions. This allows a freedom to gain other perspectives and ideas concerning how best to help you reach your goals in group. No identifying information is shared in such consultations unless a release has been obtained from you as a group member.

OTHER SAFETY FACTORS
- Members of a group may not use drugs or alcohol before or during group
- Members of a group should not engage in discussion of group issues outside of group
- Members of group should remember that keeping confidentiality allows for an environment where trust can be built and all members may benefit from the group experience

ATTENDANCE
Your presence in group is highly important. A group dynamic is formed that helps create an environment for growth and change. If you are absent from the group this dynamic suffers and affects the experience of you and other members of the group. Therefore, your facilitator(s) would ask that you make this commitment a top priority for the duration of the group. It is understood that occasionally an emergency may occur that will prevent you from attending group. If you are faced with an emergency or sudden illness, please contact your facilitator(s) before group begins let them know you will not be present. Because it usually takes several group sessions for clients to "settle in" and receive the full benefits a therapy group provides, we ask incoming members to make a week commitment when they

join a group. We also ask members to give a ___ week notice when they decide to leave a group. We ask this because each member of a group is important and your presence and your absence impacts members and facilitators. We want to allow time for members to process when members choose to leave.

WHAT TO EXPECT

Group time consists of both teaching and processing. Processing may revolve around an issue one member of the group is working on with time for structured feedback and reactions by other members of the group. At times the group may focus on a topic with all members verbally participating. In either case, the group dynamic offers a place where you can experience support, give support, understand more clearly how you relate to others, and examine your own beliefs. These dynamics provide a very powerful environment for change. Remember, the more you give of yourself during the sessions, the more you will receive. The more honest and open you are, the more you allow for insight and growth.

FEES

The fee for this group is $_____ per _____ minute session with a reduced fee of $_____ per session if you are in individual counseling at the time you attend group. You must sign a release form for your individual counselor in order to participate in this group. You are responsible to pay for each session except in the case of a true emergency.

REMEMBER TO:
Include appropriate lines for signature and date; Keep a copy of any document that was signed by a client in the client's file (hardcopy or electronic); Copy to client optional, unless they request a copy.

RESEARCH
Sample Group Therapy Consent
- **What would you change? Delete? Add?**
- **What sample text in the above consent do you strongly agree with? Why?**
- **What sample text do you strongly disagree with? Why?**

*Informed consent is vital
and if at all possible,
it should be obtained
before the onset of
assessment and treatment*

INFORMED CONSENT

Informed consent is one of the most difficult issues with which counselors must contend. Legal requirements for informed consent to treatment and informed refusal of treatment can vary according to jurisdiction. There are often instances in which clients are subjected to interventions that are contrary to their voluntary consent. For example, a person who is actively suicidal, homicidal, or gravely disabled may, depending on applicable law for the jurisdiction, be involuntarily hospitalized. However, clients are generally accorded rights to informed consent or informed refusal.

INFORMED CONSENT: THE CORNERSTONE OF HEATH CARE...
- In its simplest form, informed consent is the treatment authorization given by a client to a counselor. Legally, it is an intentional authorization in that it must be given knowingly, rationally, with volition, and without coercion. By informed, it is meant that the decision must be based on knowledge of the situation and potential consequences.
- Consent must be voluntary. Consent also must be rational, implying that an intellectually competent and mature individual renders it. Both counselor and client have roles and responsibilities in the consent process.
- Informed consent is more than legality; it is a moral responsibility on the part of healthcare providers, based in the recognition of individual autonomy, dignity, and the capacity for self-determination.

PRINCIPLES OF INFORMED CONSENT...
ROLE OF THE COUNSELOR:
- Find out what the problem is
- Find out how it can be treated
- Consider alternatives in terms of benefits and risks to the patient
- Explain the problem, treatment, and the risks and benefits to the patient
- Get consent from the patient
- Carry out the treatment

ROLE OF THE PATIENT:
- Give valid information and access to one's body
- Listen to the information the physician provides
- Consider the information in a logical, rational manner
- Consider the risks versus the benefits in terms of personal factors in his or her life

ETHICAL STANDARDS & CLINICAL FORMS

- Consent if the patient wants to do so
- Cooperate with treatment if consent is given

EXCEPTIONS TO THESE PRINCIPLES:
- In emergencies when there is no time for the physician and patient to fulfill these roles
- When the patient is not competent to fulfill his or her role at the time a decision about treatment is to be made

WHO GIVES CONSENT IN THESE EXCEPTIONS?
- In emergencies, the doctor and treatment team decide about treatment
- In other situations, the family and close friends, or the court

CONSENT ISSUES AND CONFIDENTIALITY

Who's the client? Who do you have a "duty" to?
- The minors, the parent(s), a couples, the families, or the individual
- The agencies, a supervisor(s), or another professional

Lack of confidentiality issues must be disclosed: harm to self or others, homicide plans, insurance companies, supervisors. Confidentiality is weakened whenever there are more than two people in the room.

INFORMED CONSENT:
- Provide services to clients only in the context of a professional relationship based, when appropriate, on valid informed consent.
- Use clear and understandable language to inform clients of the purpose of the services, risks related to the services, limits to services because of the requirements of a third-party payer, relevant costs, reasonable alternatives, clients' right to refuse or withdraw consent, and the time frame covered by the consent.

RESEARCH
- **Check the Internet for your state's policies and laws regarding informed consent**
  - Does your state disagree with these above statements?
  - Does your state's information on informed consent include any additional items then what is covered in this "consent overview" section?

- 398 -

INFORMED CONSENT: CONTENT

INFORMED CONSENT OFTEN INCLUDES THE FOLLOWING ITEMS...
- Counselor's identifying information and license number
- Services are provided to [who are your clients?]
- Type of Counseling Being Provided (Modality, Theoretical Orientation, Interventions)
- Statement of confidentiality
- When Disclosure Is Required By Law (Mandatory Reporting)
- When Disclosure May Be Required (Additional limits of confidentiality the counselor has included)
- Confidentiality of records
- Litigation Limitation
- Consultation disclosure
- E-mails, Cell phones, Computers and Faxes
- Contact Outside the Office
- Medical Records and Your Right to Review Them
- Telephone and Emergency Procedures
- Payment and Insurance Reimbursement
- Mediation and Arbitration
- Process of Therapy
- Appointment information
- Scope of Practice
- Risks of Therapy
- Discussion of Treatment Plan
- Termination
- Cancellation Policies
- Agreement and Signature

FINANCIAL ARRANGEMENT IS A PART OF INFORMED CONSENT

See the section "Financial Arrangements" for more detailed information

INFORMED CONSENT: COUNSELOR'S RESPONSIBILITIES...
- Secure written acknowledgment of all documents received by client
- Retain client's written acknowledgment of receipt
- Keep copies of document available at service delivery site for clients to request and receive a copy

- Post document in a clear and prominent location at service delivery site where it is reasonable to assume a client could read it
- Whenever document is revised, make the revised document available upon request
- Retain copies of all versions of document
- If you maintain a practice web site, this document should be available on your website. While provision of an electronic version fulfills your requirements, if requested by the client, a paper copy must also be provided
- Whenever a material change occurs to: 1) Permitted uses or disclosures; 2) Clients' rights; and/or 3) Counselor's legal duties or other privacy practices described in this document, the counselor must promptly revise and distribute the document

REQUIRED INCLUSIONS:
- Name of firm, business, agency, counselor's practice name, and/or counselor's name counselor's business address and telephone number
- Statement of client's right to refuse treatment
- An accurate description of the extent of a client's confidentiality rights
- Description of types of uses and disclosures the counselor is permitted to make for purposes of treatment, payment, and operations of the practice, with examples of each type
- A clear and detailed description of other purposes for which the counselor is permitted or required to disclose Protected Health Information (PHI) without a client's written authorization
- An acknowledgment that other uses and disclosures will be made only with client's written authorization and that client is legally permitted to revoke such authorization
- An acknowledgment of the counselor's intention or practice (if applicable) of contacting clients to provide appointment reminders, or to provide any information about treatment alternatives or other health-related benefits and services that may be of interest to clients

REQUIRED INCLUSIONS REGARDING CLIENT'S RIGHTS:
- Right to refuse treatment
- An accurate description of the client's rights with respect to their Protected/Private Health Information (PHI), and a brief description of how the client may exercise those rights
- Right to request restrictions on certain uses and disclosures of their PHI along with the caveat that the counselor is not obligated to agree to a requested restriction

- Right to receive confidential communications regarding PHI
- Right to inspect and copy their written health record
- Right to amend their written health record
- Right to receive an accounting of disclosures made of their PHI
- Right to receive a paper copy of the counselor's informed consent

REQUIRED INCLUSION REGARDING CLIENT'S RESPONSIBILITIES:
- Statement that it is the responsibility of client to choose the counselor and treatment modality that best meets their needs.

REQUIRED INCLUSIONS REGARDING COUNSELOR'S RESPONSIBILITIES:
- Statement that counselor is required by law to maintain privacy of client's Protected Health Information (PHI) and to provide client with notice of counselor's legal duties and privacy practices as they relate to the client's PHI (Private Health Information)
- Statement that the counselor is required to abide by terms of their current Privacy Disclosure and Notice document
- Statement that counselor reserves the right to both change the terms of their document, and to make the new provisions effective for all PHI maintained

RESEARCH
- **Check the Internet for your state's policies and laws regarding informed consent (Professional Disclosure)**
  - Does your state disagree with these above statements?
  - Does your state's information on informed consent include any additional items then what is covered in this "consent overview" section?

CAVEAT: Counselors take reasonable steps to ensure that client understands the implications of any diagnosis, the intended use of tests and reports, and the methods, techniques and interventions of treatment.

INFORMED CONSENT: WHAT TO EXPECT IN COUNSELING...

Sample text ideas [about counseling and the counseling process] for inclusion in a consent form or for discussing with clients.

CONFIDENTIALITY:
- Discussions between the counselor and client are private.
- It is the counselor's goal to protect the client's confidentiality.
- In almost all cases, it is the counselor's intent to use the client's PHI (Private Health Information) only for the purpose of providing treatment, appropriate and ethically required consultation with colleagues, arranging for payment of services, or for business functions referred to as TPO (Treatment, Payment and Operations).
- The client, may at times, give the counselor written authorization to use your PHI or to disclose or speak with another person for the purposed you designate.
- There may be times when disclosure of your PHI or testimony will be compelled by law, such as mandatory reporting of child or vulnerable adult abuse or neglect; duty to warn and protect in lie of a threat, or to help keep the client safe from harm.
- A counselor may use or disclose PHI to defend a complaint to the licensing board or a negligence suit brought against them by the client.

COURSE OF TREATMENT:
- Assessments are initially done to determine the most appropriate treatment plan, based on a diagnosis [when one is required].
- Clients are assessed for readiness for counseling, client's responsibility for problems and solutions, client's problem-solving style, and ability to define the problem (presenting issues).
- Assessment and diagnosis are the beginning of the process, an estimate and not wholly accurate. Errors can result due to unknown variable.

INTERVIEWS CAN COVER:
- Biological factors: genetic, potential predisposition's, biochemical agents
- Development factors: physical development, psychosocial development, cognitive development and psychogenetic predispositions
- Social-interactive factors: culture, family or system, parent/child relationship, family attitudes, socioeconomic and community

- Psychological vulnerabilities: person response to stress, arousal rate, intensity, temperaments and cognitions
- Socioenvironmental stresses: status of current primary relationships, use of substance, socioeconomic status and changes

DATA BASES CAN COVER:
- Cross-sectional items: (a point in time) are presenting complaints, relevant history and mental status (consciousness, attention span, orientation, memory, concentration and judgment).
- Longitudinal items: (over a lifetime) include family constellation and history, psychosocial history, educational history, employment history, legal problems, drug and alcohol history and medical history.

TESTING CAN INVOLVE:
- Counselor must administer test under the same conditions that were established in their standardization.
- Counselor does not permit unsupervised or inadequately supervised use of tests or assessments unless the test or assessments are designed, intended and validated for self-administering and/or scoring.
- Counselor recognizes the effect of age, color, race, culture, disability, ethnic group, religion, sexual orientation and socioeconomic status on test administration and interpretation and place test results in proper perspective with other relevant factors.
- Counselor indicates any reservations that exist regarding the validity of a test in norms for the person being tested.

TREATMENT PLANNING:
- It is a negotiation between Counselor and client.
- It is a decision for direction based on assessed and reported information.
- Distortions can exist due to defense mechanism (e.g., justification, rationalization, projection, transference) that are not consciously recognized by the client or lack of information presented to counselor.
- Treatment is the specific application of intervention to assist client in change (e.g., behavioral, cognitive, affective, relational and/or spiritual change).
- Treatment plans are discussed with the client and are revised or amended as needed and as treatment proceeds over time.

ETHICAL STANDARDS & CLINICAL FORMS

ASSESSMENT AND DIAGNOSIS:
- Diagnosis and assessment are initially done to determine the most appropriate treatment plan. Initial assessments include interview, and behavioral observation; it can also include personality inventories and relevant psychological testing.
- Clients are assessed for readiness for counseling, client's responsibility for problems and solutions, client's problem-solving style, and ability to define the problem (presenting issues).
- Assessment and diagnosis are the beginning of the process, an estimate and not wholly accurate.

See "diagnosing" and "assessments" sections for more information.

ABOUT COUNSELING
Sample text ideas [about counseling] for inclusion in a consent form or for discussing with clients.

These statements can be put in first person or third person language
- Counseling, as in the context of a therapeutic relationship, cannot guarantee saved marriages, continued employment, social acceptance, or elimination of presenting symptoms. Nor, is it a guarantee that symptoms will not worsen.
- You, as the client, are ultimately responsible for change or non-change.
- Although no one can solve problems for you, it is hoped that you will be better able to understand your situation and feelings and move toward resolving your problems.
- Many clients remain "stuck" due to external influences beyond the therapeutic relationship or lack of commitment to explore options and try alternatives.
- Everyone has periods in their life of difficulty, change and transition, when personal issues affect their work and relationships. Issues such as family, marital, career, financial, physical, abuse of alcohol/drugs, or a variety of mental issues.
- Counseling can help with incongruent thoughts, difficult relationships, career issues, over-whelming emotions, fears, disturbing memories, bad habits, confusion, chemical dependencies, violence and anger issues, adjustment issues and depression.

- The counselor is to use his/her knowledge of human development and behavior to make observations about your situation and suggestions for new ways to problem solve.
- It is a multi-level process that requires you to have the ability, desire and willingness to see yourself objectively.
- Drugs and alcohol create false realities and self-images, interfering with the underlying issues and the ability to gain deeper insights. Individuals actively using drugs or alcohol must go through assessment and be referred to a recovery program, or Chemical Dependency Counselor first.
- It is important for you, the client, to share with me the goals you have for therapy and realize that entering therapy does not always guarantee anticipated outcomes.
- Counseling provides options for change. Change can be the catalyst for growth and personal maximization.
- It is the counselor's responsibility to listen, understand and be helpful to the fullest extent of their professional ability. It is the client's responsibility to help the counselor understand their life situation, thoughts, feelings, and to have the courage to try new approaches in order for change to occur.
- You will benefit the most from counseling if you explore options and pursue solutions to your hopes and aspirations.
- The input and active participation from the client is essential in order to ensure your individuality and personal style.

RESEARCH

- **What would you say "about counseling" in general?**
  - Add as many statements as you can to list on pages 404-405

CAVEAT: Throughout the counseling process as necessary, counselors inform the client of the purposes, goals, techniques, procedures, limitations, potential risks and benefits of services to be preformed, and clearly indicate limitations that may affect the therapeutic relationship.

INFORMED CONSENT: TYPES OF INTERVENTION...

Sample text ideas [about counseling and the counseling process] for inclusion in a consent form or for discussing with clients. Below are a few common samples.

CAVEAT: There are hundreds of interventions. A simple web search for "counseling theories" or "mental health interventions" will produce multiple pages and information.

PSYCHOANALYTIC THERAPY/INTERVENTIONS:
- BASIC PHILOSOPHIES: Human beings are basically determined by early experiences. Unconscious motives and conflicts are central in present behavior. Early development is of crucial importance, because later personality problems have their roots in repressed childhood conflicts.
- TECHNIQUES AND INTERVENTIONS: Key techniques are interpretation, dream analysis, free association, analysis of resistance and transference. All are designed to help the client gain access to their unconscious conflicts, which lead to insight and eventually assimilation of new material.

BEHAVIOR THERAPY/INTERVENTIONS:
- BASIC PHILOSOPHIES: Behavior is a product of learning. We are both the product and the producer of the environment. Behavior can be changed.
- TECHNIQUES AND INTERVENTIONS: A pragmatic approach based on validation of results. The main techniques are systematic desensitization, relaxation methods, reinforcement techniques, modeling, cognitive restructuring, assertion and social-skills training, self-management programs, behavior rehearsal and coaching.

COGNITIVE-BEHAVIOR THERAPY/INTERVENTIONS:
- BASIC PHILOSOPHIES: Individuals tend to incorporate faulty thinking, which leads to emotional and behavioral disturbances. Cognitions are the major determinants of how we feel and act. Therapy is a learning process, including acquiring and practicing new skills, learning new ways of thinking, and acquiring more effective ways of coping with problems.
- TECHNIQUES AND INTERVENTIONS: Therapy uses a variety of cognitive, and behavioral techniques. Some techniques include socratic dialogue, debating irrational beliefs, homework assignments, gathering data on assumptions, keeping record activities, forming alternative interpretations, learning new coping skills, changing one's thinking and speaking patterns, role playing, imagery and confronting faulty beliefs.

FAMILY SYSTEMS THERAPY/INTERVENTIONS:
- BASIC PHILOSOPHIES: The family is viewed as an inactive and systemic unit. They are connected in a living system; change in one part of the system will result in a change in other parts. The family provides the context for understanding how individuals function in relationship to one another. Treatment is focus on the family unit. An individual's dysfunctional behavior grows out of the interactional unit of the family and out of larger systems as well.
- TECHNIQUES AND INTERVENTIONS: Useful for marital distress, communication problems among family members, power struggles, crisis situations in families and enhancing the overall functioning of the family. Interventions may target behavior change, perceptual change or both. Techniques include using genograms, teaching, asking questions, family sculpting, joining the family, tracking sequences, issuing directives, anchoring, family mapping, reframing, restructuring, enactments and setting boundaries.

RESEARCH

Search the Internet for, at least, ten more theoretical orientations. Be sure to include some of the complementary or alternative therapies. If standard interventions are not effective, there are alternative such as: Medications (Medical Management), Hypnotherapy, Naturopathic Medicine, Bio-Feedback, Medical Evaluations, Group Therapies, 12-Step Groups, Specialized Counseling, In-Patient Treatment Programs.
- Write sample BASIC PHILOSOPHIES sections (try to keep it short) and sample TECHNIQUES/INTERVENTIONS sections (try to keep it short) for all ten.
- Write the same for the type, or types, of counseling you provide
- What would an eclectic counselor say about the types of intervention they use?
  - Write two samples from an eclectic viewpoint...

ETHICAL STANDARDS & CLINICAL FORMS

INFORMED CONSENT:
EXPLAINING "CONTACT OUTSIDE THE OFFICE"

Sample text ideas for inclusion in a consent form or for verbal discussion with clients.

- There may be occasions when you see your counselor outside the office. In an effort to protect your confidentiality and privacy, the counselor will not initiate conversation. At no time will counselor discuss clinical issues with you in social settings. Your relationship with your counselor is professional and therapeutic. Personal and/or business relationships undermine the effectiveness of therapy and should be avoided.

RESEARCH
- **Rewrite the above statement in to your own words**
- **What would be another example of "contact outside the office"?**
  - **Write a statement regarding it**

See "Clinical Relationships" section for more information on this topic.

INFORMED CONSENT:
EXPLAINING "GIFTS"

Sample text ideas for inclusion in a consent form or for verbal discussion with clients.

- The organization I work for does not allow me to accept gifts from clients.

or...

- Often, clients wish to bring a gift to their counselor. Gifts of a small monetary value, and symbolic in nature may be accepted by your counselor. Expensive gifts are exploitive in nature or could undermine effective therapeutic relations. Please understand that the non-acceptance of a gift is done so as to help maintain appropriate therapeutic boundaries. At no time does your counselor want you to feel obligated to give a gift. If you have further questions regarding this, please talk with your counselor.

or...

- Our organization understands that our clients may choose to give a gift of appreciation to their therapeutic team. As a client, you are never expected to give a gift for the services you receive; however, if you wish to do so please ensure that the gift is under $50.00 in value and is appropriate for and intended for all those involved in your care. Please do not give a gift to any one single caregiver. If you have questions or concerns regarding this matter, please speak to your counselor.

RESEARCH

- **What is your policy regarding gift receiving? Rewrite the above statements in to your own words.**
- **What would you do if:**
  - **A client brings you a $200.00 gift card for an electronics store. (It's a card someone gave them and they don't want it)**
  - **A client brings you a hand-made pillow for your office? (You think the pillow is ugly)**

ETHICAL STANDARDS & CLINICAL FORMS

INFORMED CONSENT:
ADDITIONAL LIMITS TO CONFIDENTIALITY...

> **This can be controversial. There are counselors who firmly believe that listing additional limits of confidentially (aside from those that are mandatory or required by law) diminishes what counseling is about. If imposed, be sure to verbalize them to clients.**

Sometimes counselors want to add additional limits of confidentiality to their consent form. (You may want to see the section on "minors" and some of the sample consents that have included the below items). A counselor can add additional limits of confidentiality to their consent form and when working with minors or other special populations, it can make sense.

SAMPLE TEXT FOR ADDITIONAL LIMITS OF CONFIDENTIALITY

In addition to: 1) Mandatory Duty to Warn/Protect; and 2) Child Protective Services (CPS), [Vulnerable] Adult Protective Services (APS), some typical examples are:

- **Risky behavior that is not mandatory (e.g., duty to warn/protect and CPS):** If you engage in and tell me about risky behaviors not covered under mandatory reporting laws, such as fire starting, severe eating disorders, self-injurious behaviors, harming animals, drug and/or alcohol use combined with safety sensitive activities, where there is a substantial likelihood of harm to yourself or others, I reserve the right to report to appropriate sources to keep you and others safe.
- **Criminal activities (e.g., past murders, bank robberies, etc.)** If you speak to me of your direct involvement in a past criminal offense, I reserve the right to report to appropriate sources.

RESEARCH
ADDITIONAL LIMITS TO CONFIDENTIALITY Sample Text Ideas
- Would you consider adding any of these statements?
- What are additional examples?
- What additional situations exist that a counselor might want to impose additional limits of confidentiality?

INFORMED CONSENT SAMPLE

> **DISCLAIMER: All samples & sample texts are intended as a guideline only. For use in your own setting, forms must be personalized to reflect your state's relevant laws and your own actual policies. Sample forms are designed for training purposes. Modify sample forms or sample text according your state's requirements and to the client, setting, and context of the work you do. Sample Forms and Sample Text ideas are provided "as is," without warranty of any kind; they are not intended to be a substitute for legal, ethical, or clinical advice or consultation.**

SAMPLE INFORMED CONSENT

CAVEAT: For use in your own setting, forms must be personalized to reflect your state's relevant laws, ethical requirements for your licensing, and your own actual policies.

Office Policy and Disclosure Statement: Welcome to _____.
It is a pleasure to assist you with your health care needs. This document contains important information about our professional services and business policies. It is important that you read this document carefully. When you sign this document, it will represent an agreement between us. You may revoke this Agreement in writing at any time. The revocation will be binding unless we have relied on it to take actions required of us by your insurance company, or your financial obligations to us have not been met at the time of your notice of Agreement revocation. We can discuss any questions you may have about this agreement at any time.

Quality of Care: We will make every reasonable effort within the scope of our abilities and expertise to help you resolve your presenting problems. Of course, you must understand that despite the fact that you will receive competent care by a well trained licensed counselor, there is no guarantee that the help provided will resolve your presenting problem(s). To utilize the mental health benefits of some insurance policies and ensure the quality of client care, we may ask you to complete a short questionnaire at the beginning, during, or at the end of treatment. This allows us to check the effectiveness of our work. There is no fee for this, and you may have access to the results of the questionnaire. Moreover, you have the right to decline if you so choose.

Voluntary Participation:
- Your participation in this counseling experience is voluntary. You may choose not to participate and you may withdraw your consent to participate at any time. You will not be penalized in any way should you decide to withdraw from your involvement in professional counseling with me. Your signature also indicates that you are willingly consenting to receive counseling services. I too reserve the right to end the counseling relationship should it be indicated, and the necessary referral and termination processes will be followed.
- It is understood that the counseling received on the part of the client is voluntary
- The client is responsible for selecting their mental health practitioner and thereby mode of counseling used.
- By signing at the first session, client is entering into a counseling contract with Counselor.
- Client agrees to be present, talk and be honest.

As a client in a [state], you have the following rights:
- **To expect that a licensee has met the minimal qualifications of training** and experience required by state law
- To examine public records maintained by the Board and to have the Board confirm credentials of a licensee
- To obtain a copy of the Code of Ethics
- To report complaints to the Board
- To be informed of the cost of professional services before receiving the services
- To be assured of privacy and confidentiality while receiving services as defined by rule and law, including the following exceptions: a) Reporting suspected child abuse; b) Reporting imminent danger to client or others; c) Reporting information required in court proceedings or by client's insurance company, or other relevant agencies; d) Providing information concerning licensee case consultation or supervision; and e) Defending claims brought by client against licensee
- To be free from being the object of discrimination on the basis of race, religion, gender, or other unlawful category while receiving services

Treatment Approach: Our treatment approach recognizes that each person is an individual with biological, psychological, sociological, and spiritual aspects of their being. Depending on your needs and preferences, we blend family systems, dynamic, solution focused, interpersonal, cognitive, and behavioral treatment approaches. We will also refer you to appropriate specialists when indicated, such as when medication is likely to be helpful, or medical testing seems necessary. We will discuss treatment goals and the proposed course of treatment with you periodically throughout your treatment. If you have any questions or concerns, please bring them to our attention. You have the right at any time to refuse treatment, change counselors, or request a change in therapy approach. You will not be discriminated against due to race, age, religion, national origin, handicap, gender, or sexual preference. Effective psychotherapeutic treatment requires openness, honesty, an attitude for collaboration, trust, and your willingness to invest both time and effort between sessions for working toward personal and/or family change. Your counselor cannot guarantee the success of treatment, because the outcome is, in part, your responsibility. We will utilize our experience, education, and training to work with you productively, and we will perform our services in a professionally competent, caring, and confidential manner.

Appointments: Individual treatment sessions typically last 45-50 minutes in length with the remaining 10-15 minutes devoted to treatment planning and record keeping. It is important to be on time, because your appointment will not be extended beyond the scheduled time as a result of your late arrival. Your appointment time is held exclusively for you. If you are unable to keep your appointment for any reason, you must give at least a 24-HOUR ADVANCED NOTICE to cancel. Otherwise, you WILL BE CHARGED THE FULL AMOUNT for the time reserved for you. Insurance companies will not reimburse you or us for the missed appointment. It is our office policy to attempt to contact our clients on the day prior to their scheduled appointment to confirm their appointment. This is a courtesy and not a requirement of our office staff.

Fees: Fees will be discussed at the time of our initial meeting and will be consistent with those of my colleagues practicing in this area with similar qualifications and experience and in the context of other service provision rates. I do not offer sliding scale fees. Payment is expected at the time of service, and failure to make payment will be considered a termination of the counseling relationship initiated by you and respected by me. Payment is required at the time of service.

Confidentiality: The law requires reporting of confidential information in three situations: suspected child abuse, threatened harm to self or others, or if individuals are gravely disabled and not able to care for themselves. Furthermore, based on the Uniform Healthcare Information Act, we may confer with others who are providing healthcare services to you as a means of ensuring quality and continuity of care. In most instances, confidential information can be subpoenaed by a court if you become involved in a lawsuit. We cannot be held responsible for maintaining the confidentiality of information about you should you become involved in litigation. If disclosure is required without your authorization, we will attempt to discuss the situation with you to clarify the situation and look for alternative solutions. Information to be disclosed that requires your authorization will not be released without a Release of Information form signed by you. The Release of Information form is valid for _____ days from the date of your signature, unless otherwise noted. Confidentiality does not cover sessions with two or more persons (couples or families), since we cannot assure that others present will keep the information in confidence. However, confidentiality does apply when one of those persons is seen individually. In some cases, it might be useful to your therapy for us to discuss your situation with others, such as a physician. In that case, we will seek your written permission for this exchange of information. On all occasions in which confidentiality is an issue, we will attempt to meet the ethical, clinical, and legal responsibilities we have with you.

Confidentiality of Adults: You have [privileged] or [confidential] communication with your counselor under the laws of the State of _____. That means that, with few exceptions, anything you disclose in therapy and any information we obtain about you from any source, including the simple fact that you are in treatment, is confidential and can only be disclosed to others with your written consent.

Disclosure without your authorization can be made if the disclosure is:
- To a current healthcare provider
- To a former or future healthcare provider, unless you request in writing that we not do so
- To immediate family members or any person with whom you have a close personal relationship, unless you request in writing that we not do so
- To public health authorities when required or when needed to protect the public or your safety
- To proper authorities if we should have reason to suspect that a child, a disabled adult, or an elderly person has been abused or neglected or if we feel you are a danger to yourself or others
- To licensing/certification boards if we are under disciplinary investigation

> **CAVEAT:**
> ***CONSENT INFORMATION REGARDING MINORS MUST BE COMPLETED BASED ON YOUR STATE'S APPLICABLE LAWS REGARDING MINORS AND THEIR RIGHTS TO HEALTH CARE.***
> If a minor, who is old enough to consent to counseling without parental involvement, chooses to use their parent's insurance, then the parent also need to sign the consent form.
> *****You must know the laws for your state*****

Confidentiality of Minors: In the case of children under _____ years of age, the parent(s) or legal guardian holds the communication privilege. This means that the parent is entitled to information about the child and so is the person who authorizes any release of information about the child. We will discuss with parents their child's general progress and case specifics if indicated. We will attempt to act in the child's best interests in deciding to disclose confidential information without the child's consent.

Minors _____ years of age or older have the right to consent to mental health treatment without their parent's knowledge and they can consent to disclosure of treatment records. Thus, the consent of the minor (___ years and older) is required in order to release information, except in the situations listed below.

Disclosure without your authorization can be made if the disclosure is:
- To a current healthcare provider
- To a former or future healthcare provider, unless you request in writing that we not do so
- To immediate family members or any person with whom you have a close personal relationship, unless you request in writing that we not do so
- To public health authorities when required or when needed to protect the public or your safety
- To proper authorities if we should have reason to suspect that a child, a disabled adult, or an elderly person has been abused or neglected or if we feel you are a danger to yourself or others
- To licensing/certification boards if we are under disciplinary investigation

Risks and discomforts: It is possible that during our work together you might share with me some experiences that might be painful to recall. As we proceed with your goals, you might notice yourself feeling uncomfortable. This is to be expected, since change can create feelings of discomfort, and I would ask that should you notice any discomfort, you share with me that you are having that experience. It is likely that as we continue to work together, these symptoms will diminish.

Information About Your Treatment Records: We will keep a record of the mental healthcare services that we provide you. You may ask to see and/or correct that record. You may see your record or get more information about it by contacting and/or setting up an appointment with us. You may be charged an appropriate fee for the time and costs involved with an information request. Counselors in this office are not authorized to release your records to anyone without your permission unless the law authorizes or causes us to do so. If you are utilizing a third-party payer, such as an insurance company, we may be required to submit information about you to them in order to obtain reimbursement or authorization for treatment services. You will be asked to give permission for this release on the Insurance/Patient Information Form given to you with this Policy Statement. If there is any information that you DO NOT wish to have recorded in your chart, please inform the counselor.

Consultation: The competent and ethical practice of psychotherapy dictates that we participate in case consultation with other licensed professionals when necessary. Should we obtain consultation regarding aspects of your treatment, we will omit identifying information (including name, employment, etc.) so that confidentiality will be preserved to the best of our ability. Your signature on this policy statement serves as your consent that we may pursue consultation regarding your treatment without obtaining additional written consent from you to do so. Currently, we (or I) consult with:
[LIST EACH PERSON…]
NAME: License Number; Education; Focus of Work
NAME: License Number; Education; Focus of Work
NAME: License Number; Education; Focus of Work

Duration and termination of counseling: The amount of time you attend therapy with me will be determined by both or one of us, and can be influenced by a variety of conditions, including financial resources, achievement of determined objectives, and many other variables which are too numerous to list, but about which I will be happy to answer questions, and provide you with hypothetical examples.

Contacting Your Counselor: We are not available by telephone on evenings and weekends. If you cannot reach us, or you feel that you cannot wait for us to return your call, you should call your family physician, an emergency room at the nearest hospital, a crisis line at _____ or _____ or dial 911. If we are unavailable for an extended time, we will provide you with the name of a trusted colleague whom you can contact if necessary.

Emergencies: Should you have an emergency and are unable to contact me during my normal business hours, you should contact your Primary Care Physician or go to the nearest Emergency Room or dial 911.

Complaints: If you have any concerns or complaints about the course of your evaluation or treatment, please contact my/our office and discuss them with me/us first. You have the right to discontinue your treatment or ask for a referral to another counselor at any time. If after discussing your concerns with us you are still dissatisfied and feel you have been treated unprofessionally or unethically, you may contact the Department of Licensing at _____.

> **CAVEAT: MANY STATES REQUIRE THE FOLLOWING (BUT NOT ALL)...**
> *Mental health professionals are required to report themselves or any other healthcare provider in the event of a final determination of an act of unprofessional conduct; and, a determination of risk to patient safety due to mental or physical condition, or if they have knowledge of unprofessional conduct by another licensed provider. Mental healthcare providers have to report a client who is a healthcare provider who may pose a clear and present danger to his or her clients. If you have questions or concerns about this requirement, please discuss them with your care provider.*

Consent for treatment—*the process of therapy/evaluation and scope of practice*: Participation in therapy can result in a number of benefits to you, including improving interpersonal relationships and resolution of the specific concerns that led you to seek therapy. Working toward these benefits, however, requires effort on your part. Psychotherapy requires your very active involvement, honesty, and openness in order to change your thoughts, feelings and/or behavior. [Counselor] will ask for your feedback and views on your therapy, its progress and other aspects of the therapy and will expect you to respond openly and honestly. Sometimes more than one approach can be helpful in dealing with a certain situation.

During evaluation or therapy, remembering or talking about unpleasant events, feelings, or thoughts can result in you experiencing considerable discomfort or strong feelings of anger, sadness, worry, fear, etc., or experiencing anxiety, depression, insomnia, etc. [Counselor] may challenge some of your assumptions or perceptions or propose different ways of looking at, thinking about, or handling situations, which can cause you to feel very upset, angry, depressed, challenged or disappointed. Attempting to resolve issues that brought you to therapy in the first place, such as personal or interpersonal relationships may result in changes that were not originally intended. Psychotherapy may result in decisions about changing behaviors, employment, substance use, schooling, housing or relationships. Sometimes a decision that is positive for one family member is viewed quite negatively by another family member. Change will sometimes be easy and swift, but more often it will be slow and even frustrating. There is no guarantee that psychotherapy will yield positive or intended results. During the course of therapy, [counselor] is likely to draw on various psychological approaches according, in part, to the problem that is being treated and his assessment of what will best benefit you. These approaches include, but are not limited to, behavioral, cognitive-behavioral, cognitive, psychodynamic, existential, system/family, developmental (adult, child, family), humanistic or psycho-educational. As stated, there are benefits and risks in all mental health counseling. Common risks include the following: *presenting symptoms/concerns do not improve; or, they worsen. Possibly, new symptoms/concerns might arise during the therapeutic process.* [Counselor] will check with you regularly as to your assessment of the benefits of counseling. Please share any concerns you have on an on-going basis with [counselor].

Termination: Ethically, the counselor always assesses the benefit of counseling to you. If at any point during psychotherapy your counselor assesses that he/she is not effective in helping you reach the therapeutic goals, or that you are non-compliant to the process, he/she is obligated to discuss this with you and, if appropriate, to terminate treatment. In such a case, he/she would give you a number of referrals that may be of help to you. If you request it, and authorize it in writing, [counselor] will talk to the counselor of your choice in order to help with the transition. If at any time you want another professional's opinion or wish to consult with another counselor, [counselor] will assist you with referrals, and with your written consent, he/she will provide her or him with the essential information needed. You have the right to terminate therapy at any time.

We reserve the right to refuse service to anyone without reason, provided that a referral to an appropriate treatment provider is made at the time of refusal of services.

Agreement to Participate in Services: If you have any questions, please feel free to discuss them with us prior to signing this form. Your signature indicates that you have read, understand, and agree with our policies and accept responsibility for payment of our fees in accordance with our terms and conditions. Furthermore, you hereby authorize the mental healthcare provider to provide you psychological services. This authorization constitutes informed consent without exception.

REMEMBER TO:
Include appropriate lines for signature and date; Keep a copy of any document that was signed by a client in the client's file (hardcopy or electronic); Copy to client optional, unless they request a copy.

RESEARCH
Sample Informed Consent
- **What would you change? Delete? Add?**
  - **What sample text in the above consent do you strongly agree with? Why?**
  - **What sample text do you strongly disagree with? Why?**
- **Does this consent form have all the basic information required for "best practice" or per your state's requirements?**
- **What, if anything, does your state require that is not in this sample?**

INFORMED CONSENT: CHECKING THE VALIDITY OF INFORMED CONSENT

INFORMED CONSENT
- Counseling services should only be provided when valid informed consent can be obtained, except in emergent situations. Therefore, clients must know the exceptions before consenting to treatment or other services.
- Informed consent is a legal construct intended to ensure that individuals entering a process of treatment have adequate information to fully assess whether they wish to participate.
- This concept of informed consent is closely linked with the value of self-determination.

GENERALLY, POTENTIAL THREATS AND FACTORS TO BE CONSIDERED IN ENSURING THE "VALIDITY OF INFORMED CONSENT" ARE:
- Language and comprehension
- Capacity for decision-making
- Limits of service refusal by involuntary clients (e.g, court-mandated clients)
- Limitations and risks associated with electronic media services
- Audio and videotaping

INFORMED CONSENT: DO CLIENTS READ THEM?
CHECKING THE VALIDITY...

A short verbal discussion with a new client, before they sign the consent form, and before any assessment and treatment, using clear and understandable language is recommended.

In instances when clients are not literate or have difficulty understanding the primary language used in the practice setting, take steps to ensure a client's comprehension. This may include providing clients with a detailed verbal explanation or arranging for a qualified interpreter or translator.

Counselors should discuss with new clients and other interested parties the nature of confidentiality and limitations of a client's right to confidentiality. Counselors should review with clients circumstances where confidential information may be requested and where disclosure of confidential information may be legally required. This discussion should occur as soon as possible in the relationship and as needed throughout the course of the relationship.

CHECKING THE VALIDITY OF INFORMED CONSENT TEMPLATE

- It is considered "best practice" to verbally discuss with new clients the following items [preferably before the consent form is signed, but certainly before the onset of assessment and treatment, unless the situation involves an emergency]. **TALK WITH THEM ABOUT:** *client's rights, your commitment to your ethical codes, about the type of counseling you do, what they can expect in the course of counseling, the risks of counseling, the reason why therapy could be terminated, and the client's part.* **It is ethically required that counselors verbally discuss with new clients all "limits of confidentiality" such as mandatory reporting requirements.** Again, it is preferable to have this discussion before a consent form is signed, but certainly before the onset of assessment and treatment, unless the situation involves an emergency.

NOTE: The following are suggested templates/text. Take these suggestions and put them in your own words. Then take the time to verbally discuss this information with clients, preferably before the onset of assessment/treatment.

CLIENT'S RIGHTS
- **SAMPLE TEXT:** You have the right to self-determination; a right to privacy concerning medical information; a right to participate in treatment decisions. Other rights include**:** *dignity; quality service provided by concerned, trained, professional and competent staff; to expect complete confidentiality within the limits of the law; to full, knowledgeable, and responsible participation in the ongoing treatment plan to the maximum extent feasible; to obtain information and to have this information explained clearly and directly; to request info and/or consultation to refuse and to be advised of the consequences; to a safe environment free of emotional, physical and sexual abuse.* **The PATIENT'S RIGHTS ACT is an important document; take the time to read it...see the "Patient's Rights Act" section for more detail.**

COMMITMENT TO ETHICS
- **SAMPLE TEXT:** "I have an ethical responsibility not to… or to…" [You can talk more about situations that are relevant or of concern to you, your client or your situation such as living in a rural area; potential conflicts of interest, concerns regarding dual relationships, etc.
- **SAMPLE TEXT:** As a professional mental health practitioner I abide by the Code of Ethics of [the state's licensing board and any associations you belong to]. I must abide by all state mandated reporting requirements.

ABOUT COUNSELING
What do you have to say about counseling in general and about the type of counseling you do specifically?
- **SAMPLE TEXT:** The counseling relationship cannot guarantee [saved marriages, continued employment, social acceptance]… ***See the section "Informed consent: What to Expect in Counseling" in this book for more ideas***
- **SAMPLE TEXT:** My belief is that an individual will seek assistance when their usual coping mechanisms have become ineffective and they are interested in exploring other avenues and increasing their own resources. I believe that each individual will bring with them very unique perspectives and experience, thus I do not offer a generic statement regarding types of support offered.
- **SAMPLE TEXT:** Commonly, concerns relating to relationships, employment, addiction and/or addiction recovery, death and loss, sexuality, and ways in which to integrate the past experience with the present circumstances to create a rich understanding with insights that can assist in future decision making, are brought for examination and in that undertaking, deeper associated concerns may, but do not necessarily always, arise.

WHAT TO EXPECT
- **SAMPLE TEXT:** Let me explain a few key points regarding what to expect…
  - Discuss duration of sessions, payment plans/fees, emergency procedures, and any other items that are important to you.
  - **Provide a short list of reasons for TERMINATING COUNSELING:** *client not benefiting from counseling, outside counselor's area of expertise, client needs a different type of counseling, or client needs a higher level of care than you can provide.* (See next page: ***REASONS WHY THERAPY COULD END***, for more sample text ideas)

RISKS

- **SAMPLE TEXT:** There are risks and benefits with counseling, some risks are: presenting symptoms/issues are not resolved, or they could worsen. And possible, during counseling, new symptoms or concerns could arise. If you ever feel counseling is not helping you, please talk to me. There are many options we can discuss.

REASON WHY THERAPY COULD END

- **SAMPLE TEXT:** There are several reasons for ending counseling. When a client no longer needs a counselor or is not benefiting from counseling then it is time to end. Sometimes a specific treatment might be more harmful than helpful or a client might need a higher level of care than I can provide. As counseling proceeds, issues outside my area of expertise could arise that require a referral to another care provider. If I, or you, identify any conflicts of interests, we will discuss them. If the concern cannot be resolved then again, a referral would need to be made. We will periodically assess how counseling is working for you and measure your progress against the treatment plan and the therapy goals. I will make every attempt to assist you in establishing with another care provider; however, sometimes if another can't be found due to insurance or financial needs, or for any other reasons, then you may need to seek help from your primary care provider, a local emergency room, or a community mental health agency. It is unethical for me to continue counseling when, in my clinical judgment, your needs are not being met.

CLIENT'S PART

- **SAMPLE TEXT:** You'll help the process by being present, talking and sharing, and being honest.
- **SAMPLE TEXT:** Counseling requires your very active involvement. It requires your best efforts to explore your awareness, and change thoughts, feelings, and behaviors. For example, I want you to tell me about important experiences, what they mean to you, and what strong feelings are involved. This is one of the ways you are an active participant in counseling.
- **SAMPLE TEXT:** Certain expectations exist within the counseling relationship parameters, and these include the assumption that their is a willingness to work during and between sessions, on goals and objectives. Communication and negotiation is expected by both the client, or clients, and the counselor.

CLIENT'S PART (Continued)

- **SAMPLE TEXT:** I request 24 hours notice before missing a session, whenever at all possible, since the time I schedule for you is a commitment I make to you. I will, of course, call you in the event that I have an incident that prevents me from meeting with you.

LIMITS OF CONFIDENTIALITY

- **SAMPLE TEXT:** I will take every precaution to protect your confidentiality, however if you share with me harmful intentions toward yourself or toward others, or speak of abuse or neglect of children or vulnerable adults, you could place me in the position of having to report to appropriate sources according to the laws. HOWEVER, please do not withhold such thoughts and feelings—*I am here to help and support you as needed*.
- **SAMPLE TEXT:** Most of what we talk about is private. If you talk about abuse of children or vulnerable adults or harm to others, I am required to report these to appropriate agencies. If you speak of harm to yourself, I must take steps to help keep you safe. If these come up, we'll also talk about the best way for us to talk about the problem(s) with others, for the best potential for helping you…

RESEARCH
CREATE YOUR OWN TEMPLATE for: *CHECKING THE VALIDITY OF INFORMED CONSENT*
What would you say? How would you say it?
- CLIENT'S RIGHTS...
- COMMITMENT TO ETHICS...
- ABOUT COUNSELING...
- WHAT TO EXPECT...
- RISKS...
- REASON WHY THERAPY COULD END...
- CLIENT'S PART...
- LIMITS OF CONFIDENTIALITY...

IMPORTANT: If you have added any additional "limits of confidentiality" to your consent form, you need to verbalize that to the client.
Risky behaviors that are not covered under mandatory...
SAMPLE TEXT: If you are involved in fire starting, injury to animals, excessive drinking/drug abuse, severe eating disorders, cutting... where there is a "Substantial Likelihood" of harm to self or others, I reserve the right to speak with your parents/legal guardian to help keep you and others safe.
Criminal activities...
SAMPLE TEXT: If you speak of an involvement with a past murder I reserve the right to report to law enforcement.

RESEARCH
- There is disagreement between counselors regarding adding "additional limits of confidentiality" to a consent form.
    - Why do you think this is?

ETHICAL STANDARDS & CLINICAL FORMS

INTAKE
INFORMATION TYPICALLY COVERED IN AN INTAKE DOCUMENT

CAVEAT: For use in your own setting, forms must be personalized to reflect your state's relevant laws, ethical requirements for your licensing, and your own actual policies.

DEMOGRAPHIC INTAKE INFORMATION (items to include)
Clients Information (Identification, Insurance, Contact Information, etc.)
Photocopy of photo identification and Insurance Card
Primary language: [ ] English [ ] Spanish [ ] other _____
Disabilities: [ ] mobility [ ] sight [ ] hearing [ ] other _____
Client's address [street or PO Box, city, state, zip]
Phone number(s) [home, work, cell, other]
E-mail address:
Client's employment:
Emergency contact [name, [hone number(s), relationship to client]:
Primary care physician [name, city, phone number]:
How do you want to be contacted?   Yes No–Home Phone   Yes No–Work Phone
Yes No–Cell Phone   Yes No–Text Message (Cell phone)   Yes No–E-mail
If you have answered YES to e-mail or Text, you will need to sign The Use of e-mail and Texting Consent Form
Amount of information I can leave on a recorder or with another person:
[ ] appointment reminder only [ ] other: _____
Current and Past Medical History (health conditions, past surgeries, chronic conditions, past counseling an/or psychiatric care]:
You were referred to me by? [ ] Internet search [ ] healthcare provider [ ] family or friend [ ] other: _____
Billing Information:
INSURANCE [IF YOU HAVE YOUR INSURANCE CARD, PRESENT IT PLEASE]
Primary Insurance Company Name: [ ] Employer Plan vs. Individual Plan
Policy Number _____
Responsible Party [ ] SELF   [ ] EAP Referral by _____ [ ] OTHER:
(Secondary Insurance Information)

INTERVAL HISTORY FORM

Pediatricians, for years, have utilized a form that parents complete at each visit, prior to seeing the physician. The document asks about key information, issues and concerns. Counselors can use a form like this. Clients would complete the form prior to their counseling session.

The Benefit is threefold:
- Gets the client thinking about what's going on in their life right now and what they want to focus on.
- Helps the counselor because a quick glance at the form can let the counselor know where the client is at and what needs to be discussed.
- Ethically, such a form helps assess regularly if counseling is helping, or not.

SAMPLE INTERVAL HISTORY FORM

CAVEAT: For use in your own setting, forms must be personalized to reflect your state's relevant laws and your own actual policies. Always consult with supervisors or legal advice before implementing a new document

Name, Date

Ask about changes in health (e.g., traumas, accidents, emergency care, medication changes, etc…) since last appointment

SUGGESTED QUESTIONS:

ANY SPECIFIC REACTION FROM YOUR LAST APPOINTMENT

What insights did you gain from our last session?

What behavioral change, if any, have you made? What was the result?

Overall since my last visit, I am (circle one) BETTER   NO CHANGE   WORSE

CURRENT EMOTIONAL WELL-BEING _____ (Please rate: 1 being worst; 10 is the best)

CURRENT FAMILY/MARITAL LIFE _____ (Please rate: 1 being worst; 10 is the best)

CURRENT WORK/CAREER LIFE _____ (Please rate: 1 being worst; 10 is the best)

PROBLEM LIST: (What do you see as your current concerns; please list in order of importance)

    1. _____   2. _____   3. _____   4. _____

What particularly would you like to discuss today?

How would you describe the need for today's visit?

Complete this sentence: Without today's visit I would be…

LIMITING ACCESS TO RECORDS

Access to Records
- Counselors should provide clients with reasonable access to records concerning the clients. Counselors who are concerned that clients' access to their records could cause serious misunderstanding or harm to the client should provide assistance in interpreting the records and consultation with the client regarding the records.
- Counselors should limit clients' access to their records, or portions of their records, only in exceptional circumstances when there is compelling evidence that such access would cause serious harm to the client. Both clients' requests and the rationale for withholding some or all of the record should be documented in clients' files.
- When providing clients with access to their records, counselors should take steps to protect the confidentiality of other individuals identified or discussed in such records.

SAMPLE TEXT FOR LIMITING ACCESS TO RECORDS

CAVEAT: For use in your own setting, forms must be personalized to reflect your state's relevant laws and your own actual policies.

Statements you may want to include in an informed consent:
- [Counselor] reserve the judgment call as to whether or not to provide exact copies of a client's records. If you request a copy of your records, [counselor] may choose to summarize the information for the client.

MANDATORY REPORTING

Mandatory reporting: When the law compelled breaches of confidentiality.

> **CAVEAT: States vary in laws, statutes, and State Boards' ethical codes**—*readers need to know their state's health & safety codes/laws/statutes relevant to: minors' rights, protective services, mandatory reporting, and licensing board's ethical guidelines. You must modify the forms so they comply with your state laws, professional organizations' codes of ethics and your State Licensing Board's guidelines.*

PROTECTIVE SERVICES

Counselors are mandated in all states to report suspected abuse under penalty of criminal charges. They are required by law to report the reasonable suspicion of abuse, even in the absence of hard evidence.

- The ethical decision lies in deciding if you must report. Being a mandatory reporter requires judgment, and being directed by law to report means being alert to the potential need to report
- State statutes vary slightly in language, but the meaning is generally the same and reads similarly.
- Counselors are mandatory child abuse reporters, which means they:
  - Have an absolute duty to report; do not have to be certain; suspicion is enough to establish a duty; have a duty that is not discretionary but is absolutely clear
  - Are protected as good faith reporting is assumed
  - Understand that there is not a statute of limitations on child abuse reporting

WHO MUST REPORT? Any person who reasonably believes that a minor or vulnerable adult is or has been the victim of physical injury, abuse, child abuse, a reportable offense or neglect that appears to have been inflicted on the minor or vulnerable adult by other than accidental means or that is not explained by the available medical history as being accidental in nature, or who reasonably believes that there has been a denial or deprivation of necessary medical treatment or surgical care or nourishment with the intent to cause or allow the death, shall immediately report or cause reports to be made of this information to a peace office or to Child Protective Services or Adult Protective Services.

The following persons are required by law to report: Every state defines who the mandatory reporters are. Check your state. However, counselors are listed as mandatory reporters in all states. A person making a report or providing information about a child is immune from civil or criminal liability unless such person has been charged with, or is suspected of, the abuse or neglect in question. A person acting with malice, who either knowingly or intentionally makes a false report of child abuse and neglect or who coerces another person to make a false report, is guilty of a crime. A person who knowingly and intentionally falsely accuses another of maliciously making a false report of child abuse and neglect is also guilty of a crime.

RESEARCH
- **Every state defines who the mandatory reporters are. Check your state.**
- **What constitutes child abuse in your state?**
- **What's the difference between "bad parenting" and abuse?**

DUTY TO WARN AND PROTECT
SERIOUS THREAT OF HARM TO SELF OR OTHERS:
The core innovation of the legal case of Tarasoff was the creation of a new exception to counselor-client confidentiality. Although the duty to warn often is standard among jurisdictions, not all states have adopted the "protection standard" which requires counselors to attempt to contact a specific, identifiable third party. Counselors should be familiar with laws in their jurisdictions. Knowing your state's statutes is critical.

See "Assessment" or "Clinical Relationship" section for more information.

RESEARCH
- **Counselors should be familiar with laws in their jurisdictions.**
  - **Does your state require counselors to make a reasonable attempt to contact a potential victim?**
  - **Or, does your state have a permissive or no statutory language standard?**

MINORS

States vary regarding minors' rights. Use this information as a template and always follow the specific policies of the company you work for and/or your state's laws and regulations.

THE CONCEPT OF INFORMED CONSENT WITH CHILDREN:
- Although minors may have appropriate decision-making capacity, they usually do not have legal empowerment to give informed consent. Therefore, parents or other surrogate decision-makers may give informed permission for diagnosis and treatment of a child, preferably with the assent of the child whenever possible.
- In most cases, parents are assumed to act in the best interest of their child. But circumstances may occur where there is a conflict between what the parents and the healthcare providers feel is in the best interest. State laws cover some of these areas of potential dispute, for example, in cases of suspected child abuse
- Other disagreements in care may result in court orders that specify what treatment should occur (for example, blood transfusions), or in the court-ordered appointment of a guardian to make medical decisions for the child.
- Most states also give decision-making authority to otherwise unemancipated minors with decision-making capacity (mature minors) who are seeking treatment for certain medical conditions, such as drug or alcohol abuse, pregnancy, or sexually transmitted diseases

EMANCIPATED MINOR REQUIREMENTS, EACH STATE CAN VARY. HERE ARE COMMON FACTORS:
- Self-supporting and/or not living at home
- Married
- Pregnant or a parent
- In the military
- Declared emancipated by a court

LEGAL AND ETHICAL ISSUES WHEN COUNSELING CHILDREN:
- Age issues
- Aloneness with issues
- Suggestibility issues
- Legal parent(s)
- Non-custodial parent(s)
- Parenting plans

MINORS AND INFORMED CONSENT

The process of informed consent becomes more complicated when considering minors because there is only limited direct application of the doctrine of informed consent in pediatrics. Those with legal entitlement and decisional capacity only can give informed consent, so typically a parent or guardian must provide permission.

- The fundamental issue in informed consent for minors is a question of how decisions should be made for those who are not fully competent to decide for themselves.
- Parents or guardians are entitled to provide permission because they have legal responsibility and, in the absence of abuse or neglect, are assumed to act in the best interests of the child.
- Part of why consent issues are so difficult with minors is that the best interests of the child are hard to define, and are often subjective.
- Additional issues include questions of how to define and assess decision-making capacity.

WHO CAN GIVE CONSENT FOR A MINOR

- The legal parent(s)
- Non-custodial parents
  - Get a copy of the parenting plans

CAVEAT: Where a child or adolescent is the primary client, or the client is not competent to give consent, the interests of the minor or the incompetent client shall be paramount. Where appropriate, a parent(s) or guardian(s) may be included in the counseling process. The mental health counselor must still take measures to safeguard the client's confidentiality.

MINORS AND CUSTODY AGREEMENTS

> **CAVEAT:** It is necessary to understand clearly the court-ordered arrangements about legal custody, regardless of who has physical custody of the child. It applies when parents seek outpatient mental health evaluation or treatment for their minor child. States vary in their laws regarding minors and the minor's rights to consent to health care. If a minor seeks outpatient therapy on his/her own, the provider must make a case-by-case judgment about whether it is appropriate to work with the minor without parental consent, or over a parent's objection. This would involve weighing the clinical and ethical issues, and obtaining consultation about legal implications, especially if the family is engaged in a custody dispute.

WHEN IN DOUBT ABOUT ETHICAL OR PROFESSIONAL ISSUES
- Ethics texts recommend making it a rule to involve both parents whenever mental health services are being provided to a child.
- Even if one parent lives far away, it is possible to obtain written consent and gather information from that parent by phone.
- Doing so can often prevent the absent parent from later objecting to the mental health services, becoming angry about being ignored, or complaining to the licensing board about the professional's conduct.
- Exceptions to this rule may be necessary if the parent is inaccessible, unwilling to participate, or guilty of abuse or neglect and his/her involvement would be harmful to the child.

UNDERSTANDING CUSTODY AGREEMENTS
- Sole legal custody: The parent with sole legal custody has the right to seek mental health evaluation and/or treatment of child without consent from the non-custodial parent.
- Joint legal custody: When parents have joint legal custody, ask to see the actual court-ordered custody agreement to determine whether the other parent must be notified if one parent seeks mental health services for the child, and/or whether they must both agree about obtaining mental health evaluation and/or treatment. In some cases, depending on the custody agreement, parents who disagree can have a judge determine whether mental health services are in the child's best interest.

ETHICAL STANDARDS & CLINICAL FORMS

WHEN IN DOUBT ABOUT A PARENT'S LEGAL RIGHTS:
- It is recommended that, if there is any question about whether the parent initiating the evaluation and/or treatment has the legal right to do so, we do the following:
    - Ethics texts recommend making it a rule to involve both parents whenever mental health services are being provided to a child.
    - Even if one parent lives far away, it is possible to obtain written consent and gather information from that parent by phone.
    - Doing so can often prevent the absent parent from later objecting to the mental health services, becoming angry about being ignored, or complaining to the licensing board about the professional's conduct.
    - Exceptions to this rule may be necessary if the parent is inaccessible, unwilling to participate, or guilty of abuse or neglect and his/her involvement would be harmful to the child.

WHEN THE INDIVIDUAL CLAIMS TO BE THE SOLE LEGAL CUSTODIAL PARENT:
- Get a letter from his/her attorney stating that there is nothing in the custody agreement that would prevent this individual from seeking evaluation and/or treatment of this child; OR get evidence in the form of a copy of the section of the legal custody agreement verifying that this is the sole legal custodian who has the right to make decisions regarding the child's mental health.

WHEN THE INDIVIDUAL CLAIMS TO BE A JOINT LEGAL CUSTODIAN:
- Get evidence of the joint legal custody agreement (see above) AND get consent from both parents in writing.

WHEN THE INDIVIDUAL CLAIMS TO BE THE NON-LEGAL-CUSTODIAL PARENT:
- The individual has the right to access the child's medical records
- The individual can seek emergency medical treatment only, which probably does not include mental health treatment
- The individual can petition a court for an order prohibiting the evaluation and/or treatment because it is not in the child's best interest.

ETHICAL CONCERNS ASSOCIATED WITH CHILDREN (MINORS):
- Suggestibility
- Vulnerability

SAMPLE SEPARATED-DIVORCED PARENTS AGREEMENT

CAVEAT: For use in your own setting, forms must be personalized to reflect your state's relevant laws, ethical requirements for your licensing, and your own actual policies.

I have brought my/our child _____, age _____, to [counselor], for evaluation and/or treatment. I understand that my child is [counselor's] client— *not me, any other sibling, or my ex-spouse or current spouse.* This is true no matter who pays [counselor] for the evaluation/treatment of my child. I have the authority to bring my child to and consent for psychological/mental health counseling. I have provided [counselor] with a copy of the court document that grants me this permission. I understand that [counselor's] primary responsibility is my child's best interest and that he/she may decide to involve me in my child's evaluation/treatment at her sole discretion. I understand that if payment is not received promptly for services rendered, the services may be suspended or terminated at counselor's discretion, pursuant to the ethical guidelines governing psychological care. I understand that [counselor] is not agreeing to be an expert witness or to testify on my behalf or on the behalf of any other individual other than my child at any deposition, court proceeding, or in any other way. I understand that [counselor] may or may not agree to with my attorney, or any other party in any custodial or divorce proceeding at his/her sole discretion. He/she may also charge for the receipt of any correspondence or acceptance of any telephone calls, other than those directly from the court or counsel for my child. I have read the above paragraphs and understand them. By signing below, I agree to the above. This authorization constitutes informed consent without exception. I have read, understand, and agree to the above stated policies.

REMEMBER TO: Include appropriate lines for signature and date.

RESEARCH
Sample Separated-Divorced Parent Agreement
- **What would you change? Delete? Add?**
  - **What sample text in the above consent do you strongly agree with? Why?**
  - **What sample text do you strongly disagree with? Why?**

MINORS: AGE OF CONSENT...In the U.S., state legislation requiring parental consent for medical treatment reflects the conception that minors (typically, commonly, those under the age of 18) are incapable of understanding and making decisions about medical treatment. The state recognizes that the legal age of majority is arbitrary and that there are minors who are competent and others, of legal age, who are not; however, legislation is designed to protect minors from the consequences of poor decisions.

MINORS ARE VIEWED AS INCOMPETENT DECISION MAKERS WITH A FEW EXCEPTIONS:
- Mature minors
- Emancipated minors

MATURE MINOR DOCTRINE: Mature minors are those who meet the conditions set forth by the mature minor rule, legal doctrine that enables minors who are deemed mature (able to understand the nature and consequences of medical treatment) to consent to or refuse treatment. Determination of maturity requires an assessment of the minor's capacities, as well as his or her understanding of the nature of treatment and the potential consequences. Usually the determination of maturity is left to physicians or judges. In some states, mature minor legislation extends older minors the authority to provide informed consent for all general medical treatment, with ages varying by state. The difficulty of the mature minor doctrine lies in assessing maturity; there are no firm guidelines for assessing maturity or decision-making capacity.

EMANCIPATED MINORS: Emancipated minors are those who live independently of their parents. Emancipated minors may consent to medical care, and refuse it, as if they were adults. The criteria for emancipation vary by state, but generally include the following situations: marriage, military service, parental consent (parents who have surrendered their rights and responsibilities), parenthood, judicial order, and financial independence.

RESEARCH
- **Conduct a search for information on the:**
  - 1) **Mature Minor Doctrine and 2) Emancipated Minors' Laws for your state**
  - *You must understand the laws in your state regarding minors' rights*

MINORS: RIGHTS TO CONSENT...
(Without parental involvement)
- Most states allow minors ages 13 through 18 to provide consent for some medical care, including contraception, sexually transmitted diseases, pregnancy, alcohol and drug abuse, and psychiatric problems, varying by state.
- The nature of these health issues is such that some minors would choose to go without treatment rather than seek parental consent (e.g., adolescents may not want parents to be aware of the problem).
- Allowing minors to give consent in these instances ensures unrestricted access to care for those who otherwise might have been deterred from seeking help.

RESEARCH

- **Go to: www.guttmacher.org**
    - **The Alan Guttmacher Institute has periodically reviewed state laws pertaining to minors' authority to consent to medical care and to make other important decisions without their parents' knowledge or permission. Recently, its review was expanded to also take into account state court decisions and attorneys general opinions that affect young people's access to confidential services.**

IS THE MINOR YOUR CLIENT?
If a minor is old enough to sign the consent and they are paying for the care then confidentiality is owed to the minor—they are your client. However, they cannot use their parent's insurance or have their parents pay privately for the counseling and still be considered the sole client. If the parent is paying, then both minor and parent(s) should sign the consent. In addition, if a minor is old enough to sign the consent then they are also able to refuse treatment [Patient's Rights Act}. Counselors who work with minors should have policies [or a consent addendum] that outline the counseling relationship between counselor and parent(s) and minor.

ETHICAL STANDARDS & CLINICAL FORMS

HAVE AND FOLLOW POLICIES
- If you are in private practice and thinking about working with minors, consult with colleagues who provide services to minors. See what they are doing!
- If you are employed by an agency or organization that works with minors, follow the company's policies.

MINORS AND CONSENT FORMS
Some details you may want to cover in a consent or letter of agreement are:
- What information you would share with parent(s)
- What type of information, shared by the minor, that's kept confidential
- Any additional limits to confidentiality you've establish

CAVEAT: There is a wide variance in state laws regarding parental access to records. Both parents and the child, even in states where parents have sole decision-making authority, can sign another variation. The counselor should note that contract ratification, particularly the parents' or client's agreement to discourage subpoenas from attorneys, is not legally binding and may not prevent a judge from issuing a subpoena. However, sufficient anecdotal evidence suggests that such a contract discourages the utilization of child counselors in the divorce process. Such a contract also serves to remind the court of the strong correlation between privacy and therapeutic effectiveness.

SAMPLE CHILD THERAPY CONTRACT
CAVEAT: For use in your own setting, forms must be personalized to reflect your state's relevant laws, ethical requirements for your licensing, and your own actual policies.

Child Therapy Contract
Prior to beginning treatment, it is important for you to understand my approach to child therapy and agree to some rules about your child's confidentiality during the course of his/her treatment. The information herein is in addition to the information contained in my regular consent document. Under HIPAA, I am legally and ethical

responsible to provide you with informed consent. As we go forward, I will try to remind you of important issues as they arise. One risk of child therapy involves disagreement among parents and/or disagreement between parents and counselor regarding the best interests of the child. If such disagreements occur, I will strive to listen carefully so that I can understand your perspectives and fully explain my perspective. We can resolve such disagreements or we can agree to disagree, so long as this enables your child's therapeutic progress. If you decide to terminate treatment, I have the option of having a few closing sessions with your child to properly end the treatment relationship. You are waiving your right to access to your child's treatment records. I will inform you if your child does not attend the treatment sessions. At the end of treatment, I will provide you with a summary that includes a general description of goals, progress made, and potential areas that may require intervention in the future. If necessary to protect the life of your child or another person, I have the option of disclosing information to you without your child's consent. You agree that my role is limited to providing treatment and that you will not involve me in any legal dispute, especially a dispute concerning custody or custody arrangements (visitation, etc.). You also agree to instruct your attorneys not to subpoena me or to refer in any court filing to anything I have said or done. If there is a court appointed evaluator, and if appropriate releases are signed and a court order is provided, I will provide general information about the child which will not include recommendations concerning custody or custody arrangements. If, for any reason, I am required to appear as a witness, the party responsible for my participation agrees to reimburse me at the rate of $_____ per hour for time spent traveling, preparing reports, testifying, being in attendance, and any other case-related costs.

REMEMBER TO: Include appropriate lines for signature and date; Keep a copy of any document that was signed by a client in the client's file (hardcopy or electronic); Copy to client optional, unless they request a copy.

RESEARCH
Sample Child Therapy Contract
- **What would you change? Delete? Add?**
  - **What sample text in the above consent do you strongly agree with? Why?**
  - **What sample text do you strongly disagree with? Why?**

ETHICAL STANDARDS & CLINICAL FORMS

SAMPLE COUNSELING MINORS CONSENT

CAVEAT: For use in your own setting, forms must be personalized to reflect your state's relevant laws, ethical requirements for your licensing, and your own actual policies.

> **CAVEAT: Take appropriate steps to know which parent or whether both parents need to sign. If the minor is at an age, in your state, that they can sign their own consent independently of their parents (and they are paying for the counseling themselves), then confidentiality is due to them alone.**

COUNSELING MINORS

Minors in therapy: If you are under eighteen years of age, please be aware that the law may give your parents or guardians the right to obtain information about your treatment and/or examine your treatment records. It is my policy to request a written agreement from your parents or guardians indicating that they consent to give up access to such information and/or to your records. If they agree, I will provide them only with general information about our work together subject to your approval, or, if I feel it is important for them to know in order to make sure that you and people around you are safe.

If I think it is appropriate, I will involve them if I feel that there is a high risk that you will seriously harm yourself or another/others. Before giving them any verbal or written information, I will discuss the matter with you, if possible.

I will do the best I can to resolve any differences that you and I may have about what I am prepared to discuss. I understand that all material discussed during the psychotherapy sessions is confidential and can be released only with the permission of the holder of the privilege.

I, _____ [client] have been informed of the limitations to confidentiality relevant to mandatory reporting laws (duty to warn and protect; child and adult protective services) that are in the counselor's main consent form, which I have read and signed. In counseling minors, special sensitivity may be required in releasing information about certain topics such as drugs and sex. I will accept [counselor's] judgment in regard to releasing or sharing information obtained during the course of psychotherapy with the minor that may endanger or jeopardize the patient's well being.

Additional limits of confidentiality that I include are as follows: *If the minor speaks to me about their involvement in dangerous behaviors (not covered under mandatory reporting), such as fire starting, hurting animals, excessive drug/alcohol abuse, severe eating disorders, or any other activities where there is a substantial likelihood of harm to themselves or others, and if they speak to me about their direct involvement in a previous capital crime, I reserve the right to report these to appropriate sources.*

REMEMBER TO: Include appropriate lines for signature and date; Keep a copy of any document that was signed by a client in the client's file (hardcopy or electronic); Copy to client optional, unless they request a copy.

RESEARCH
Sample Counseling Minors Consent
- **What would you change? Delete? Add?**
  - **What sample text in the above consent do you strongly agree with? Why?**
  - **What sample text do you strongly disagree with? Why?**

SAMPLE ADOLESCENT CONSENT FORM

CAVEAT: *For use in your own setting, forms must be personalized to reflect your state's relevant laws, ethical requirements for your licensing, and your own actual policies.*

What to expect: The purpose of meeting with a counselor is to get help with problems in your life that are bothering you or that are keeping you from being successful in important areas of your life. You may be here because you wanted to talk to a counselor about these problems. Or, you may be here because your parent, guardian, doctor or teacher had concerns about you. When we meet, we will discuss these problems. I will ask questions, listen to you and suggest a plan for improving these problems. It is important that you feel comfortable talking to me about the issues that are bothering you. Sometimes these issues will include things you don't want your parents or guardians to know about. For most people, knowing that what they say will be kept private helps them feel more comfortable and have more trust in their counselor. Privacy, also called confidentiality, is an important and necessary part of good counseling.

As a general rule, I will keep the information you share with me in our sessions confidential, unless I have your written consent to disclose certain information. There are, however, important exceptions to this rule that are important for you to understand before you share personal information with me in a therapy session. In some situations, law requires me to disclose information whether or not I have your permission. I have listed some of these situations below.

Confidentiality cannot be maintained when:
- You tell me you plan to cause serious harm or death to yourself, and I believe you have the intent and ability to carry out this threat in the very near future. I must take steps to inform a parent or guardian of what you have told me and how serious I believe this threat to be. I must make sure that you are protected from harming yourself.
- You tell me you plan to cause serious harm or death to someone else who can be identified, and I believe you have the intent and ability to carry out this threat in the very near future. In this situation, I must inform your parent or guardian, and I must inform the person who you intend to harm.
- You are doing things that could cause serious harm to you or someone else, even if you do not intend to harm yourself or another person. In these situations, I will need to use my professional judgment to decide whether a parent or guardian should be informed.
- You tell me you are being abused-physically, sexually or emotionally-or that you have been abused in the past. In this situation, I am required by law to report the abuse to the state's Department of Social Services.
- You are involved in a court case and a request is made for information about your counseling or therapy. If this happens, I will not disclose information without your written agreement unless the court requires me to. I will do all I can within the law to protect your confidentiality, and if I am required to disclose information to the court, I will inform you that this is happening.

One goal of treatment is to promote a stronger and better relationship between children and their parents. However, it is often necessary for children to develop a "zone of privacy" whereby they feel free to discuss personal matters with greater freedom. This is particularly true for adolescents who are naturally developing a greater sense of independence and autonomy. By signing this agreement, you will be waiving your right of access to your child's treatment records.

Communicating with your parent(s) or guardian(s):
I have explained to your parent(s)/legal guardian that you may reveal sensitive information regarding sexual contact, alcohol and drug use, or other potentially problematic behaviors. Sometimes these behaviors are within the range of normal adolescent experimentation, but at other times they may require parental intervention. We must carefully and directly discuss your feelings and opinions regarding "what is acceptable behavior" and concerns for your safety. If I ever believe that you are at serious risk of harming yourself or another, I will inform your parents or other appropriate reporting to help keep you and others safe. Except for situations such as those mentioned above, I will not tell your parent or guardian specific things you share with me in our private therapy sessions. This includes activities and behavior that your parent/guardian would not approve of—*or would be upset by*—but that do not put you at risk of serious and immediate harm. However, if your risk-taking behavior becomes more serious, then I will need to use my professional judgment to decide whether you are in serious and immediate danger of being harmed. If I feel that you are in such danger, I will communicate this information to your parent or guardian.

Communicating with other adults:
- **School:** I will not share any information with your school unless I have your permission and permission from your parent or guardian. Sometimes I may request to speak to someone at your school to find out how things are going for you. Also, it may be helpful in some situations for me to give suggestions to your teacher or counselor at school. If I want to contact your school, or if someone at your school wants to contact me, I will discuss it with you and ask for your written permission. A very unlikely situation might come up in which I do not have your permission but both I and your parent or guardian believe that it is very important for me to be able to share certain information with someone at your school. In this situation, I will use my professional judgment to decide whether to share any information.
- **Doctors:** Sometimes your doctor and I may need to work together; for example, if you need to take medication in addition to seeing a counselor. I will get your written permission and permission from your parent/guardian in advance to share information with your doctor. The only time I will share information with your doctor even if I don't have your permission is if you are doing something that puts you at risk for serious and immediate physical/medical harm.

ETHICAL STANDARDS & CLINICAL FORMS

PARENT/GUARDIAN AGREEMENT REGARDING CONFIDENTIALITY:
Signing below indicates that you have reviewed the policies described above and understand the limits to confidentiality. If you have any questions as we progress with therapy, you can ask your counselor at any time. [Add minor's signature line]

Parent/Guardian: *Check boxes and sign below indicating your agreement to respect your adolescent's privacy*

- I/we will refrain from requesting detailed information about individual therapy sessions with my/our child. I understand that I/we will be provided with periodic updates about general progress, and/or may be asked to participate in therapy sessions as needed. ___/___ (initial)
- Although I/we know that I/we have the legal right to request written records/session notes since my child is a minor, I agree NOT to request these records in order to respect the confidentiality of my adolescent's treatment and progress in therapy. ___/___ (initial)
- I/we understand that I/we will be informed about situations that could endanger my/our child. I/we know this decision to breach confidentiality in these circumstances is up to the counselor's professional judgment and may sometimes be made in confidential consultation with her consultant/supervisor. [Parent(s) Signatures]

REMEMBER TO:
Include appropriate lines for signature and date; Keep a copy of any document that was signed by a client in the client's file (hardcopy or electronic); Copy to client optional, unless they request a copy.

RESEARCH
Sample Adolescent Consent Form
- **What would you change? Delete? Add?**
    - **What sample text in the above consent do you strongly agree with? Why?**
    - **What sample text do you strongly disagree with? Why?**

NO CHARGE INITIAL SESSION

Some counselors have a "no charge" first session so the counselor and the potential client can meet and talk without forming a fiduciary relationship. If this is done best practice is to have a simple consent form explaining the nature of the session and its limitations.

SAMPLE "NO CHARGE" INITIAL SESSION CONSENT

CAVEAT: For use in your own setting, forms must be personalized to reflect your state's relevant laws and your own actual policies.

There will be no charge for this 20-minute session. This session is an opportunity for counselor and potential client to meet and determine if entering a counseling relationship would be beneficial and in the best interests of the potential client. No fiduciary relationship is being formed. A fiduciary relationship would be established if the potential clients wishes to continue and signs [counselor's] informed consent document. Also, if [counselor] believes that the potential client will be better served by another counselor, another type of modality, a different level of care, or a different therapeutic approach, the counselor will discuss this with potential client and provide suggestions. What you, as a potential client, shares is confidential except for the following: *If you speak of harm to yourself or others, counselor must report to appropriate sources to keep you and others safe according to mandatory reporting laws. If you speak of abuse, neglect, abandonment or exploitation of children or vulnerable adults, counselor will need to report to appropriate agencies according to the law.* I have read, understand, and agree to the above statements.

REMEMBER TO:
Include appropriate lines for signature and date.

RESEARCH
- **Have you ever considered a no-charge initial session?**
  - What could be potential risks or complications with doing this?

ETHICAL STANDARDS & CLINICAL FORMS

NON-SUBPOENA CONTRACT

CAVEAT: Although this is not a legally binding contract, it does emphasize the importance of protecting the confidentiality of the therapeutic relationship. It also can greatly reduce the likelihood of the client trying to use the information from the counseling sessions in a subsequent court case. Some courts give consideration to this agreement when making a determination about whether to quash a subpoena.

SAMPLE NON-SUBPOENA CONTRACT

CAVEAT: For use in your own setting, forms must be personalized to reflect your state's relevant laws and your own actual policies.

LETTERHEAD

This contract is an agreement between the counselor and client(s) that no one involved in the counseling with [counselor] shall attempt to subpoena the counselor or the counselor's records for a deposition or court hearing of any kind for any reason. The goal of psychotherapy is the improvement of psychological distress and interpersonal conflict, and that this process depends on trust and openness during the counseling sessions. Therefore it is understood by all that if they request counselor's services as a counselor, they are expected not to use the information given during therapy for their own legal purposes or against any of the other parties in a court or judicial setting of any kind. I have read, understand, and agree to the above statements.

REMEMBER TO:
Include appropriate lines for signature and date.

RESEARCH
- **Which counselors, and in which settings, would be more likely to use a document like this?**
- **Do you think it would be worthwhile to execute a document like this given the above caveat information?**

NOTICE OF PRIVACY PRACTICES (HIPAA)

The HIPAA document contains summary information about the Health Insurance Portability and Accountability Act (HIPAA), a federal law that provides privacy protections and patient rights with regard to the use and disclosure of your Protected Health Information (PHI). HIPAA requires that we provide you with a Notice of Privacy Practices for use and disclosure of PHI for treatment, payment, and healthcare operations. This notice, which is given along with this agreement, explains HIPAA and its application to your personal health information in greater detail. The law requires that we obtain your signature acknowledging that we have provided you with this information.

NOTICE OF PRIVACY PRACTICES

Healthcare and Mental Health Professionals disclose confidential information without the consent of the individual only as mandated by law, or where permitted by law for a valid purpose such as to:

- Provide needed professional services
- Obtain appropriate professional consultations
- Protect the client/patient, psychologist, or others from harm
- Obtain payment for services from a client/patient, in which instance disclosure is limited to the minimum that is necessary to achieve the purpose

RESEARCH
Understanding HIPAA
- A general web search on the topic will produce samples of the HIPAA Notice of Privacy Practice document or pick up 10 different samples from local hospitals, counseling centers, or healthcare offices
- Compare the samples that you have acquired
- Is the "Notice of Privacy Practices" you're using (if you are in practice) sufficient? How does it compare to the other samples?

ETHICAL STANDARDS & CLINICAL FORMS

NOTICE OF PRIVACY PRACTICES: OVERVIEW LETTER (HIPAA)

SAMPLE OVERVIEW LETTER

CAVEAT: For use in your own setting, forms must be personalized to reflect your state's relevant laws, ethical requirements for your licensing, and your own actual policies.

[LETTERHEAD]
Dear Client:
Counselors have always protected the confidentiality of health information. We and other [your state] healthcare providers are currently bound by our professional ethics and the strict standards of the Uniform Healthcare Information Act to protect your health information. The federal government has published regulations under HIPAA, the Health Insurance Portability and Accountability Act of 1996 ("HIPAA"), designed to provide further protection of the privacy of your health information. This "privacy rule" protects health information that is maintained by counselors. These rules protect virtually all clients regardless of where they live or where they receive their healthcare. All health information including paper records, oral communications, and electronic formats are protected by the privacy rule. The privacy rule also provides you certain rights, such as the right to have access to your medical records. However, there are exceptions; these rights are not absolute. We also take precautions in our office to safeguard your health information such as training our employees and employing computer security measures. Please feel free to ask your counselor about exercising your rights or how your health information is protected in our office. The Notice of Private Practices document you have been given/will be given explains privacy practices. It contains very important information about how your confidential health information is handled. It also describes how you can exercise your rights with regard to your protected health information. Please let us know if you have any questions about our Notice of Privacy Practices. [If applicable] You may contact our Privacy Officer at _____, or discuss any questions you may have with your counselors.

Note: Overview letter is optional.

PATIENT'S RIGHT ACT

patient's/client's bill of rights is a list of guarantees for those receiving medical care. It may take the form of a law or a non-binding declaration. Typically a bill of rights guarantees clients information, fair treatment, and autonomy over medical decisions, among other rights.

A bill of rights comes from policies and laws established in the Patient's Right Act.
- For Information and links to this act go to: www.wikipedia.org OR keyword search: "Patient's Rights Act"

THE PATIENT'S RIGHTS ACT ADDRESSES A PERSON'S RIGHT TO:
- Dignity
- Participate in treatment decisions
- Refuse treatment
- Autonomy and self-determination
- File a complaint

THE PATIENT'S RIGHTS ACT COVERS INFORMATION ON:
- Living Wills
- Power of Attorney
- Euthanasia

RESEARCH
Patient's Rights Act
- **Internet search for a copy of the Patient's Rights Act**
  - **It's important to be familiar with this document; take the time to read through it**
- **What additional information (other than what is listed above) does it cover?**

*Records are a working
document for recording
client care*

PROFESSIONAL DISCLOSURE STATEMENTS
SUGGESTED GUIDELINES

WHAT IS IT?
- The Professional Disclosure Statement (PDS) is a written document that a counselor gives to clients to tell the client information about the licensee/intern and his/her practice.

WHO MUST HAVE THEM?
- Mandatory requirement depends on your state's licensing requirements. Some licensing boards required practicing professionals to have a copy of the PDS on file at their state licensing board.
- What is considered "practicing"? Practicing means to perform any of the activities relevant to your licensing including identifying, assessing, and treating behavioral conditions, applying theories and techniques, researching, reporting, and consulting.

CONTENTS OF A PDS:
- Identification: Counselor's name, business or employer's name (if applicable), business address and telephone number.
- Philosophy and approach to counseling: Description of counselor's proposed course of treatment (if known). There should be sufficient detail to enable the client to make an informed decision about whether (or not) to accept treatment from the specific counselor.
- Include: A statement that you will abide by the code of ethics for your state licensing board and any associations that you belong to.
- Formal training and education: List the highest relevant degree, subject, school granting degree, and subsequent and significant continuing education or certifications.

CAVEAT: Counselors do not solicit testimonials from current therapy clients because their particular circumstances are vulnerable to undue influence.

SAMPLE WORKSHEET
PDS (Professional Disclosure Statement)

CAVEAT: For use in your own setting, forms must be personalized to reflect your state's relevant laws and your own actual policies.

BACKGROUND
I obtained my degree in _____ from _____. Currently, I provide the following services:
State of _____, License Number _____
I am a member of _____ Association(s)
Code of Ethics Adherence: *As a licensed counselor, I will abide by the Codes of Ethics of [association], codes of professional conduct per [state] licensing board, and all [state] mandated reporting requirements.*

Continuing Education/Supervision: I maintain a network of mental health professionals and attend many workshops for my continued professional growth.

PHILOSOPHY: I believe [whatever you want to say about counseling in general, about the utilization of counseling, reasons individuals seek counseling, and about the type of counseling you provide]

APPROACH: It is my belief that [whatever you want to say about counseling in general, about the utilization of counseling, reasons individuals seek counseling, and about the type of counseling you provide]
From experience, I have found _____.
My approach to counseling is: _____.

RESEARCH
- **Work on your PDS (Professional Disclosure Statement)**
  - **Use the above form to guide you in creating your Professional Disclosure Statement**

SAMPLE PROFESSIONAL DISCLOSURE STATEMENT

CAVEAT: For use in your own setting, forms must be personalized to reflect your state's relevant laws and your own actual policies.

Philosophy and Approach

I work with both individuals and families, and have experience working with minors as well as adults. My belief is that an individual will seek assistance when their usual coping mechanisms have become ineffective and they are interested in exploring other avenues and increasing their own resources. I believe that each individual will bring with them very unique perspectives and experience, thus I do not offer a generic statement regarding types of support offered. Commonly, concerns relating to relationships, employment, addiction and/or addiction recovery, death and loss, sexuality, and ways in which to integrate the past experience with the present circumstances to create a rich understanding with insights that can assist in future decision making, are brought for examination and in that undertaking, deeper associated concerns may, but do not necessarily always, arise. The adage that "the best predictor of future behavior is past behavior", and the belief that the past behavior is no longer yielding satisfying results is often the cornerstone for new growth and development. The client will be considered a collaborator and the treatment will be mutually agreed upon.

Expectations

- Certain expectations exist within the counseling relationship parameters, and these include the assumption that a willingness to work during and between sessions, on goals and objectives, communication and negotiation is upheld by both the client or clients, and myself.
- I request 24 hours notice before missing a session, whenever at all possible, since the time I schedule for you is a commitment I make to you, and I would of course, call you in the event that I have an incident that prevents me from meeting you. If you miss 2 sessions consecutively I will send a reminder note to the address given at the time of intake. If I do not hear from you, the file will be closed and I will assume that you are no longer interested in pursuing counseling at this time.
- I may suggest that you consult with a medical healthcare provider regarding ruling out any possible physiological causes for any distressing symptoms. If another healthcare provider is working with you, I may ask

ETHICAL STANDARDS & CLINICAL FORMS

you to sign a release of information form so that I may communicate with that person about your care. Sometimes I also recommend a support or counseling group as an adjunct to our individual work. Of course, you have the right to carefully consider and to say "yes," "no," or "not now" to anything I suggest.
- Counseling requires your very active involvement. It requires your best efforts to explore your awareness, and change thoughts, feelings, and behaviors. For example, I want you to tell me about important experiences, what they mean to you, and what strong feelings are involved. This is one of the ways you are an active participant in counseling.

Formal Education and Training
I have worked in human service agencies in [state] for the past ___ years and qualified with my Masters in Applied Psychology in _____, from _____ University. I have extensive experience in case management, alcohol and drug concerns and family and individual work, including trauma focused treatment modalities. I am a National Certified Counselor.

Code of Ethics Adherence
As a professional mental health practitioner I will abide by the Codes of Ethics of National Board of Certified Counselors and all State mandated reporting requirements.

Continuing Education/Supervision
As a Licensed Counselor, I am required to attend trainings and seminars on subjects relevant to my profession on an ongoing basis. I consult with colleagues on a regular basis and as needed.

> ## RESEARCH
> **Sample Professional Disclosure Statement**
> - What would you change? Delete? Add?
> - What sample text in the above consent do you strongly agree with? Why?
> - What sample text do you strongly disagree with? Why?

PROFESSIONAL WILL

The purpose of a professional will is to execute your ethical responsibilities related to a transfer plan or record custodian. When a counselor is incapacitated (unable to provide counseling) or has deceased, the counselor needs to have a transfer plan in place explaining who will take possession of the clients' records, how the clients are to be notified, and what needs to be done.

See the "Transfer Plans" or "Record Custodian" sections for more details.

Every professional counselor in private practice needs to have procedures in place detailing what will happen to current clients and records should the professional counselor leave the practice, die, or become disabled and unable to practice.

For this reason, as well as client welfare, there is an importance of creating a will or other instructions addressing record disposition. Make arrangements with a professionally responsible colleague for the care and management of the records.

If you work for someone else, the agency or company is the custodian of the records. However, if you work for yourself [private practice] then you must name another counselor who will become the custodian of your clients' charts. If you have ever been in a private practice and have client flies in your possession, then you must have a transfer plan that is outlined in your professional will and designates a record custodian.

The record custodian does not have to see your clients. They do take possession of the charts and notify your clients of your death. They provide copies of a client's chart with appropriate authorization to do so by the client or in response to appropriate legal actions. They retain the charts according to the required number of years for your state. This is referred to a "transfer plan" and having one is an ethical requirement.

SAMPLE PROFESSIONAL WILL

CAVEAT: Always get legal advice regarding wills.

CAVEAT: For use in your own setting, forms must be personalized to reflect your state's relevant laws, ethical requirements for your licensing, and your own actual policies.

Place of practice…
- Place(s) where records are stored and ways to access them (keys, combination locks, etc.)…
- Place(s) where list(s) of present clients' names, addresses or phone numbers are located
- Location of digital records, access to computer, backups, and the location of all your financial records…

This document intends to direct the executor of my estate, as stated in my Living Trust, in dealing with the confidential records of my psychotherapy clients in the event of my death. After my death the executor should contact [record custodian] and accompany him/her to my office. Once there, my record custodian will take possession of my clients' records, appointment book, office computer (if clinical records are in digital format), and any other clinical relevant records. The record custodian will need to notify my clients ASAP about my death or incapacitation and give them a couple of referrals that they may wish to contact. I have included the names of colleagues and their areas of specialties. The record custodian should notify the referral sources about my death or incapacitation and check for their availability to consult with new clients. All the clinical records should be given in full to the record custodian who is aware of his/her clinical, ethical, and legal responsibilities and duties in regard to the clinical records. Neither the executor nor anyone else except my record custodian should read the clinical records or any part of them. My executor should receive a written statement from the record custodian that he/she has taken possession of all the above items.

This document should be notarized

REMEMBER TO:
- Include appropriate lines for signature and date
- Keep a copy with your will or other important documents
- Provide a copy to your record custodian

See the "Transfer Plans" and "Record Custodians" sections for more details.

PSYCHOTHERAPY NOTES

Before discussing what psychotherapy notes are, let's discuss what they are not.
- Non-psychotherapy notes are anything you maintained in the client's chart.

Psychotherapy Notes are a very specific form of documentation that is maintained separate from the client's chart. It is important that counselors understand the difference.

Under HIPAA there is a difference between regular Personal Health Information and "psychotherapy" notes." Here is HIPAA's definition of psychotherapy notes:
- Psychotherapy notes means notes recorded (in any medium) by a healthcare provider who is a mental health professional documenting or analyzing the contents of conversation during a private counseling session or a group, joint, or family counseling session and that are separated from the rest of the individual's medical record. Psychotherapy notes excludes medication prescription and monitoring, counseling session start and stop times, the modalities and frequencies of treatment furnished, results of clinical tests, and any summary of the following items: diagnosis, functional status, the treatment plan, symptoms, prognosis, and progress to date.
- Mental health professionals are permitted to maintain psychotherapy notes separately from the rest of the client's chart.
- These psychotherapy notes may represent personal notes used to record or analyze group, individual or family therapy, and unlike the rest of the chart do not have to be disclosed to the client.
- They are solely for the use of the provider that created them.

ANYTHING KEPT IN A CLIENT'S CHART IS NOT A PSYCHOTHERAPY NOTE.

RESEARCH
- **Research psychotherapy notes: what additional information can you find?**
  - When would they be helpful/useful to keep?
- **Are they discoverable?**
  - Check the legal case "Jaffee vs. Redmond", 1996 Supreme Court Case. What does it have to do with psychotherapy notes?

*Good records
should begin the moment
a record is created*

RECORD CUSTODIAN

Good records management begins the moment a record is created. If you work for someone else, the agency/company is the custodian of the records. However, if you work for yourself [private practice] then you must name another counselor who will become the custodian of your clients' charts. The record custodian does not have to see your clients. They do take possession of the charts and notify your clients of your death. Then provide copies of a client's chart with appropriate authorization to do so by the client or in response to appropriate legal actions. They retain the charts according to the required number of years for your state. This is referred to as a "transfer plan" and having one is an ethical requirement.

COUNSELOR INCAPACITATION OR TERMINATION OF PRACTICE
Every professional counselor in private practice needs to have procedures in place detailing what will happen to current clients and records should the professional counselor leave the practice, die, or become disabled and unable to practice. For this reason, as well as client welfare, there is an importance of creating a will or other instructions addressing record disposition. One alternative could involve an arrangement with a professionally responsible colleague for the care and management of the records.

WHO SHOULD BECOME THE RECORDS CUSTODIAN?
When counselors become incapacitated or leave a practice, they follow a prepared plan for transfer of clients and files. Counselors prepare and disseminate to an identified colleague or 'records custodian' a plan for the transfer of clients and files in the case of their incapacitation, death or termination of practice. Even beginning counselors need to have a transfer plan. You may be young, healthy and starting a new practice, and the last thing on your mind is thinking about illness or death. But what if you get hit by a car and can't resume work for a month or more? Who will see your clients? There has to be a transfer plan in place to ensure that your clients have access to both counseling and their records during your period of incapacitation. This is important for all counselors, but it is especially critical in a private practice.

"Counselor Incapacitation" or "Termination of Practice" standards are offered in the spirit of preventing a sense of abandonment, protecting client welfare and preserving confidentiality as best as possible in a difficult situation.

ETHICAL STANDARDS & CLINICAL FORMS

WHAT ARE THE RESPONSIBILITIES OF THE RECORDS CUSTODIAN?
THE RECORDS CUSTODIAN'S PRIMARY DUTIES:
1) Help determine retention and disposition policies.
2) Make decisions about who can access records.

RECORD CUSTODIANS AND INFORMED CONSENT:
- This relates to the issue of informed consent. The transfer plan needs to be incorporated into the informed consent process. Clients should be given the plan in writing so that they know whom to contact if the counselor suddenly becomes unavailable. Counselors can easily do this by incorporating a transfer plan into their written informed consent document and making sure that clients receive a copy of this document.
- There is no one particular format. A counselor just needs to make sure that the important points are covered. The plan needs to state what clients should do to access their records and facilitate continued services if the counselor becomes inaccessible through death, disability or change of location. This would include explicitly stating in your informed consent brochure that the custodian of your records will be _____ and include the complete contact information for that person. This custodian should then notify active clients upon receipt of the records.
- An administrative assistant, receptionist or another counselor within your practice should be informed about the plan so that he or she knows where to transfer the records. This colleague or staff member can also give out the custodian's contact information if clients have misplaced their copy of the informed consent brochure.

CHOOSING A RECORD CUSTODIAN
What are the options for choosing a custodian? Ideally, it should be another mental health professional. The most logical person would be the colleague you use for backup or on-call purposes when you are away or otherwise unavailable. Using a professional counselor or other mental health professional as your records custodian speaks to the need for confidentiality. Whoever the custodian is, the arrangement should be in writing.

See "Transfer Plans" and "Professional Will" sections for more details.

RECORD RETENTION

- States vary. Contact your state's association or licensing board for requirements. Typically it has been 7 years from the last time you saw a client [and 7 years after a client turns 18] for mental health records. You can only destroy records by burning or shredding. Electronic records are typically stored forever.
- Many insurance companies are requiring preferred providers to keep records for 10 years from the last time they saw a client or 10 years from when a minor client turns 18.
- Records retention can vary depending on practice setting. If you work for an organization then adhere to their record retention policies.

RECORDS: KEEP OR TOSS...
One of the thornier issues of counseling today involves the why, when, and where of keeping clinical records. While hospitals and social service agencies invariably follow strict procedures requiring the indefinite retention of records, solo or group practitioners are often left hoping for a bit more leeway. And why not? A thriving practice can quickly accumulate documents, resulting in a storage problem within a matter of years. While it's tempting to consider weeding out the old to free up space for the new, the prudent practitioner will think twice before moving toward the shredding machine.

QUESTIONS TYPICALLY CENTERS ON FOUR ISSUES:
- How long should counselors retain their records?
- Where and how should inactive files be stored?
- What are the guidelines for retaining electronic (computer-based) records?
- What is the potential downside should old records be prematurely disposed of?

OFF-SITE STORAGE IS LESS PRICEY AND BURDENSOME THAN A LEGAL DEFENSE.
- Given the potential legal fallout stemming from premature disposal, adopting the minimally accepted standards in today's litigious environment seems unwise. Better to have a file and not need it, than to need it and not have it. In short, anticipate the unexpected—be prepared.

ETHICAL STANDARDS & CLINICAL FORMS

RECORDS SUMMARIES

See "record retention" for more information.

RECORDS: KEEP OR TOSS...
- If a counselor in private practice decides to shred old files (after they have met the record retention requirement for their state), then an option is a record summary. Before destroying the file, a counselor can transfer key information into a short summary. If this is done, then the short record summaries continue to be protected health information and these summaries must be stored with appropriate security measures.

SAMPLE RECORD SUMMARY

CAVEAT: For use in your own setting, forms must be personalized to reflect your state's relevant laws and your own actual policies.

[Letterhead]
SUMMARY OF RECORD
CLIENT'S NAME:
Seen between _____ and _____
Diagnosis _____
Have not seen since _____
SUMMARY: *type in a short summary of key information*

All other records obtained in the course of treating this person have been destroyed by [ ] shredding [ ] incineration by [ ] myself or [ ] other (a licensed, bonded company), on the following date: _____. This summary will be kept as the only record from this point on regarding this person's past care with me.

REMEMBER TO:
Include appropriate lines for your signature and date

RECORDINGS

VOICE AND/OR VIDEOS

- Before recording the voices or images of individuals to whom counselors provide services, counselors obtain permission from all such persons or their legal representatives.

ETHICAL PROCEDURES

- Ask the client if they would be receptive to being videotaped. If they decline, then simple move on. If they agree, use clinical judgment to gauge whether the client is actually comfortable or just agreeable. Counselors must take into consideration the client's condition and the appropriateness of involving the client in videotaping.
- Inform the client of all the details relevant to videotaping the session. Who will be viewing the taping and how it will be used are important details that must be shared with the client. The client needs to know who will be viewing the tape postproduction: only the counselor, supervisor(s), counseling interns for educational purposes, and/or other colleagues for continuing education.
- Use an "Informed Consent to Videotape" agreement, which will cover all of the terms and conditions of the videotaping.
- Get confirmation from the client the day before the session to ensure that the client is still comfortable with the session being videotaped.

CAVEAT: Erase the video once it is done being reviewed by whoever was to view it. If it is being kept for training/educational purposes, take every measure possible to secure its safety from an unauthorized release. As a counselor, you are responsible for this highly confidential media, and the leaking of the video could potentially lead to a lawsuit and the loss of your license. If you delete the video file, make sure that the file is deleted from the camera, the memory card, and the computer that it may have been uploaded to, then delete it from the computer's recycle bin. If a cassette tape was used, use a magnetic tape eraser to permanently erase any residue on the film.

ETHICAL STANDARDS & CLINICAL FORMS

SAMPLE RECORDING A SESSION CONSENT

CAVEAT: For use in your own setting, forms must be personalized to reflect your state's relevant laws and your own actual policies.

Informed Consent to Videotape: I understand that [counselor] routinely videotapes therapy sessions. I am aware that I am under no obligation to have my sessions videotaped. I understand that such recording(s) will be used only for educational purposes and that the professionals involved will respect and protect the confidential nature of the sessions. I understand that only my first name will be used in association with the video of my session. I understand that the tapes will be the property of [counselor]. I also understand that if I object to be videotaped, it will in no way jeopardize my relationship with [counselor] or the therapy being provided. I understand that I can have a copy with a written request; however, if I have a copy I understand that my confidentiality could be compromised since a copy exists outside the counselor's copy.

Agreement to Participate in Services: If you have any questions, please feel free to discuss them with counselor prior to signing this form. Your signature indicates that you have read, understand, and agree with the policies. Furthermore, you hereby authorize the mental healthcare provider to provide you psychological services. This authorization constitutes informed consent without exception. I have read, understand, and agree to the above stated policies.

REMEMBER TO: Include appropriate lines for signature and date; Keep a copy of any document that was signed by a client in the client's file (hardcopy or electronic); Copy to client optional, unless they request a copy.

RESEARCH
Sample Recording a Session Consent
- Search the Internet for another sample consent form and compare it to this one.
- What would you change? Delete? Add?
  - What sample text in the above consent do you strongly agree with? Why?
  - What sample text do you strongly disagree with? Why?

RELEASE OF INFORMATION

Counselors who conduct assessments are gatekeepers of sensitive information that may have profound and lasting effects on the life of the person who was assessed. The gate-keeping responsibilities exist within a complex framework of federal (HIPAA) and state legislation and case law as well as other relevant regulations, codes, and contexts.

Requests for client's records can come from many sources:
- PCP (Primary Care Providers) or other relevant care providers
- Parents, Foster Care, Legal Guardians
- Employers (Worker's Compensation)
- Attorneys, The Courts
- Another counselor

It is unfortunately all too easy, with the demands of a busy schedule or a hurried lapse of attention, to release data to those who are not legally or ethically entitled to it, sometimes with disastrous results.

> **CAVEAT:** Clarifying release of information issues while planning an assessment is important because if the counselor does not clearly understand them, it is impossible to communicate the information effectively as part of the process of informed consent and informed refusal. Information about who will or won't have access to an assessment report may be the key to a client's decision to give or withhold informed consent for an assessment. It is the counselor's responsibility to remain aware of the evolving legal, ethical, and practical frameworks that effect information release decisions.

ETHICAL STANDARDS & CLINICAL FORMS

RESEARCH

RESEARCH AND EVALUATION REQUIRES KNOWLEDGE:
- Counselors need to understand how to critically evaluate research relevant to the practice of counseling.

RESEARCH AND EVALUATION REQUIRES SKILLS AND PRACTICE:
- Counselors apply relevant research findings to inform the practice of counseling. They develop measurable outcomes, interventions, and treatments and they analyze and use data to increase the effectiveness of counseling programs.

RESEARCH AND PROGRAM EVALUATION includes all of the following:
- The importance of research in advancing the counseling profession
- Research methods such as qualitative, quantitative, single-case designs, action research, and outcome-based research
- Statistical methods used in conducting research and program evaluation
- Principles, models, and applications of needs assessment, program evaluation
- The use of findings to effect program modifications; the use of research to inform evidence-based practice
- Ethical and culturally relevant strategies for interpreting and reporting the results of research and/or program evaluation studies

CAVEAT: Counselor in the research field must be knowledgeable of all ethical codes relevant to the research work they are involved with. They must adhere to their research ethical guideline strictly and document all their work accurately and consistently. Always follow the policies and procedures outlined by the agency or organization you work for (unless they are asking you to do something unethical). If you are every asked to do something that is unethical (or illegal), you are ethically required to make known your commitment to your ethics. Consult legal advise as needed.

RESPONDING TO A SUBPOENA

A counselor does not need to automatically respond to the subpoena and uncritically send the records, unless it is accompanied by a signed authorization of release that was executed by your client or a court order appropriately executed. Even then, it is considered best practice to contact the client and discuss the situation. Make note of the discussion in the client's clinical record.

CAVEAT: Always get legal advice regarding subpoenas.

SAMPLE RESPONDING TO A SUBPOENA

CAVEAT: For use in your own setting, forms must be personalized to reflect your state's relevant laws and your own actual policies.

[LETTERHEAD]
Re: _____ Civil
Action File No. _____

Dear [Attorney]

In response to the Subpoena I received on [date], please be advised that all counseling communications between a licensed counselor and a client are legally privileged and/or confidential communications and cannot be released without the written permission by the client or proper legal authority. With respect to federal law, all communication between a counselor and a client is protected. I cannot, and will not, release any information without a court order signed by a judge or by written authorization from my client or their legal representative.
Sincerely,

RESEARCH

- For your state, is privileged communication extended to licensed mental health professionals?
- What is the difference between a subpoena and a court order?
- Would you word this letter differently? How? Why?

The structure of session notes can come from organizational policies, private practitioners' preferred format, or electronic record format

SESSION NOTES

STRUCTURE

The structure of session notes can result from organizational policy and procedure, private practitioner's preferred format, or electronic record formats.

CONTENT

The type of counseling being done, the setting, relevant cultural factors, etc., can affect the content in session notes.

SOME KEY ELEMENTS OF EXCEPTIONAL DOCUMENTATION:
- Symptoms and Progress Toward Goals: Specific DSM symptom cited; detailed frequency, duration, and progress; sophisticated linking of symptoms to personal dynamics, interventions, and all other aspects of note
- Interventions: Sophisticated choice of interventions consistent with symptoms, addiction status, and diversity needs; demonstrates clear understanding of counseling model
- Plan: Thoughtful adjustment of plan based on client response to treatment; modification demonstrates sensitivity to client needs, diversity issues
- Crisis Issues: Clear evidence of ability to identify ethical issues, dilemmas, ethical decision making; sophisticated management of crisis, legal, ethical issues, addiction; sophisticated safety plan; mandated reporting handled smoothly
- Case Consultation/Supervision: Proactive use of consultation, supervision, especially for legal, ethical issues; specific integration of feedback into treatment; insightful attention to personal issues that affect treatment
- Collateral Contact: Thoughtful and sensitive collaborative work with other stakeholders; obtains needed consents; clearly respects multiple perspectives of all involved; collaborates when making diagnosis as necessary
- Legal Issues: Case notes consistently timely; in exact accordance with legal, ethical requirements

ETHICAL STANDARDS & CLINICAL FORMS

WHAT SHOULD BE IN SESSION NOTES?

- Person's Name (Record the first name, last name, and middle initial of the person)
- Record Number (If applicable)
- Person's DOB (Date of birth)
- Modality (individual, family or couple) [List name(s) of person(s) present]
- Person's Report of Progress Towards Goals/Objectives Since Last Session (Document person's self-report of progress towards goals since last session including other sources of information, such as family, case manager, etc.)
- New Issue(s) Presented Today (New concerns presented)
- Person's Condition (Mood/affect Thought Process/Orientation Behavior Functioning Medical Condition)
- Substance Use
- Risk Assessment
- Goal(s) Addressed as Per Individualized Treatment/Action Plan
- Therapeutic Interventions Delivered in Session
- Person's Response to Intervention
- Progress Toward Goals and Objectives
- Additional Information/Plan

RESEARCH

- **What else can you think of to add to the above list**
- **Find ten samples of session notes from various sources:**
  - **Online**
  - **Other counselors**
- **Create your session note format**

S.O.A.P. NOTE FORMAT:
What about the amount of detail in a clinical record?
- The amount of detail is often determined by your employer, the electronic record format, or your personal choice.

CLINICAL RECORDS, REGARDLESS OF THE AMOUNT OF DETAIL, SHOULD REFLECT:
1) What the client is thinking (Subjective)
    Subjective is symptoms—what a client can feel and therefore what they complain about
2) How the counselor is thinking (Objective)
    Objective is signs—what a counselor can see when looking at a client
3) Counselor's clinical judgment(s) (Assessment)
4) The proposed direction(s) (Plan)

S.O.A.P. NOTES
SUBJECTIVE-OBJECTIVE-ASSESSMENT-PLAN
Counselors are required to accurately document what occurred during a counseling session; counselors need to ask:
- What are the mental health needs of this client?
- How can they best be met?

SUBJECTIVE: (Suggestions)
- Keep client quotations to a minimum
- When client quotations are overused it makes the record more difficult to review for client themes and to track the effectiveness of interventions
- If used, record only key words or a very brief phrase

OBJECTIVE: (Suggestions)
- Information should be factual
- What is seen, smelled, counted, or measured
- Counselor observations include any physical, interpersonal, or psychological findings that the counselor witnesses
- Information is stated in precise and descriptive terms
- Avoiding labeling observations with value-laden language

ETHICAL STANDARDS & CLINICAL FORMS

S.O.A.P. NOTE FORMAT: (Continued)

ASSESSMENT: (Suggestions)
- A summarization of the counselor's clinical thinking regarding the client's problem(s)
- Serves to synthesize and analyze the date from the subjective and objective portions of the notes
- Include clinical impressions (some counselors keep personal or shadow notes separate from the client's file. See Psychotherapy Notes)

PLAN: (Suggestions)
- Described as the parameters of counseling interventions used
- Includes two parts: the action plan (interventions, educational instruction, treatment progress, and treatment direction) and the prognosis (the probable gains to be made by the client given the diagnosis, the client's personal resources, and the motivation for change)

S.O.A.P. SIMPLIFIED:
- Subjective = Client's report
- Objective = Therapist's observation of client
- Assessment = Therapists assessment and interpretations
- Plan = Interventions

NOTE: Many electronic records are formatted around the S.O.A.P. note concept. They are called D.A.P. notes. The D stands for DATA (includes both the Subjective and Objective); the A is for ASSESSMENT; and, the P is for PLAN.

SUICIDE SAFETY PLAN

See "Assessments" and "Clinical Relationships" sections for sample suicide safety plans.

There is no pure legal duty to prevent suicide—the duty is to intervene appropriately. The law recognizes limits in the ability to stop a determined person from suicide.

SUICIDE ASSESSMENT
Assessment of suicidal risk involves gathering information from multiple sources across a number of key variables.

ESSENTIAL QUESTIONS FOR DETERMINING THE NEED TO INTERVENE:
1) Is this person at risk for committing suicide, and if so, 2) How serious is the risk?

EVALUATE SUICIDE RISK ACROSS KEY VARIABLES:
Risk for suicide increases according to...
- Past suicide attempts and their seriousness
- Communication of intent/denial of intent
- Assessing the violent-angry-impulsive person
- Professional counselor liability for suicide cuts across two issues:
- The setting in which the crisis arises and the nature of the alleged harm
- Whether it involved failure to take preventive action to avoid suicide or whether the clinical behavior caused the suicide

RESEARCH
- **What would delete from the list and why?**
- **What would you add to the list and why?**

CAVEAT: No suicide document is a substitute to thorough clinical assessment, referrals, consultations, etc. Counselors must continue to monitor the situation and evaluate options even when client signs a safety plan.

*Supervision
helps improve
competency and confidence*

SUPERVISION

Supervisors may be responsible for the acts of those who perform work under their supervision. This can include everything from interns providing therapy or administrative assistants helping with record-keeping and billing.

Supervisors must continually assess their supervisee's competence and make sure they are managing them appropriately. Supervision should cover everything from the informed-consent process being done correctly to the termination of a clinical relationship.

SUPERVISORS MUST HAVE TRAINING IN SUPERVISION:
Supervisors also...
- Establish timely and specific processes for providing feedback, and provide information about these processes at the beginning of supervision
- Outline the nature and structure of the supervisory relationship in writing before supervision begins
- Document their experience with the supervisee(s), including supervision dates, discussions they've had and other relevant facts. Such information will help if ethical dilemmas arise later

THE IMPORTANCE OF SUPERVISION:
- It's a socializing process to help teach and educate new professionals. But supervision is not just for beginners. Supervisors play a critical role in the ethical practices of counselors over the lifetime of the professional
- The role is to support, challenge, and encourage—to reflect on their work and help counselors continue to grow
- The supervisory relationship is a hierarchical relationship with evaluation as a key component with no choice. Evaluation and choice are key differences between supervision and consultation

PURPOSE OF SUPERVISION:
- Supervisors review supervisee's work in order to improve competency and effectiveness so clients can receive the highest quality of service possible, and prevent any harm

DIFFERENCE BETWEEN SUPERVISION AND ADMINISTRATIVE SUPERVISION:
The main difference is the purpose.
- Clinical supervision is focused on the supervisee's actions in the counseling work and organization activities. This is ruled by ethical codes and standards for the profession.
- Administrative supervision is focused on the supervisee's actions in the organization. (This is often governed by the laws, rules, and regulations from legislation)

SUPERVISION IS A BALANCING ACT
- NEEDS OF SUPERVISEES: helping them be and become the most competent and skillful in their services to clients (mentoring, teaching, training, etc.)Help supervisees prevent burnout and handle compassion fatigue.
- NEEDS OF CLIENTS: Assuring that clients are receiving the best service and care possible. Assure the health and welfare of the clients. Monitoring carefully so as to do no harm (monitoring the case/gate keeping functions)

QUESTIONS TO CONSIDER:
- What are the needs of my supervisees?
- What are the needs of their clients?
- What are my needs?
- What are the organization's needs?

SUPERVISOR AS GATE-KEEPER:
Challenges...
- Competence to understand client's problems and not to underestimate the seriousness of client's problems
- Appropriately addressing and managing potential/actual dual/multiple relationships with a focus on appropriate boundary crossings vs. inappropriate boundary violations.
- Demonstrate, manage, and expect clear communication and adherence to confidentiality requirements (expectations and exceptions as required by law).
- Be aware and discuss with supervisees personal issues that could affect their counseling work and encourage good self-care
- Ensure good, ethical, and appropriate documentation

QUESTIONS FOR SUPERVISORS TO ANSWER:
- What is harm? How can a supervisee harm a client?
- What is enough supervision?
- How do I know what my supervisees are doing with their clients?
- What do I want the supervisor/supervisee relationship to be like? My approach?
- What do I want my supervisees to get out of this experience with me? To remember? To learn? To take away?

INFORMED CONSENT AND SUPERVISEES:
- Make certain that clients understand that the supervisee [counselor] is in training and give client the name(s) of the supervisor(s).
- Note that billing may be under a supervisor's name, not the supervisee's, so that clients don't accidentally report billing problems when there are none.

CONTENT OF THE SUPERVISION INFORMED CONSENT:
- Professional Disclosure
- Practical Issues
- Supervision Process
- Administrative Talks
- Ethical and Legal Issues
- Evaluation Procedures
- Means to Resolve Conflicts
- Statements of Agreement
- Signatures and Date of Agreement

INCLUDE THESE STATEMENTS IN A SUPERVISION INFORMED CONSENT:
- "Supervisee agrees to practice ethically, professionally, and legally while in supervision."
- "Supervisee agrees to practice in the clients' best interests and protect clients from harm."
- "Supervisee will actively participate in supervision to promote skill development."
- "Supervisee will be honest and open, share deficits, and report mistakes."

ETHICAL STANDARDS & CLINICAL FORMS

SAMPLE SUPERVISION CONSENT AGREEMENT

CAVEAT: *For use in your own setting, forms must be personalized to reflect your state's relevant laws and your own actual policies.*

Counseling Supervision Contract

This contract serves as verification and a description of the counseling supervision provided by _____ (Supervisor) and _____ (Supervisee) for the period of time beginning _____ and ending _____.

PURPOSE, GOALS, AND OBJECTIVES:
The supervisor will monitor and ensure welfare of clients seen by supervisee and promote development of supervisee's professional counselor identity and competence. Supervisor will help fulfill requirements in preparation for supervisee's licensure application.

CONTEXT OF SERVICES:
____ clock hour(s) of individual supervision _____ [daily, weekly, etc.] or as needed. Supervision will revolve around counseling conducted with adults, adolescents and children. Individual supervision will be conducted in the supervisor's office at selected time. The developmental model for supervision, the supervisee's case conceptualization based on his/her theoretical preference, progress notes, and tape review will be used in supervision.

METHOD OF EVALUATION:
Feedback will be provided by the supervisor during each session, and a formal evaluation, using the supervisor's standard evaluation of supervisee's clinical skills, will be conducted each _____ [Week, month, etc.]. A narrative evaluation will also be provided at that time and at the end of the contracted supervision time. Specific feedback provided by supervisor will focus on supervisee's demonstrated counseling skills and clinical documentation, as well as knowledge of and adherence to ethical and legal requirements. Supervisee will evaluate supervisor at the end of the contracted supervision period. Supervision notes will be shared with supervisee at supervisors discretion and at the request of the supervisee.

DUTIES AND RESPONSIBILITIES OF SUPERVISOR:
- Examine client presenting complaints and treatment plans
- View videotapes of supervisee's counseling sessions
- Sign off on all client documentation
- Challenge supervisee to justify approach and techniques used
- Monitor supervisee's basic attending skills
- Present and model appropriate directives
- Intervene when client welfare is at risk
- Ensure that ethical guidelines are upheld
- Maintain weekly supervision case notes

DUTIES AND RESPONSIBILITIES OF SUPERVISEE:
- Uphold ethical guidelines
- View counseling during supervision session
- Be prepared to discuss all client cases; have client files, current and completed client case notes, and counseling session videotapes ready.
- Justify client case conceptualizations made and approach and techniques used.
- Complete case notes.
- Consult with supervisor in cases of emergency.
- Implement supervisory directives in subsequent sessions.

PROCEDURAL CONSIDERATIONS: Supervisee's written case notes, treatment plans, and videotapes will be reviewed and evaluated in each session. Issues related to supervisee's professional development will be discussed. Sessions will be used to discuss issues of conflict and failure of either party to abide by directives outlined here in contract. If concerns of either party are not resolved in supervision, a third party can be consulted. In event of emergency, supervisee is to contact supervisor at _____ or _____. In event of emergency, and supervisor is not available, please contact _____.

TERMS OF CONTRACT: This contract is subject to revision at any time, upon the request of either the supervisor or supervisee with the agreement of both. We agree to the best of our ability, to uphold the directives specified in this supervision contract and to conduct our professional behavior according to the ethical principles of our professional association.

ETHICAL STANDARDS & CLINICAL FORMS

REMEMBER TO:
Include appropriate lines for signature and date; Keep a copy of any document that was signed by a client in the client's file (hardcopy or electronic); Copy to client optional, unless they request a copy.

RESEARCH
Sample Supervision Consent Agreement
- **What would you change? Delete? Add?**
  - **What sample text in the above consent do you strongly agree with? Why?**
  - **What sample text do you strongly disagree with? Why?**

SAMPLE SUPERVISION LOG

CAVEAT: For use in your own setting, forms must be personalized to reflect your state's relevant laws and your own actual policies.

Supervisee Name:

Date: _____ Time: _____ Duration of meeting: _____

Modality of meeting: [ ] individual meeting [ ] group meeting

Case reviewed:

Details of Case Review:

Supervisee's assessment of client's presenting problem:

Important history or environmental factors (especially multicultural issues)

Short summary of supervisee's session with client:

Tentative assessment or problem conceptualization (diagnosis):

Plan of action and goals for therapy (treatment plan)

Suggested Actions:

Concerns surrounding the case:
[ ] Risk management
[ ] Ethical, legal issues
[ ] Therapeutic readiness
[ ] Substance abuse
[ ] Other:

REMEMBER TO:
Include appropriate lines for signature and date; Keep a copy of any document that was signed by a client in the client's file (hardcopy or electronic); Copy to client optional, unless they request a copy.

RESEARCH
Sample Supervision Log
- **What would you change? Delete? Add?**
  - **What sample text in the above consent do you strongly agree with? Why?**
  - **What sample text do you strongly disagree with? Why?**

*Technology is an
integral part of
our professional work*

TECHNOLOGY AND INFORMATION SECURITY

COMPUTERS ARE AN INTEGRAL PART OF COUNSELING: Business and administrative management, document and recordkeeping, psychological assessments, e-mail, web pages, online counseling.
- Benefits: increased organization and time efficiency in tracking client's progress, and decreased space needed for file storage. Quick generation of case conceptualization and treatment plans
- Drawbacks: security, computer crashes, backing up, "canned" client case summaries and treatment plans

SOFTWARE PROGRAMS/SECURE SIGN-IN ONLINE SITES ARE AVAILABLE FOR...
- Managing client records and documentation
- Assessments and treatment planning
- Client homework tools and progress archive
- Third-party billing
- Computerized psychological testing

INFORMATION SECURITY

Information security is the method used to preserve the confidentiality, integrity, and availability of computer-based information. Security controls reduce the impact or probability of security threats and vulnerabilities to a level acceptable to the organization. A major focus of information security is preventing authorized and unauthorized individuals from accessing, creating, or modifying information inappropriately. Risk assessment is the identification of information resources, the threats to those resources, and the vulnerabilities that may be exploited by those threats, thus exposing the resources to a loss of confidentiality, integrity, or availability. Risk analysis is the formal process of examining potential threats and identified vulnerabilities discovered during the risk assessment and prioritizing those risks based on the probability and effect of those risks. A risk analysis may include a cost-benefit comparison to justify and determine appropriate security controls. Risks may be mitigated, transferred, researched, or accepted, depending on which option is the most reasonable for the organization. Researched decisions are typically temporary decisions that are used until additional information can be gathered about possible solutions, controls, or tools. Researched decisions should lead to a final risks strategy to mitigate, transfer, or accept the risks.

ETHICAL STANDARDS & CLINICAL FORMS

RISK MANAGEMENT is the ongoing process of managing identified risks to an acceptable level by applying security controls and measures to maintain a predetermined level of risk. Security systems cannot withstand every possible threat, so there is no such thing as absolute security. Instead, health information professionals must weigh risks to their systems against the criticality and confidentiality of the information they contain and focus on developing, implementing, and maintaining appropriate security controls.

COST-EFFECTIVE SECURITY CONTROLS AND SAFEGUARDS appropriate to the level of risk should be implemented. Good security measures do not have to be expensive, and they should not affect system speed or performance or make legitimate access to systems a hassle. The HIPAA security rule clearly indicates that cost alone does not relieve a covered entity of the responsibility of applying appropriate security measures to its systems.

TYPES OF CONTROLS
Broadly speaking, there are three types of controls used in information security: management controls, operational controls, and technical controls
- Management controls are issues that must be addressed by management in the organization's information security program. Generally, these issues focus on management of the information security program and the management of risk within the organization. Management controls include security policies, procedures, and plans that incorporate all applicable laws and regulations and meet the organization's needs.
- Operational controls are implemented and executed by staff at all levels of an organization; sometimes consultants and vendors also are asked to do this work. Operational controls include contingency planning, user awareness and training, physical and environmental protections, computer support and operations, and management of security breaches.
- Technical controls focus on controls that are executed by information systems. These controls include user identification and authentication, access control, audit trails, cryptography (encryption), firewalls, intrusion detection and prevention systems, virus protection, access (port) point security, audit logging and reporting, and many other controls.

TECHNOLOGY: THREATS AND VULNERABILITIES...
- Threats are potential events or dangers that may cause damage or inappropriate access to information systems and the sensitive information they contain. Threats may be malicious or accidental, but they can damage a system or cause loss of confidentiality, integrity, or availability. Vulnerabilities are system weaknesses that can be exploited by a threat. Reducing system vulnerabilities can reduce the risk and impact of threats to the system significantly.

THREATS TO INFORMATION SECURITY INCLUDE BUT ARE NOT LIMITED TO:
- AUTHORIZED USERS: The greatest number of security breaches involves authorized users who use information inappropriately, such as viewing records without a justifiable need. Examples would include breaches of privacy or confidentiality or identity theft.
- THEFT OR LOSS: Desktop and laptop computers and the data they contain are vulnerable to theft and/or loss from inside and outside the organization. The increasing use of laptops, tablets, smartphones and other handheld devices, along with portable media such as external hard drives and USBs, thumb drives, makes potential inappropriate access to PHI a greater threat, especially if these devices lack encryption. Measures must be implemented to ensure that patient and corporate data are protected in the event devices are lost, stolen, or misplaced by users. Measures such as encryption and limiting USB usage are strongly recommended practices to enhance information security.
- OTHER THREATS: Disgruntled employees, malicious code (viruses), hackers

ESTABLISHING SECURITY POLICIES
- Create their information security program and assign responsibility for it
- Outline their approach to information security
- Address specific issues of concern to the organization
- Outline decisions for managing a particular system
- Define sanctions
- Set expectations for all staff

RESEARCH
- **Research HIPAA for required security measures. What are they?**
- **Does your practice have appropriate security measures?**
  - **If not, what needs to be implemented?**

TECHNOLOGY AND MOBILE DEVICE LIABILITY

MOBILE LIABILITY

- Mobile devices such as laptop computers, flash or thumb drives, personal digital assistants. Smartphones have become an integral part of the professional lives of working Americans, including mental health practitioners.
- The lack of attention given to securing the confidential data stored on laptops is in stark contrast with the professional standards set for mental health professionals regarding client records.
- Password protection is certainly a step in the right direction, but encryption is better whenever possible.
- The same is true of individual file encryption, which does not address the vulnerability associated with temp files, hibernation files, or erased files.

FULL DISK ENCRYPTION: Full-disk encryption offers far greater security, and most applications have the added benefit of extending encryption to all removable and portable media (external hard drives and flash drives) and also include components that allow for complete erasure of deleted files.

SECURITY MEASURE OPTIONS: Although there are programs that break encryption codes, it requires a degree of determination that the average laptop thief might lack. A potentially safer alternative to keeping client records on a laptop is to store them on an encrypted external drive. There are HIPAA compliant file storage providers that offer the service at reasonable rates. While more laptops are coming with built-in global positioning systems (GPS), tracking devices can be installed in laptops that locate the stolen laptop if or when the thief connects to the Internet. There are also software programs that allow the owner of a lost or stolen laptop to shut it down remotely and erase the hard drive. It should go without saying that, to reduce the risk of theft of a laptop that contains confidential information, it should never be left in an unattended car.

RESEARCH

- **Research your options for securing confidential information on your mobile devices. What have you found?**

TECHNOLOGY: INTERNET SEARCHES

INTERNET SEARCHES

Is it acceptable for counselors to search their clients on the Internet? Only with informed consent.

SAMPLE TEXT REGARDING INFORMED CONSENT AND INTERNET SEARCHES: "At times I may conduct a web search on clients. If you have concerns or questions regarding this practice, please discuss it with me."

TECHNOLOGY: SOCIAL MEDIA

Some counselors may choose to add a statement to their office policies stating that they do not engage in social networking with clients. If you do interact with clients on social media website, define the parameters of such involvement in your consent form or have a separate document that clients can sign.

INFORMED CONSENT AND SOCIAL NETWORKING: "I do not accept friend requests from current or former clients on social networking sites due to the fact that these sites can compromise clients' confidentiality and privacy. For the same reason, I request that clients do not communicate with me via any interactive or social networking websites."

> **RESEARCH**
> - Search the Internet using these key words: mental health counseling and social media policies
> - You will find various samples, some short and other quite lengthy
>   - Read one of each
>   - Compare them to the sample policy on the next page
> - What is (or would be) your policy regarding social media and mental health clients?

If you plan to or are interacting with clients via social media, then explain the reasons for doing so (or not doing so), the limits relevant to such interactions, and all other relevant policies in a consent form. ***See the next page for a sample.***

SAMPLE SOCIAL MEDIA CONSENT

CAVEAT: For use in your own setting, forms must be personalized to reflect your state's relevant laws and your own actual policies.

PRIVATE PRACTICE AND SOCIAL MEDIA POLICY

- Please read it to understand how I conduct myself on the Internet as a mental health professional and how you can expect me to respond to various interactions that may occur between us on the Internet.
- If you have any questions about anything within this document, I encourage you to bring them up when we meet. As new technology develops and the Internet changes, there may be times when I need to update this policy. If I do so, I will notify you in writing of any policy changes and make sure you have a copy of the updated policy.

FRIENDING

I do not accept friend or contact requests from current or former clients on any social networking sites (e.g., Facebook, Linkedin). I believe that adding clients as friends or contacts on these sites can compromise your confidentiality and our respective privacy. It may also blur the boundaries of our therapeutic relationship. If you have questions about this, please bring them up when we meet and we can talk more about it. My personal Facebook Page is for families and friends only and I block others from viewing.

FOLLOWING

I publish a blog on my website and I post psychology news on Twitter. I have no expectation that you as a client will want to follow my blog or Twitter stream. However, if you use an easily recognizable name on Twitter and I happen to notice that you've followed me there, we may briefly discuss it and its potential impact on our working relationship.

My primary concern is your privacy. If you share this concern, there are more private ways to follow me on Twitter (e.g., RSS feed or a locked Twitter list), which would eliminate your having a public link to my content. You are welcome to use your own discretion in choosing whether to follow me. Note that I will not follow you back. I only follow other health professionals on Twitter and I do not follow current or former clients on blogs or Twitter. My reasoning...I believe casual viewing of clients' online content outside of the therapy hour can create confusion in regard to whether it's being done as a part of your treatment or to satisfy my personal curiosity. In addition, viewing your online activities without your consent and without our explicit arrangement towards a specific purpose could potentially have a negative influence on our working relationship. If there are things from your online life that you wish to share with me, please bring them into our sessions where we can view and explore them together, during the therapy hour.

INTERACTING

Please do not use messaging on social networking sites, such as Twitter, Facebook, or Linkedin, to contact me. These sites are not secure and I may not read these messages in a timely fashion. Do not use Wall postings, @replies, or other means of engaging with me in public online if we have an already established client/counselor relationship. Engaging with me this way could compromise your confidentiality. It may also create the possibility that these exchanges become a part of your legal medical record and will need to be documented and archived in your chart.

If you need to contact me between sessions, the best way to do so is by phone. Direct e-mail at _____@_____.com is second best for quick, administrative issues such as changing appointment times. See the e-mail section below for more information regarding e-mail interactions.

USE OF SEARCH ENGINES

It is NOT a regular part of my practice to search for clients on Google or Facebook or other search engines. Extremely rare exceptions may be made during times of crisis. If I have a reason to suspect that you are in danger and you have not been in touch with me via our usual means (e.g., appointments, phone, or e-mail) there might be an instance in which using a search engine (to find you, find someone close to you, or to check on your recent status updates) becomes necessary as part of ensuring your welfare. These are unusual situations and if I ever resort to such means, I will fully document it and discuss it with you when we next meet.

GOOGLE READER

I do not follow current or former clients on Google Reader and I do not use Google Reader to share articles. If there are things you want to share with me that you feel are relevant to your treatment whether they are news items or things you have created, I encourage you to bring these items of interest into our sessions.

BUSINESS REVIEW SITES

You may find my psychology practice on sites such as Yelp, Healthgrades, Yahoo Local, Bing, or other places which list businesses. Some of these sites include forums in which users rate their providers and add reviews. Many of these sites comb search engines for business listings and automatically add listings regardless of whether the business has added itself to the site. If you should find my listing on any of these sites, please know that my listing is NOT a request for a testimonial, rating, or endorsement from you as my client.

It is unethical for counselors to solicit testimonials from current therapy clients because of their particular circumstances are vulnerable to undue influence.
Of course, you have a right to express yourself on any site you wish. But due to confidentiality, I cannot respond to any review on any of these sites whether it is positive or negative. I urge you to take your own privacy as seriously as I take my commitment of confidentiality to you. You should also be aware that if you are using these sites to communicate indirectly with me about your feelings about our work, there is a good possibility that I may never see it.

If we are working together, I hope that you will bring your feelings and reactions to our work directly into the therapy process. This can be an important part of therapy, even if you decide we are not a good fit. None of this is meant to keep you from sharing that you are in therapy with me wherever and with whomever you like. Confidentiality means that I cannot tell people that you are my client and my Ethics Code prohibits me from requesting testimonials. But you are more than welcome to tell anyone you wish that I'm your counselor or how you feel about the treatment I provided to you, in any forum of your choosing. If you do choose to write something on a business review site, I hope you will keep in mind that you may be sharing personally revealing information in a public forum. I urge you to create a pseudonym that is not linked to your regular e-mail address or friend networks for your own privacy and protection.

LOCATION-BASED SERVICES

If you used location-based services on your mobile phone, you may wish to be aware of the privacy issues related to using these services. I do not place my practice as a check-in location on various sites such as Foursquare, Gowalla, Loopt, etc. However, if you have GPS tracking enabled on your device, it is possible that others may surmise that you are a therapy client due to regular check-ins at my office on a weekly basis. Please be aware of this risk if you are intentionally "checking in," from my office or if you have a passive LBS app enabled on your phone.

E-MAIL

I prefer using e-mail only to arrange or modify appointments. Please do not e-mail me content related to your therapy sessions, as an e-mail is not completely secure or confidential. If you choose to communicate with me by e-mail, be aware that all e-mails are retained in the logs of your and my Internet service providers. While it is unlikely that someone will be looking at these logs, they are, in theory, available to be read by the system administrator(s) of the Internet service provider. You should also know that any e-mails I receive from you and any responses that I send to you become a part of your legal record.

CONCLUSION

If you feel I have done something harmful or unethical and you do not feel comfortable discussing it with me, you can always contact the licensing board at _____ which oversees licensing, and they will review the services I have provided. Thank you for taking the time to review my Social Media Policy. If you have questions or concerns about any of these policies and procedures or regarding our potential interactions on the Internet, do bring them to my attention so that we can discuss them.

REMEMBER TO: Include appropriate lines for signature and date; Keep a copy of any document that was signed by a client in the client's file (hardcopy or electronic); Copy to client optional, unless they request a copy.

RESEARCH
Sample Social Media Consent
- **Search the Internet for another sample social media consent form and compare it to this one.**
- **What would you change? Delete? Add?**
  - **What sample text in the above consent do you strongly agree with? Why?**
  - **What sample text do you strongly disagree with? Why?**

ETHICAL STANDARDS & CLINICAL FORMS

*Records allow for
continuity of care*

TERMINATION AND REFERRALS
REASON TO TERMINATE OR MAKE A REFERRAL

CLIENT REASONS:
- Client can no longer benefit from treatment/service
- Client needs a higher level of care
- Client needs counseling outside counselor's area of expertise
- Client is no longer benefiting from counseling
- Client may be harmed by the treatment
- Client no longer needs therapy

COUNSELOR REASONS:
- There are conflicts of interest that are unresolvable
- Counselor's objectivity has been compromised
- The client has threatened the counselor

FINANCIAL REASONS: (always have a clear financial arrangement agreement that is signed by the client)
- Counselor's in a "fee-for-service" setting may terminate services to clients who are not paying for the services they've received. Counselor needs to discuss a past due account with the client and provide an opportunity for the client to bring their account current.
- Client has changed insurance carriers and counselor is not a preferred provider, and the client does not want to pay any extra out-of-pocket charges.

RESEARCH
- **What other reasons can you add to the above lists?**

When a referral is made, the referring counselor is obligated to determine the appropriateness of the referral, including the abilities of the receiving professional or agency, and should follow up on the client's progress wherever possible and permitted. Finally, mental health counselors should continue to refer to their professional association's ethical code guidelines and state laws regarding a related issue: the disposition of client records upon termination, referral, or practice closure.

TERMINATION: REFERRALS

Counselors should make reasonable efforts to ensure continuity of services in the event that services are interrupted by factors such as unavailability, relocation, illness, disability, or death.

- Counselors who are leaving an employment setting should inform clients of appropriate options for the continuation of services and of the benefits and risks of the options.
- Counselors who anticipate the termination or interruption of services to clients should notify clients promptly and seek the transfer, referral, or continuation of services in relation to the clients' needs and preferences.
- Counselors should not terminate services to pursue a social, financial, or sexual relationship with a client

See the "Transfer Plans" section for more detailed information

CLIENT TRANSFERS

When an individual who is receiving services from another agency or colleague contacts counselors for services, the counselor should carefully consider the client's needs before agreeing to provide services.

- If another agency or colleague has served a new client, counselors should discuss with the client whether consultation with the previous service provider is in the client's best interest.

TERMINATION: INTERRUPTIONS OF SERVICES

Paramount consideration must be given to the welfare of the client and to the continuity of care.

- Counselors (in solo or private practice) ethically are required to have a transfer plan in place to ensure continuity of care in the event that services are interrupted by factors such as counselor unavailability due to relocation, illness, disability, or death.

See the "Transfer Plan" section for more details.

TERMINATION: ABANDONMENT CONCERNS

TERMINATION VS. ABANDONMENT
First, know the difference between abandonment and termination. Abandonment is not the same as treatment termination. Counselors should have a clear understanding of when a therapeutic relationship should end.

THE THERAPEUTIC RELATIONSHIP CAN BE DISCONTINUE WHEN CLIENTS...
- The client is not benefiting from therapy
- The client may be harmed by the treatment
- The client needs a higher level of care
- Client's issues are outside of counselor's expertise
- Client no longer needs therapy
- There are conflicts of interest that are unresolvable
- Counselor's objectivity has been compromised
- The client has threatened the counselor

ABANDONMENT
Client abandonment is defined as the premature termination of the professional treatment relationship by the counselor without adequate notice, without therapeutic reason, or without the client's involvement. This unilateral termination of the clinical relationship is a form of negligence.

Abandonment occurs when a counselor inappropriately ends treatment, such as halting needed therapy with no notice. In comparison, many times counselors and clients continue with therapy beyond the point of necessity. While dependent clients can make it difficult to end treatment appropriately, the counselor must sometimes make the therapeutic decision to appropriately end the clinical relationship.

TERMINATION: INFORMED CONSENT

One of the reason information on termination and referrals is in the consent form is to help educate the client. Counselors should take some time, as early on as possible in the clinical relationship, to verbally discuss with the client this information. This can help head off termination and/or referral dilemmas. During this discussion, cover the differences between short- and long-term therapy and all the other reasons that can and do lead to treatment termination. Talk with your clients periodically about this topic. Counselors and clients, often, both don't like to talk about termination/referrals, because it brings up uncomfortable feelings for clients and counselors alike. Many of our life endings (breakups, divorces, graduations, broken friendships, being fired, death) provoke feelings of sadness, anger, rejection and abandonment. Counseling often results in a meaningful relationship and evokes difficult emotions when therapy ends. Instead, counseling can be a place to discuss these feelings to promote a healthy closure.

TERMINATION: PRE-TERMINATION COUNSELING

Counselors should provide pre-termination counseling and suggest alternative service providers. This may not be possible in all cases, such as if or when a client abruptly stops attending therapy. Pre-termination counseling could include explaining to the client the benefits of new services or alternative counselors and why the current treatment is no longer helpful. Counselors often have to address the client's feelings of separation by emphasizing the transfer is not a personal rejection, and identifying practical issues in transferring the client. Strive to involve the client in the termination or transfer plan—empower them to feel confident and competent; help the client understand that the transition is a constructive step toward achieving their goals.

TERMINATION AND REFERRAL

Termination/referral is a time to evaluate the work that has (or has not) been accomplished. Celebrate the progress and talk about the goals that have not been reached. Treatment plans are vitally important; they are the roadmap, as well as the gauge, to monitor progress and weigh the appropriateness or necessity for terminating the clinical relationship or making a referral.

TERMINATION: DUE TO COUNSELOR VARIABLE

ENDING THERAPY DUE TO COUNSELOR VARIABLES

Counselors are to be objective. This can be a difficult task because counselors are people. The cornerstones of ethics: do no harm, do not exploit clients, and do not continue counseling if your professional judgment is impaired. These are foundational to good therapeutic care. Impairment comes in many forms, such as a counselor's bias or judgmental attitude, or their misuse of prescription medications and/or abuse of other substances. Counselors can become impaired when their own life stressors are too great. Compassion fatigue and burnout can lead to impairment. When a counselor loses objectivity (for any of the above reasons, or others) and their integrity, they ethically need to consult with colleagues, seek self-care, and determine if they need to step out from counseling for a time.

A crucial part of many counselors' ethics is to remain unjudgmental. Counselors need to explore their judgments of clients; analyze them; and, understand why they are critical. This requires looking at personal flaws and failings. But don't get stuck there. Also worthy of exploration are: 1) What is inside you, the counselor, that might help you better understand the client's experience? 2) What might you, the counselor, be failing to see as a result of personal bias? If a counselor is unable to get through certain feelings, then they can choose to express their concern about their difficulty, and give the client a choice about whether or not to continue therapy or have the counselor assist them in finding a new counselor.

When a counselor, for whatever reason, cannot tolerate, accept, or remain objective regarding a client's behavior, it often is best to be open with the client about it (but choose your words carefully), frame it as your problem, and then refer them to someone who you believe can work with the issues better. Acknowledge that you're having trouble giving them the therapy that you think they need. Refer the client—far better to refer the client after one or two sessions, than to decide well into treatment that it's a poor match.

Be careful to refer the client in a way that is not damaging to the client. Don't view referral as a failure. It's impossible for counselors to help every client who comes through the door. Finding a counselor who is a good match, as soon as possible, is in the client's best interest.

Therapy is a two-person process. There are times when a client's difficulties fall outside a counselor's expertise, or the client needs a higher level of care—these are situations that make termination and referral an easier discussion. But counselors are human beings, with their own religious and moral convictions. Always remaining neutral (objective), being the "blank screen" (Freud) reflecting back only a client's issues and not the counselor's personality, is a challenging task; even considered to be unrealistic. And some clients may be so taxing that they deplete a counselor's energy for the rest of their clients, so, if possible, limit the number of emotionally exhausting clients at any one time. How should counselors deal with a client they don't like? Reframe the question and ask yourself: "Can I provide competent service? Can I overcome my opposition? Can I use my feelings to move therapy forward?" Raise questions in therapy with the client to explore the relationship dynamics, such as: "You [client] seem angry with me [counselor]?" or "Does it seem to you [client] that we're not making progress?" And don't forget to consult with colleagues. If feelings toward a client are getting in the way of providing good treatment, seek help. If you are having a tough time with a client, discuss with trusted colleagues and explore if it is because of something in your own history? And then explore whether or not you can use your personal feelings to better understand the client's challenges.

RESEARCH

Consider these questions carefully:
- What if you have a client whose lifestyle opposes your significant personal beliefs, and that client is seeking validation from you? Or you have a client you don't like?
- What if you do not wish to work with clients who are involved in pornography, child abuse, or drug dealing?

What is the role of the counselor? Is it to affirm a client's belief(s), or to offer support and guidance, even to clients that a counselor personally finds distasteful or morally wrong?

- Is it unrealistic to suggest that counselors be unbiased? Is that the counselor's job—*to affirm any choice that a client makes?*
- Could referring a client be a lost opportunity to make meaningful contact with the client and also with important parts of the counselor's internal life?

How can a counselor's Professional Disclosure Statement help in heading off or avoiding some of the above issues?

SAMPLE TERMINATION SUMMARY

CAVEAT: *For use in your own setting, forms must be personalized to reflect your state's relevant laws, ethical requirements for your licensing, and your own actual policies.*

Client name, date of last session, etc.

Reason(s) for termination:
[ ] The treatment was completed
[ ] This is a planned pause as part of an intermittent long-term treatment
[ ] The client refused to continue in therapy
[ ] There was little or no progress in treatment
[ ] The client needs services not available here, must be referred out.
[ ] Others:

Decision to terminate was:
[ ] Client initiated [ ] Therapist-initiated [ ] A mutual decision
[ ] Other (specify):

ALSO INCLUDE: General description of treatment, Treatment goals, Outcomes and progress, Clinical impression at termination, Description of client's state at termination, Concerns with danger, Medications, Compliance, Reason for referral(s), Follow up (Letters, calls, contacts, and Future Appointments), and any relevant additional comments.

REMEMBER TO: *Include appropriate lines for signature and date; Keep a copy of any document that was signed by a client in the client's file (hardcopy or electronic); Copy to client optional, unless they request a copy.*

RESEARCH
Sample Termination Summary
- **What would you change? Delete? Add?**
  - **What sample text in the above summary do you strongly agree with? Why?**
  - **What sample text do you strongly disagree with? Why?**

THERAPY IS TERMINATED (BY COUNSELOR)
REASON: Various (select the reason as appropriate)

CAVEAT: For use in your own setting, forms must be personalized to reflect your state's relevant laws, ethical requirements for your licensing, and your own actual policies.

Dear [client],

This letter is to follow up our previous discussion(s) regarding the completion of our working together. From the onset of all my counseling relationships, I strive to explain to my clients the various reasons that can precipitate the termination of a therapeutic relationship. **Those reasons can include any of the following:** *the client is not benefiting from therapy; the client needs a higher level of care; the client's issues are outside of counselor's expertise; or the client no longer needs therapy, to name a few. Further, if a counselor's objectivity is compromised due to a conflict of interest, or for any other reason, ethically a counselor must refer the client.* Counseling is a two-person process; however, counselors sometimes must make a clinical judgment to end therapy and provide referral options that are for the client's best interest. Please follow through with the referral options I have provided. If you need copies of your records or would like me to consult with your next counselor, please contact me. With the appropriate authorization from you, I will do either. If you have any additional question do not hesitate to call.

Sincerely,

REMEMBER TO: Include appropriate lines for signature and date; Keep a copy of any document that was signed by a client in the client's file (hardcopy or electronic); Copy to client optional, unless they request a copy.

RESEARCH
Sample Termination Letter: Terminated by Counselor (various reasons)
- **What would you change? Delete? Add?**
  - What sample text in the above letter do you strongly agree with? What sample text do you strongly disagree with? Why?

THERAPY IS TERMINATED (BY COUNSELOR)
REASON: LACK OF COMPLIANCE

CAVEAT: For use in your own setting, forms must be personalized to reflect your state's relevant laws, ethical requirements for your licensing, and your own actual policies.

Dear [client],

As we discussed at previous sessions, it is clear that our ongoing work together has not been beneficial to you. Although I understand your desire to continue under my care, I strongly believe it will be in your best interest for us to end our clinical relationship. It is my ethical mandate to appropriately discontinue therapy if it is not beneficial to my clients. As we discussed, I will be providing you with referrals. Each of these professionals are licensed and are located in your local area. I hope you will contact them and make arrangements to begin treatment. If you would like me to discuss your circumstances and our treatment with them you will need to provide that authorization in writing. I am available to assist in this transition. I will meet with you up to four more times to assist you during this time of transition. Please contact me as soon as you can to further discuss this matter and set up remaining appointments.

Sincerely,

REMEMBER TO: Include appropriate lines for signature and date; Keep a copy of any document that was signed by a client in the client's file (hardcopy or electronic); Copy to client optional, unless they request a copy.

RESEARCH
Sample Termination Letter: Terminated by Counselor (lack of compliance)
- **What would you change? Delete? Add?**
  - **What sample text in the above letter do you strongly agree with? What sample text do you strongly disagree with? Why?**

ETHICAL STANDARDS & CLINICAL FORMS

THERAPY IS TERMINATED (BY COUNSELOR)
REASON: INSURANCE COMPANY NOT PAYING

CAVEAT: *For use in your own setting, forms must be personalized to reflect your state's relevant laws, ethical requirements for your licensing, and your own actual policies.*

Dear [client],

As we discussed during your most recent appointment, your insurance company [managed care company _____] has rejected the treatment plan submitted, stating that your treatment needs are not found to be medically necessary according to their utilization review or other criteria. This means that [insurance company] will not reimburse any additional treatment expenses at this time. However, this does not mean that additional treatment is not needed or that you would not benefit from continued counseling. Upon your request, I will help you to find more affordable services, if they are available in this area. Or, if you prefer, we can work out a private payment plan so you may continue treatment under my care. Please let me know how I can best assist you at this time.

Sincerely,

REMEMBER TO: Include appropriate lines for signature and date; Keep a copy of any document that was signed by a client in the client's file (hardcopy or electronic); Copy to client optional, unless they request a copy.

RESEARCH
Sample Termination Letter: Terminated by Counselor (insurance company not paying)
- **What would you change? Delete? Add?**
  - What sample text in the above letter do you strongly agree with? What sample text do you strongly disagree with? Why?

THERE ARE MANY REASONS TO TERMINATE OR MAKE A REFERRAL

The following does not constitute a complete list. What would you add?

RECAP...

CLIENT REASONS:
- Client can no longer benefit from treatment/service
- Client needs a higher level of care
- Client needs counseling outside counselor's area of expertise
- Client is no longer benefiting from counseling
- Client may be harmed by the treatment
- Client no longer needs therapy

COUNSELOR REASONS:
- There are conflicts of interest that are unresolvable
- Counselor's objectivity has been compromised
- The client has threatened the counselor

FINANCIAL REASONS:
- Financial reasons (counselors in a fee-for-service settings may terminate services to clients who are not paying an overdue balance)
- Client has changed insurance carriers and counselor is not a preferred provider (and client does not want to pay any extra out-of-pocket charges)

RESEARCH
- **Search the Internet for additional sample letters**
  - **Use these key words: "mental health counseling and termination letter samples"**

Always follow your state's laws, regulations, and licensing board's policies; follow best practices, and standard of care, when creating documents

TOUCH IN THERAPY

Ethical and clinical guidelines about touch in counseling.

THE GENERAL SIGNIFICANCE OF TOUCH:
- Touch is one of the most essential elements of human development
- A form of communication, critical for healthy development and one of the most significant healing forces
- The effects of touch deficiencies can have lifelong serious negative ramifications
- Touch has a high degree of cultural relativity

TYPES OF TOUCH IN PSYCHOTHERAPY:
- Ritualistic or socially accepted gestures
- Conversational Marker
- Consoling or reassuring
- Playful touch
- Grounding or reorienting
- Task-Oriented
- Instructional or modeling
- Celebratory or congratulatory
- Experiential
- Referential
- Inadvertent
- Preventing someone from hurting self or others
- Various forms of touch related to various therapeutic interventions

INAPPROPRIATE TOUCH:
- Inappropriate, unethical and probably illegal forms of touch include sexual, hostile-violent and punishing touch.

CONTRA-INDICATIONS FOR THE USE OF TOUCH:
- Touch is usually contra-indicated for clients who are highly paranoid, actively hostile or aggressive, highly sexualized or who implicitly or explicitly demand touch. Special care should be taken in the use of touch with people who have experienced assault, neglect, attachment difficulties, rape, molestation, sexual addictions, eating disorders, and intimacy issues.

ETHICAL and CLINICAL CONSIDERATION:
NON-SEXUAL TOUCH IN THERAPY...

- Touch in therapy is not inherently unethical. None of the professional organizations code of ethics view touch as unethical.
- Touch should be employed in therapy when it is likely to have positive therapeutic effect.
- Ethical touch is the touch that is employed with consideration to the context of the therapeutic relationship and with sensitivity to clients' variables, such as gender, culture, history, diagnosis, etc.
- Ethical counselors should thoroughly process their feelings, attitudes and thoughts regarding touch in general and the often, unavoidable attraction to particular clients.
- Critical thinking and thorough ethical-decision making are important processes preceding the ethical use of touch in therapy. Documentation of type, frequency and rationale of extensive touch is an important aspect of ethical practice.
- The meaning of touch can only be understood within the context of who the client is, the therapeutic relationship, and the counseling setting.

CAVEAT: Western culture places an emphasis on autonomy, independence, separateness and privacy. It also tends to sexualize most forms of touch. In a litigious culture that emphasis resulting risk management and defensive medicine practices, touch presents concerns. However, avoiding touch in therapy on account of fear of boards or attorneys is unethical and, rigidly withholding touch from children and other clients who can benefit from it, such as those who are anxious, dissociative, grieving or terminally ill can be harming and therefore unethical. Sexual, erotic or violent touch in therapy is always unethical. Seeking ethical consultation is important in complex and sensitive cases. Due to the absence of attention to touch in most training programs, clinical supervision, research and testing, the majority of counselors tend not to incorporate the use of touch in therapy.

GUIDELINES FOR THE CLINICAL AND ETHICAL USE OF TOUCH IN THERAPY:
- Touch should be employed in therapy if it is likely to be helpful and clinically effective.
- Touch in therapy must always be employed with full consideration to the context of therapy and clients' factors: presenting problems and symptoms, personal touch and sexual history, ability to differentiate types of touch, the clients level of ability to assertively identify and protect boundaries as well as the gender, and cultural influences of both the client and the counselor.
- Touch should be used according to the counselors training and competence.
- Extensive touch should be incorporated into the written treatment planning.
- The decision to touch should include a thorough deliberation of the clients' potential perception and interpretation of touch.
- Counselors must be particularly careful to structure a foundation of client safety and empowerment before using touch.

CAVEAT: Use a written consent. Counselors should state clearly that there will be no sexual contact and they need to be clear about the process and type of touch that will be used. Permission to touch should be obtained from clients in a form of a written consent if therapy involves extensive use of touch.

RESEARCH
- What types of touch in a clinical relationship are commonplace?
- When it comes to touch: What importance does client culture have? Client's sex? Age? Condition or diagnosis? Type of counseling being done?
  - What types of touch are specific to various therapeutic orientations?
  - Find examples of various therapeutic interventions, philosophies or modalities that incorporate touch. (Example: EMDR and bilateral touch)

ETHICAL STANDARDS & CLINICAL FORMS

SAMPLE TEXT: TOUCH IN THERAPY

CAVEAT: For use in your own setting, forms must be personalized to reflect your state's relevant laws, ethical requirements for your licensing, and your own actual policies.

[Counselor] may incorporate non-sexual touch as part of psychotherapy. Sexual touch of clients by counselors is unethical and illegal. [Counselor] will ask your permission before touching you, and you have the right to decline or refuse to be touched without any fear or concern about reprisal. Touch can be very beneficial, but can also unexpectedly evoke emotions, thoughts, physical reactions or memories that may be upsetting, depressing, evoke anger, etc. Sharing and processing such feelings with the counselor, if they arise, may be a helpful part of therapy.

REMEMBER TO: Include appropriate lines for signature and date; Keep a copy of any document that was signed by a client in the client's file (hardcopy or electronic); Copy to client optional, unless they request a copy.

RESEARCH
Sample Text: Touch in Therapy
- **The consent should always explain the therapeutic reason(s) for the touch. Why?**
- **What therapeutic interventions require touch?**
  - **Research and list several.**

TRANSFER PLANS

See the "Record Custodian" and "Professional Will" sections for more information.

TRANSFER PLANS
- A transfer plan is a notarized document that names another mental health professional or practice as "custodian" to provide the services in the event of a counselor's incapacitation, death or retirement.

ESSENTIAL COMPONENTS OF THIS DOCUMENT INCLUDE:
- Access information or protocol provided to custodian. The professional counselor will provide the custodian location(s), keys, passwords, access codes and other information necessary or a protocol to obtain this information in order to execute the transfer plan.
- Notify all active clients of inability to practice. The custodian will send a letter to all active clients notifying the client of your inability to practice. The custodian will offer to provide on going counseling services (if clinically appropriate) or provide referrals to the most appropriate service provider.
- Possession of clinical records: The custodian will take possession/responsibility of the clinical records and inform all active clients on procedures to access their clinical records.
- Requests for information: The custodian will respond to a request for information in concert with state laws, HIPAA guidelines and code of ethics.
- Maintaining and destruction of clinical records, according to state laws for record retention requirements.

THE RECORD CUSTODIAN'S CONTACT INFORMATION SHOULD BE INCLUDED IN YOUR INFORMED CONSENT DOCUMENT

For example: "In the unlikely event that I am unable to provide ongoing services John Smith, will provide those services or will refer you to the appropriate resource. He will maintain your records for a period of ____ years. John Smith, [credentials] may be contacted at 1-555-123-4567."

Beyond the transfer plan, consideration should be given to the business side of the practice in the event of your incapacitation. Who will be empowered to write checks, make withdrawals or deposits, pay bills and collect fees? Some practice consultants recommend a power of attorney document naming those individuals who can conduct business if you cannot.

Good records support
good client care and are
a road map of where you've been
and where you need to go

TREATMENT PLANNING

It is a negotiation between Counselor and client (unless court-ordered) and it is a decision for direction based on assessed and reported information

ETHICAL CONSIDERATIONS FOR TREATMENT PLANNING:
- Within a reasonable period of time after the initiation of treatment, [counselor] will discuss with client their working understanding of the problem, treatment plan, therapeutic objectives and their view of the possible outcomes of treatment.
- Distortions can exist due to defense mechanism (e.g., justification, rationalization, projection, transference) that are not consciously recognized by the client or lack of information presented to counselor
- Treatment is the specific application of intervention to assist client in change: behavioral, cognitive, affective, relational and/or spiritual change
- Treatment plans are discussed with the client and are revised or amended as needed and as treatment proceeds over time
- Treatment plans provide a rationale for treatment
- Constructed a treatment plan as soon as possible after treatment is started
- Ideally, the treatment plan is discussed and agreed upon with the client because this increases compliance and promotes positive outcomes
- Client should sign that they have reviewed and agreed to the treatment plan
- Treatment plans do not need a DSM diagnosis; they are needed with existential, spiritual, developmental or any other concerns or problems, whatever the focus of treatment is going to be
- The interventions used by a counselor should have a research or theoretical backing or rationale
- Interventions are matched specifically to each level of achievement of goals
- As goals change, so will interventions

When crisis or potential harm is the presenting problem, crisis intervention must be the intervention of choice and safety, harm prevention, volatility and containment are the focus of treatment.

TREATMENT DECISIONS:
Treatment decision are based on...
- Severity and acuteness of presenting symptoms
- Curability with counseling (increased coping skills)
- Invasiveness of the presenting symptoms
- Degree of counselor's knowledge
- Degree of counselor's competence

LET CLIENTS KNOW WHY YOU'RE ASKING SO MANY QUESTIONS:
Say something similar to this... "If you have any unanswered questions about any of the procedures used in the course of your therapy, their possible risks, [counselor's] expertise in employing them, or about the treatment plan, please ask and you will be answered fully. You also have the right to ask about other treatments for your condition and their risks and benefits."

STANDARD OF CARE AND TREATMENT INTERVENTIONS:
In a field that is comprised of hundreds of therapeutic orientations, consensus is hard to come by. Refer to professional associations, general practice guidelines for additional information on treatment interventions.
- To follow the standard of care, counselors are expected to also be aware of the contents of their professional associations' official publications, such as newsletter and journal articles.
- While counselors are not required to follow the recommendations or guidelines in such publications, they are expected to be aware of them and, when appropriate, consider them in their clinical and ethical decision-making.
- The standard of care is a particularly difficult issue in counseling, as there are hundreds of different orientations and approaches to treatment. Each is based on a different theoretical orientation, a different methodology, philosophy, belief system and even worldview. Beyond the agreements of do not harm, do not exploit your client, or impair your judgment.
    - For example there is no one standard, or method or way for the treatment of anxiety. Psychoanalysis, cognitive-behavioral, existential, biologically based psychiatry, Gestalt and pastoral counseling all define, explain and treat the anxiety in very different terms. Not one of them will follow the others' standards.

STANDARD OF CARE AND CHOICE OF INTERVENTIONS:

An additional complexity for standard of care has to do with interventions that fall into the called "respected minority" doctrine. This doctrine may apply if the scientific or research support of the technique is not well established. An example is the employment of existential counseling for major depression. While there is a lot of research to support a biological intervention in conjunction with cognitive-behavioral therapy, there is also a knowledge that provides a theoretical framework for an existential treatment of major depression. Prudent counselors can apply existential treatment for major depression without falling beneath the standard of care. However, in an ideal world the counselors' clinical notes would indicate that they are aware of and considered the other, more common, treatment options.

- The "respected minority" doctrine also applies to new techniques, which as yet do not have well established scientific or research support. This provision allows for new or "experimental" psychotherapeutic techniques to be carefully, cautiously and ethically employed even though the theories and/or practices are still being developed and tested.
- Most successful and effective techniques started out as "experimental or alternative" techniques prior to being tested, validated, recognized, and employed on a broad scale. As a result of the multitude of legitimate, established and highly diverse therapeutic orientations in the field of counseling, most experts agree that when it comes to the standard of care, majority should not rule and diversity should be upheld.

CAVEAT: Interventions should neither be determined by a counselor's "beloved" theoretical orientation, nor by any graduate school professor's or supervisor's dogma, nor by rigid protocols or guidelines. Rigidly and indiscriminately employing the same type of intervention in all circumstances with all clients for all conditions may be below the standard of care. Too many graduate school professors and supervisors are attached to a certain school of thought and rigidly adhere to that dogma. They often ignore the fact that no one orientation has proven to be superior to all others. They ignore the findings that show that counselors' flexibility is one of the most significant factor in therapeutic success. Interventions should be employed for their effectiveness to treat the specific problem, their appropriateness for the client and their likelihood to achieve the desired results.

STANDARD OF CARE AND THE COMMUNITY:

The standard of care is also bound by community norms, including culture. Consequently, different communities, which abide by different cultural customs and values, have different standards.

- Gifts, touch and attending ceremonies and rituals are normal and expected in many communities. Bartering and social dual relationships between counselor and clients are an unavoidable part of rural living.
- Complex dual relationships between counselor and clients are inherent in the military, prisons, police and fire departments, and other various institutions.

This important part of the standard of care, which is based on community standards, has often been erroneously ignored and dismissed by experts, boards and courts.

STAMDARD OF CARE AND COUNSELING OUTSIDE AN OFFICE:

Out of office counseling seldom complies with analytic or rigid risk management standards, but many forms of counseling occur outside an office.
Ethical Considerations for seeing clients outside the office include...

- Counselors do not leave the office indiscriminately or habitually. But there are reasons or instances where leaving the office is part of a clearly articulated treatment plan, which constituted the most effective intervention for the specific situation. They neither constitute dual relationships, sexual relationships, nor violate any other professional association's ethics code.
- All of the interventions where a counselor leaves an office should be preceded by thorough consideration, and the interventions should be consistent with behavioral, humanistic, and existential treatment plans and geared to enhancing client welfare.
- Out of office counseling can result in an increase of therapeutic alliance, knowledge of the clients and, most importantly, enhanced effectiveness of treatment.

Counseling outside the office and community/cultural considerations:
There are types of counseling, such as "assertive community care" or "social clubs" that require the counselor to interact with the client in the community or in a social setting. Even so, counselors need to remain thoughtful when talking with clients within their community. Some situations and peoples are not suited to this kind of work. While the analytic approach frowns upon socializing with clients, the humanistic, cognitive, or behavioral approaches may not.

COMMUNITY CONNECTIONS WITH CLIENTS:
- Community connections with clients do constitute dual relationships. They are part of communal life where people are connected and interdependent in a healthy way and are neither isolated nor insulated from each other.
- Healthy dual relationships are always non-sexual, non-exploitive, and non-harming, they should enhance therapeutic alliance, trust, and psychotherapy effectiveness.

RESEARCH
- **Explore types of counseling done outside an office. Find five examples.**
  - **When would they be appropriate? With which clients? When would they be contra-indicated? Explain.**

TREATMENT PLANS ARE REQUIRED:
- Treatment planning is one of the most important elements of psychotherapy. It is the blueprint for executing clinical interventions.
- Having a treatment plan is a first-line defense against any administrative or other legal investigations.

As discussed, there are many different theoretical orientations. Each orientation has its own strategic plan, which would be implemented in all situations, regardless of the diagnosis, personality and the condition of the client. If a counselor were behaviorally or psychoanalytically trained, they would employ their behavioral or analytical techniques accordingly with each and every patient. There is a saying that "if the only tool that you have is a hammer, every problem looks like a nail."

THE IMPORTANCE OF TREATMENT PLANNING
Counselors construct a treatment plan for each client because...
- Treatment planning is the road map of psychotherapy.
- It gives therapy direction and identifies the goals and means of the therapeutic process.
- A treatment plan in a client's chart helps with continuity of care.
- They help counselors determine progress.
- They help counselors identify when treatment is not progressing according to plan.

ETHICAL STANDARDS & CLINICAL FORMS

- They help counselors assess when termination or referral is clinically appropriate.
- A treatment plan as part of the clinical records complies with the standard of care doctrine.
- In civil, administrative and criminal proceedings, a treatment plan is a line of defense for the counselor.
- If the original counselor is not capable of continuing with a client due to death, illness, etc, a treatment plan assists the next counselor with the client's continuity of care.
- Counselors working as preferred providers with insurance companies, employee assistance programs, or managed care companies are required to submit a treatment plan before they get authorization for treatment and/or reimbursement.

TREATMENT PLANS REFLECT A COUNSELOR'S COMPETENCE...
Treatment plans should be created for each client and updated periodically and/or as needed.

COMPONENTS OF A TREATMENT PLAN:
The main components of treatment plans are...
- Focus of treatment or diagnosis
- Goals of treatment
- Means or intervention
- Assessment of progress
- Plan updates

TREATMENT PLANNING REQUIRES ASSESSMENT:
- Assessment support diagnosis or foci of treatment; diagnosis or foci supports interventions

TAKING OR REVIEWING CLIENT'S HISTORY INVOLVES...
- Getting to know, as appropriate to the situation, the client's background, history, culture, etc.
- Ruling out medical conditions that effect mental conditions and when appropriate, referring to physical or other medical exams or tests.
- Constructing a treatment plan based on patient's problem, concern, issue, diagnosis, probable diagnosis, possible diagnosis, or condition.

THERAPY GOALS:
- Crisis safety issues are very often the first step in the construction of treatment plans.
- Counselors attend to crisis or immediate issues, short-term, intermediate-term and long-term goals.
- Treatment plans do not exclusively belong to behavioral or cognitive-behavioral theories.
- Treatment plans are not always based on Evidenced-based Therapies (EBT) or based on outcome research.
- Some diagnoses may invite the use of EBT more readily than others.
- It can be part of any intervention regardless of the theoretical orientation that supports it.
- Some treatment plans can be objectively measured and observed, others may be more subtle, abstract and subjective.
- Treatment plans and updates to them should correspond to the different phases of treatment (beginning, middle and end) and to the corresponding different goals (short, intermediate and long term goals).

FOCUS OF TREATMENT:
- A treatment plan can list a diagnosis or list a description of the nature of the problem. A DSM diagnosis is not a requirement for a treatment plan.

FOCUS OF TREATMENT MAY INCLUDE ANY, OR ALL, OF THE FOLLOWING...
- Developmental (teenager ready to move out, mid-life transition, couple is facing the reality of old age, struggle with medical condition and imminent death)
- Familial (single mother, blended family, enmeshed family, chaotic family, marriage of an alcoholic and co-alcoholic)
- Existential (client is searching for more meaningful way to live, questioning current friendships)
- Spiritual (client is striving to understand relationship to God, religious confusion, faith based crisis)
- Client's concern or issues fall within a specific theoretical orientation (fragmented sense of self, shame based ego, cognitive dissonance)

GOALS OR OBJECTIVES:

Each goal in therapy should have a corresponding intervention.
The goals or objectives of treatment are the desired outcomes of psychotherapy.

- Traditionally goals were preferred to be, when possible, observable, specific, measurable or quantifiable. But, goals can be abstract: search for meaning, fulfillment or better understanding of God. (Examples of goals: Go back to work, go back to school, stop drinking, restore to previous level of functioning, decrease family conflict, increase sleep quality, decrease isolation, stop domestic violence, reduce suicidal thoughts, feel closer to God, discover one's calling, etc.)
- Goals must be realistic and achievable within the context of the patient's life
- Attending to safety, crisis and danger issues, must be part of the most immediate goals of treatment
- Goals are important to, desired by, and need to be understood by the client; and, the client agrees with the plan
- Treatment goals are often listed in one of three categories: immediate (or crisis), intermediate and long-term goals

TREATMENT GOALS ARE ALSO DIVIDED BETWEEN:

- Initial stage of counseling
- On-going stage of counseling
- The termination stage of counseling

INTERVENTION OR TREATMENT METHODS:

- Interventions are the means used to achieve the stated goals and they should reflect what is done, how, who did it, and when.
- Include the specific intervention, methods, or techniques used (relaxation, thought stopping, therapeutic alliance, insight enhancement, systematic desensitization, interpretation of transference, empathy, create a therapeutic alliance, create a safe environment, educate about mental illness, discuss the cycle of violence, uncover childhood trauma, XYZ behavior modification, cognitive restructuring, read a specific book, attend a training program, look up XYZ information on the Internet, suicide contract, free association, hypnosis, meditation, dream interpretation).
- State the theoretical orientation of the counselor (Object Relations, Gestalt, Cognitive Behavior, Humanistic, Hypnotherapy, Family System, etc.)

FACTORS TO HELP DETERMINE INTERVENTION CHOICE:
- Client Factors: culture, gender, class, psychological mindedness, expectations, motivation, social skills
- Environmental factors: social-familial support, spiritual community
- Mobility: can the client make a weekly appointment without a car or access to public transportation?
- Financial situation: ability and willingness to pay
- Who is the patient? Individual, couple, family, adult, child, geriatric person or any combination of the above
- Human diversity issues: culture, recent immigration, language, acculturation, discrimination or racism
- Client's psychotherapy history: what was effective or ineffective in the past and concerns with past compliance
- Client's presentation: understanding of the problem as well as client's ideas of what might be helpful
- Setting: outpatient or inpatient, rural, church, military or disabled community, isolated setting, or office location

RESEARCH
- **Take the time to search the Internet for a listing of theoretical orientations for mental health counseling.**
  - How many did you find?
- **Which diagnoses would invite Evidenced Based Therapies (EBT)?**
  - Give ten examples of conditions and best practice interventions based on EBT findings
- **List ten additional client concerns or issues that would fall within a specific theoretical orientation**
  - List the specific orientation

REFERRALS:
Referrals are an important part of intervention and treatment planning. Effective counselors are aware of the many resources available to their clients beside their own; they include appropriate referrals in the treatment plan.

See the "Termination and Referrals" section for more information.

ASSESSMENT OF PROGRESS AND TREATMENT PLAN UPDATE

Assessment of progress is an on-going part of treatment and often a neglected part in the treatment plan. Counselors must evaluate how effective their interventions are through determining how well the goals have been achieved. Only through the assessment of progress can the treatment plan be updated and the next set of goals be formulated.

ONE CAN USE A WIDE VARIETY OF ASSESSMENT APPROACHES TO DETERMINE CLIENT'S PROGRESS, SUCH AS:
- Self-report
- Reports by family members, friends, teachers
- Reports from other healthcare providers
- Objective and subjective testing

RESEARCH
- **Take the time to search the Internet for a list of objective and subjective mental health tests.**
  - How many did you find?

UPDATING THE TREATMENT PLAN

Treatment planning must be updated according to the client and the situation (depending on the client and the situation this could be daily, weekly, monthly, bi-monthly, bi-annually, or annually.
- Each update is comprised of the following components:
  - Assess how well the original or last set of goals were achieved
  - Assess that the original or last diagnosis or client's concern/issue/condition is still valid; If not, then make changes as needed
- Identify the next goal or set of goals
- With a new therapy goal or the setting of new goals, a new treatment plan is needed and must be formulated

TREATMENT PLAN SAMPLE

CAVEAT: For use in your own setting, forms must be personalized to reflect your state's relevant laws and your own actual policies.

TREATMENT PLAN: DATE_____
ASSESSMENT HAS COVERED:
[ ] Getting to know, as appropriate to the situation, the client's background, history, culture, etc.
[ ] Ruling out medical conditions that effect mental conditions and when appropriate, referring to physical or other medical exams or tests.
[ ] Constructing a treatment plan based on patient's problem, concern, issue, diagnosis, probable diagnosis, possible diagnosis, or condition

FOCUS OF TREATMENT OR DIAGNOSIS
[ ] Diagnosis is...
[ ] Description of the nature of the problem is...

Current maladaptive coping includes: (List)

Current Adaptive Coping Skills
[ ] Mindfulness skills
[ ] Stress tolerance skills
[ ] Emotional regulation skills
[ ] Radical acceptance skills
[ ] Interpersonal relationship skills

EGO-SYNTONIC vs. EGO-DYSTONIC
[ ] **EGO-SYNTONIC:** "emotionally responsive to surroundings" describes somebody who's emotionally attuned to his/her environment. According to beliefs in ego psychology; ego-syntonic is used to describe behavior that does not conflict with their basic attitudes/beliefs and, therefore, is not anxiety provoking.
[ ] **EGO-DYSTONIC:** denoting aspects of a person's thoughts, impulses, and behavior that are felt to be repugnant, distressing, unacceptable, or inconsistent with the self-conception, or inconsistent with the rest of the personality. Describing elements of a person's behavior, thoughts, impulses, drives, and attitudes that are unacceptable to him/her and cause anxiety.

CURRENT LEVEL IN THE "STAGES OF CHANGE"
[ ] Pre-contemplation
[ ] Contemplation
[ ] Action
[ ] Relapse

FOCUS OF TREATMENT
[ ] Developmental
[ ] Familial
[ ] Existential
[ ] Client's concern or issues falls with a specific theoretical orientation (fragmented sense of self, shame based ego, cognitive dissonance)
[ ] Other description that completes the picture or is the focus of treatment: _____

GOALS OF TREATMENT
[ ] Crisis or immediate issues _____
Attending to safety, crisis and danger issues, must be part of the most immediate goals of treatment
[ ] Short-term goals _____
[ ] Intermediate-term goals _____
[ ] Long-term goals _____

Goals, objectives or desired outcome of treatment
[ ] Client's desired outcomes of psychotherapy _____
Goals must be realistic and achievable within the context of the patient's life

FACTORS TO HELP DETERMINE INTERVENTION CHOICE
Client Factors, the following have been considered:
[ ] Culture, gender, class, psychological mindedness, expectations, motivation, social skills
[ ] Environmental factors, social-familial support, spiritual community
[ ] Client's psychotherapy history, what was effective or ineffective in the past and concerns with past compliance

Setting for therapy will be:
[ ] Outpatient or inpatient
[ ] Rural, church, military or disable community
[ ] Isolated setting
[ ] Office location
[ ]Other: _____

REFERRALS
Reasons for referrals:
[ ] Medical check up
[ ] Higher level of care is needed
[ ] Client's issues is outside counselor's area of expertise
[ ] Support group attendance
[ ] Assistance from other care providers: *welfare office, community mental health agency, drug treatment program, pastoral counseling/spiritual counseling, psychological testing needed, family therapy, vocational counselor needed, online support group, 12-step programs, etc.*

MEANS OR INTERVENTION(S)
Intervention, methods, or techniques used:
[ ] Relaxation
[ ] Thought stopping
[ ] Therapeutic alliance
[ ] Insight enhancement
[ ] Systematic desensitization
[ ] Interpretation of transference
[ ] Empathy; create a therapeutic alliance, create a safe environment
[ ] Educate about mental illness
[ ] Discuss the cycle of violence
[ ] Uncover childhood trauma
[ ] XYZ behavior modification
[ ] Cognitive restructuring
[ ] Read a specific book
[ ] Attend a training program
[ ] Look up XYZ information on the Internet
[ ] Suicide contract
[ ] Free association
[ ] Hypnosis
[ ] Meditation
[ ] Dream interpretation
[ ] Other

THEORETICAL ORIENTATION
[ ] Object Relations
[ ] Gestalt
[ ] Cognitive Behavior
[ ] Humanistic
[ ] Hypnotherapy
[ ] Family System
[ ] Other

ASSESSMENT OF PROGRESS
DATE: _____
[ ] Self-report
[ ] Reports by family members, friends, teachers
[ ] Reports from other healthcare providers
[ ] Objective and subjective testing
[ ] Noted DECREASE in maladaptive coping

Noted INCREASE in adaptive coping, such as:
[ ] Mindfulness skills
[ ] Stress tolerance skills
[ ] Emotional regulation skills
[ ] Radical acceptance skills
[ ] Interpersonal relationship skills

Noted changes in EGO-SYNTONIC vs. EGO-DYSTONIC
[ ] Ego-Syntonic
[ ] Ego-Dystonic

Noted ADVANCE in the STAGES OF CHANGE
[ ] Pre-contemplation
[ ] Contemplation
[ ] Action
[ ] Relapse

TREATMENT PLAN UPDATES

DATE: _____
[ ] Assess how well the original or last set of goals were achieved
[ ] Assess that the original or last diagnosis or client's concern/issue/condition is still valid; If not, then make changes as needed
[ ] Identify the next goal or set of goals
[ ] New goal or set of goals, then a new treatment plan is needed and must be formulated. COMPLETED: _____

REMEMBER TO:
Include appropriate lines for signature and date; Keep a copy of any document that was signed by a client in the client's file (hardcopy or electronic); Copy to client optional, unless they request a copy.

RESEARCH
Treatment Plan Sample
- **What would you change? Delete? Add?**
- **Search the Internet for three additional samples**
  - **Compare them to this sample**
- **Ask three counselors for a copy of their treatment plan form**
  - **Compare them to each other**
- **Create your treatment plan template**
  - **Customize it for the type of therapy you do (or plan to do)**

ETHICAL STANDARDS & CLINICAL FORMS

VISITOR TO A SESSION

Many times clients will show up for a counseling appointment with a friend or family member. Should counselors allow the visitor into session without any special procedures or consent? In the medical profession, when a patient brings someone with them to a doctor's appointment, and that person goes in the room with them, consent is assumed because the patient brought the other person with them. However, in the mental health field it is considered best practice to speak with the client (alone) first and double check—make sure they want the person in the room with them. The use of a simple consent addendum can be useful in these situations.

SAMPLE TEXT: VISITOR TO A SESSION

CAVEAT: For use in your own setting, forms must be personalized to reflect your state's relevant laws, ethical requirements for your licensing, and your own actual policies.

- I, _____ [client's name] understand that if I choose to invite a person or persons to be present during a session with my counselor that my confidentiality may be compromised
- I do want to bring a person or person to session on this day _____
- I do so with the understanding that my counselor will use his or her clinical discretion when he or she chooses to share or reveal confidential and/or sensitive information
- I understand that my counselor will use his or her clinical discretion and reasoning in sharing any information
- Unless specified in writing, this consent does not give permission to the counselor to discuss any confidential information with the visitor any time after the visit
- I have clarified to my counselor that the following topics should NOT be mentioned during the time that the visitor come to the session:

    _____

REMEMBER TO:

Include appropriate lines for signature and date; Keep a copy of any document that was signed by a client in the client's file (hardcopy or electronic); Copy to client optional, unless they request a copy.

RESEARCH
Sample Text: Visitor to a Session
- **What would you change? Delete? Add?**
    - **What sample text in the above do you strongly agree with? Why?**
    - **What sample text do you strongly disagree with? Why?**

RESEACH

State-by-State Research

Codes of Ethics

Ethical Decision Making

ETHICAL STANDARDS & CLINICAL FORMS

STATE-BY-STATE RESEARCH FORM

WORKSHEET: STATE-BY-STATE RESEARCH (photocopy as needed)

TOPIC: _____

RELEVANT WEBSITE ADDRESSES:

http://www._____
[ ] Information useful [ ] Copied information to file _____
[ ] Printed out information and filed under _____

http://www._____
[ ] Information useful [ ] Copied information to file _____
[ ] Printed out information and filed under _____

http://www._____
[ ] Information useful [ ] Copied information to file _____
[ ] Printed out information and filed under _____

http://www._____
[ ] Information useful [ ] Copied information to file _____
[ ] Printed out information and filed under _____

Key points included:

Relevancy to my practice:

Does any of the information need to be added to my consent form?
[ ] No [ ] Yes
If yes, what statement(s) should be added:

Misc. Comments:

STATE-BY-STATE RESEARCH

*The following Website Addresses were working when the 2019 ediition was published.
If there is a Webpage Address that has been disabled, search the "key words" listed.*

ETHICAL STANDARDS & CLINICAL FORMS

RESEARCH: YOUR STATE
SEARCH ENGINE KEY WORDS
Use the following title in a key words:
[Your State] Mental Health Laws / Rules
[Your State] Social Worker Laws / Rules
[Your State] Psychologists Laws / Rules
[Your State] [Any Profession] Laws / Rules
[Your State] Revised Codes relevant to Mental Health Care
[Your State] Administrative Codes relevant to Mental Health Care
[Your State] State Statutes relevant to Mental Health Care
[Your State] District Court Rules relevant to Mental Health Care
[Your State] Superior Court Rules relevant to Mental Health Care
[Your State] Health Department or Mental Health Department (Division)
[Your State] Mental Health Licensing Board
[Your State] Legal Court Finding affecting Healthcare or Mental Health Care
and Federal Legal Court Finding affecting Healthcare or Mental Health Care

STATE-BY-STATE RESEARCH
Check out these websites: (Please note that websites may have changed since publication)
State Mental Health Laws (Try: megalaw.com)
States Boards Standard of Professional Conduct and Sanctions (Try: your state licensing board website)
Your state's mental health professional's association (Look for a page on legislative bills/laws relevant to practice) NOTE: You may need to be a member to access.
State and Federal Laws/Codes: Federal and State Resources (Try: lawsonline.com)
Minors and Rights to Consent (Try: guttmacher.org)
State Laws: State-by-State (Try: justlaws.org)
Licensure for Counselors State-by-State (Try: counseling.org/counselors/licensure)

NATIONAL RESEARCH
Check out these websites: (Please note that websites may have changed since publication)
Duty to Warn Laws (Key word search)
Child Abuse Laws (Try: acf.hhs.gov)
National Hotline Toll Free Mental Health Support and/or Self-Help Numbers
Disability Laws (Try: ada.gov)

UNDERSTANDING HIPAA

Check out these websites: (Please note that websites may have changed since publication)
Try: hipaa.com
Try: hipaa-dsmo-org
Try: hhs.gov/ocr/hipaa
Try: www.hhs.gov/ocr/privacy/hipaa/understanding...from their home page use their in-site search for various topics, such as:

Research HIPAA updates
- Covered entities
- Business associate agreements
- Electronic health records
- Privacy disclosure document
- Informed consent
- Psychotherapy notes
- Authorizations for release of information
- Other:

STANDARDS FOR PARTICULAR DISCIPLINE

Check out these websites: (Please note that websites may have changed since publication)
Ethics and Mental Health Research (Try: emdr.com)
Ethical Standards and School Counselors (Try: schoolcounselors.org)
Ethics in Religious and Spiritual Therapy (Try: aapc.org; Try: aacc.org)
Ethics and Managed Care [key work search]
Ethics and Emergency Care [Try: acep.org]
Ethics and Employee Assistance Programs (EAPs) (Try: eapassn.org)
Ethics and Coaching (Try: certifiedcoach.org; Try: coachfederation.org)
Ethics and Technology (Try: ethicscenter.net)
Ethics and Business (Try: Business-ethics.com)
Ethics: Military and heir Families [key word search]
Ethics and Administrators in Mental Health [key word search]

GLOBAL

Check out this website: (Please note that website may have changed since publication)
Global Ethics (Try: globalethics.org)

ETHICAL STANDARDS & CLINICAL FORMS

IN YOUR STATE
YOU NEED TO KNOW THE ANSWERS TO THESE QUESTIONS...
Use the Internet to search for the following information:

LICENSING BOARDS
- Who is in charge of the counseling profession and licensing in your state?
- Where are they located? How do you get in touch with them?
- What are the various counseling credentials for my state?
- What is the information regarding counselor licensing examination and internship hours?
- Do I need to take an HIV/AIDS class and where can I attend?
- How much clinical supervision is required for licensing?
- Starting your own counseling practice in your state?
- Look for the following information: doing business in your state; professional liability insurance; private practice pointers; supervision; consultation requirements for counselors in private practice.

ETHICAL CODES FOR YOUR LICENSING
- Look up and review any administrative or revised codes relevant to your licensing.
- Get a copy of your licensing's standard of professional conduct.

ADMINISTRATIVE/LICENSING BOARDS SANCTION POLICIES
- Sanctions: administrative or revised code number; general provision information regarding sanctions for misconduct for your state; practice below standard of care; sexual misconduct or contact; physical and emotional abuse; diversion of controlled substances or legend drugs; substance abuse; criminal convictions; aggravating and mitigating factors.

STATE MENTAL HEALTH PROFESSIONAL ASSOCIATIONS
- Go to your states mental health counseling associations and look for information regarding legislative updates that affect the mental health counseling profession for your state.
- This information should include the various legislative bill numbers and bill names and a brief description of each bill placed before the legislation for your state.

CONTINUING EDUCATION
- Continuing education requirements: who is required to have continuing education? What courses are acceptable?
- What are industry-recognized local, state, national, international organizations or institutions of higher learning?
- How many hours do I need and in what time.?
- How are credit hours determined for preparation and presentation of a lecture or an educational course?
- How should you document courses taken?

SCOPE OF PRACTICE FOR YOUR LICENSING
- Scope of practice: know and understand the scope of practice for your specific professional designation, certification, and/or licensing in your state and understand the standard of care to which you will be held.

PRIVILEGED COMMUNICATION
- **Privileged communication:** administrative or revised code number; definition of privileged communication for your state; who are disqualified; frequently asked questions regarding privileged communication for your state; changes in law or legislation affecting privileged communication for your state; when are you required to release information? Seek information regarding your states disclosure laws.

MANDATORY REPORTING LAWS (Relevant to Child/Vulnerable Adult Abuse)
Key Word Search:
- [Your State] Child Abuse Reporting Numbers
- [Your State] Child Abuse Reporting Laws
- [Your State] Vulnerable Adult Abuse Reporting Laws
- [Your State] Duty To Warn And Protect Laws
- Mandatory reporting of child and vulnerable adult abuse and neglect: state statute number; standard for reporting; persons required to report; failure to report; privileged communication relevant to mandatory reporting laws.

ETHICAL STANDARDS & CLINICAL FORMS

MANDATORY REPORTING LAWS (Relevant to Duty to Warn and Protect)
Key Word Search:
- [Your State] Duty To Warn And Protect Laws
- Tarasoff 1 and Tarasoff 2 court cases. Also check out these relevant court cases:
- Lipari vs. Sears, Roebuck and Company, US District Court, Nebraska, 1980 (Duty to detain dangerous people)
- Jablonski by Pahls vs. United States, United States Court of Appeals, Ninth Circuit, 1983 (Foreseeable harm of an identifiable victim)
- Ewing vs. Goldstein 2004, CA Supreme Court (Communication from a family member to a counselor, made for the purpose of advancing a patient's therapy, is a "patient communication" creating a duty to warn a victim)
- Naidu vs. Laird, Supreme Court of Delaware, 1988 (Foreseeable harm to any third party target)
- The core innovation of Tarasoff was the creation of a new exception to counselor-client confidentiality: Warn the intended victim, to notify the police, or to take whatever steps are reasonably necessary under the circumstances. In Tarasoff, the court declared, "once a counselor does in fact determine, or under applicable professional standards reasonably should have determined, that a client poses a serious danger of violence to others, the counselor bears a duty to exercise reasonable care to protect the foreseeable victim of that danger." Although the duty to warn often is standard among jurisdictions, not all states have adopted the "protection standard" which requires counselors to attempt to contact a specific, identifiable third party.

MANDATORY REPORTING OF IMPAIRED COLLEAGUES
- Check your state counseling association or state licensing board. As an example, many states require the following statement in your consent form: *I am required to report myself to _____ in the event of an act of unprofessional conduct, a determination of risk to patient safety due to a mental or physical condition, or disqualification from participation in the federal Medicare or Medicaid programs. I am also required to report other healthcare providers if I have actual knowledge of a finding, conviction or determination of an act constituting unprofessional conduct or if the healthcare provider may be unable to practice his or her professional with reasonable skill and safety due to a mental or physical condition. If you have any questions or concerns about these requirements, please feel free to discuss them with me.*

LAWS RELEVANT TO SEXUAL RELATIONS WITH CLIENTS
Key word search:
- [Your State] Sexual abuse of clients by counselors
- [Your State] Sexual misconduct of counselor/counselors
- **Sexual misconduct:** administrative or revised code number; definitions and examples of sexual misconduct for your state; disciplinary action relevant to sexual misconduct for your state. Sexual contact of any kind between a counselor and the client is universally regarded as unethical, is considered in every jurisdiction to constitute malpractice, and in some states is a criminal offense. Has your state criminalized sexual relations between a counselor and client? What conditions apply is there is such a law in your state?

MINORS AND CONSENT
Key Word Search:
- [Your State] Minors And Consent Laws
- [Your State] Marriage Age Requirements
- [Your State] Consensual Sex Laws
- Visit: *www.guttmacher.com*
  Minors and consent: Providing health care to minors in your state... What is the age of majority for health care in your state? When can a minor receives services without parental consent in your state in the following areas: emergency medical services, non-emergency medical services, immunizations, treatment for sexually transmitted diseases and or testing including HIV, birth control services, abortion services, prenatal care services, outpatient mental health treatment, inpatient mental health treatment, outpatient substance abuse treatment, inpatient substance-abuse treatment, abortion, and mental status. Web search for "important information to parents and guardians of minor children" for your state for more information.

EMANCIPATION OF MINORS
Key word search:
- [Your State] Emancipation Laws
- Emancipation: how does your state defined emancipation? Who qualifies for emancipation? Some states do not recognize emancipated minors; does your state? What are the administrative or revised code numbers?

ETHICAL STANDARDS & CLINICAL FORMS

KINSHIP LAWS AND CONSENT
- Consent to health care for a child in your care or sometimes referred to as kinship caregivers declaration of responsibility for a minor's health care. Does your state have such a program that allows relatives who are raising a family member's child in your state to consent for that minor's health care?
- Check for "aging and disability services" information for your state.

STATUTORY RAPE LAWS
Key Word Search:
- [Your State] Statutory Laws
- **Statutory rape laws:** some states do not specifically use the term statutory rape, instead they use designations such as sexual assault and sexual abuse to identify prohibited activity. Regardless of the designation, crime is based on the premise that until a person reaches a certain age, they are legally incapable of consenting to sexual intercourse. What are the statutory rape laws for your state? What are the statute numbers? What are the penalties?

INVOLUNTARY COMMITMENTS
Key word search:
- [Your State] Involuntary Commitment Laws
- **Involuntary commitment:** what are the laws regarding involuntary commitment for your state. What is the basis for involuntary commitment? What are that patient's rights? Initial detention? 14 day hearing? 90 day hearing? 180 day hearing? Are there less restrictive alternatives?

OTHER
- [Your State] Medical Records Disclosure Laws
- [Your State] Sodomy Laws
- [Your State] Parity Laws
- [Your State] Obscenity and Pornography Laws

The following Website Addresses were working when the 2019 ediition was published. If there is a Webpage Address that has been disabled, search the "key words" listed.

STATE-BY-STATE CHARTS and LISTS:
CHART Child Abuse Reporting Numbers
https://www.childwelfare.gov/pubPDFs/manda.pdf
https://apps.rainn.org/policy/
CHART Commitment by States
http://www.treatmentadvocacycenter.org/storage/documents/State_Standards_Charts_for_Assisted_Treatment_-_Civil_Commitment_Criteria_and_Initiation_Procedures.pdf
CHART Crisis Hotlines by State
www.recovery-world.com/National-Hotline-Phone-Numbers
CHART Elder Abuse Resources by State
https://www.justice.gov/elderjustice/elder-justice-statutes-0
CHART GUTTMACHER-Minors and Consent
http://www.guttmacher.org/graphics/gr030406_f1.html
CHART Licensure for Counselors
http://www.counseling.org/Counselors/LicensureAndCert/TP/StateRequirements/CT2.aspx
CHART Mandatory Reporting Statutes Elder Abuse
https://www.seniorhomes.com/elder-abuse-hotlines/
CHART Marriage Age Requirements
http://law.jrank.org/pages/11840/Marriage-Age-Requirements.html#ixzz1HokVWfMa

USEFUL CLINICAL FORMS
FORM Cultural Formulation Interview
http://www.multiculturalmentalhealth.ca/wp-content/uploads/2013/10/2013_DSM5_CFI_InformantVersion.pdf

FORMS DSM5 Assessment Tools
https://www.psychiatry.org/psychiatrists/practice/dsm/educational-resources/assessment-measures

ETHICAL STANDARDS & CLINICAL FORMS

ETHICAL CODES-Research:
Regardless of your licensing and particular field of counseling, review a few different associations' codes of ethics:

- **Read the American Counseling Association (ACA) Code of Ethics**
- **Read the American Mental Health Counseling Association (AMHCA) Code of Ethics**
- **Read the National Board of Certified Counselors (NBCC) Code of Ethics**
- **Read the Association for Multicultural Counseling and Development (AMCD) Code of Ethics**
- **Read the American Psychological Association (APA) Code of Ethics**

- Read your state licensing board's code of professional conduct
    - Your Licensing Board: _____
- Read the code of ethics from any and all association(s) you belong to:
    - Name the association: _____
    - Name the association: _____
- Read the code of ethics from associations relevant to your practice that you do not belong to:
    - Name the association: _____
    - Name the association: _____
- What field of counseling are you interested in? Find any or all association(s) relevant to your interest(s) and review their code of ethics:
    - Name the association: _____
    - Name the association: _____
- Are you a faith-based counseling? Find a couple associations relevant to your faith-based practice and review their codes of ethics:
    - Name the association: _____
    - Name the association: _____

ETHICAL DECISION MAKING

ETHICAL DECISION MAKING

ETHICAL DILEMMAS
- Situations in which a decision maker must choose between alternatives in which the following conditions exist: significant value conflicts among differing interests, real alternatives that are equally justifiable, and significant consequences on stakeholders in the situation.
- Different professionals can (and do) implement different courses of action,
when choosing between two or more options, each having its own ethical merits

RIGHT vs. RIGHT
- Ethical concerns pose some of the most challenging questions; and, these questions change with each advancement in technology and each new piece of legislation—bringing a fresh barrage of vexing ethical dilemmas.
- To complicate matters, a true ethical dilemma is one that struggles with "right vs. right."

TO DEAL WITH SUCH ETHICAL DILEMMAS, EACH COUNSELOR NEEDS TO FIND THE ANSWERS TO THESE QUESTIONS:
- How do you define a dilemma?
- What values are at stake in the dilemma?
- What principles are at stake in the dilemma?
- What personal issues are at stake in the dilemma?

ETHICAL ISSUES THAT VIOLATE ETHICAL STANDARDS AND ESTABLISHED LAWS ARE NOT A "RIGHT VS. RIGHT," BUT RATHER "RIGHT VS. WRONG."
- Counselors should always remain alert to and avoid conflicts of interest that interfere with the exercise of professional discretion and impartial judgment.
- Counselors should not take unfair advantage of any professional relationship or exploit others to further their personal, religious, political, or business interests.
- Counselors only provide services to clients in the context of a professional relationship based on valid informed consent.
- Counselors take all reasonable steps to ensure that documentation in records is accurate and reflects the services provided.
- Counselors should always base practices on recognized knowledge, including empirically based knowledge, relevant to counseling and ethics.

- Counselors refrain from initiating an activity when they know, or should have known, that there is a substantial likelihood that their personal problems will prevent them from performing their work-related activities in a competent manner.

"Right vs. Right" decisions often involve truth vs. loyalty, individual vs. community, short term vs. long term, and justice vs. mercy.

ETHICAL DECISION MAKING
WHAT VALUES ARE AT STAKE?
- Explore the relevant values in the authorities' literature of the case. Individuals may validate their basic ethical values from such sources as laws, social science research, and holy books.
- Some of the issues concerning values are:
  - The right or wrong of an action
  - The acceptance, reputation or embarrassment of an action
  - Qualification and disqualification of a person, with reasons
  - Virtues such as integrity, love, forgiveness, respect, purity, trust, sanctity of life

WHAT PRINCIPLES ARE AT STAKE?
- Select the relevant principles that apply to the case and explain the reasoning process that you used to arrive at a tentative solution.
- Some relevant principles may be:
  - Protection of life etc.
  - Conflict avoidance
  - Greatest good of group, etc.
  - Truth telling
  - Acceptance of faith/belief command
  - Accountability

WHAT PERSONAL ISSUES ARE AT STAKE?
- Consider what personal issues of people or populations may affect the outcome of the case to such an extent that a particular ethical position is required. Reconsider your tentative solution in light of the personal issues involved and suggest a final solution.
- In some cases, the loyalty for one group takes precedence over the other group. Some groups include the:
  - Victim, family, employer, profession, community

It is good to remember that the dilemmas you face are often complex, so a useful guideline is to examine the problem from several perspectives and avoid searching for a simplistic solution.

ETHICAL DECISION MAKING PROCESS

IDENTIFY THE PROBLEM.
IF A LEGAL QUESTION EXISTS, SEEK LEGAL ADVICE.
- Is it an ethical, legal, professional, or clinical problem?
- Is it a combination of more than one of these?
- Is the issue related to me, and what I am doing or am not doing?
- Is it related to a client and/or the client's significant others and what they are or are not doing?
- Is it related to the institution or agency and their policies and procedures?
- If the problem can be resolved by implementing a policy of an institution or agency, you can look to the agency's guidelines.

APPLY YOUR RELEVANT CODE OF ETHICS.
- After you have clarified the problem, refer to relevant Code of Ethics to see if the issue is addressed there.
- If there is an applicable standard or several standards and they are specific and clear, following the course of action indicated should lead to a resolution of the problem.
- If the problem is more complex and a resolution does not seem apparent, then you probably have a true ethical dilemma and need to proceed with further steps in the ethical decision making process.

DETERMINE THE NATURE AND DIMENSIONS OF THE DILEMMA.
- There are several avenues to follow in order to ensure that you have examined the problem in all its various dimensions.
- Consider the moral principles of autonomy, non-maleficence, beneficence, justice, and fidelity.
- Decide which principles apply to the specific situation, and determine which principle takes priority for you in this case. In theory, each principle is of equal value, which means that it is your challenge to determine the priorities when two or more of them are in conflict.

REVIEW THE RELEVANT PROFESSIONAL LITERATURE TO ENSURE THAT YOU ARE USING THE MOST CURRENT PROFESSIONAL THINKING IN REACHING A DECISION.

- Consult with experienced professional colleagues and/or supervisors. As they review with you the information you have gathered, they may see other issues that are relevant or provide a perspective you have not considered. They may also be able to identify aspects of the dilemma that you are not viewing objectively. Consult your state or national professional associations to see if they can provide help with the dilemma.
- Generate potential courses of action. Brainstorm as many possible courses of action as possible. Be creative and consider all options. If possible, enlist the assistance of at least one colleague to help you generate options.
- Consider the potential consequences of all options and determine a course of action.
- Considering the information you have gathered and the priorities you have set, evaluate each option and assess the potential consequences for all the parties involved. Ponder the implications of each course of action for the client, for others who will be affected, and for yourself as a counselor.
- Eliminate the options that clearly do not give the desired results or cause even more problematic consequences. Review the remaining options to determine which option or combination of options best fits the situation and addresses the priorities you have identified.

SELF-REFLECTION ON DECISION MAKING

The process is to learn more about oneself as a decision maker or to better understand the lens one wears to make decisions.

The "person-in-environment perspective" argues that to understand human behavior, one must understand the context of the environment that colors, shapes, and influences behavior.

Prior socialization, cultural values and orientations, personal philosophy, world views, organizational context, professional context, and societal context (societal norms) all play a role in influencing moral decision making.

REFERENCES

PREAMBLE (ACA)

The American Counseling Association (ACA) is an educational, scientific, and professional organization whose members work in a variety of settings and serve in multiple capacities.

- Counseling is a professional relationship that empowers diverse individuals, families, and groups to accomplish mental health, wellness, education, and career goals.
- Professional values are an important way of living out an ethical commitment.
- The following are core professional values of the counseling profession: enhancing human development throughout the life span; honoring diversity and embracing a multicultural approach in support of the worth, dignity, potential, and uniqueness of people within their social and cultural contexts; promoting social justice; safeguarding the integrity of the counselor–client relationship; and practicing in a competent and ethical manner.

REFERENCES

MENTAL HEALTHCARE ASSOCIATIONS:

- American Association for Marriage and Family Therapy (AAMFT), Code of Ethics, www.aamft.org American Counseling Association (ACA), Code of Ethics, www.aca.org
- American Psychologists Association (APA), Code of Ethics, www.apa.org
- National Association of Social Workers (NASW), Code of Ethics, www.nasw.org
- American Mental Health Counseling Association (AMHCA), Codes of Ethics, www.amhca.org
- American Association for Marriage and Family Therapy (AAMFT), Code of Ethics, www.aamft.org
- American Counseling Association (ACA), Code of Ethics. www.aca.org
- American Psychologists Association (APA), Code of Ethics, www.apa.org
- National Association of Social Workers (NASW), Code of Ethics, www.nasw.org
- Association for Multicultural Counseling and Development (AMCD), Codes of Ethics, www.amcdaca.org
- American Association of Christian Counselors (AACC), Codes of Ethics, www.aacc.org

HEALTHCARE and MENTAL HEALTHEALTH Associations - LIST with LINKS

- American Association for Marriage and Family Therapy, www.aamft.org
- American Counseling Association, www.counseling.org
- American Association for Nurse Practitioners https://www.aanp.org
- American Alternative Medicine Association https://joinaama.com
- American Counseling Association, www.counseling.org
- American Chiropractors Association https://www.acatoday.org
- American Dental Association https://www.ada.org/en
- Association for LGTBQ issues in counseling, www.algbtic.org
- American Massage Therapist Association https://www.amtamassage.org
- American Medical Association www.ama-assn.org
- American Nurses Associations https://www.nursingworld.org/ana/
- Association for Multi-Cultural Counseling/Development www.multiculturalcounseling.org
- American Mental Health Counselors Association, www.amhca.org
- American Pharmacists Association https://www.pharmacist.com
- American Physical Therapy Association https://www.apta.org
- American Psychiatric Associations https://www.psychiatry.org
- American Psychological Association, www.apa.org
- American Psychological Association Ethics Office www.apa.org/ethics
- Commission on Rehabilitation Counseling Org., www.crcertification.com
- International Association of Marriage/Family Counselors www.iamfconline.org
- National Association for LPNs https://nalpn.org
- National Association of Mental Health Counselors www.namch.org
- National Association of Social Workers, www.socialworkers.org
- National Board of Certified Counselors, www.nbcc.org
- National Center for Cultural Competence https://nccc.georgetown.edu

PROFESSIONAL ARTICLES/PAPERS

- Aadam, Bani, Melissa Petrakis. 2019. Ethics, Values, and Recovery in Mental Health Social Work Practice. Mental Health and Social Work, pages 1-21. Aadam, Bani, Melissa Petrakis. 2020. Ethics, Values, and Recovery in Mental Health Social Work Practice. Mental Health and Social Work, pages 1-21. Bani Aadam, Melissa Petrakis. 2020. Ethics, Values, and Recovery in Mental Health Social Work Practice. Mental Health and Social Work, pages 23-43.
- Brandl, Eva J., Stefanie Schreiter, Meryam Schouler-Ocak. (2020) Are Trained Medical Interpreters Worth the Cost? A Review of the Current Literature on Cost and Cost-Effectiveness. Journal of Immigrant and Minority Health 22:1, pages 175-181.
- Bhola, Poornima, Santosh K. Chaturvedi. (2017) Through a glass, darkly: ethics of mental health practitioner-patient relationships in traditional societies. International Journal of Culture and Mental Health 10:3, pages 285-297.
- Beaulieu, Lauren, Joshua Addington, Daniel Almeida. (2019) Behavior Analysts' Training and Practices Regarding Cultural Diversity: the Case for Culturally Competent Care. Behavior Analysis in Practice 12:3, pages 557-575.
- Dransart, Dolores Angela Castelli, Elena Scozzari, Sabine Voélin. (2017) Stances on Assisted Suicide by Health and Social Care Professionals Working With Older Persons in Switzerland. Ethics & Behavior 27:7, pages 599-614.
- George, Riya Elizabeth, Karl Smith, Michelle O'Reilly, Nisha Dogra. (2019) Perspectives of Patients With Mental Illness on How to Better Teach and Evaluate Diversity Education in the National Health Service. Journal of Continuing Education in the Health Professions 39:2, pages 92-102. George, Riya Elizabeth, Nisha Dogra, Bill Fulford. (2015) Values and ethics in mental-health education and training: a different perspective. The Journal of Mental Health Training, Education and Practice 10:3, pages 189-204.
- Ngui, Emmanuel M., Lincoln Khasakhala, David Ndetei, Laura Weiss Roberts. (2010) Mental disorders, health inequalities and ethics: A global perspective. International Review of Psychiatry 22:3, pages 235-244.
- Quartiroli, Alessandro, Justine Vosloo, Leslee Fisher, Robert Schinke. (2020) Culturally Competent Sport Psychology: A Survey of Sport Psychology Professionals' Perception of Cultural Competence. The Sport Psychologist 34:3, pages 242-253.
- Pelts, Michael D., Abigail J. Rolbiecki, David L. Albright. (2014) Implication for Services With Gay Men and Lesbians Who Have Served. Social Work in Mental Health 12:5-6, pages 429-442.

- Penn, Claire. (2019) Cultural Safety and the Curriculum: Recommendations for Global Practice. Perspectives on Global Issues in Communication Sciences and Related Disorders 1:1, pages 4-11.
- Ramathuba, Dorah U., Hulisani Ndou. (2020) Ethical conflicts experienced by intensive care unit health professionals in a regional hospital, Limpopo province, South Africa. Health SA Gesondheid 25:0.
- Rensburg, André J van, Dingie J van Rensburg. (2013) Nurses, industrial action and ethics. Nursing Ethics 20:7, pages 819-837.
- Roberts, Laura Weiss, Daryn Reicherter. 2015. Questions with Narrative Answers. Professionalism and Ethics in Medicine, pages 85-112.
- Roos, Vera, Jacobus Hoffman, Vanessa van der Westhuizen. (2017) Ethics and Intergenerational Programming: A Critical Reflection on Historic Environment Education in South Africa. Journal of Intergenerational Relationships 11:4, pages 449-458.
- Schultz, Tammy, Hana Yoo, Mandy Kellums Baraka, Terri Watson. (2020) Does this apply here?: Ethical considerations in transnational supervision settings. Ethics & Behavior 0:0, pages 1-14.

BIBLIOGRAPHY/REFERENCES
- Arredondo, P., Toporek, M. S., Brown, S., Jones, J., Locke, D. C., Sanchez, J. & Stadler, H. (1996; updated 2019). Operationalization of the Multicultural Counseling Competencies capitalization of title I believe is incorrect. Alexandria.
- Bossman, D. M. (2017). Teaching pluralism: Values to cross-cultural barriers. In M. L. Kelley (Ed.), Understanding cultural diversity: Culture, curriculum, and community in nursing (pp. 55–66). Sudbury, MA: Jones and Bartlett.
- Corey, G., Corey, M., Corey, C., & Callahan, P. (2016). Issues and ethics in the helping professions. (9th ed.) Stamford, CT: Cengage Learning.
- Donner, M. B., VandeCreek, L., Gonsiorek, J. C. & Fisher, C. B. (2008; revised 2018). Balancing confidentiality: Protecting privacy and protecting the public. Professional Psychology: Research and Practice, 39, 369-376.
- Epstein, R. S. (2018). Keeping boundaries: Maintaining safety and integrity in the psychotherapeutic process. Washington, DC: American Psychiatric Press.
- Epstein, R. S., & Simon, R. I. (2020). The Exploitation Index: An early warning indicator of boundary violations in psychotherapy. Bulletin of the Menninger Clinic, 54, 450–465.
- Hawley, K. M. & Weisz, J. R. (2018). Child and therapist (dis)agreement on target problems in outpatient therapy: The therapist's dilemma and implications. Journal of Consulting and Clinical Psychology, 71, 62-70.
- Kotsopoulou, A., Melis, A., Koutsompou, C., & Koutsompou, V. I. (2015). E-therapy: The ethics behind the process. Procedia Computer Science, 65, 492-499.
- Kottler, J. A., & Carlson, J. (2019). Bad therapy: Master therapists share their worst failures. New York, NY: Routledge.
- McCurdy, K. G. & Murray, K. C. (2018; Web paper 2018). Confidentiality issues when minor children disclose family secrets in family counseling. The Family Journal, 11, 393-398.
- Moleski, S. M. & Kiselica, M. S. (2015). Dual relationships: A continuum ranging from the destructive to the therapeutic. Journal of Counseling & Development, 83, 3-11.
- Remley, T. P. & Huey, W. C. (2019). Ethics. Professional Counseling, 6, 3-11.
- Welfel, E. R., Danzinger, P.R & Santoro, S. (2017). Mandated reporting of abuse/maltreatment of older adults: A primer for counselors. Journal of **Counseling** & Development, 78, 284- 292.
- Wheeler, A.M.N., & Bertram, B. (2018; Updated 2020). The Counselor and the law: A guide to legal and ethical practice. (6th ed.) Alexandra, VA: ACA

ETHICAL STANDARDS & CLINICAL FORMS

ADDITIONAL PAPERS/RESOURCES:
- American Art Therapy Association (AATA). Ethical Principle for Art Therapists. ETHICAL PRINCIPLES FOR ART THERAPISTS. 2020. http://www.arttherapy.org/pdf/EthicalPrincipals.pdf
- American Association for Marriage and Family Therapy (AAMFT), Codes of Ethics. 2020. www.aamft.org/resources/LRM_Plan/Ethics/ethicscode2001.htm.
- American Counseling Association (ACA), Code of Ethics. 2020. http://www.counseling.org/Resources/aca-code-of-ethics.pdf.
- American Psychiatric Association (APA), Principles of Medical Ethics With Annotations Especially Applicable to Psychiatry, 2020. http://www.psych.org/MainMenu/PsychiatricPractice/Ethics/ResourcesStandards/Principles-of-Medical-Ethics-2010-Edition.aspx?FT=.pdf. Retrieved.
- American Psychological Association (APA), APA Statement on services by phone, teleconferencing. 2020. www.apa.org/ethics/stmnt01.html.
- American Psychological Association (APA), Ethical Principles of Psychologists and Code of Conduct. 2020. www.apa.org/ethics/code.html.
- American Psychological Association (APA), Ethical Principles of Psychologists and Code of Conduct 2019. www.apa.org/ethics/code.html.
- Association of State and Provincial Psychology Boards (ASPPB), Consumers. 2019. www.asppb.org/Consumers/sexintro.htm.
- Board of Behavioral Sciences (BBS), Notice to Licensees Regarding Psychotherapy on the Internet. 2018. http://www.bbs.ca.gov/licensees/psych_online.shtml.
- Canter, M., Bennett, B., Jones, S., & Nagy, T. Ethics for psychologists. Washington, DC: American Psychological Association. 2020.
- Doverspike W. F. The APA Ethics Code: An Overview. 2018. www.division42.org/MembersArea/ Nws_Views/articles/Ethics/ethics_code.html.
- Harris, E. A. Legal and Ethics Risks and Risk Management in Professional Psychological Practices. Workshop reader, March, LA. 2018.
- Hill, M. Barter: Ethical considerations in psychotherapy. Women and therapy, 22 (3), 81-91. 2019.
- National Association of Social Workers (NASW). 2020. Code of Ethics. http://www.naswdc.org/Code/ethics.htm
- National Association of Social Workers Code of Ethics (NASW) 2020. www.ssc.msu.edu/~sw/ethics/nasweth.html#105.

INDEX

Abandonment: 55, 495
Academic Settings: 263
Academic Settings SAMPLE CONSENT: 266
Accepting Employment: 203
Administrators: 268
Alternative and Complementary Interventions: 102, 345
Alternative and Complementary Treatment SAMPLE CONSENT: 345
Amending Records: 315
Amending Records REQUEST SAMPLE: 317
Apologizing: 131
Assessing Yourself: 270
Assessment: 127, 275
Assessment SAMPLES FORM: 287
Assessment and Homicide Risk: 279
Assessment and Suicide Risk: 279
Assessment and Testing: 277
Attorneys (working with): 293
Audio Recordings: 463
Authorization for Release of Information: 49, 72
Authorization for Disclosure SAMPLE: 294
Bartering: 96, 297
Bartering SAMPLE AGREEMENT: 299
Bill of Rights: 301
Board Investigation: 15, 17
Board Investigations-Responding to: 15
Board Investigators: 16
Boundaries: 328
Boundaries-Appropriate Boundary Crossings: 149
Boundaries-Gifts: 152
Boundaries-Making Boundary Decisions: 38, 149
Boundaries-Small Towns or Small Communities: 150
Boundaries-Social Interactions: 151
Boundary Crossing: 36, 329
Boundary Crossing AGREEMENT SAMPLE: 331
Boundary Violations: 41, 42
Boundary Violations and Issues of Impairment: 155
Burnout: 156
Breaches of Confidentiality: 302

Breaches of Confidentiality SAMPLE NOTIFICATION: 302
Burnout: 353
Business Associate Agreement: 305
Business Associate AGREEMENT SAMPLE: 306
Checking the Validity of Informed Consent TEMPLATE: 420
Child Protective Laws: 77, 79
Client Self-Determination: 321
Clients-Their Vulnerable Nature: 34, 187
Clinical Care Settings: 109
Clinical Notes: 90, 469
Clinical Records: 31, 89, 90, 92, 93, 311
Clinical Relationships: 115, 321
Clinical Relationships and Therapy Impasses: 335
Clinician's Presence: 116
Clinician's Professionalism: 115
Clinicians-Differences: 101
Clinicians-Explore Your Vocation: 110
Clinicians-Self-Assessment: 110, 111, 113
Coaching: 341
Coaching SAMPLE CONSENT: 341
Codes of Ethics: 177, 539
Colleague Impairment: 156, 355
Codes of Ethics-Need to know: 540
Codes-How are Codes Used: 14
Cognitive Justifications: 13
Colleagues-Ethical Responsibilities: 157
Colleagues-Working with Other Professionals: 132
Collection Agencies: 379
Compassion Fatigue: 155, 353
Competence in Accepting Employment: 203
Competence in Providing Services: 203
Competence-Defining Competence: 168
Competence-Ethical Requirements: 167, 168
Competence-Three Dimensions: 172
Competencies and Assessments: 127, 199
Competencies and Codes of Ethics: 177
Competencies and Diagnosis: 127, 201
Competencies and Education: 198

Competencies and Group Work: 197
Competencies and Multiculturalism: 213
Competencies and Research: 200
Competency Domains: 171
Competency Obligations: 168, 193
Competency Profiles: 209
Competency-Retaining: 203, 204
Complaints: 29
Complimentary Treatments: 345
Complementary Treatment CONSENT SAMPLE: 345
Confidentiality: 326, 410
Confidentiality SAMPLE STATEMENTS: 347
Confidentiality-Client Records: 62
Confidentiality-Counseling: 76
Confidentiality-E-Counseling: 65, 67
Confidentiality-Exceptions: 71
Confidentiality-Exceptions-Clinician Imposed: 75
Confidentiality-Exceptions-HIPAA's Notice of Privacy Practice: 71
Confidentiality-Exceptions-Involuntary Commitment: 74
Confidentiality-Exceptions-Mandatory Reporting Laws: 71, 76
Confidentiality-Expectations: 57
Confidentiality-Four Principles: 59
Confidentiality-History of: 57
Confidentiality-Mandatory Exceptions: 76, 77, 80
Confidentiality-On-Line Issues: 65
Confidentiality-Statement for Transmissions: 347
Conflicts of Interest: 134
Conflicts Between Codes & Laws: 348
Consent Comprehension: 53
Consent Form: 50
Consent-Helping Clients Understand What to Expect: 159
Consultations: 141, 201, 349
Consultation CONSENT SAMPLE: 351
Contact (with clients) Outside the Office: 408
Continuation of Counseling: 61
Continued Professional Growth: 195
Cornerstones of Ethics: 20
Counseling Errors: 207

Counseling Goals: 125, 126
Counseling-Sometimes We Can't Help: 207
Counselor Impairment: 353
Counselor Safety: 61
Counselor Self-Disclosure: 122, 123
Counter-Transference: 119
Couples Counseling: 351
Couples Counseling CONSENT SAMPLES: 360, 361, 362
Court Ordered Treatment: 73
Cultural Competence: 38, 195, 223, 254, 365
Cultural Competence and the DSM: 190
Cultural Competence-Common Errors: 221
Cultural Competency-Awareness, Knowledge, and Skills: 224
Cultural Competency-Interventions: 196
Cultural Diversity and Ethical Standards: 195, 196, 213, 215
Cultural Formulation Interview (CFI): 249
Cultural Identity: 223
Cultural Responsiveness: 220, 252
Culturally Appropriate Intervention Strategies: 247
Culture in Psychotherapy Practice: 223
Culture-Counselor Self-Assessment: 254
Culture-Multiculturalism: 213, 214, 225
Culture-Self-Reflections and Self-Assessments: 254
Cultures-Increase Your Knowledge: 222
Dangerous People: 285
Developmental Perspectives: 195
Diagnosing: 127, 170, 190, 201, 367
Diagnosis Errors: 358
Diagnosing Clients' Conditions: 127, 170
Domains of Competency: 171
DSM-Definition of Mental Disorder: 190
Dual-Concurrent Relationships: 140
Dual (Multiple) Relationships: 330, 332
Dual (Multiple) Relationships CONSENT SAMPLE: 331
Duty to Warn and Protect: 80, 430
Duty to Warn-Clear and Imminent Danger : 82
Duty to Warn-Serious and Foreseeable Harm: 82
E-Counseling-Consent Considerations: 66, 369

E-Counseling-Ethical Issues and Confidentiality: 65, 67
E-Counseling-Future of Online Counseling: 67
E-Counseling CONSENT SAMPLE: 374
E-Mail : 67, 373
E-Mail Confidentiality STATEMENT SAMPLE: 347
Education-Competencies: 198
Elements of Good Therapy: 191, 192
Emergencies: 73
Emotional Competence: 171
Empathy and Warmth: 35
Enduring Principles of Counseling: 157
Errors: 130, 206, 221, 366, 339
Ethical Assessments: 276
Ethical Competence: 168, 171
Ethical Competencies-Required: 167
Ethical Decision Making: 541
Ethical Decision Making Model: 161, 287
Ethical Decision Making Principles: 161, 268
Ethical Dilemmas: 6
Ethical Dilemmas-the A.B.C.s of Getting Help: 160
Ethical Responsibilities to Colleagues: 157
Ethical Standards: 6
Ethics Codes-History of: 11
Ethics Differs from The Law: 19
Ethics-Mental Health Care: 210
Ethics-Overview: 7, 8, 14, 163
Ethics-the Real World: 209
Extratherapeutic: 28
Faith-Based Counseling-Competencies: 198, 324
Familiarity-Issues of: 34
Family Counseling: 357
Family Counseling CONSENT SAMPLES: 379, 382, 383
Family Stories and Legacies: 243
Fee Structures: 95
Fiduciary Duty: 27, 170
Fiduciary Relationship: 170
Financial Arrangements: 52, 95
Forensic Psychology: 385

ETHICAL STANDARDS & CLINICAL FORMS

Forensic Assessment CONSENT SAMPLE: 389
Forensic CONSENT SAMPLE: 387
Fraud-Issues of: 29
Freedom of Inquiry: 175
Functional Competencies: 173, 189
Gifts and the Therapeutic Relationship: 152, 409
Group Therapy: 73, 133, 197, 391
Group Therapy CONSENT SAMPLE: 393
Harm: 46
Helping Clients: 125, 207
HIPAA Authorizations: 49, 72
HIPAA Notice of Privacy Practices: 49, 71
HIPAA Privacy Disclosure: 48
Homicide Risks: 82, 284, 334
Humor in Therapy: 325
Impairment of Colleagues: 156, 355, 354
Impairment-Boundary Violations Concerns: 155
Influential Position and Multiple Relationships: 140
Information Security: 783
Informed Consent: 47, 50, 53, 55, 397, 349
Informed CONSENT SAMPLE: 411
Informed Consent-Additional Limits of Confidentiality: 410
Informed Consent-Checking the Validity of: 420
Informed Consent-Contact (with clients) Outside the Office: 408
Informed Consent-Gifts: 409
Informed Consent-Professional Disclosure: 51
Informed Consent-Risks of Counseling: 54
Informed Consent-Termination of Services: 496
Informed Consent-Types of Interventions: 406
Informed Consent-What to Expect in Counseling: 53, 402
Insurance Coverage: 17
Intake: 426
Internet Searches and Confidentiality: 68, 487
Intentional Harm: 338
Interruption of Services: 56, 494
Interval History Form: 293, 427
Interventions: 196, 247, 406
Intervention Strategies-Culturally Appropriate: 247

Interventions and Ethics: 107
Interventions are Purposeful: 101
Interventions-Categorizing: 103
Interventions-Complementary and Alternative: 102
Interventions-Culture and Therapeutic Interventions: 247
Interventions-Hundreds of Therapeutic Orientations: 107
Involuntary Commitment and Confidentiality Exceptions: 74
Labeling-the Concern for Caution: 187
Law Differs from Ethics: 19
Law, Ethics, and Practice: 22
Laws and Codes: 7
Licensing Boards: 10, 15, 16
Licensing Boards vs. Civil vs. Criminal: 30
Licensing Requirements: 173
Limiting Access to Client Records: 428
Location of Work: "Out-Of-Office" Settings: 147
Mandatory Exceptions To Confidentiality: 76
Mandatory Reporting: 76, 429
Marginalization: 188, 215, 277
Mature Minor Doctrine: 99
Media and the Mental Health Profession: 33
Mental Health: It's a Unique Profession: 33
Microaggressions: 215, 278
Minors: 431
Minors-Age of Consent: 436
Minors-Custody Agreements: 433
Minors-Rights to Consent: 437
Minors-Ethical Considerations: 99
Minors-Mature Minor Doctrine: 99
Minors-Who's The Client: 100
Minors SAMPLE CONSENT FORMS: 435, 438, 440, 441
Misdiagnosis: 367
Mobile Device Liability: 486
Moral Principles: 21, 174
More than One Person in the Room; 132, 133
Multicultural Approach for your Practice: 212
Multicultural Counseling: 211
Multicultural Counseling-Operationalization of Competencies: 225, 230

Multicultural Counseling-Personal Dimensions Of Identity: 225
Multiculturalism: 211
Multiculturalism-Debates, Diversity and Ethics: 215
Multiculturalism-Discrimination: 217
Multiculturalism-Diversity: 214, 215
Multiculturalism-Gender and Sexual Identity: 217
Multiculturalism-Marginalization: 215
Multiculturalism-Microaggressions: 215
Multiculturalism-Oppression: 215
Multiculturalism-Principles: 219
Multiculturalism-Sex Differences: 217
Multiculturalism-Terms: 214
Multiple Relationships: 137, 330, 331, 333
Multiple Relationships-Accidental: 144
Multiple Relationships-Avoiding: 141
Multiple Relationships-Concluding Thoughts: 145
Multiple Relationships-Incidental: 143
Multiple Relationships-Intentional: 143
Multiple Relationships-Myths: 145
Multiple Relationships-the Influential Position: 140
Multiple Relationships-Types of: 139
Negligence: 338
No Charge Initial Session: 445
No Charge Initial Session CONSENT SAMPLE: 445
Non-Subpoena CONTRACT SAMPLE: 446
Notice of Privacy Practices (HIPAA): 446
Notice of Privacy Practices OVERVIEW SAMPLE: 447
On-line Issues and Confidentiality: 65
Oppression: 188, 216, 217
Patient's Rights Act: 48 , 448
Phone Counseling: 374
Pre-termination Counseling: 496
Professional Disclosure Statement: 51, 451
Professional Disclosure Statement SAMPLE: 453
Professional Disclosure Statement WORKSHEET: 452
Professional Will: 455
Professional Will SAMPLE: 456
Protective Services: Child and Vulnerable Adult: 77, 429

Providing Services-Competence : 203
Psychotherapy Notes: 62, 91, 457
Questionable Behavior: 12
Questionable Therapy-Warning Signs of: 205
Records are Very Important: 31
Record Custodians: 98, 455, 459
Record Guidelines: 90, 312
Record Retention: 94, 313, 461
Record Summaries: 462
Recordings (Video/Audio) 463
Records-Amount of Detail: 93
Records-Clinical: 31, 62, 89, 92, 93
Records-HIPAA (Three Key Forms): 319
Records-Inspect, Copy & Amend: 315
Records-Limit Access: 428
Records-Reflect Clinician's Competence: 93
Records-S.O.A.P. Notes: 90
Records-Suggested Documents: 318
Referrals: 394
Release of Information: 465
Relationships of Concern: 142
Relationships-Dual-Concurrent Relationships: 140
Relationships-Multiple Relationships: 137
Relationships-Sequential Relationships: 140
Required Ethical Competencies: 165
Research: 466
Research-Competencies: 200
Responding to a Subpoena: 467
Retaining Competency: 203
Risks of Counseling: 54
Session Notes: 469
S.O.A.P. Notes: 90, 471
Scope of Practice: 22
Self-Assessment-for Clinical Skills: 110
Self-Assessment-Your Areas of Strength: 111
Self-Disclosure: 120, 121
Self-Disclosure-Concerns Associated with: 124
Self-Disclosure-Different Rationales: 123, 124

ETHICAL STANDARDS & CLINICAL FORMS

Self-Disclosure-Types of: 121
Self-Reflection-Decision-Making: 255
Self-Reflection-Your Own Identity: 255
Self-Reflection-Gender and Ethnicity: 256
Sequential Relationships: 140
Sexual Boundary Violations: 42
Social Diversity: 365
Social Interactions: 151
Social Media: 487
Social Media CONSENT SAMPLE: 488
Social Media and Confidentiality: 68
Special Exceptions: 142
Spirituality: 245
Standard of Care: 23, 169, 512, 513, 514
State-to-State Information and Research: 9, 261
Subpoenas: 467
Suicide Assessment: 280
Suicide Risks: 83, 279, 334
Suicide Safety Plans: 84, 282, 473
Supervision: 475
Supervision CONSENT SAMPLE: 487
Supervision LOG SAMPLE: 480
Technology: 486
Technology-Information Security: 483
Technology-Internet Searches: 487
Technology-Mobile Device Liability: 486
Technology-Social Media: 486
Technology-Social Media CONSENT SAMPLE: 488
Termination of Services: 54, 55, 128, 493, 496, 503
Termination LETTER SAMPLES: 500, 501, 502
Termination SUMMARY SAMPLE: 499
Termination-Abandonment Concerns: 55, 495
Termination-Due to Counselor Variable: 497
Termination-Informed Consent: 496
Termination-Interruption of Services: 494
Termination-Pre-termination Counseling: 496
Termination-Referrals: 493, 494
Testing and Assessment: 277

Texting: 373
Text Messages: 67
Texting CONSENT SAMPLE: 374
The A.B.C.s of Getting Help with Ethical Dilemmas: 160
The A.R.T.Ful Counselor: 158
Therapeutic Impasses: 335
Therapeutic Interventions: 101, 102, 103, 107
Therapeutic Relationships: 322
Therapy Errors-Good Therapy Is Imperfect: 206
Therapy Impasses: 335
Touch in Therapy: 45, 505
Touch in Therapy CONSENT SAMPLE: 508
Transfer Plans: 511
Transference: 118
Treatment Plans: 129, 144, 511
Treatment Plan SAMPLE: 521
Video Recordings: 463
Unethical Behavior: 205
Unethical Counseling-Warning Signs of: 205
Unique Profession: 5, 33
Unprofessional Behavior: 12
Visitor to a Session: 134, 526
Vulnerable Nature of Clients: 34, 187
What to Expect in Counseling: 402
Working with an Attorney: 293
Working with Other Professionals: 132
Workplace Violence: 286

RESEARCH: 529
State-by-State WORKSHEET: 530
State-by-State "Need to Know": 531-539
Codes of Ethics "Need to Know": 540

ETHICAL DECISION MAKING: 541-545
REFERENCES: 547-554
INDEX of topics: 555-567

BULK BOOK ORDERING INFORMATION: 568

ETHICAL STANDARDS & CLINICAL FORMS

BULK ORDERS & SPECIAL PRICING
for your academic program

Bulk order discount wholesale pricing through:

www.samdia.com

Select the CONTACT tab
to contact the publisher/author

You'll also find this book online:
www.amazon.com
www.kindle.com

If you have any questions
CONTACT ME at:
www.samdia.com

*Thank you,
Samara*

Made in the USA
Columbia, SC
16 June 2022